Lecture Notes in Computer Science 7983

Commenced Publication in 1973
Founding and Former Series Editors:
Gerhard Goos, Juris Hartmanis, and Jan van Leeuwen

Jens Heidrich   Markku Oivo
Andreas Jedlitschka
Maria Teresa Baldassarre (Eds.)

Product-Focused Software Process Improvement

14th International Conference, PROFES 2013
Paphos, Cyprus, June 12-14, 2013
Proceedings

 Springer

Volume Editors

Jens Heidrich
Fraunhofer IESE, Fraunhofer-Platz 1, 67663 Kaiserslautern, Germany
E-mail: jens.heidrich@iese.fraunhofer.de

Markku Oivo
University of Oulu, P.O. Box 3000, 90014 Oulu, Finland
E-mail: markku.oivo@oulu.fi

Andreas Jedlitschka
Fraunhofer IESE, Fraunhofer-Platz 1, 67663 Kaiserslautern, Germany,
E-mail: andreas.jedlitschka@iese.fraunhofer.de

Maria Teresa Baldassarre
University of Bari, Via E. Orabona 4, 70125 Bari, Italy
E-mail: mariateresa.baldassarre@uniba.it

ISSN 0302-9743   e-ISSN 1611-3349
ISBN 978-3-642-39258-0   e-ISBN 978-3-642-39259-7
DOI 10.1007/978-3-642-39259-7
Springer Heidelberg Dordrecht London New York

Library of Congress Control Number: 2013941298

CR Subject Classification (1998): D.2.8-9, D.2, K.6, J.1, H.3-4, C.2.4, J.3

LNCS Sublibrary: SL 2 – Programming and Software Engineering

Typesetting: Camera-ready by author, data conversion by Scientific Publishing Services, Chennai, India

Printed on acid-free paper

Springer is part of Springer Science+Business Media (www.springer.com)

Preface

On behalf of the PROFES Organizing Committee, we are proud to present the proceedings of the 14th International Conference on Product-Focused Software Process Improvement (PROFES 2013) held in Paphos, Cyprus.

Since 1999, PROFES has established itself as one of the recognized international process improvement conferences. The main theme of PROFES is professional software process improvement (SPI) motivated by product, process, and service quality needs. PROFES 2013 addressed both quality engineering and management topics, including processes, methods, techniques, tools, organizations, and enabling SPI. Solutions found in practice and relevant research results from academia were presented.

The technical program was selected by a committee of leading experts in software process improvement, software process modeling, and empirical software engineering research. This year, 41 papers were submitted, with each paper getting at least three reviewers. After a thorough evaluation, the Program Committee finally selected 22 technical full papers (54% acceptance rate). The topics addressed in these papers indicate that SPI is a vibrant research discipline and is also of high interest for industry. Many papers report on case studies or SPI-related experience gained in industry.

The technical program consisted of the following tracks: Decision Support in Software Engineering, Empirical Software Engineering, Managing Software Processes, Safety-Critical Software Engineering, Software Measurement, Software Process Improvement, and Software Maintenance.

Since the beginning of the PROFES conference series, the purpose has been to highlight the most recent findings and novel results in the area of process improvement. We were proud to have three keynote speakers at the 2013 edition of PROFES: Prof. Dr. Stefan Wagner (University of Stuttgart, Germany) gave a talk on "Making Software Quality Visible." Dr. Alexis Ocampo (ECOPETROL S.A., Colombia) gave a talk on "ECO-MAPS: Information Quality Driven Enterprise Modeling." Christos Xenis (LogiSoft, Cyprus) gave a talk on "Implementation of an Online Multi-Level and Device-Independent Time & Attendance System."

Furthermore, several events were co-located with PROFES 2013: the tutorial "Model-Based Transition from Requirements to High-Level Software Design," presented by Prof. Dr. Hermann Kaindl (Vienna University of Technology, Austria). The tutorial "Software Effort Estimation and Risk Management," presented by Dr. Jens Heidrich (Fraunhofer IESE, Germany).

We are thankful for the opportunity to have served as Program Co-chairs for this conference. The Program Committee members and reviewers provided excellent support in reviewing the papers. We are also grateful to the authors, presenters, and Session Chairs for their time and effort in making PROFES 2013 a success.

In addition, we sincerely thank Dr. Andreas Jedlitschka for his work as General Chair of PROFES 2013 and the Organizing Chair, Prof. Dr. George Angelos Papadopoulos (University of Cyprus, Cyprus), for his professionalism and drive in making PROFES a successful event. Last, but not least, we would like to thank the Short Papers Chair, Dr. Maria Teresa Baldassarre (University of Bari, Italy), the Doctoral Symposium Chair, Prof. Dr. Barbara Russo (Free University of Bolzano, Italy), the Tutorial Co-chairs, Andreas Andreou (Cyprus University of Technology, Cyprus) and Michael Kläs (Fraunhofer IESE, Germany), and the Publicity Chair, Christos Mettouris (University of Cyprus, Cyprus).

May 2013   Jens Heidrich
                                                     Markku Oivo
                                              Andreas Jedlitschka

Preface to the Short Papers Track

The PROFES 2013 short papers present recent ideas or current work-in-progress based on research, practice, or experience. Contributions to this track serve a distinct purpose and are subject to requirements different than those of full technical papers. Short papers may represent research work still in progress with preliminary results, ideas that might not be mature enough to be featured in a full technical paper, or experience with existing approaches or technologies that can be told in a compact form.

This year we received 19 short paper submissions. The submissions underwent a rigorous review process by a separate, international Program Committee consisting of ten members. Each submission received at least three reviews. Based on these reviews and the Program Committee's overall assessments, ten submissions were accepted for presentation at the conference and for inclusion in these proceedings.

The accepted papers cover a relevant range of topics: software process reference models; process reliability; software process; performance management; process modeling; software quality.

The session was literally an international event, with authors coming from Sweden, Germany, Finland, Italy, Ireland, as well as Brazil, Australia, and Japan.

We hope that the short papers will be of interest to the attendees, and that the authors will receive relevant feedback.

Special thanks go to the Program Committee for their diligence in reviewing the submissions and for their help with the selection process.

May 2013   Maria Teresa Baldassarre

Organization

General Chair

Andreas Jedlitschka   Fraunhofer IESE, Germany

Program Co-chairs

Jens Heidrich   Fraunhofer IESE, Germany
Markku Oivo   University of Oulu, Finland

Short Papers Chair

Maria Teresa Baldassarre   University of Bari, Italy

Doctoral Symposium Chair

Barbara Russo   Free University of Bolzano, Italy

Tutorial Co-chairs

Andreas Andreou   Cyprus University of Technology, Cyprus
Michael Kläs   Fraunhofer IESE, Germany

Organizing Chair

George Angelos Papadopoulos   University of Cyprus, Cyprus

Publicity Chair

Christos Mettouris   University of Cyprus, Cyprus

Program Committee

Silvia Abrahao   Universitat Politècnica de València, Spain
Sousuke Amasaki   Okayama Prefectural University, Japan
Maria Teresa Baldassarre   University of Bari, Italy
Andreas Birk   SWPM, Germany
Sjaak Brinkkemper   Utrecht University, The Netherlands
Luigi Buglione   Engineering.IT / ETS Montréal, Canada

Daniel Rodriguez   Universidad de Alcalá, Spain
Barbara Russo   Free University of Bolzano, Italy
Outi Salo   Nokia, Finland
Klaus Schmid   University of Hildesheim, Germany
Kurt Schneider   Leibniz Universität Hannover, Germany
Katsutoshi Shintani   Information-technology Promotion Agency, Japan
Michael Stupperich   Daimler, Germany
Marco Torchiano   Politecnico di Torino, Italy
Guilherme Travassos   COPPE/UFRJ, Brazil
Adam Trendowicz   Fraunhofer IESE, Germany
Burak Turhan   University of Oulu, Finland
Sira Vegas   Universidad Politécnica de Madrid, Spain
Matias Vierimaa   VTT, Finland
Stefan Wagner   University of Stuttgart, Germany
Hironori Washizaki   Waseda University, Japan

Additional Reviewers

Caballero, Ismael
Fernández, Adrián
Mayr, Alois
Monteiro, Paula
Palomares, Cristina
Pereira, Antonio
Salgado, Carlos
Takai, Toshinori

Short Papers Program Committee

Maria Teresa Baldassarre   University of Bari, Italy (Chair)
Marcela Genero   University of Castilla-La Mancha, Spain
Mahmood Niazi   King Fahd University of Petroleum and Minerals, Saudi Arabia
Giuseppe Scanniello   Unisalerno, Italy
Philipp Diebold   Fraunhofer IESE, Germany
Sylwia Kopczynska   Poznan University of Technology, Poland
César Pardo   University of San Buenaventura, Colombia
Felix Garcia   University of Castilla-La Mancha, Spain
Lutz Prechelt   Freie Universität Berlin, Germany
Dietmar Winkler   Vienna University of Technology, Austria

Table of Contents

Keynote Talks

Making Software Quality Visible 1
   Stefan Wagner

ECO-MAPS: Information Quality-Driven Enterprise Modeling 3
   Alexis Eduardo Ocampo Ramírez

Implementation of an Online Multi-level and Device-Independent
Time and Attendance System 4
   Christos Xenis

Empirical Software Engineering

How Applicable Is ISO/IEC 29110 in Game Software Development? 5
   Jussi Kasurinen, Risto Laine, and Kari Smolander

Supporting Cognitive Work in Software Development Workflows 20
   Jarkko Hyysalo, Jari Lehto, Sanja Aaramaa, and Markus Kelanti

Impediments in Agile Software Development: An Empirical
Investigation 35
   *Kristian Wiklund, Daniel Sundmark, Sigrid Eldh, and
   Kristina Lundqvist*

Are Happy Developers More Productive? The Correlation of Affective
States of Software Developers and Their Self-assessed Productivity 50
   Daniel Graziotin, Xiaofeng Wang, and Pekka Abrahamsson

A Model-Driven Approach to Specifying and Monitoring Controlled
Experiments in Software Engineering 65
   *Marília Freire, Paola Accioly, Gustavo Sizílio,
   Edmilson Campos Neto, Uirá Kulesza,
   Eduardo Aranha, and Paulo Borba*

Beyond Herding Cats: Aligning Quantitative Technology Evaluation
in Large-Scale Research Projects 80
   Michael Kläs, Thomas Bauer, and Ubaldo Tiberi

Software Process Improvement

Software Process Improvement in Inter-departmental Development
of Software-Intensive Automotive Systems – A Case Study 93
   Joakim Pernståhl, Tony Gorschek, Robert Feldt, and Dan Florén

Improving Requirements Engineering by Artefact Orientation   108
  Daniel Méndez Fernández and Roel Wieringa

Managing Constant Flow of Requirements: Screening Challenges
in Very Large-Scale Requirements Engineering   123
  Sanja Aaramaa, Tuomo Kinnunen, Jari Lehto, and Nebojša Taušan

Managing Software Processes

Who Cares About Software Process Modelling? A First Investigation
About the Perceived Value of Process Engineering and Process
Consumption   138
  Marco Kuhrmann, Daniel Méndez Fernández, and Alexander Knapp

Modeling Variabilities from Software Process Lines with Compositional
and Annotative Techniques: A Quantitative Study   153
  Fellipe A. Aleixo, Uirá Kulesza, and Edson A. Oliveira Junior

SMartySPEM: A SPEM-Based Approach for Variability Management
in Software Process Lines   169
  *Edson A. Oliveira Junior, Maicon G. Pazin, Itana M.S. Gimenes,
  Uirá Kulesza, and Fellipe A. Aleixo*

Software Measurement

Aligning Corporate and IT Goals and Strategies in the Oil and Gas
Industry   184
  *Victor Basili, Constanza Lampasona, and
  Alexis Eduardo Ocampo Ramírez*

Evaluating Maintainability of MDA Software Process Models   199
  *Bruno C. da Silva, Rita Suzana Pitangueira Maciel, and
  Franklin Ramalho*

The Evaluation of Weighted Moving Windows for Software Effort
Estimation   214
  Sousuke Amasaki and Chris Lokan

Decision Support in Software Engineering

Identifying Potential Risks and Benefits of Using Cloud in Distributed
Software Development   229
  *Nilay Oza, Jürgen Münch, Juan Garbajosa, Agustin Yague, and
  Eloy Gonzalez Ortega*

A Cloud Adoption Decision Support Model Based on Fuzzy Cognitive
Maps   240
  Andreas Christoforou and Andreas S. Andreou

Modeling and Decision Support of the Mobile Software Development
Process Using Influence Diagrams   253
Pantelis Stylianos Yiasemis and Andreas S. Andreou

Safety-Critical Software Engineering

Authoring IEC 61508 Based Software Development Process Models   268
Ivan Porres, Jeanette Heidenberg, Max Weijola,
Kristian Nordman, and Dragos Truscan

Challenges in Flexible Safety-Critical Software Development – An
Industrial Qualitative Survey   283
Jesper Pedersen Notander, Martin Höst, and Per Runeson

Software Maintenance

Improving Process of Source Code Modification Focusing on Repeated
Code   298
Ayaka Imazato, Yui Sasaki, Yoshiki Higo, and Shinji Kusumoto

Assessing Refactoring Instances and the Maintainability Benefits
of Them from Version Archives   313
Kenji Fujiwara, Kyohei Fushida, Norihiro Yoshida, and Hajimu Iida

Short Papers

Evaluation of Standard Reliability Growth Models in the Context
of Automotive Software Systems   324
Rakesh Rana, Miroslaw Staron, Niklas Mellegård, Christian Berger,
Jörgen Hansson, Martin Nilsson, and Fredrik Törner

A Tool for IT Service Management Process Assessment for Process
Improvement   330
Anup Shrestha, Aileen Cater-Steel, Wui-Gee Tan,
Mark Toleman, and Terry Rout

Making Sense Out of a Jungle of JavaScript Frameworks: Towards
a Practitioner-Friendly Comparative Analysis   334
Daniel Graziotin and Pekka Abrahamsson

Software Processes with BPMN: An Empirical Analysis   338
Andre L.N. Campos and Toacy Oliveira

A Generalized Software Reliability Model Considering Uncertainty and
Dynamics in Development   342
Kiyoshi Honda, Hironori Washizaki, and Yoshiaki Fukazawa

Orienting High Software Team Performance: Dimensions for Aligned
Excellence 347
   Petri Kettunen

An Experience Report: Trial Measurement of Process Independency
between Infrastructure Construction and Software Development........ 351
   Noriko Hanakawa and Masaki Obana

How to Configure SE Development Processes Context-Specifically? 355
   Philipp Diebold

Improving IT Service Operation Processes........................... 359
   Marko Jäntti and Terry Rout

A Security Assurance Framework for Networked Medical Devices....... 363
   Anita Finnegan, Fergal McCaffery, and Gerry Coleman

Tutorials

Model-Based Transition from Requirements to High-Level Software
Design... 367
   Hermann Kaindl

Software Effort Estimation and Risk Management.................... 370
   Jens Heidrich

Author Index 373

Making Software Quality Visible

Stefan Wagner

University of Stuttgart
Institute of Software Technology
Stuttgart, Germany
`stefan.wagner@informatik.uni-stuttgart.de`

Abstract. Software quality is hard to comprehend and grasp. Therefore, we need to support developers by giving them quick and frequent
feedback so that they can control the quality of their software systems.
This talk discusses existing techniques, tools and quality models as well
as directions for future research.

1 Motivation

Quality is an essential property of any product, and its importance is still increasing in comparison to functional properties. Many products cannot differentiate
themselves by features but by superior quality characteristics.

Quality in general, however, is a very difficult concept with many different
facets. Also software is hard to comprehend because it is intangible which is not
intuitive for humans. Therefore, software quality is even more difficult to capture
and understand. This becomes visible in many unreliable or unmaintainable
software systems existing today.

What can we do to help software developers to control the quality of their
software systems? Software development is a human-centric task. Although we
are able to automate many aspects of it, the abilities of the developers determine largely the outcome. Humans need feedback to control and improve their
actions, in our case the development process. This feedback is best when it is
fast. Therefore, we need fast feedback about the quality of the software: We need
to make software quality visible.

2 Quality Assurance Techniques

There are many established techniques in analytical quality assurance that help
us in finding quality problems. The most used technique is testing with its various specialisations. Test automation allows us to repeat the tests frequently and,
thereby, give rapid feedback. Reviews and inspections can give the earliest feedback, because they can be applied to any artefact including specifications and
designs. Also for reviews, automation can facilitate a more frequent application.
Comparably cheap to apply and, hence, also well suited for frequent feedback

J. Heidrich et al. (Eds.): PROFES 2013, LNCS 7983, pp. 1–2, 2013.

is automated static analysis. Various analyses for control flow defects or bug patterns show problematic parts of the code to the developer. We discuss in particular the static analysis technique "clone detection" which can automatically find duplications in the code. We will look into the possibilities to use these techniques in making quality visible.

In addition, many software measures have been proposed to better understand software systems and their quality. Some of them, such as the number of failed test cases, measure the results of the techniques above. Others, such as fan-out our inheritance depth, aim to capture the properties of the code itself. To comprehend the large amount of data we can get from all these measures, we use visualisations such as trend chars or treemaps, often contained in a dashboard.

3   Quality Models

The visualisations, however, cannot give you an interpretation of the data. What constitutes good or bad quality still needs to be decided. For that, we can apply quality models. They break down quality in its quality factors and, if operationalised, also concrete measurements. In particular, we will discuss the quality models and the modelling approach created in the research project Quamoco. In the project, we built an explicit meta-model for quality model which captures not only abstract quality factors but also properties of the product ("product factors") and corresponding measures. Using this meta-model, we built a quality base model operationalising quality for the source code of Java and C# systems. This allows us a comprehensible and repeatable quality evaluation of such systems.

4   Outlook

In an outlook, we will look into how we can integrate the different techniques and results into an ever more comprehensive visualisation for the developers. For example, repository mining has reached a level of maturity that allows us to analyse and integrate aspects not possible before. Finally, we will propose "interactive quality control" as approach to give all quality information directly to the developers at the time they create and change artefacts. This contains many additional challenges we will need to solve in the future.

Nevertheless, with the ever-growing size and complexity of software systems, we need to make quality more visible so that developers will be able to handle them.

ECO-MAPS: Information Quality-Driven Enterprise Modeling

Alexis Eduardo Ocampo Ramírez

ECOPETROL S.A.
Bogotá, Colombia
alexis.ocampo@ecopetrol.com.co

Abstract. Fluctuating cash flows, shortage of qualified people, and strict laws demanding safer processes and systems are some examples of challenges that organizations in the oil and gas domain have to cope with in order to remain competitive in the market. The IT domain of these organizations has historically installed best-of-class technology. However, some essential information capabilities, which are important for making strategic, tactical, and operational decisions, are still missing. This missing information can jeopardize the whole operation of a major oil company. To avoid this risk, ECOPETROL has designed and implemented the ECO-MAPS approach, consisting of an enterprise architecture model, an enterprise modeling methodology, and tool support. With this approach, the driver for making decisions is the explicit identification of information that adds value to the business processes and mitigates relevant risks. In practice, this has changed the paradigm at ECOPETROL from "technology first, information last" to "information of high quality first, technology last." This presentation provides insights about the approach, the measurement of information quality, and the current results of the implementation.

Biography

Alexis Ocampo is the Enterprise Architecture Leader at ECOPETROL S.A., Colombia. ECOPETROL is a corporate group headquartered in Colombia, focused on petroleum, gas, petrochemicals, and alternative fuels, and recognized for its international positioning, its innovation, and its commitment to sustainable development. Alexis Ocampo received his doctoral degree in computer science from the University of Kaiserslautern, Germany. He has experience in industry in the area of enterprise architectures, software development, software processes, software evolution, and variability.

J. Heidrich et al. (Eds.): PROFES 2013, LNCS 7983, p. 3, 2013.
© Springer-Verlag Berlin Heidelberg 2013

Implementation of an Online Multi-level and Device-Independent Time and Attendance System

Christos Xenis

LogiSoft
Limassol, Cyprus
christos@logisoft-cy.com

Abstract. A time & attendance system can be implemented at various levels of complexity, from just recording the IN and OUT of employees for attendance and payroll purposes to a sophisticated system recording various events for costing, such as department, job, project, and even item costing. By monitoring live working processes we can create alarms to prevent conflicts and delays. During this keynote we will describe the various levels of a time & attendance system, the necessary integration with recording devices (both biometric and non-biometric), and the methodologies for showing real-life data.

Biography

Christos Xenis studied Computer Science and Physics at Johann Wolfgang Goethe Universität Frankfurt am Main (Germany), where he earned his "Diplom-Informatiker" degree in 1991 under the renowned Professor Dr. Ernst W. Mayr. In 1992, he joined LogiSoft Computer Systems as a partner and has since then been the Research and Development Managing Director of the company. Under his supervision and with his active participation, LogiSoft has created a number of commercial applications that have been very successful in the Cyprus market and beyond. Specific attention is given to human resources applications, such as job scheduling, allocation of man-hours to projects and products, recording of personnel attendance, access control management, monitoring of work execution, and payroll calculation. As a project manager, Xenis successfully completed a number of EU- and government-funded projects and is currently involved in new projects regarding the development of innovative products.

J. Heidrich et al. (Eds.): PROFES 2013, LNCS 7983, p. 4, 2013.
© Springer-Verlag Berlin Heidelberg 2013

How Applicable Is ISO/IEC 29110
in Game Software Development?

Jussi Kasurinen, Risto Laine, and Kari Smolander

Department of Software Engineering and Information Management,
Lappeenranta University of Technology, P.O. Box 20, 53851 Lappeenranta, Finland
{jussi.kasurinen,risto.laine,kari.smolander}@lut.fi

Abstract. Software development in a small development team is a challenge, as people have to fulfill several roles, which in larger groups would have separate, dedicated people for the work. To help small development teams to organize their activities, ISO/IEC standardization body has developed the standard ISO/IEC 29110, Lifecycle profiles for Very Small Entities. Our study focuses on the application of this model in the game industry, an industry that develops software. However, the game industry has its own set of unusual features in software development, such as the demand for artistic vision, need for novelty and demand for creative designs. In this study we analyze how the standard would work in seven different game industry companies and identify a set of additions that would help these organizations to apply the standard in practice. Based on our results, the ISO/IEC 29110 should incorporate more support for iterative development to allow easier adaptation to real-life organizations.

Keywords: game development, game industry, ISO/IEC 29110, software process, empirical study.

1   Introduction

The standardization work and standardized systems are important for many business areas, and the video game industry is not an exception [1]. The video game industry has a number of large international operators such as Sony and Nintendo, which form strong de facto standards for the entire industry [2]. The game industry has also been a constantly growing business for the last decade, having grown in the United States from the annual sales of 6.9 billion in 1999 [1] to 25.1 billion USD in 2010 [3]. Based on this background, it is hardly surprising that the video game industry has more and more new startup companies entering the market.

Fundamentally, video game development is a form of software development, although with several added requirements like visual presentation, artistic aspects and creative design [4, 5]. Game developers may have problems with their technical frameworks, but more often their project management practices need improvement [4]. It seems that game developers should and could learn more from the software engineering discipline in general [5]. In this sense the new ISO/IEC 29110 standard, Lifecycle profiles for Very Small Entities [6], could benefit the game industry. The standard is aimed towards small

J. Heidrich et al. (Eds.): PROFES 2013, LNCS 7983, pp. 5–19, 2013.

and very small software-developing organizations, which, according to the standard, are enterprises, organizations, departments or projects having up to 25 people. The standard introduces a general development process model for development activities, which could be utilized also to organize team activities towards a more systematic and efficient approach to game development.

In this paper we study game industry organizations, compare them against the ISO/IEC 29110 standard, and evaluate how the standard model could be applied in the case organizations. Our research question can be presented as in the title "How applicable is ISO/IEC 29110 in Game Software Development?" Although game development is also software development, it has several unusual features such as the drive for novelty factors, creativity and artistic impression [2], which complicates the software design and development work. Taking this into an account, we wish to understand if the ISO/IEC 29110 standard can cater to the needs of game developing organizations. Based on our results we also develop a revised lifecycle model which should further assist organizations to utilize the current model. This study is also a continuation of our earlier empirical studies in the software industry, in which we, for example, have assessed the problems of software testing [7] and assessed the technical infrastructures of software development companies [8].

The rest of the paper is constructed as follows; Section 2 provides an overview on the related research in game development from the viewpoint of software engineering and introduces the ISO/IEC 29110 model, Section 3 presents the results from the data analysis and observations, while Section 4 discusses these results and their implications. Finally, Section 5 closes the paper with conclusions.

2   Related Research

The research of game development from the viewpoint of software engineering is currently quite active. There are several studies discussing software development processes of game developing organizations. For example, game development lifecycles has been studied by Peltoniemi [2] from the viewpoint of creativity and other intrinsic features. This analysis compared game software development to other domains and concluded that in general game software development is not very mature. Peltoniemi also argues that game development differs from the traditional software industry because of the relatively stable hardware platform and the extensive demand for creativity. Because of these differences, the established life-cycle models are not directly applicable to game development. However, Kultima & Alha [9] observed that the game industry has been moving from the "creative chaos" towards process thinking, and that the larger industry operators have reduced innovation and creativity to a publicity act. Successful game products generate game brands, where innovation and creativity are limited, although innovation in game industry is still necessary in the development of new products.

The challenges of game development have been studied by Kanode and Haddad [10]. According to them, the game industry needs to adopt more advanced software engineering strategies in areas such as management of assets, definition of project requirements and team management. The game industry could benefit from adopting process improvement, project management and development process designs from software engineering. Blow [4] also reports similar findings, emphasizing the need for the game industry to follow software engineering specific project management.

Outside the scope of the game industry, there is a study by Kautz, Hansen and Thaysen [11], which discusses the application of process models in software organizations. Their main finding was that organizations can adjust to given models, provided that the model itself is sound and allows adjustment to fit for the organization. Similarly, Dybå [12] conducted a study on software process improvement in different types of organizations. He found that the company size does not hinder or restrict the process improvement activities. Small organizations are at least as effective as large ones in applying process models and doing process improvement. The rationale for this observation was that small organizations tend to be less formal and loosely defined and can adapt to change needs more quickly in turbulent business environments.

This study discusses the ISO/IEC 29110 lifecycle profiles and the general process model defined for very small entities (VSE) [6]. The standard is created to cater to the needs of the VSE software developers, which, according to the OECD study [13], accounts for over 95% of the worldwide business population. The standard defines life cycle processes, a framework, taxonomy and an assessment guide for small organizations to understand and develop their practices. The standard is meant to allow organizations to develop towards more mature software process models such as ISO/IEC 12207 [14] regardless of the current approach in the organization. The activities defined by the standard are divided to the management and software implementation processes. These processes are interconnected, the management steering the implementation and the implementation providing feedback to the management, both with their own separate phases. The model is illustrated in Figure 1.

The management process has four main activities, project planning, project plan execution, project assessment and control, and project closure. These activities run roughly in this order as the project proceeds, with plan execution and assessment and control as parallel activities. These management activities steer the implementation process, which has six activities. These activities are software implementation initiation, where the project plan is reviewed, necessary creative tasks for designs are done and the implementation is started, software requirements analysis, where the work

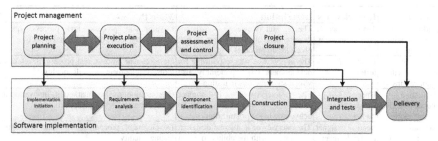

Fig. 1. ISO/IEC 29110 processes. The most important inter-process influences are marked with arrows.

team determines the task assignments and analyses the requirements, software component identification, where architecture is designed, software construction, where the software is developed, software integration and tests, where the construct is tested against the requirements, and product delivery, where the product is finalized and delivered to the customer. Unlike the management process, these activities are not meant to be parallel; the phases advance as product matures.

It is apparent that the game industry could benefit from the project management practices developed for the general software industry, as identified by Petrillo et al. [5], Peltoniemi [2] and Blow [4]. The ISO/IEC 29110 standard offers a general model for software development, which promotes the best practices of the other existing process standards, and is lightweight enough for application use in very small development organizations. In this sense, ISO/IEC 29110 could be an ideal model for the game industry to allow more mature approaches to software development.

3   Research Process

Software development, including the design, development and testing of a commercial product is a complex phenomenon with varying solutions even in similar organizations [8]. Acknowledging this we decided to apply empirical qualitative analysis and apply the grounded theory method to understand the practices of game software development and make conclusions on the applicability of the standard in real-life game development [15-17]. We applied the grounded theory research method as introduced by Glaser and Strauss [15] and later by Strauss and Corbin [17] to systematically codify and analyze the interview data regarding the ISO/IEC 29110 model and related concepts such as game development or management activities in practice.

3.1   Data Collection

The initial population and population criteria were decided based on the prior research made by our research group [for example 7, 8]. In this study, the population ranges from very small (less than 10 people [18]), startup companies making their first products to large and medium-sized companies with extensive product libraries.

Table 1. Interview rounds and themes

Interviews	Interviewee s	Description	Main themes
Qualitative interview with 7 organizations	Team leader or project manager	The interviewee manages development of one product, or one phase for all products.	Development process, test process, quality, outsourcing, tools, organizational aspects.
Qualitative interview with 7 organizations	Developer or tester	The interviewee was responsible for development tasks, preferably also with responsibilities in testing.	Development process, test process, development tools, development methods, quality.
Qualitative interview with 7 organizations	Upper management or owner	The interviewee is upper management, or owner with an active role in the organization.	Organization, quality, marketing, innovation and design process, development process.
Qualitative interview with 7 organizations	Lead designer or Art designer	The interviewee is a game designer, or manager with the ability to affect the product design.	Development process, design and innovation, testing, quality

We carried out four interview rounds in our study (Table 1). The sample of the interview rounds consisted of seven organizations collected from our research partners and supplemented with volunteering organizations to achieve a heterogeneous group of different target audiences, development platforms and organizational backgrounds. The interviews were collected from spring to fall of 2012 by seven different researchers from two different research laboratories.

The seven organizations in the study group are all full-time professional software producers, with game development as their main activity and source of income. The smallest organization in the study was a startup with three persons; in the largest organization several hundred people contributed to the product development by directly working in the organization or by producing bought content. The organization sizes in Table 2 vary from small to large according to the EU SME definition [18], where a company is small when it has less than 50 employees, but in fact all small organizations in the study had less than 25 employees and so they fit to the ISO/IEC 29110 VSE definition. The group of organizations included different target platforms and different sizes of development teams. The organizations varied (Table 2) from mobile game developers to developers of browser-based, PC and console games. Their distribution channels included internet stores, general digital distribution, and boxed copies sold at game stores. The objective of this diverse approach was to gain a broader understanding of the practices in the organization to identify the most important factors affecting how the organization felt about the ISO/IEC 29110 standard [6]. To succeed in this objective, the research questionnaires included themes such as development methods, quality requirements, test phases, applied tools and design principles, which helped us to understand the case organizations. The questionnaires were also refined between the interview rounds to gain more role-oriented information and test our observations from the organizations made on the earlier rounds. Before interviews, the questionnaire questions were reviewed by a number of peers from the research group to assess the first round interview questions. The complete questionnaires are available at http://www2.it.lut.fi/project/SOCES/material.

The interviews contained semi-structured questions, and the whole sessions were tape-recorded for qualitative analysis. We also allowed the interviewees to get access to the data collection instruments before the interview, ask questions on the topics and gave a brief introduction to the interview themes prior to the actual interview.

Table 2. Description of the interviewed organizations

Organization	Release platforms	Team size[1]	Intended distribution channels for products	Number of released games in history
Case A	PC, game consoles	Large	Digital distribution, boxed copies	More than 10 released products
Case B	Mobile platforms	Small	Platform store	Less than 5 released products
Case C	Game consoles, PC	Large	Boxed copies, digital distribution	More than 10 released products
Case D	Mobile platforms, PC	Medium	Platform store, digital distribuiton	Less than 5 released products
Case E	Mobile platforms	Small	Platform store	Less than 5 released products
Case F	PC	Medium	Digital distribution	Developing first product
Case G	Browser games	Small	Separate service site	Developing first product

[1]Number of people contributing to the released product, size by SME definitions [18]

All interviews lasted in average about one hour. The interviews were arranged face-to-face with one or two organization participants and one or two researchers present.

The decision to interview project managers during the first round was based on the objective to understand the organizational processes and gain understanding of the operational level of software development in the case organizations. We also wanted to test whether our earlier observations from general software industry [7,8] would be applicable in the game industry context, and gain some insight into the organization.

The interviewees in the second round were selected from a group of developers, who directly contributed to the game product and had experience with the technical details of the developed product. The second round interview topics were heavily focused towards programming techniques, process activities and applied tools.

In the third round, the focus of the interviews was to collect general data of the company and focus on the managerial and business aspects. During this round additional themes such as marketing, innovation and financing were collected to better understand the context in which the game industry operates.

In the fourth round, the focus was on the creative aspects of development, in the game design work. During this round the interviewed employees were game designers or management-level personnel with the ability to affect the designs. Additional topics were change management, testing and external influences on the products.

3.2   Data Analysis

The grounded theory method contains three data analysis steps: open coding, where categories and their related codes are extracted from the data; axial coding, where connections between the categories and codes are identified; and selective coding, where the core category is identified and described [17].

The objective of the open coding is to identify leads in the data and classify the observations. This process was started with "seed categories" [19], which in our case, were derived from our prior studies on general software industry [7,8]. These seed categories were also used to define the main themes for the questionnaires. We used Atlas TI as the tool to manage codings in the interview transcripts. In open coding, the classified observations are organized into larger categories. New categories appear and are merged because of new information that surfaces during the coding and analysis work. For example, we revised our initial choice of collecting data on applied standards as a separate category as the interviews proved that the organizations were not as process-oriented or highly organized as originally thought, not even the larger or older ones. At the end of the open coding, the number of codes was 172. They came from 1572 observations from over 1400 minutes of recorded interview data.

The objective of the axial coding, which starts when the categories start to emerge and runs somewhat parallel with the open coding [17], is to further develop the categories by looking for causal conditions or any kind of connections between the categories. In this phase, the analysis focuses on identifying the relationships between larger concepts. For example, codes such as "Design process: refining designs", "Development process: knowledge transfer" and "Problem: Documentation/knowledge transfer related to design" form a chain of evidence for observing organizational documentation practices and the problems associated to the communication between stakeholders. By following these leads in the data, the relationships were identified.

The third phase of grounded analysis, selective coding, is used to identify the core category [17] and relate it to the surrounding categories. As defined in [17], the core category is sometimes one of the existing categories, and at other times no single category is broad or influential enough to cover the central phenomenon. In this study, the core category "applicability of the ISO/IEC 29110 standard" resulted to the identification of the four different scenarios which could enable better applicability of the standard in game development organizations. This core category was formed by collecting the case organization views on the standard, collecting the existing development process issues and comparing them against the organizational backgrounds. For example, we observed that the most common consideration with the standard was that it was not considered as important in the very small organizations, but more important in the "small-medium" organizations with ten to twenty members. Similarly, the organizations with the background in software industry were the most critical towards the standard itself. Overall, we adjusted the core category to include all issues that explained the opinions on the ISO/IEC 29110 standard and based on this analysis, created an initial model that could combine the simplicity of the ISO/IEC 29110 standard with the concerns the case organizations presented.

4   Results

In this section we first introduce the categories created in the analysis, present the main observations we made on the applicability and usability of ISO/IEC 29110 [6], discuss the implications of the observations and finally present a revised draft for a model that combines the observations with the standard.

4.1   Categories

The core category, *Applicability of ISO/IEC29110* (Table 3), describes our interpretation of how the organization saw that ISO/IEC 29110 could be applied in their organization. The core category was identified from the data because it explained well the differences between the organizations and enabled us to create four scenarios of using the ISO/IEC 29110 process model.

Our analysis identified four scenarios. In scenario 1, named *"As is"*, the organization considers the model to be applicable "as is", with little to no modifications. In scenario 2, *"development iteration"*, the organization considers that the model is applicable, but the development phase activities from component identification to testing should be modeled iteratively or at least allow iterations over the existing plan-driven definition. In scenario 3, *"full iteration"*, the model is seen applicable, but only if it is used only as a definition of one iteration round. In scenario 3, the entire process model is executed several times, for example once for product design to deliver a design prototype, in development to deliver an alpha release candidate and so on. In each iteration there would all activities from design to delivery. Finally the scenario 4, *"reference tool"*, basically considers the model to be unsuitable for the organization, but applicable as a glossary, reference or teaching tool.

The category *Opinion on ISO/IEC 29110 applicability in own organization* describes the overall attitude of the organization towards the ISO/IEC 29110 software process model, should it be applied in the current organization. The category *Most important development need* for the standard describes the most important area or shortcoming, which should be revised to enable better applicability.

The category *Applied development method* defines what kind of development process the organization applies. The applied scale is undefined agile, where the organization uses basically an open-form approach, with little documentation and planning, defined agile, where the organization follows the principles of an established agile practice – also named if followed officially – and plan-driven, if the organization considers itself to follow a more traditional design-first approach.

The category *Typical design deliverables* summarizes the deliverables the organization usually produces before it commits to the construction of a new game product. The term functional prototype denotes to a proof-of-concept prototype that features the main gameplay elements, core features and concept art means that the organization has decided on the main features and the artistic direction. Basic gameplay elements simply means that the organization has decided on the game type and some of the most important features for the product.

The category *External or publisher influence on the development* categorizes the extent and type of influence the external organizations or partners have on the developed product. Low influence means that an external partner, usually a publisher,

Table 3. Summary of the essential categories in organizations

Category	Case A	Case B	Case C	Case D	Case E	Case F	Case G
Applicability of ISO/IEC29110	Scenario 3, "full iteration"	scenario 1, "As is"	Scenario 4, "reference tool"	Scenario 2, "development iteration"	Scenario 1, "As is"	Scenario 2, "development iteration"	Scenario 4, "reference tool"
Opinion on ISO/IEC 29110 applicability in own organization	Game development has additional issues	Management-part is close to current state,	Basis for contracts, problematic to implement	More or less defines the basic activities done in each project.	Too close to waterfall model.	Would limit design.	Overtly rigid, too close to waterfall model.
Most important development need for the standard	Too generic model to be directly usable.	Too generic model to be directly usable.	Design cannot be finalized before development	Needs experienced crew to use.	Design cannot be finalized before development	Design cannot be finalized before development	Too close to waterfall model
Applied development method	Defined agile, SCRUM	Plan-driven	Defined agile, SCRUM	Undefined agile	Undefined agile	Defined agile, SCRUM	Defined agile
Typical design deliverables	Functional prototype	Basic gameplay elements	Functional prototype	Core features, concept art	Basic gameplay elements	Core features, concept art	Basic gameplay elements
External or publisher influence in development	Medium/Large: Some features dictated by the publisher	Low/Medium: Some requested features, negotiable	Large: rejected features, cuts project schedules	Medium: Own testing, requested features	Low: Rarely requested features	Medium: Some requested features and changes	-
Project size	Large	Small	Large	Medium	Small	Medium	Small
Organizational experience	More than 10 products	Less than 5 products	More than 10 products	Less than 5 products	Less than 5 products	Developing first products	Developing first products
Key personnel background	Media	Academic	Media	Media	Software Industry	Academic	Software Industry

[1]See SME definitions [18]

recommends only few additions or changes, medium that some wanted features are demanded and large that the external influence may reject features, enforce changes, or even dictate themes or genre of the designed product.

The categories *Project size* and *Organizational experience* express the size and the experience of the development team. The project size is small when there are less than ten people, medium when ten to fifty and large when more than fifty developers contribute to the game product. Third-party members such as insourced musicians, artists or asset developers are also included to the size estimate. Organizational experience expresses the experience of the organization in game development. The experience is evaluated with the number of commercially launched products, excluding expansion disks or other additional content developed for earlier product. The applied scale is "developing the first products", "less than five", "less than ten" and "ten or more" to give a rough estimate on how experienced the organization is.

The category *Key personnel background* lists the business domain from which the key personnel such as company owners or founding members have emigrated to the company. The backgrounds were classified to three domains: media which includes areas such as advertisement agencies or journalism, academic which includes university-level students or teachers and software industry which means software business domains other than entertainment or video games.

4.2   Observations

ISO/IEC 29110 Should Offer a More Iterative and Flexible Approach to Development

The ISO/IEC 29110 standard was introduced and discussed with the representatives of the seven study organizations. In most organizations the standard was considered to be at least somewhat useful, although in need of some revisions. Cases A and B considered the model to be too generic to apply as such, while organizations E and G considered it to resemble too much the classical waterfall approach. However, several case organizations (A, B, D, E and F) considered the model to be adjustable with some revisions to cater to their organization.

"Yes, I do recognize stuff from our current processes, but I think that in game development design cannot be finalized beforehand." ..."We should try to be more Agile than this." – Case C, Project manager

"The first thing I see here is that requirement analysis is completely done before construction. So design is finished before anything is implemented... that's just not the way it happens." – Case G, Designer

Interestingly, the most critical outlook against the ISO/IEC 29110 standard in its current form came from the organizations with background in the software industry. Both this kind of organizations criticized the model for steering the process activities towards waterfall model, which in their opinion is very unsuitable for the game industry. In both organizations, cases E and G, the main concern was that the waterfall-like approach would lock the design too early in the development process.

"I think that the current tools have made that approach redundant"… *"Why should we bother with strict decisions when we can make a prototype in two hours to test things out?"* – Case E, Developer

"I think that the [waterfall] model is no longer feasible approach for any kind of development project." – Case G, Designer

Game Development Has Many Stakeholders, But They Are Not Interested in Certification or Process Standards

In all organizations with the sole exception of the Case G the interviewees reported that they get regularly requests from their external stakeholders. The requests varied between negotiable feature additions (for example cases B and E), to large interventions where the requests could determine the features and dictate project schedules. However, these external stakeholders did not require defined development processes. In fact the opposite was observed: the organizations (cases B and E) which had most limited external influence on their products were also the most positive towards the ISO/IEC 29110 model, while case organizations A and C with the most external interference were also very critical towards the standard.

"Well, practically this is how we work. All the stuff we do is in this model somewhere." – Case E, Developer

"Considering our team I think this would be good to use as a backbone"…*"I think this should be usable in the game industry. At least I do not see why it would not be."* – Case B, Project manager

It is also worthwhile to notice that even if the external organizations would promote standardization for game development, the developers are rather critical towards using it in small organizations. All organizations expressed that their organization either was too small for such a rigid model (cases B, D, E and G) or that very small organizations in general do not require defined process models (cases A, C and F).

"In our team everyone does a bit of everything, there really is no separate project management organization." – Case B, Project manager

"If our team was 10 people, our approach would be hard, with 20, probably impossible. But since we are still so small, we can go with ad hoc." – Case D, Upper management

Game-Developing Organizations Have Problems in Following the Current ISO/IEC 29110 Process Model because of the Nature of the Industry

In almost all organizations the design process was considered to be at least somewhat problematic area in the standard. Cases C, E and F expressed their concern over how the standard enables design activities. In many organizations product design is not very specific, and the decisions are made based on the usability, playability and "fun factor" tested with product prototypes.

"If a tester comes to say that this does not work, there is not fun in it, you really cannot leave that in the game, you have to fix it." – Case E, Designer

"When the production started, the specifications went out of the window"…*"There simply is not enough knowledge to make a full design at the early stages."* – Case G, Designer

"We sometimes have to make drastic changes [to keep the game fun]." – Case F, Designer

Another common concern with the standard was the level of abstraction. Case organizations A and C considered the standard very abstract to the point of being hard to implement as a development guideline. Case D considered the standard to be generally close to what they are already doing, adding that the standard would require an experienced team to work properly. Case B mentioned that the management model is a rather accurate representation of the project management tasks in their organization.

"With these states and arrows... pretty much every step we take with development falls into some of the [ISO/IEC 29110] model categories." – Case D, Project manager

Besides general comments, case organizations A, B and C considered the standard to be usable in software development, but lacking the features and parts that are specific to the game industry. Features like design with prototypes, demo versions to attract business partners and art design were mentioned to be such features missing.

"The management parts, that's OK, but the implementation [is not]." – Case B, Developer

"I do identify parts of our current work, but in my opinion game programming with this is difficult." – Case C, Project manager

4.3   Implications

Based on the observations it is apparent that the ISO/IEC 29110 standard is a reasonable start for creating a model for small and very small software organizations. However, for the game industry in particular there are some troublesome areas which require further attention. For example, the model needs to be able to support iterative development, like in the scenarios 2 and 3. In addition, the game industry has some unusual features such as the requirement for late changes to designs and focus on fine-tuning the user experience. It seems that the most useful standard for the game industry would be a lean iterative process standard for development tasks, targeted at small and small-medium sized organizations. Very small organizations operate with highly informal and flexible methods, and do not benefit from the standard as much as a small to small medium (roughly ten to twenty participants) sized organizations would. ISO/IEC 29110 can be developed to meet the needs of these organizations, but that requires revisions to allow more iterative approaches. The requirements for a VSE model suitable for application should have the following changes:

- Design should not be finalized before the implementation.
- Varying amounts of details should be allowed in the initial design.
- Changes in the product should be allowed even near the end of the project.
- The standard should support iterative approaches.
- The standard should define all of the main activities to allow its use as the basis for business contracts, but leave the definition of details to organizations.
- The standard should support delivery-phase activities such as acceptance testing and planning phase activities such as proof-of-concept prototypes.

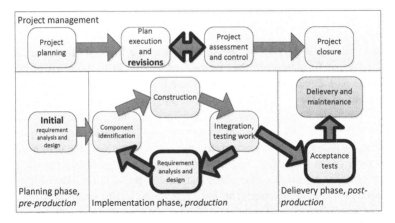

Fig. 2. The revised model based on the analysis, revised elements bolded

A draft model based on these requirements is illustrated in Figure 2. The most important difference between the standard and the revised model is the implementation of iterative development and separating the process to three phases. Initial requirements analysis and design, which includes experimenting new ideas with functional prototypes before the implementation is located in the planning phase (also called pre-production by the game industry), while the implementation phase (production in game industry) has its own requirement analysis and design phase to allow revisions to the plans during the development. Finally the finalization activities such as acceptance testing or identification of reusable assets are separated to a new phase called delivery phase (post-production).

The management process is kept relatively intact, as it was considered to be the most accurate part of the model. The project planning is done before the development starts, and in the plan execution process some minor revisions can be done to the project plans to cater to the change needs during development. Project closure happens in the delivery phase, when final adjustments and quality assurance activities to validate the requirements are done. With these additions the model is still conceptually similar to the standard. Iteration is not necessary but it is allowed. Varying degrees of design are allowed and if revisions are not needed, the process is similar to the original.

5   Discussion

A common opinion was that a life-cycle standard for very small organizations could be beneficial. Out of the seven organizations only two considered ISO/IEC 29110 as unsuitable for their use, but the others considered the standard at least as a useful basis for contracts. The most common problem with the standard was the apparent lack of support for iterative development especially in design. The ISO/IEC 29110 documentation mentions that it can be applied with any methodology, like agile, evolutionary, incremental, test driven or other [6], but this is not very evident from the viewpoint of the organizations. The model design steers the development towards plan-driven principles, or at least does not support agile development well.

The interviewed organizations also considered the model target audience to be problematic; very small organizations can operate with an ad-hoc structure. However, most organizations agreed that a small-medium organization (roughly ten to twenty developers) needs a more or less defined process model. Overall, the conclusions for the applicability and the suitability of the ISO/IEC 29110 standard can be summarized as follows: *For very-small-sized game development companies the standard should promote more agility. For the current standard the best target audience seems to be small and small-medium-sized organizations.*

Many interviewees were happy with their informal and, to some degree, unstructured approach to software development. The small organization size and unstructured process also affected the assessment of the standard. The smallest organizations represented the key demographic of the standard, while the larger, more experienced organizations provided insight into the general applicability. Interestingly, the more the organization had external stakeholders like financers and publishers, the more they considered the model to need changes. On the other hand, this could also indicate that the model is suitable for small, autonomous developer teams such as case organizations B and E, should there be any incentive like an external publisher or a financer requiring the implementation of some process model. However, since expertise with process models or process development was not required for participating in this study, these results should be considered more like indications or recommendations.

Based on all of the identified needs and observations, the ISO/IEC 29110 standard can be considered to be somewhat difficult to implement in a game organization as is. However, dividing the process model to three main phases, the design phase, the implementation phase and the delivery phase, with added support for iteration in implementation, the model caters to the most of the identified game industry problems. In addition, should the implementation phase be completed without iteration, the revised model should still be compatible with the original ISO/IEC 29110 standard.

There are threats that should be acknowledged when addressing the validity of this type of qualitative research [20,21]. Whittemore et al. [20] lists integrity, authenticity, credibility and criticality as the most important attributes that are universally required for a qualitative study. In their conclusion, the most important aspect of presenting validity is to present enough evidence for the reader to accept that the researchers truly understand the phenomena they are observing, "know what they claim to know". The most common threat is personal biasing, disregarding the patterns and observations which do not fit or support their own theories [21]. In this study these risks have been taken into account when planning and implementing the study with several cautionary actions. The study questionnaires were designed by seven researchers to avoid personal bias, the data collection was conducted by six researchers and the analysis process for this paper was conducted by two and validated by three researchers working separately on the same data. The two analyzers did their work independently, and the different interpretations were discussed and resolved in meetings during the study.

Additionally, all interviewed organizations were small and medium size game organizations, located in Southeastern Finland. This can be considered a threat, as some phenomena can be caused by the geographical proximity, such as local policies or support from the local educational institutions. However, the game business is international and all our organizations aimed their products at international markets. The possibility for the bias caused by the cultural similarity was addressed by selecting the organizations to represent different release platforms, company backgrounds, different maturity levels as businesses and different production sizes.

6   Conclusions

In this paper we have presented our study on seven game software development organizations with the purpose of evaluating the applicability of the ISO/IEC 29110 standard. The results indicate that very small game developing organizations do not tend to follow any systematic development method, working mostly ad hoc. The application of the ISO/IEC 29110 standard could be possible, but the model should support an iterations, as in the game business product design is mostly a guideline, which changes throughout the development process. The current standard version is reasonably accurate for the management tasks, but does not support the continuous design or the approach where late changes to the product features are expected. The applicability of the current version can be summarized as follows: Should the target audience of VSE-sized companies be kept, the model should promote more agile approaches, and should the current model be kept, the best target audience in the game industry would be not a VSE, but small and medium-sized organizations.

The results of this study can be used to help very small new game developing organizations to understand how they could apply the ISO/IEC 29110 standard, or at least the concepts presented in the standard to help in managing development. For the future work, the applicability of the revised model should be assessed with the game developing organizations. Another interesting direction could also be the inclusion of creative elements to the process thinking; how game organizations actually work, and how they could be supported with the existing software engineering knowledge.

Acknowledgements. This study was supported by the European Union Regional Development Fund projects number A31814, "Kaakon Peliklusteri" administered by the Council of Southern Karelia and number A32139 "Game Cluster" administered by the Council of Päijät-Häme. We would also like to thank all the interviewed organizations and the project partners, namely Cursor and Innovire research team at LUT Kouvola.

References

1. Gallagher, S., Park, S.H.: Innovation and competition in standard-based industries: a historical analysis of the US home video game market. IEEE Transactions on Engineering Management 49(1), 67–82 (2002), doi:10.1109/17.985749
2. Peltoniemi, M.: Life-cycle of the Games Industry The Specificities of Creative Industries. In: Proceedings of the Mindtrek 2008, Tampere, Finland, October 7-9 (2008)

3. Entertainment Software Association: 2011 Sales, demographic and usage data: Essential facts about computer and video game industry (2011)
4. Blow, J.: Game Development: Harder Than You Think. Queue 1(10), ss.28–ss.37 (2004)
5. Petrillo, F., Pimenta, M., Trindade, F., Dietrich, C.: Houston, we have a problem...: A survey of Actual Problems in Computer Games Development. In: Proceedings of SAC 2008, Fortaleza, Brazil, March 16-20 (2008)
6. ISO/IEC: ISO/IEC 29110 Software Engineering – Lifecycle Profiles for Very Small Entities (VSEs), Part 5-1-2: Management and engineering guide:Generic profile group: Basic profile ISO/IEC JTC1/SC7, Technical Report dated 2011-05-15 (2011)
7. Kasurinen, J., Taipale, O., Smolander, K.: Analysis of Problems in Testing Practices. In: Proceedings of the 16th Asia-Pacific Software Engineering Conference (APSEC), Penang, Malaysia, December 1-3 (2009), doi:/10.1109/APSEC.2009.17
8. Kasurinen, J., Taipale, O., Smolander, K.: Software Test Automation in Practice: Empirical Observations. In: Advances in Software Engineering, Special Issue on Software Test Automation. Hindawi Publishing Co. (2010), doi:10.1155/2010/620836
9. Kultima, A., Alha, K.: Hopefully Everything I'm Doing Has to Do with Innovation: Games industry professionals on innovation. In: 2009, Proc. 2nd International IEEE Consumer Electronics Society's Games Innovation Conference, Hong Kong, China (2010)
10. Kanode, C.M., Haddad, H.M.: Software Engineering Challenges in Game Development. In: Sixth International Conference on Information Technology: New Generations ITNG 2009, pp. ss.260–ss.265 (2009)
11. Kautz, K., Hansen, H.W., Thaysen, K.: Applying and adjusting a software process improvement model in practice: the use of the IDEAL model in a small software enterprise. In: Proceedings of the 22nd International Conference on Software Engineering, Limerick, Ireland, pp. 626–633 (2000), doi:10.1145/337180.337492
12. Dybå, T.: Factors of software process improvement success in small and large organizations: an empirical study in the scandinavian context. In: Proceedings of the 9th European Software Engineering Conference Held Jointly with 11th ACM SIGSOFT International Symposium on Foundations of Software Engineering, Helsinki, Finland, pp. 148–157 (2003), doi:10.1145/940071.940092
13. OECD: OECD SME and Entrepreneurship Outlook, 2005 Edition, Organisation for Economic Co-operation and Development, Paris (2005)
14. ISO/IEC: ISO/IEC 12207:2008 Systems and Software engineering - Software life cycle processes (2008)
15. Glaser, B.G.: Constuctivist Grounded Theory? Forum: Qualitative Social Research (FQS) 3(3) (2002)
16. Glaser, B., Strauss, A.L.: The Discovery of Grounded Theory: Strategies for Qualitative Research. Aldine, Chicago (1967)
17. Strauss, A., Corbin, J.: Basics of Qualitative Research: Grounded Theory Procedures and Techniques. SAGE Publications, Newbury Park (1990)
18. EU: SME Definition, European Commission (2003)
19. Seaman, C.B.: Qualitative methods in empirical studies of software engineering. IEEE Transactions on Software Engineering 25, 557–572 (2002)
20. Whittemore, R., Chase, S.K., Mandle, C.L.: Validity in Qualitative Research. Qual. Health Res. 11, 522–537 (2001), doi:10.1177/104973201129119299
21. Golafshani, N.: Understanding Reliability and Validity in Qualitative Research. The Qualitative Report 8(4), 596–607 (2003)

Supporting Cognitive Work
in Software Development Workflows

Jarkko Hyysalo[1], Jari Lehto[2], Sanja Aaramaa[1], and Markus Kelanti[1]

[1] University of Oulu, Department of Information Processing Science, M-Group,
P.O. Box 3000, 90014 Oulu, Finland
{Jarkko.Hyysalo,Sanja.Aaramaa,Markus.Kelanti}@Oulu.fi
[2] Nokia Siemens Networks Oy, P.O. Box 1, 02022 Nokia Siemens Networks, Espoo, Finland
Jari.Lehto@nsn.com

Abstract. Both the increasing complexity of developing software systems and the growing significance of knowledge work require new innovations to support developers' cognitive activities in product development. A workflow is one aid to the development process. Current workflow models support business process management and logical ordering of tasks, but provide insufficient cognitive support for developers' daily work. We argue that cognitive support should also be provided. This paper addresses the topic through an empirical study. A model to support cognitive work in product development workflows has been developed and validated in an action research intervention. The empirical results indicate that the model tackles the identified challenges in workflows, increases the development process's efficiency, and provides better results. The findings of this study offer new insights into workflows and work support for both scholars and practitioners.

Keywords: Work support, product development, cognitive work, workflow.

1   Introduction

In today's world, software (SW) systems are becoming ever more complex. Software development (SD), in turn, has become increasingly challenging and intellectually demanding knowledge work [1, 2]. This knowledge work is a largely cognitive activity based on a worker's internal mental processes, rather than physical labor. To support developers' cognitive work, we aim to reduce the cognitive burden—the burden of keeping unnecessary things in their minds, e.g., how to use tools, how to link information between tools, and how to search for relevant data. Similarly principles apply also to the development process and its tasks.

Furthermore, in real life, work has variables that may cause changes and unexpected events that require non-routine solutions. This places a substantial demand on developers' cognitive capacities while creating, processing, and disseminating data. SW developers face several individual and team cognition-related challenges in their work, such as complex decision making and problem solving, the handling of vast amounts of information, the creation of a shared understanding, and information and knowledge sharing.

J. Heidrich et al. (Eds.): PROFES 2013, LNCS 7983, pp. 20–34, 2013.

Workflows are one way to help companies and their workers manage processes, transferring the work and data from one to another, and to help establish a logical order for implementing tasks. However, traditional workflow approaches are quite static and do not fully address the changes and unexpected events; current workflow models also lack cognitive support [3]. The hypothesis of this paper is that having proper support for cognitive work in SD workflows will help developers use available knowledge to come up with creative solutions to non-routine situations, improving efficiency and the results of the product creation process. Cognitive support needs to be integrated into workflows to address the challenges mentioned above. This requires defining support needs and ways to provide support. Thus, the following two research questions must be answered:

RQ 1. What kind of cognitive support is needed in SD workflows?
RQ 2. How should cognitive support for SD workflows be provided?

This paper defines the aspects of cognitive work support a workflow must cover to support SD. A model for support is presented, with results from action research validating the model and demonstrating its value. The rest of the paper is organized as follows. Section 2 examines related literature; Section 3 presents the research approach; Section 4 presents the model and the empirical study with its findings and results; Section 5 discusses the results and implications of the study; Section 6 concludes the study and summarizes the key findings.

2   Related Work

Processes are built to ensure that activities in an organization are performed consistently and reliably [4]. Workflows are one way to structure processes [5]. Traditionally, workflows have been described as a sequence of working steps or logically related tasks, including the use of resources to achieve a common goal—transforming a set of inputs into outputs of value to stakeholders. Each task in a workflow is an interaction between actors and their environment, where objectives, work requirements, and resources set the boundaries of acceptable performance.

Within the processes of a workflow, the exact execution order of activities is not necessarily important. It may even be impractical, as interaction with the environment, the activities, and underlying business logic set the order, rather than predetermined, static process schema [6]. In real life, work is more variable and dynamic than current workflows can support, and workflows do not handle exceptions well [7–9]. This calls for cognitive skills that are required to respond to changes, while routine tasks can be automated. Changes and unexpected events require creativity and human problem-solving skills to overcome and solve them [10]. Experts in a given field are recognized as such because they are good at identifying problem states invoking certain solutions [11], and when the type of problem can be identified, it is easier to find a solution [12]. Thus, the ability to provide already identified and tried solutions and support for problem solving would help experts, and even more so novices who do not yet have ready problem solving schemas. However, identifying problems and situations requires substantial information.

Human cognition is the result of interactions between individuals, artifacts, and resources in their environment [13]. This knowledge-intensive teamwork is as good and efficient as actors' cognitive and cooperative abilities, requiring three kinds of cooperation [3]: Work cooperation, resource sharing, and cognitive cooperation. Work cooperation and resource sharing are currently addressed, to some extent, with workflows. However, it has been recognized that cognitive cooperation is missing in the current workflows [3], [6]. Cognitive cooperation is when individuals learn from each other, make abstractions, solve problems, and use their experience and skills [3], [14–16]. Knowledge-intensive teamwork is required in SD, which involves working with abstract knowledge instead of physical matters, but there are several challenges: knowledge is not easily transferred, unless it is made explicit; knowledge elements are context-specific; and cooperation is needed due to humans' cognitive limitations— one cannot know everything [17]. Suggested solutions include an awareness of context [18], and an awareness of others' actions, which makes it possible for developers to structure their interactions and cooperative processes, and to provide a context for one's own activities [19–20]. Other studies address the issue of cognitive workflows from different angles: cognitive support for business processes, real-time routing and strategic control of business process management [6], agent-based cognitive flow management, recording of cognitive information and passing it to others [3], and interfaces for workflows [21].

To perform knowledge-intensive tasks and creatively solve challenges, a developer must understand both the current state and the goal state, and have a way to reach the goal. This understanding is the basis of problem solving and task implementation. To address this, we suggest focusing on information content, providing practical work support and promoting awareness. Hence, this paper's main contribution is to complement traditional workflows by providing cognitive support for SD workflows. The support will help developers' in their daily tasks, with an emphasis on cognitive work with relevant information and solid reasoning for the developers' tasks, awareness support, and the provision of concrete guidance for work.

3   Research Approach

A study was conducted to build and validate the developed model. While the model was built in the pre-study following the principles of constructive research, the empirical work was done via action research intervention. Action research is one way theories are put into practice to help an organization solve concrete problems, while at the same time expanding scientific knowledge [22]. It is an iterative process, where theory-based diagnosis is followed by practical intervention through action planning, action taking, and evaluation. Learning from action and evaluation results in change, and the cycle is repeated until satisfactory results are obtained. Action research was applied to see the developed model in practice, to improve it, and to evaluate the outcome. Evaluations were made by implementing the model and applying it in its intended settings, thus providing empirical evidence on its use.

The study was conducted at a large global company that provides systems and services and that is one of the largest information and communication technology (ICT) companies in the world. Most of the company's products are considered SW-intensive systems developed as a parallel and interconnected set of processes run by different stakeholders. SW is delivered in releases, where each release can be seen as a collection of new and/or enhanced features.

Our research started with a pre-study, where the need for cognitive support was first identified by analyzing existing literature. The initial model for supporting cognitive work in workflows was then developed. The case company was studied to understand the state-of-the-practice; company material was studied and weekly workshops were arranged to understand practical needs and issues. Interview questions were formulated based on the understanding achieved. The pre-study phase was iterative in nature to ensure a solid basis for subsequent actions. After the pre-study, we proceeded to action research. The research cycle is show in Fig. 1.

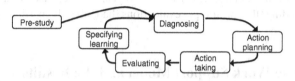

Fig. 1. Action research cycle with a pre-study [adapted from 23]

In the diagnosing phase, thematic, semi-structured interviews were conducted in which interviewees were allowed to carefully explain their views. Interviews were transcribed and then summarized to condense the main points of each answer for subsequent checking by the interviewees. The summaries did not contain conclusions or interpretations. In the data analysis, the data were grouped into topics of process visibility, cooperation and communication, information, and development environment. Common denominators were then identified. The challenges were listed for each topic, and solutions were proposed. The findings were then compared with existing literature. This provided the basis for prototype development related to the need for cognitive support in the case company's workflow.

A total of 35 qualitative interviews were conducted, over a period of 18 months at several sites in several countries. Individuals in a range of positions, from "floor level" to mid-management, were interviewed. One of the interviewees is a service capability manager, 14 are development team leaders with at least 15 years of work experience, and one was the head of the development team leaders. The rest are experienced developers from different organizational units with 10 to 20 years of work experience. Altogether, 20 different organizational units were represented covering several aspects of the products' lifecycle. Different questionnaires were used, as the interviews were targeted for each phase with relevant questions concerning interviewees' work.

Based on the identified needs, the prototype tool was built to test our model in practice. Integration into the case company's workflow was done in the action-taking phase. A part of the company's requirements development process selected as a "testbed," including the activities from recording the initial development ideas, their transformation from problem domain requests to solution domain requirements, and further bundling them into features. The prototype was then evaluated by applying participatory observation. During each evaluation session, a researcher made observational notes, and all sessions were recorded. In addition, the researcher provided guidance when needed for both on the developed method and the prototype as well. The developers were encouraged to think out loud as much as possible, and after each evaluation phase, experiences were discussed in the monthly team meeting. Gathered feedback from the experts, observed challenges, and identified bugs in the prototype were recorded into wiki. The researchers, prototype developers, and a case company representative had weekly meetings to review the results and decide further actions. These actions provided rich data to be analyzed and for specifying learning. A workshop was then held at the case company to report our initial findings and gather feedback that was also incorporated into our findings.

Eight developers participated in the prototype evaluations. Four of the developers are development team leaders, while the rest are specialists with strong experience on practical work. All of them had at least 10 to 20 years of work experience Most of the developers attending the prototype evaluations had already participated in earlier interviews.

4   Cognitive Work Support Model and the Results

To have effective developer performance, clearly defined expectations, processes, tasks, and an appropriate development environment are necessary. The high-level goals must be transformed into specific development tasks that are part of the process to produce the desired outcome. Developers can then accomplish their tasks using their knowledge and skills, which however, are not always sufficient for the task at hand and support may be needed. In addition, there is a need for tools that support cognitive work, such as communication tools to aid cognitive cooperation, and tools to reduce cognitive overhead.

4.1   Pre-study – Developing the Model

The key is to integrate all support into a workflow, facilitating the easy retrieval of information and its use, which supports knowledge creation. We link the developers and their tasks to development processes, information, knowledge, and tools, and help them understand what they need to do, why they need to do it, and how. Developers' cognitive performance is improved by providing them the necessary information and tools. The collaborative nature of development is supported by including communication channels geared toward other experts, which eases the dissemination of knowledge and improves cooperative work.

Fig. 2 shows the three levels of cognitive support, which provide three complementary views of development. "Why?", "What?", and "How?" are the basic questions defining the work. The WHY-level describes the high-level objectives and processes, sets the context for development, and defines the criteria for achieving the purposes. The WHAT-level splits these into activities and tasks that instantiate the high-level purposes. The order of operations is not strictly defined; instead the activities are synchronized and coordinated by decision points (DP). The HOW-level focuses on the ways in which the tasks can be accomplished. Each level is supported with a graphical presentation and links to data, development and collaboration tools, and guidance. The graphical presentation is used for navigating a workflow, tracking the work, and visualizing dependencies of work items. All information flows are explained by defining the needs, inputs, outputs, and data sources. For all levels, dependencies of activities and work items play an important role.

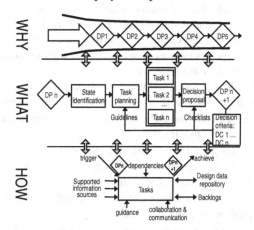

Fig. 2. Three levels of knowledge–Three complementary views of development

The need and the level for cognitive support may differ for developers with different skill levels. An expert may not require much support, whereas a novice may need comprehensive help. To address this, first and foremost, a workflow is built to make a developer produce accurate data in the correct format. The system helps users to think about what is really asked for in the tasks and guides them to produce the most relevant data. When there is a need for guidance and instructions, developers can request help. The system includes context-sensitive guidance. Users can easily check the guidance for processes, activities, and tasks. The framework is designed to be easily interpreted and should enable users to quickly understand how the process work, how information flows, and the purpose of each process element, activity, and task.

WHY-Level. At this level, the implemented model provides information about the goals and objectives of organizations' processes. Development phases are handled by describing the dependencies and relationships between different processes and phases, as well as the data flows between them. The activities in the development process are justified, and the criteria to achieve the purposes, values, and priorities are defined. To create the work context and achieve full comprehension of the whole work system, we map processes, activities, and tasks to high-level expectations (purposes, goals, and objectives) so that each activity and task belongs to a context, and tasks and work items are connected to others via a network of dependencies.

WHAT-Level. This level focuses on work activities that build a workflow. For all activities, there is a defined input that shall be available, along with information and knowledge about tasks, resources, objectives, decision criteria, and the context. Activities are loosely coupled sets of tasks that aim at producing a coherent piece of work focusing on a certain topic. As SD is inherently cooperative, it requires several developers who need to coordinate their efforts. Therefore, an important part of SD is the creation and maintenance of a shared understanding that concerns the state of project tasks, artifacts, and the activities and expertise of developers. In addition, awareness is needed to identify and understand the current conditions. Lack of awareness can be quite problematic for SW systems; therefore, information is provided about the workspace, work items, and activities of others to help create a shared understanding and to tackle awareness issues. The results of activities and tasks are presented for decision makers as proposals that are evaluated against given decision criteria defined by relevant stakeholders. Developers must also understand the intended characteristics of the end product, and why they are requested.

How and in what order the work is done is not strictly defined, and developers can choose how to reach their goals within specifically defined acceptable performance boundaries and existing constraints. Defining these boundaries and making them visible is one of the main goals at this level.

HOW-Level. This level goes into the finer details of task implementation, providing the inputs needed for tasks, and tools to support the work, including sufficient collaboration means by integrating collaboration applications into a workflow.

Guidance is provided on how things can be done, including task descriptions, and data with links to repositories and other sources is provided. Constraints, such as resources and strategies, together with acceptance criteria, guide task implementation with task descriptions per DP, including why and how information is produced. The implemented model provides this information.

Workspace awareness (e.g., information about developers' availability, instant messaging systems, and contact information) supports instant connection between people and facilitates communication and collaboration. Task management and coordination ranging from backlogs to work allocation create task-oriented awareness, providing information about the state of the artifacts and tasks.

Cognitive information is created, stored, and shared while implementing tasks. Each member will accumulate information, knowledge, and experiences. These are recorded to maintain the data, even if the member leaves the team. Different aspects of development are represented by groups of stakeholders. Behind each aspect, there is a platform of knowledge and technology to be adapted to the development process. These platforms are knowledge bases that include both products and processes. Platform managers are responsible for defining and maintaining platforms. The main role of the platform managers is to use knowledge they obtain from the platform and form guidelines and principles. Among other benefits, these data can provide solution strategies to support developers' work. They can be used to train new team members and to support team members who are unfamiliar with a particular task.

4.2   Diagnosing – Cognition Issues in the Case Company's Workflow

In the diagnosing phase, both managers and experienced developers were interviewed. Product lifecycle was covered, from initial customer contact, through different aspects of development, to disposal. Each of these phases provided requirements, either directly or indirectly, by mediating customers' or other stakeholders' requests. The interviews revealed several cognition-related issues in the case company's workflow. These issues are summarized in Table 1, along with proposals to tackle the issues and the level(s) of the model at which the proposals are to be implemented.

Table 1. Summary of identified issues and proposals to address them

Issue	Proposals to tackle the issue	Level
1. Processes are not visible	1.1 Identify the big picture and providing a justification for the work	WHY
	1.2 Increase the visibility of processes and phases	
2. Inadequate cooperation and communication	2.1 Provide an awareness of others' actions	WHAT
	2.2 Foster communication and cooperation	
	2.3 Ensure rigorous documentation	
	2.4 Create a shared understanding	
3. Inadequate information	3.1 Identify information needs	WHAT, HOW
	3.2 Provide an information flow	
	3.3 Support information usage	
	3.4 Provide a rationale	
4. Inadequate development environment	4.1 Create a common, flexible development environment to reduce cognitive load	WHY, WHAT, HOW

Issue 1) Processes are not visible. While the case company has defined and documented its processes, there seemed to be no proper overall view of processes or development phases. In some cases, interviewees did not know if there was an official process at all. Correspondingly, not all organizational units were known or taken seriously. There were also cases where an interviewee viewed cooperation possibilities as completely lacking. Cooperation among different actors and development phases indicates that apart from the different actors having, in some cases, a different perspective, the interviewees had varying understandings of a product's lifecycle. Mostly, the interviewees described cooperation among the phases of a development chain, instead of considering a product's entire lifecycle. We interpreted the interviewees' main focus and interests as being restricted to their own work phase and the immediately preceding and following phases. As a result, their own work cannot be put into the context of the whole development chain, and the dependencies are not followed all the way through. The resulting situation was one in which the real needs of processes and phases were not considered adequately, and the relationships between and even the reasons different processes and phases exist were not recognized.

Proposals: 1.1) Identify the big picture and provide a rationale for why the work is done. At a minimum, the purposes and objectives of the work should be recognized. *1.2)* The processes and phases must be visible to inform the developers about the context and dependencies between tasks and work items, even though the exact order of activities is not strictly enforced.

Issue 2) Inadequate cooperation and communication. Work conducted during the preceding or following phases was not visible anywhere in practice, or if something had been changed or work had progressed, it was not easily recognized by others, if at all. There were tracking issues as well, as there was no way to see the work's progress toward subsequent process phases. This was partly due to insufficient communication and cooperation with developers in other phases and units. Serious problems arose as a result, including an insufficient understanding of what the other activities required and a lack of feedback from others. Additionally, informal means of communication are heavily used, which poses a hindrance to documentation for further use.

Proposals: *2.1)* Provide awareness of others' actions and ensure the transparency of the work to reduce overlapping activities and to control redundancy and repetition of work. *2.2)* Enhance communication to foster cooperation. *2.3)* Ensure more rigorous documentation. *2.4)* Create a shared understanding by enhancing visibility.

Issue 3) Inadequate information. Inadequate knowledge acquisition, sharing, and utilization were identified. Information was insufficient or was not stored in a way that is accessible and useful for others. For example, requests were not sufficiently detailed for decision making and processing. Acceptance criteria in particular were not adequately defined, which made decision making problematic. Practical problems included finding relevant data, which was often scattered over several sources without proper structure, classification, or means of identification. In some cases, the information was missing, while in others, there was too much information. Instant access to all information, tools, databases, and repositories from the workflow was requested. Finally, there was no work guidance.

Proposals: 3.1) Identify the information needs required for different process elements and functions. *3.2)* Offer technical details, guidelines, and how-to descriptions within the workflow. *3.3)* Make information instantly available with proper search and filter functionalities to allow the development to be based on up-to-date facts. *3.4)* Document rationale to help in decision-making.

Issue 4) Inadequate development environment. Awareness issues with tools, documents, and work items were revealed. Tools, interfaces, and data usage caused additional cognitive load. To address these issues, the tools and environment should be sufficiently generic, rather than each individual working in an independent silo.

Proposals: *4.1)* Create a common development environment and flexible workflow to connect the phases, so that jointly processed data become more accurate, and during later phases, more complete. Properly building a development environment with cognitive support will help tackle all of the identified issues.

The present findings are aligned with the literature, suggesting that cognitive cooperation and support are missing in current workflow models. The findings are also in line with the drivers underlying the developed model. Based on these findings, the model was refined, and it was planned to be integrated into the company's workflow.

4.3   Action Planning – Planning the Integration

The research cycles were prepared based on the diagnostic results. The model was accordingly refined to include the proposals described above. The study of company processes suggested a way to implement the model. Parts of the model could easily be implemented with the current processes and workflow. We mapped the work into the relevant processes to make the existence of process models and documents clear for all; we also provided links to available documents. The original processes were retained to the greatest extent possible. After the suggested modifications were documented and the tool prototype was implemented according to the refined model, the plans were presented to company representatives for review. Following company approval, we proceeded to use the prototype in selected parts of the company. The prototype was designed to address the identified problems as follows.

Process visibility was addressed by designing the prototype to display an overview and status of documents and other development items. In addition, the prototype also clearly showed the process and phase to which each of the different documents and development items were related. To address inadequate cooperation and communication, the prototype enabled multiple users to access the documents and development items by utilizing a simple "invite to collaborate" functionality. Simultaneous work was enabled by locking from others only the data fields that were currently manipulated instead of the whole document. In addition, the prototype also allowed users to see what others were doing, and that information was constantly updated and made visible. The prototype also provided brief guidance for completing a task. More detailed guidance with elaborated instructions, including the rationale, was available upon request. Addressing the inadequate information, the prototype clearly presented what information is needed at each process and phase. In addition, the prototype provided search functionality, which was necessary for the users to search for the needed information from the documents and development items. Finally, the prototype itself is a way to address the issue of inadequate development environment.

4.4   Action Taking – Integrating the Model into the Case Company's Workflow

The integration took place in three iterations, as discussed in the following section. A company representative guided the integration in close collaboration with researchers and the tool development team. In each iteration, more functionalities were implemented in the prototype. Other company representatives also followed the work closely and offered feedback. After the initial prototype was integrated into the company's workflow, evaluations began.

Ideas for improvements emerged during the integration. Some changes were considered useful and thus implemented between iterations. These suggested improvements included graphical representation that was discussed and agreed to be very useful. Together with textual descriptions, it will create a mental model of the work and provide greater comprehension of the entirety and its parts. Clearly defined DP dependencies were requested to define the inter-process communication and to clarify the synchronization of parts. More support for information and knowledge gathering is needed, as it would provide the basis for state identification. It would also help in task planning and decision making. Strong cooperation between development phases and organizational units was also requested. In order to enable such cooperation, the communication channels need to be integrated into the workflow system to support social and organizational cognition.

4.5   Evaluating – Testing the Model

Six cases were conducted, focusing on four different aspects of product development that also provide requirements for the company: testing, environmental issues, assembly, and packaging and logistics. Three sessions for each case were organized for each iteration, for a total of 36 sessions. The evaluations were conducted at several sites and in two countries. Iterations were divided according to the DPs of the company's requirements development process. In empirical testing, the developers handled real requests and requirements. They were first asked to record initial development ideas or customer requests into the system. In the second iteration, they continued to transform the problem domain requests into solution domain requirements. Finally, they formed features by bundling requirements into a coherent whole. Feedback was gathered and further development was done in between the iterations.

4.6   Specifying Learning – Evaluating the Model's Use in the Case Company

The empirical test yielded the following understanding about how the model is useful and how it tackles the identified issues (see Table 1 for the issues).

Issue 1) At the WHY-level, developers understanding of the context of work and of the big picture was improved. Their comprehension of the whole system made developers think beyond their own tasks and immediate goals to consider their dependencies, relationships, and effects on others' work. Understanding the context made a significant difference. It prompted developers to think about different viewpoints for different stakeholders. A few developers indicated that they did not need guidance, saying that they already knew their job. However, observations indicated that some found it difficult to understand the context of the work, and here the tool supported the task at hand. A few developers noted that the concept of a request caused some trouble at first when it came to determining the impact of requests. Testing teams were thinking about value instead of how it affects different stakeholders. After they received guidance, they eventually understood the difference and recorded the correct data into the system. Alternatively, in understanding the difference between problem and solution domains, the developers realized that these were clearly different concepts than they had initially thought. Finally, developers welcomed the reasoning being provided..

Issue 2) Enhanced communication and cooperation at the WHAT-level resulted in developers' better understanding of each other's needs and work. With the prototype, the visibility of others' work was enhanced, as was the understanding of the different elements of the development process and their relationships, thereby helping developers formulate a holistic understanding of the full context. Understanding other elements and their state enhances one's awareness of a situation and produces more accurate data and results. For example, recording negative values (i.e., a requirement has a negative value or impact for another stakeholder) for a requirement forced developers to think about the effects of the requirement on others—how the implementation of a requirement impacts others' work. Overall, transparency of the work improved, and it was suggested that traceability was better than the old ways of displaying changes. In addition, acceptance criteria and decision criteria issues appeared to be helped with the support. Developers seemed to understand what was needed to create a decision proposal, and decision makers were provided with checklists for decision-making.

Issue 3) At the HOW-level, the three different levels of instruction were positively accepted. Different levels of instructions are needed, as developers have different needs. First, generic advice is provided that may then be elaborated upon based on a developer's unique needs. It was proposed that instructions and guidance should be integrated with training support. The cognitive overhead was reduced with immediate access to data, without the need to open various applications. Immediate access to needed knowledge via links was perceived as quite useful. All the necessary data were not yet available in the tool, as the case company intends to gradually gather more data at the same time as the tool is being developed further. It was clearly indicated that when sharing knowledge is easy and the responsibilities, principles, and practices for storing information are defined, it creates valuable assets for developers. One important observation was the usefulness of metadata, particularly in classifying and structuring data. The tags were used to group systems by similar function, or by a piece of equipment or materials used. Predefined data were also expected, but as the development of the support system is still in its early phases, this functionality was not available.

Issue 4) Combining the proposals to tackle issues 1–3 with other tool-related solutions also addresses the inadequate development environment issue. The idea of graphical representation was thought to be extremely useful for showing the work progress and the different flows (e.g., work, resource, information) in the process, especially for navigation purposes and as a concrete way to present the whole development context and the big picture. The need to work collaboratively was evident, which also suggests that it is essential to have communication tools in a workflow. There is a need for different types of applications, including instant messaging and video conferencing. Interfaces for other types of tools should also be integrated into the system to provide instant access to work items. However, complete communications tool support was not yet implemented in the case company.

In conclusion, these observations indicate that supported work clearly facilitated a better understanding—and thus more accurate results—than non-supported work, by providing developers with the data that are actually needed in subsequent phases. Each of the levels was considered useful for responding to changes and unexpected events, especially the HOW-level, when the system was able to offer tried and tested solutions. The implemented model would also be useful in training personnel, a conclusion the developers involved in this study made a point of noting. The action research cycle validates that the implemented model supports cognitive work in SD workflows. The prototype also improves developers' abilities to accomplish their tasks by giving proper cognitive support, and the model can even change developers' thinking to better match the intentions and purposes of the processes. The quality of work results is likewise perceived to improve with the prototype.

5   Discussion and Implications

The findings are based on our analysis of the transcribed interview material as well as observations and feedback on prototype use. The cognitive support integrated into the workflow was well accepted and found to be useful. The experts attending the evaluation appeared enthusiastic about the subject matter and were eagerly awaiting new versions of the prototype with more functionality.

RQ1 examined what kind of cognitive support is needed in SD workflows. Based on our study of the literature and empirical evidence, we can conclude the following aspects of cognition need support in workflows: work context and situation awareness, especially defining the purposes and objectives of work; knowledge management aspects, such as knowledge acquisition, knowledge sharing, and knowledge utilization; the use of experience and skills, including support for learning; and decision making and problem solving. These aspects support developers' understanding, reduce cognitive overhead, and help developers in reacting to changes.

RQ2 examined how cognitive support can be provided for SD workflows. Three levels of support are proposed. Each level provides a complementing view to development. The top level is concerned with creating the context and defining both the purposes and high-level objectives on what the work system provides and the role of the work system and its subsystems. The second level provides the criteria to measure whether a system is achieving its purposes and defines the functions that are required to achieve its purposes. The third level is concerned with how activities and tasks are implemented and what resources are needed. Together, these three levels provide a solid way of supporting cognitive work in SD workflows. Our results suggest that the model supports work and complements the other workflow aspects with proper cognitive support. The empirical evaluation proved the model's value by providing an enhanced understanding for developers and better results for development tasks. With the prototype, the developers in the case company were also able to respond to changes and solve practical development problems more efficiently. The tool provides support for cognitive workflow by bridging the gap between high-level objectives and developers' daily tasks. In sum, cognitive support is offered in several ways, as Kuutti [24] suggested: automating routines, supporting communication, making things visible, making objects manipulable, supporting transformative and manipulative actions, supporting sense-making actions within an activity, and supporting learning.

All research has limitations, however, and this study was no different. The evaluation sessions were not videotaped for more detailed analysis, due to company policy. Furthermore, only one observer was allowed to attend these sessions. The observer provided her immediate impressions after the sessions, and others validated the findings with the help of audiotapes. Another limiting factor concerning the prototype testing was that the observer was not simply observing, but also participating in discussions with developers when they requested more information or were unable to continue the work by themselves. The trade-off, however, was that we were able to obtain valuable feedback for further development.

5.1   Implications for Research and Practice

Our findings form a concept that is, according to our knowledge, not discussed in existing literature. This concept provides valuable insights for academic research, laying the foundation for further scholarly inquiry, including a validation of the findings in phases other than requirements development and domains other than ICT.

Competition in the ICT sector is fierce, and companies are constantly striving for innovative practices to gain a competitive advantage. This work would benefit the industry by providing new ideas to improve the efficiency of work and the accuracy of results. In sum, the model provides a better understanding of the context of work—in particular, the real needs of all processes, phases, and functions—that will provide better results, primarily because the produced data and results will fulfill their purpose better and provide less waste. The model can also be used as a learning tool. The effort needed to guide new developers would diminish if the proper support were available when needed, thus allowing experienced developers' efforts to be applied to places other than basic tasks.

5.2   Areas for Future Improvement

There are still issues that need more work, such as getting the level of details in guidance and instructions correct. Another obstacle involves finding ways to complement the organizational knowledge base and to encourage developers to record their feedback and their experiences for others' use. This is not a trivial task, as the knowledge must be gathered in a non-intrusive way, such that it will not hinder practitioners' work. Furthermore, the validation and management of such information needs to be studied further. Finally, the communication tool integration, the graphical representation, and the user interface all need to be finalized. With the abovementioned additions, the final product will be a full SD support integrated into organizations' workflows. This study creates the basis for developing the actual implementation of such workflows.

6   Conclusions

The development of SW systems is complex knowledge work, requiring substantial cognitive effort from developers. However, neither changes and unexpected events, nor cognitive work and cognitive cooperation, are properly supported in current workflow models. This paper presents a model, and its theoretical basis, to support cognitive work and cooperation in SD workflows.

To evaluate the model, an action research study was conducted. A tool prototype was built to apply our model in a workflow in a real requirements development environment, to be validated by empirical evaluations. In this study, the model's practical usefulness for solving problems in an organization was validated. While the research shows that further work is still needed, the results prove the significance of the developed model, as well as its high level of acceptance in the case company. In practice, the model's use increased the efficiency of the development process and the developers' understanding of their work, thus providing more accurate results from their tasks. This work provides a promising solution to the current lack of cognition support in SD workflows as well as a way to respond to changes.

Acknowledgments. This research is supported by ITEA2 and TEKES. The authors would also like to thank AMALTHEA partners for their assistance and cooperation.

References

1. Robillard, P.: The Role of Knowledge in Software Development. Communications of the ACM 42(1), 87–92 (1999)
2. Bjørnson, F.O., Dingsøyr, T.: Knowledge Management in Software Engineering: a Systematic Review of Studied Concepts, Findings, and Research Methods Used. Information and Software Technology 50, 1055–1068 (2008)
3. Zhuge, H.: Workflow- and Agent-Based Cognitive Flow Management for Distributed Team Cooperation. Information and Management 40(5), 419–429 (2003)
4. Mangan, P., Sadiq, S.: On Building Workflow Models for Flexible Processes. In: Proceedings of the 13th Australasian Database Conference (ADC 2002), pp. 103–109 (2002)

5. Workflow Management Coalition: Workflow Management Coalition Terminology and Blossary, Document Number WFMC-TC-1011, Document Status-Issue 3.0. Technical report, Workflow Management Coalition, Brussels (1999)

6. Wang, M., Wang, H.: From Process Logic to Business Logic: a Cognitive Approach to Business Process Management. Information and Management 43(2), 179–193 (2006)

7. Klein, M., Dellarocas, C.: A Knowledge-Based Approach to Handling Exceptions in Workflow Systems. Computer Supported Cooperative Work 9, 399–412 (2000)

8. Jennings, N.R., Faratin, P., Johnson, M.J., Norman, T.J., O'Brien, P., Wiegand, M.E.: Agent-Based Business Process Management. International Journal of Cooperative Information Systems 5(2,3), 105–130 (1996)

9. van der Aalst, W.M.P., Basten, T.: Inheritance of Workflows: an Approach to Tackling Problems Related to Change. Theoret. Comp. Sci. 270(1-2), 125–203 (2002)

10. van Merriënboer, J.J.G.: Training Complex Cognitive Skills. Educational Technology Publications, Englewood Cliffs (1997)

11. Sweller, J.: Cognitive Load During Problem Solving: Effects on Learning. Cognitive Science 12, 257–285 (1988)

12. Jonassen, D.H.: Toward a Design Theory of Problem Solving. Educational Technology Research and Development 48(4), 63–85 (2000)

13. Hollan, J., Hutchins, E., Kirsch, D.: Distributed Cognition: Toward a New Foundation for Human-Computer Interaction Research. ACM Transactions on Computer-Human Interaction 7(2), 174–196 (2000)

14. Gaines, B.R.: Knowledge Management in Societies of Intelligent Adaptive Agents. Journal of Intelligent Information Systems 9(3), 277–298 (1977)

15. Goel, A.K.: Design, Analogy, and Creativity. IEEE Expert 12(3), 62–70 (1997)

16. Zhuge, H., Ma, J., Shi, X.Q.: Analogy and Abstract in Cognitive Space: a Software Process Model. Information and Software Technology 39, 463–468 (1997)

17. van Leijen, H., Baets, W.R.J.: A Cognitive Framework for Reengineering Knowledge-Intensive Processes. In: 36th Annual Hawaii International Conference on System Sciences, pp. 97–106 (2003)

18. Omoronyia, I., Ferguson, J., Roper, M., Wood, M.: A Review of Awareness in Distributed Collaborative Software Engineering. Software Practice and Experience 40, 1107–1133 (2010)

19. Robertson, T.: Cooperative Work and Lived Cognition: A Taxonomy of Embodied Interaction. In: Fifth European Conference on Computer-Supported Cooperative Work ECSCW 1997, pp. 205–220 (1997)

20. Dourish, P., Bellotti, V.: Awareness and Coordination in a Shared Workspace. In: Proceedings of the ACM Conference on Computer-Supported Cooperative Work, pp. 107–114 (1992)

21. Nickerson, J.V.: Event-Based Workflow and the Management Interface. In: Proceedings of the 36th Annual Hawaii International Conference on System Sciences (2003)

22. Baskerville, R., Wood-Harper, A.T.: A Critical Perspective on Action Research as a Method for Information Systems Research. Journal of Information Technology 11(3), 235–246 (1996)

23. Susman, G., Evered, R.: An Assessment of the Scientific Merits of Action Research. Administrative Science Quarterly 23(4), 582–603 (1978)

24. Kuutti, K.: Activity Theory as a Potential Framework for Human-Computer Interaction Research. In: Context and Consciousness: Activity Theory and Human Computer Interaction, pp. 17–44 (1995)

Impediments in Agile Software Development: An Empirical Investigation

Kristian Wiklund[1,2], Daniel Sundmark[2], Sigrid Eldh[1], and Kristina Lundqvist[2]

[1] Ericsson AB, 164 80 KISTA, Sweden
{kristian.wiklund,sigrid.eldh}@ericsson.com
[2] School of Innovation, Design and Engineering, Mälardalen University, Sweden
{daniel.sundmark,kristina.lundqvist}@mdh.se

Abstract. In this paper, we report on a case study on development impediments encountered in the early phase of a transformation to agile methods in a software development organization. Drawing from literature and anecdotal evidence, it was assumed that the majority of the impediments were related to software testing. To investigate this, we performed a case study seeking qualitative and quantitative evidence from task boards, interviews, and observations. Our analysis indicates that the major challenge in the transformation undertaken by the studied organization was coordination and communication in the large, and that testing was the major challenge only when the unit of analysis was restricted to the teams in the department.

Keywords: Agile Development, Impediments, Industrial Case Study.

1 Introduction

In this paper, we report on a case study investigating impediments in an organization that recently changed its process to use agile, cross-discipline development teams. An impediment is defined by the Scrum Alliance as "anything that prevents a team member from performing work as efficiently as possible" [20]. The case study is based on quantitative analysis of the task boards of the teams in the department, its management team task board, and its improvement task board, combined with qualitative data from interviews and observations.

Approximately three months prior to this study, a transformation of the studied organization was initiated, to move from a traditional hierarchical product-based organization towards a more agile and feature-oriented way of working. The major driver behind this agile transformation was to create teams that are able to drive customer value end-to-end, from systemization via implementation and test to delivery and deployment. The goal is to produce software with as few hand-overs as possible, something that is considered to both increase quality and decrease lead-time [8].

From anecdotal evidence, personal communication, and related publications [4][5][10][15][19], it was expected that a lot of the impediments in the described

J. Heidrich et al. (Eds.): PROFES 2013, LNCS 7983, pp. 35–49, 2013.
© Springer-Verlag Berlin Heidelberg 2013

organizational transformation concerned including testing in the team responsi-bilties. For the same reasons, it was also expected that a lot of the test-related impediments would be tightly associated with test and delivery automation, in the shape of continuous integration (CI) [18], which was adopted as a central feature of the new design flow.

Contradictory to our expectations, we found that project management, such as coordination with other departments, work division and coordination between a large number of agile product owners, and delivery planning in the large, formed the greatest source for impediments when investigating the entire department as a unit. However, if the unit of analysis is changed to the teams, the test and test infrastructure activities were the largest source for impediments. The test im-pediments were primarily caused by staff being held up in previous assignments, new tasks to be learned as a consequence of the transformation, and effects from using shared test infrastructure.

A similar transformation is described by Shaye [15] who lists a large number of problems that needed solving. Their problem list includes a shortage of test engineers limiting the possibility to work on new functionality and regression tests at the same time, and a shortage in automation and test engineers. By using a shared automated test execution infrastructure, the cost of tests was sig-nificantly reduced. The downside is the risk for a higher impact on development if that mechanism fails for some reason, as many more people are impacted than if local solutions are used. Shaye points out that in order to minimize this risk, the shared resource needs to be handled like a formal production system, and that automation requires the same care as product development.

Smits and Pshigoda [17] describe a Scrum implementation project in an orga-nization of approximately the same size as the development department in our study. Initially, the observed impediments were related to people and resources, including a lack of testers, who together with tech writers and build engineers were tied up in prior projects. This was escalated by the teams, and the solution was to have the developers do testing as well. Other challenges included how to handle the overall testing of the complete product, and things that were not part of the responsibility of a specific team. To address these, a "suite validation team" was created to handle testing and quality for the entire product. Also, an "integration and automation team" was created to produce the integration environment, and monitor the scheduled builds and tests.

Puleio [10] report that the biggest challenge their team encountered was test-ing, and that the primary areas of problem were estimation, communication, and automation. The majority of the described scenarios are about an inability to communicate between people originally working in different disciplines that have been assigned to work in the same team. Dependencies to specialist skills are reported as well, testing the legacy product required skilled manual work with test setup and analysis to be able to produce a test result.

According to Talby et al. [19], testing is completely different in agile develop-ment compared to traditional development, partly because everyone in the team is expected to test the product. They also point out that making all testing fully agile will be harder and slower than it is to adopt practices that traditionally are enclosed in the development teams, such as test-driven development.

In general, there is a lack of information on how to do testing in agile development [5], in particular when moving outside the designer-near testing such as unit tests [4].

Based on our observations, we formulated two hypotheses to be investigated:

H1: *The primary source for impediments in newly formed agile software development teams is testing and test infrastructure.*

H2: *The majority of the test-related impediments are related to test infrastructure.*

To investigate these hypotheses, we performed a case study in a part of the transforming organization, using a multitude of sources to collect information, and analyzed the collected information using qualitative and quantitative methods. The primary contributions of this paper are (a) an empirical investigation on the hypotheses within the observed organization, (b) quantitative information about the work distribution and impediment distribution in the observed organization, and (c) a discussion on the reasons and possible remedies for the observed phenomena.

The paper is organized as follows: Section 2 describes the background to the study and the context, Section 3 describes the case study design, Section 4 provides an overview of the results and the threats to validity, together with answers to the research questions and hypotheses. Finally, Section 5 contains the over-all conclusions and recommendations of the study.

2   Study Object

The organization described in the study produces software components that are integrated into a very large telecommunications system. It is a development department in a larger organization that is transforming from traditional development methods to "end-to-end agile using cross-discipline feature-oriented development teams" [8]. In the department's parent organization, there are several parallel departments that produce related software that is integrated together with the studied components into a larger system. Within the department, there are five cross-discipline agile development teams, with 8-10 team members each, and a support function that mainly consists of the line management.

Teams A-C are working mainly with Java software, developing components that execute both in an embedded system and on desktop computers. Teams E-F are primarily working with embedded software, written in C++.

In the department's parent organization, there is a project office providing large scale coordination and process support. There is also a technical coordination office responsible for coordinating the long-term development strategy and the architecture of the products. Major HR issues, major financial issues, sourcing, legal, IT infrastructure, et cetera, are handled as part of the corporate central functions and require a relatively small effort from the local organizations compared to the design work.

Outside the immediate parent organization, there is a high-level system design organization, and a test organization that perform system testing, system release verification, as well as supply the test and design tools and infrastructure used by the design organizations. The test organization responsibilities is roughly comparable to the responsibilities of the "suite validation team" and the "integration and automation team" described by Smits and Pshigoda [17], but on a larger scale.

Prior to the transformation, the majority of development teams in the studied organization were working according to the Scrum principles, implementing software and performing design tests, typically unit tests and component tests. The teams could be described as "semi-cross-discipline" - while some systemization and testing was performed, it was not the end-to-end activity that is the target of the organizational transformation.

As part of the lean and agile transformation, new teams were formed, moving people from the system design teams and the integration and verification teams, to the new cross-discipline software development teams. In doing this, the scope of the work for the development teams was expanded, to enclose a larger part of the system development V-model [13] as shown in Figure 1, to avoid hand-overs and enable greater flexibility.

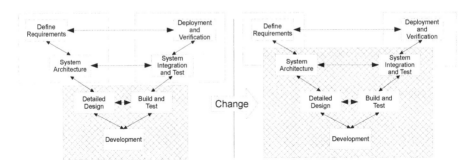

Fig. 1. V-model showing the increase in scope for a cross-discipline team

The teams are expected to solve the majority of the encountered impediments by themselves. To enable them to do this they are supported by the agile product owner, who sets the priorities for the work, an agile coach who coaches the organization through the change, the department management team, and an improvement mechanism that handles escalated impediments.

3   Case Study Design

The objective of the study was to investigate the hypotheses presented in the introduction, and to gather information about the proportions between different types of work in the sprints in the studied teams. The study is organized as a case study [11] examining recently deployed agile software development teams using a multitude of information sources. The guidelines by Runeson and Höst[12] were used when designing and performing the study.

3.1 Research Questions

RQ1: What types of impediments are encountered in a newly formed agile software development organization?

RQ2: Does any activity type have a higher amount of impediments per work unit than the others?

RQ3: Does any activity type have a higher amount of impediments than the others?

3.2 Data Collection

Data was collected from several sources and by several methods.

Participant Observation

1. "RCA Light" - Analysis of existing impediment investigations.
   The principal researcher participated as an observer in a workshop with mixed participation from all teams within the department, with the purpose to identify the top impediments for implementation progress and product quality. Information was collected as written notes.
2. Direct observation of team A Scrum meetings. When working according to Scrum, the team has open-door daily Scrum meetings to discuss progress and problems [14], which were observed with permission from the team. The observations were collected as written notes.

Artifact Inspection

1. **Team Task Boards:** The purpose of the Scrum task board is to visualize the sprint backlog in a useful way [6]. It provides an always available representation of the current status of the sprint, what is the progress, what are we working on, what is done, what are our problems, and what is not done. The task board is the centerpiece in the Scrum meetings, and the discussions are centered on how to move tasks to completion. From the team task boards we collected information about impediments, what type of tasks the teams are working with at the moment, and how much work is estimated for the tasks.
2. **Improvement Task Board:** If the team is unable to solve an impediment, or if the problem solution is expected to be of some kind of general interest, it is escalated to get team-external help. The escalated impediments form an improvement backlog which is handled through its own task board.

From this task board we collected information that allowed us to analyze the distribution of impediments between different parts of the process and work flow in the organization.

3. **Management Team Task Board:** The management team (MT) board contains items that the management team perform as parts of their daily work. We used this information to analyze what types of impediments and improvements required management attention.

Interviews. To get deeper information about the results from the "RCA light" workshop, we conducted semi-structured interviews with a developer in team E, an environment specialist in the studied organization, and a developer in the organization producing the shared build and integration system. Of these, the environment specialist had participated in the "RCA light" workshop. The interviews were recorded with participant permission and transcribed for analysis.

3.3 Data Classification

To be able to classify the tasks, impediments, and actions according to known principles, we used the "disciplines" of the Rational Unified Process (RUP) to avoid inventing our own code book. In RUP, "a discipline is a collection of related activities that are related to a major area of concern" [16].

RUP defines six engineering disciplines:

- Business Modeling - The business modeling discipline describes the business process using business use cases. This work is done outside the studied organization, and there are no tasks mapped to this code in our study.
- Requirements - The requirements discipline adresses what the system shall do, and produces use-cases, functional, and non-functional requirements that form the basis for further work.
- Analysis and Design - The analysis and design discipline focuses on how the system shall realize its requirements. The outcome is a design model that can be used for implementation.
- Implementation (including design tests) - During implementation, the requirements are implemented in source code, and the source code is organized, tested, and integrated to form a working system.
- Test (excluding design tests) - The test discipline includes testing to identify defects, component integration, and verifying that the requirements have been implemented.
- Deployment - The deployment tasks includes packaging, acceptance, build of release candidates, and other activities that are related to producing a product that can be delivered to the end users.

There are also three supporting disciplines:

- Configuration and Change Management - Configuration and CM includes revision control, baselining of preconditions and deliverables, document handling, and other activities that are done to keep order in the artifacts used and produced during product development.
- Project Management - Planning, executing, and monitoring development projects. We include work done by scrum masters and agile product owners.
- Environment - Activities related to production and maintenance of test and development tools, environments, and infrastructure.

We also added the following codes to cover the remaining tasks and actions:

- Product Maintenance - Activities related to the maintenance of delivered products, such as corrections, support, and customer relations.
- Training and Competence - Activities related to competence development and competence planning.
- Resource planning - Activities such as organizational resource plan, role descriptions, and resource forecasting.

4   Results

4.1   Task Board Contents

To get insight in what work is performed by the teams and what the majority of the escalated impediments are, we collected information from the team task boards, the improvement task board, and the management team (MT) task board. The tasks on the boards were coded according to the principles in Section 3.3.

For the MT task board, we identified which tasks were related to impediment solving and which were not. We used the Scrum Alliance definition [20], "anything that prevents a team member from performing work as efficiently as possible" to do this analysis. Only the tasks related to impediment solving, 54% of the total number of tasks on the MT task board, are included in the statistics.

We have also analyzed the tasks on the the improvement board and separated work that is related to enterprise scrum, that is, how to coordinate a large organization, from work that is related to work performed fully within or between the teams in the department. In doing this, we discovered that approximately 50% of the improvement tasks are purely team-related. In Table 1, columns marked "All Tasks" shows the entire contents of the improvement board, while columns marked "Team Related" shows the tasks that are purely team-related.

The improvement board and management team board content was not time-estimated, the number of sticky notes for a given topic were used to calculate the percentages in Table 1.

Some tasks were not uniquely connected to one topic, leading to an overlap of topics. In those cases the sum of percentages will be over 100.

The original intent was to track the planned estimates, the progress of the work, and the actually worked time, and compare them. This was not possible, we found that some tasks related to "product maintenance" and "environment" were not estimated. Also, the actual time worked was not recorded by the teams, if a task was completed it was simply marked as "done" and removed.

To be able to investigate the hypotheses, we combined the results for the test and the environment disciplines, which is shown at the bottom of Table 1 and Table 2. Investigating hypothesis 1, that test and test infrastructure is the dominating source for impediments, we found that it holds on a team level but not on a department level, as the project management discipline was the dominating source for impediments when the department was the unit of analysis. Investigating hypothesis 2, that infrastructure formed the majority of the test and test infrastructure impediments, we find that the environment impediment percentage is slightly lower or equal to test discipline impediments depending on the unit of analysis. This means that the quantitative data from the task boards does not support the hypothesis. However, by combining it with the qualitative data described further on in the paper, we consider the hypothesis to be valid.

Investigating the amount of impediments per estimated work unit, as shown in Table 2, we found that test had the highest number of impediments per estimated work unit of the engineering disciplines. Configuration and Change Management had the highest number of impediments per estimated work unit of the supporting disciplines, which we believe can be explained by both the low estimate and the fact that it is a new task to the teams, something new that is done seldom is likely to cause impediments. There were no tasks related to project management present on the team task boards, which is the reason for the missing data in the table.

Table 1. Percentage of total impediments per topic on the Management Team (MT) task board, Improvement Board (IB), and Team Task boards. The top areas per board type is highlighted.

	MT		IB			Total	
	All Tasks	Team Related	All Tasks	Team Related	Team Boards	All Tasks	Team Related
Requirements	3.7	4.0	0.0	0.0	0.0	1.3	1.9
Analysis & Design	3.7	4.0	0.0	0.0	0.0	1.3	1.9
Implementation	7.4	8.0	4.7	9.1	0.0	5.3	7.7
Test	8.0	12.0	16.3	22.7	0.0	13.3	15.4
Deployment	0.0	0.0	0.0	0.0	0.0	0.0	0.0
Configuration & CM	7.4	4.0	7.0	4.5	0.0	6.7	5.8
Project Management	18.5	16.0	**46.5**	31.8	0.0	**33.3**	23.1
Environment	7.4	8.0	9.3	13.6	100.0	12.0	15.4
Product Maintenance	0.0	0.0	4.7	0.0	0.0	2.7	0.0
Training & Competence	18.5	20.0	14	13.6	0.0	14.7	15.4
Resource Management	**22.2**	**24.0**	2.3	4.5	0.0	9.3	13.5
Test and Environment	15.4	20.0	25.6	**36.3**	**100.0**	25.3	**30.8**

Table 2. Impediments in Relation to Estimated Work

| | Estimated Work | | All | Impediment per | |
	Tasks (%)	Time (%)	Imped. (%)	Task (%/%)	Time (%/%)
Requirements	5.1	3.7	1.3	0.25	0.35
Analysis &Design	9.3	9.9	1.3	0.14	0.13
Implementation	21.6	23.8	5.3	0.25	0.22
Test	24.8	22.3	13.3	0.54	0.60
Deployment	4.8	5.8	0.0	0.0	0.0
Configuration & CM	2.5	1.5	6.7	2.68	4.47
Project Management			33.3		
Environment	16.3	13.6	33.3	0.74	0.88
Product Maintenance	10.3	13.9	12.0	0.26	0.19
Training & Competence	8.1	8.6	14.7	1.81	1.71
Test and Environment	41.1	35.8	9.3	0.23	0.26

4.2   RCA Light – "Top Impediments Investigation"

The researcher participated in an impediment investigation workshop as an observer. The workshop was facilitated by an external facilitator, who produced an Ishikawa diagram by asking "5 Whys" to the participants [3].

There is a risk for context effects [1] in this result. The workshop facilitator was asked what he considered to be "impediments", and answered "for example, if you have problems with your test tools". By clarifying what to do by mentioning test systems, the focus of the workshop could have become test systems instead of impediments in general.

The outcome of the workshop was that there were significant impediments present that were related to the build, test, and delivery systems, as well as to test competence. The infrastructure impediments were related to taking on new types of tasks, and to centralization and reuse of shared systems. The competence impediments were related both to lack of time for training and to a shortage of experienced testers in the teams.

Reuse of test systems and equipment is recommended by several authors [7] [2], and is one of the main strategies for handling the environment in the studied organization. While some frameworks and systems, such as unit test frameworks, are possible to handle within the teams, a lot of the equipment needed for telecommunication system testing is both expensive and complex, and require specialist skills for installation and configuration. These systems are then made available to the teams through a continuous integration (CI) system [18], capable of executing the necessary system integration test suites to gain confidence in the product prior to delivery to the deployment organization.

Shared infrastructure can be a great benefit to the developers, as there is no need to spend team time on production and maintenance of tools. It is also considered by the studied organization to be an enabler for staff mobility between teams and product areas, as one do not have to retrain to be able to use new tools.

However, sharing a resource also means that any problems with that resource will impact a lot of people, who no longer can fix the problems themselves.

> *"One problem is that we depend on the [centralized] build engine. If we didn't, we wouldn't have the problem. At delivery time, when we actually depend on this, they do maintenance, introduce changes; it magically stops working when we need it. We could live with the problems if it is stable when we need it. It requires coordination."*

By using centralized infrastructure, the team is pushed into a product management situation. Instead of developing their own toolset when it is needed, they have to put requirements on the infrastructure organization to be able to get what they want when they want it, and that is a clear change from the previous ways of doing things.

In addition to the infrastructure challenges, it was indicated that testing competence was an issue - the teams were not prepared for the increased test responsibilities. We also found that the lack of competence was not clearly escalated, some teams and agile product owners did not know if they had to solve this issue themselves as part of being a self-organizing team, or if they should escalate it to management.

> *"We haven't received training – particularly in verification – on things that we are supposed to do. Why no training? Lack of time. The testers that should work with us are used in the earlier project that still isn't finished. We need time to adjust."*

Smits and Pshigoda [17] report on a similar situation in their study: "The initial teams were made up primarily of developers. There was a lack of testers, tech writers and support (build) people, as they were tied up in another project".

This is not a surprising phenomenon, if one considers the phased behavior of traditional development projects. When the system developers and programmers are starting on a new feature, the testers are still working on the release testing of the previous features. This means that line management face the choice of either reorganizing everyone immediately and risk whatever work is ongoing in the old system, or keep to commitments and wait for people to be available when they have finished their previous assignments.

4.3   Interviews

We conducted semi-structured interviews in both the studied organization, and the organization producing and deploying the tools. The interviews were recorded with subject permission and transcribed prior to analysis. There is a risk for acquiescent behavior in the interviews, as the subjects were aware of the test focus of the researcher's work. Acquiescent behavior occurs when the subjects report what they believe that the interviewer wants to know, rather than what they should report [1].

The interviews indicated the same trends as in the RCA Light investigation, that there were challenges with the responsibilities for and handling of the centralized infrastructure. The most dominating finding was a dependency to key people and that the communication between organizations needed improvement.

> *"Planned maintenance is coordinated informally, we [the infrastructure organization] give key people a heads up when something will happen."*

> *"..we [the product development organization] don't see the [infrastructure] backlog, we could probably get access if we asked for it. Still, we have... I have, a pretty good view of the situation, I'm talking to them [the infrastructure developers] daily."*

We also discovered a difference in the views of the interview subjects on what the responsibility of the respective organizations should be with respect to environment, and also a lack of knowledge about what the official purpose was. One subject from the design organization said that

> *"We don't really know what they are supposed to do. They own the lab equipment, and a lot of our former colleagues have moved there to work with the tools, but our interfaces to them are not clear. We don't know what help we will get."*

This is in contrast with the very clear view of the interview subject from the infrastructure organization:

> *"In our view, we deliver a solution and decide what we will include in the solution. The design organizations do not really see it that way and want to have their own solutions, regardless of our long-term plans. Sometimes this results in a lot of effort on things that we are phasing out instead of working on the new things. We have noticed that the information about our roadmap and plans don't reach the developers, what is communicated and what is not varies a lot between organizations."*

This also indicates that communication needed improvement. All subjects expressed a desire for better communication and an awareness that everyone involved are responsible for improving the communication.

> *"We have to take at least part of the blame for not coordinating with the tool team about important deliveries, when the system must be stable. Of course, they should also ask us how we are impacted when they want to do an update of the environment"*

4.4   Team Observations

Team A was observed for three sprints, a total of nine weeks, during their daily stand-up Scrum meeting, which was held in the open office area.

The majority of the observed impediments were related to work new to the team. Delivery handling of the finished product had earlier been handled in another unit and needed to be learned quickly as the person responsible moved to a new assignment. Deploying and stabilizing the new CI system required learning the system, coordination with the infrastructure teams, and a lot of testing. Most of the environment work in the team during the observed sprints was related to the CI system.

4.5   Answering the Research Questions and Hypotheses

RQ1: *What types of impediments are encountered in a newly formed agile software development organization?*

During the study, it was clear that the centralized infrastructure was perceived by the subjects as the primary source of impediments for the development teams. Further analysis indicates that this was due to insufficient communication and coordination. That communication and coordination is a challenge is also indicated by the majority of the improvement requests, 46.5%, that are connected to the project management discipline, as shown in Table 1.

For the department as a unit of analysis, the main impediments were related to coordination on all levels, internally between agile product owners and teams, externally between departments or outside the parent line organization. Things that previously had been handled by the development projects, such as delivery planning and coordination of changes, needed to be redefined.

If the unit of analysis is changed to the teams, the test and test infrastructure activities were the largest source for impediments. Test competence in the teams was impacted since test engineers were held up in previous assignments, and there was a lack of time for training during the early phases of the organizational change.

RQ2: *Does any activity type have a higher amount of impediments per work unit than the others?*

Since the teams were not tracking actual work effort for the tasks, we had to use estimates only for this analysis.

By analyzing the task boards for the teams included in the study, together with the improvement handling task board and the management team task board, we found that we found that test had the highest number of impediments per estimated work unit in the engineering disciplines, followed by implementation and requirement analysis. Ignoring "project management", for which no tasks were present on the team scrum boards, "configuration and change management" had the highest number of impediments per estimated work unit of all disciplines. This can be explained by the combination of low estimates and the fact that it is a new task to the teams, as something new that is done seldom is likely to cause impediments. The results are further described in Table 2.

RQ3: *Does any activity type have a higher amount of impediments per work unit than the others?*

In Table 1, we have highlighted the activity types with the highest percentage of impediments per source and in total. For the entire organization, the project management discipline with 33.3% of the improvement tasks is the largest source of impediments. If restricted to team activities only, removing enterprise effects such as coordination between development organizations, the combined test and test infrastructure area is the largest source of impediments, with 30.8% of the improvement tasks.

H1: *The primary source for impediments in newly formed agile software development teams is testing and test infrastructure.*

The quantitative data in Table 1 indicate that the hypothesis is invalid in the observed organization, as project management forms the majority of the improvement requests with 33.3% of the total. However, if one restrict the observations to the teams, the hypothesis is valid, as the combined test and environment disciplines becomes dominating with 30.8% of the improvement requests.

H2: *The majority of the test-related impediments are related to test infrastructure.*

The combination of the qualitative and quantitative data indicates that the hypothesis is valid. The qualitative data, shown in Table 1, indicate that infrastructure-related impediments form approximately 50% of the combined test and environment improvement requests. Combining this with qualitative data from the team observations, the interviews, and the RCA light investigation we consider the hypothesis to be valid, as the majority of the impediments seen from those sources are traceable to environment and infrastructure issues.

4.6   Validity

- **Construct validity** addresses if the study measures what we intend it to measure [11]. The largest threat to construct validity in this study is using the number of improvement tasks for each discipline to estimate the amount and type of impediments encountered. In doing this, we do not take the effort into account as the tasks on the management team and improvement boards were not time-estimated or followed up for consumed time or resolution lead-time. Hence, the actual effect on the teams in terms of lost hours cannot be estimated, what we see is a measure of the number of annoyances that have been encountered.
- **Internal validity** addresses the conclusions of the study [12]. We have used multiple sources of information, both qualitative and quantitative, to minimize the threats to internal validity. One of the main threats is related to the time-frame of the study. While the task board analysis and the team

observations were performed during a well defined time period, the improvement and management team backlogs span over a longer time. This could impact the comparison between the amount of impediments and work effort in Table 2, where the distribution of impediments could change if restricted to the time period of the team observations.

- **External validity** addresses generalization of the findings [12]. We have provided context information in Section 2 to enable comparison to other organizations and studies.
- **Reliability** addresses the repeatability of the study [12]. The data classification principles are well-defined, and are based on RUP, which is a known and widely used process. We have also included quotations from the qualitative data to support the conclusions. The risk for context effects in the RCA Light material was reported in Section 4.2, and the risk for acquiescence in the interviews was reported in Section 4.3.

5   Conclusions

Contrary to the initial assumptions in the organization, test and test infrastructure impediments did not constitute the majority of the encountered impediments. Using empirical methods we have shown that, for the observed organization, the majority of the impediments during the early phase of the agile transformation were related to project management, coordination and communication. From the observations, it is likely that a larger focus on these disciplines had been needed prior to the transformation. This is in line with the findings of Lindvall *et al.* [9], who write that "individual projects in a large organization often depend on their environment in several ways". This environment can be too complex for a team of software developers to handle, and may in our opinion require the attention of a project manager or other specialists, even after transforming to an agile way of working.

A large part of the observed test infrastructure impediments could have been avoided by defining the division of responsibility between the infrastructure organization and the development organization earlier, and when doing so, also appointing the contact persons between the organizations. An agile way of increasing the contact between teams is to use "communities of practice" [21] to enable engineers from different organizations to meet in an informal, but still organized, way for knowledge sharing and problem solving.

We observed that test competence was missing in some teams, and that this was the source of many of the test impediments. Some teams did not know if they had to solve the competence issues themselves or not, as part of the responsibilities of being a self-organizing team. It should have been escalated, training and staffing is a manager responsibility in the organization. To avoid similar situations and to enable the transforming organization to learn what the team responsibilities are, we recommend that teams are actively encouraged to escalate all potential impediments, and that a large part of the scrum meetings during the initial sprints in a transformation are observed by managers.

References

1. Biemer, P., Lyberg, L.: Introduction to survey quality. Wiley Publishing, New York (2003)
2. Fewster, M., Graham, D.: Software test automation: effective use of test execution tools. ACM Press/Addison-Wesley (1999)
3. George, M.L., Rowlands, D., Price, M., Maxey, J.: The Lean Six Sigma Pocket Toolbook. McGraw-Hill (2005)
4. Itkonen, J., Rautiainen, K., Lassenius, C.: Towards understanding quality assurance in agile software development. In: ICAM 2005 (2005)
5. Kettunen, V., Kasurinen, J., Taipale, O., Smolander, K.: A study on agility and testing processes in software organizations. In: Proceedings of the 19th International Symposium on Software Testing and Analysis, ISSTA 2010, pp. 231–240. ACM Press, New York (2010)
6. Kniberg, H.: Scrum and XP from the Trenches. InfoQ Enterprise Software Development Series (2007)
7. Koomen, T., Pol, M.: Test process improvement: a practical step-by-step guide to structured testing. Addison-Wesley Professional (1999)
8. Larman, C., Vodde, B.: Scaling Lean & Agile Development: Thinking and Organizational Tools for Large-Scale Scrum. Addison-Wesley (2009)
9. Lindvall, M., Muthig, D., Dagnino, A., Wallin, C., Stupperich, M., Kiefer, D., May, J., Kahkonen, T.: Agile software development in large organizations. IEEE Computer 37(12), 26–34 (2004)
10. Puleio, M.: How Not to Do Agile Testing. In: Chao, J., Cohn, M., Maurer, F., Sharp, H., Shore, J. (eds.) Agile Conference, pp. 305–314. IEEE (July 2006)
11. Robson, C.: Real world research, 3rd edn. John Wiley & Sons (2011)
12. Runeson, P., Höst, M.: Guidelines for conducting and reporting case study research in software engineering. Empirical Software Engineering 14(2), 131–164 (2008)
13. Ruparelia, N.B.: Software development lifecycle models. ACM SIGSOFT Software Engineering Notes 35(3), 8 (2010)
14. Schwaber, K.: Scrum development process. In: Sutherland, J., Casanave, C., Miller, J., Patel, P., Hollowell, G. (eds.) 10th Annual Conference on Object-Oriented Programming Systems, Languages, and Applications (OOPSLA 1995), Business Object Design and Implementation, pp. 10–19 (1995)
15. Shaye, S.D.: Transitioning a Team to Agile Test Methods. In: Melnick, G., Kruchten, P., Poppendieck, M. (eds.) Agile Conference, pp. 470–477. IEEE (2008)
16. Shuja, A., Krebs, J.: IBM Rational Unified Process Reference and Certification Guide: Solution Designer. IBM Press (2008)
17. Smits, H., Pshigoda, G.: Implementing Scrum in a Distributed Software Development Organization. In: Eckstein, J., Maurer, F., Davies, R., Melnik, G., Pollice, G. (eds.) Agile Conference, pp. 371–375. IEEE (August 2007)
18. Stolberg, S.: Enabling Agile Testing through Continuous Integration. In: Dubinsky, Y., Dyba, T., Adolph, S., Sidky, A. (eds.) Agile Conference, pp. 369–374. IEEE (August 2009)
19. Talby, D., Keren, A., Hazzan, O., Dubinsky, Y.: Agile software testing in a large-scale project. IEEE Software 23(4), 30–37 (2006)
20. The Scrum Alliance: Glossary of Scrum Terms
21. Wenger, E.C., Snyder, W.M.: Communities of practice: The organizational frontier. Harvard Business Review 78(1), 139–145 (2000)

Are Happy Developers More Productive?

The Correlation of Affective States of Software Developers and Their Self-assessed Productivity

Daniel Graziotin, Xiaofeng Wang, and Pekka Abrahamsson

Free University of Bozen-Bolzano, Bolzano, Italy
{daniel.graziotin,xiaofeng.wang,pekka.abrahamsson}@unibz.it

Abstract. For decades now, it has been claimed that a way to improve software developers' productivity is to focus on people. Indeed, while human factors have been recognized in Software Engineering research, few empirical investigations have attempted to verify the claim. Development tasks are undertaken through cognitive processing abilities. Affective states – emotions, moods, and feelings - have an impact on work-related behaviors, cognitive processing activities, and the productivity of individuals. In this paper, we report an empirical study on the impact of affective states on software developers' performance while programming. Two affective states dimensions are positively correlated with self-assessed productivity. We demonstrate the value of applying psychometrics in Software Engineering studies and echo a call to valorize the human, individualized aspects of software developers. We introduce and validate a measurement instrument and a linear mixed-effects model to study the correlation of affective states and the productivity of software developers.

Keywords: Productivity, Human Factors, Software Developers, Software Development, Affective States, Emotion, Mood, Feeling.

1   Introduction

For more than thirty years, it has been claimed that a way to improve software developers' productivity and software quality is to focus on people [4]. In more recent years, the advocates of Agile software development stress this to the point that "If the people on the project are good enough, they can use almost any process and accomplish their assignment. If they are not good enough, no process will repair their inadequacy – 'people trump process' is one way to say this." [6, p. 1].

Although research in productivity of software developers is well-established and rich in terms of proposals, little is still known on the productivity of individual programmers [30]. Nevertheless, there is an increasing awareness that human-related factors have an impact on software development productivity [29].

Arguably, human-related factors play an important role on software development, as software artifacts are the result of intellectual activities. It is established but underestimated that software development is carried out through cognitive processing

J. Heidrich et al. (Eds.): PROFES 2013, LNCS 7983, pp. 50–64, 2013.

activities [10, 16]. On the other hand, the role of affective states - i.e., emotions, moods, and feelings - in the workplace received significant attention in Management research and Psychology [1, 23, 36]. Affective states have an impact on cognitive activities of individuals [16]. Thus, it is necessary to understand how affective states play a role in software development.

In Software Engineering research, the inclination to study the human aspect of developers has also been translated to a call for empirical Software Engineering studies using psychometrics [9]. In particular, there is a call for research on the role of the affective states in Software Engineering [16, 31].

The research question that this study aims to answer is: how do the affective states related to a software development task in foci influence the self-assessed productivity of developers? To this end, we examine the variations of affective states and the self-assessed productivity of software developers while they are programming.

The main results of the study are two-fold. 1) The affective states of software developers are positively correlated with their self-assessed productivity. 2) The investigation produces evidence on the value of psychometrics in empirical Software Engineering studies.

This study offers an understanding, which is part of basic science in Software Engineering research rather than leading to direct, applicable results. However, with the added understanding on how affective states influence software developers, we are in a much better position to continue the pursuit for improving Software Engineering methods and practices.

The rest of this paper is structured as follows. Section 2 provides the background theory, the related work and the hypotheses of the study. Section 3 describes the research methodology, in order to be easily evaluated and replicated. Section 4 reports the outcomes of the experimental design execution. Section 5 contains the discussion of the obtained results and the limitations of the study. Section 6 concludes the paper with the theoretical implications of the study and suggestions for future research.

2   Related Work

2.1   Background Theory

Psychology and Cognitive Science have got a long history of studies in the field of psychometrics, affective states, and how individuals process information.

It is difficult to differentiate terms like affective states, emotions, and moods. Emotions have been defined as the states of mind that are raised by external stimuli and are directed toward the stimulus in the environment by which they are raised [25]. Moods have been defined as emotional states in which the individual feels good or bad, and either likes or dislikes what is happening around him/her [24]. However, there is still no clear agreement on the difference between emotion and mood. Many authors consider mood and emotion as interchangeable terms (e.g., [3], [8]). In this paper, we adopt the same stance and use the term affective states as a generic term to indicate emotions, moods, or feelings.

There are two main theories to categorize affective states. One theory, called the discrete approach, seeks a set of basic affective states that can be distinguished uniquely [25]. Examples include "interested", "excited", "upset", and "guilty". The other theory groups affective states in major dimensions, which allow clear distinction among them [28]. With this approach, affective states are characterized by their valence, arousal, and dominance. Valence (or pleasure) can be described as the attractiveness (or adverseness) of an event, object, or situation [20]. Arousal is the sensation of being mentally awake and reactive to stimuli, while dominance (or control, over-learning) is the sensation by which the individual's skills are higher than the challenge level for a task [7]. The dimensional approach is common in human-machine interaction and computational intelligence studies (e.g., [13, 33]). It is commonly adopted to assess affective states triggered by an immediate stimulus [5, 22]. Therefore, the dimensional approach is adopted in this study.

The measurement of affective states is usually achieved using questionnaires and surveys. One of the most used questionnaire for the dimensional approach is the Self-Assessment Manikin (SAM) [5, 18]. SAM is a non-verbal assessment method, based on pictures. SAM measures valence, arousal, and dominance associated with a person's affective reaction to a stimulus. A numeric value is assigned to each rating scale for each dimension. For a 5-point rating scale, a value of 5 for valence means "very high attractiveness and pleasure towards the stimulus". SAM is not uncommon in Computer Science research where the affective states towards a stimulus must be studied (e.g., [13]).

These scales and similar other psychometrics present issues when employed in within- and between-subjects analyses. There is not a stable and shared metric for assessing the affective states across persons. For example, a score of 1 in valence for a person may be equal to a score of 3 for another person. Nevertheless, it is sensible to assume a reasonable, stable metric within a person. To overcome this issue, the scores of each participant are converted to Z-scores (a.k.a. standard scores). An observation is expressed by how many standard deviations it is above or below the mean of the whole set of an individual's observations. In this way, the measurements between participants become dimensionless and comparable with each other [19].

The affective states of individuals have impact on work-related behaviors and capacities [1, 11, 15, 21]. Additionally, the positive-Psychology branch defines the mental status of flow as fully focused motivation, energized focus, full involvement, and success in the process of the activity [7]. The correlation with productivity seems straightforward. In fact, evidence has been found that happier employees are more productive [11, 23, 36].

2.2   Related Studies

The literature shows that the affective states have an impact on various cognitive activities of individuals and many of these activities are linked with software development.

Fisher and Noble [11] employ Experience Sampling Method [19] to study correlates of real-time performance and affective states while working. The study recruited different workers (e.g., child care worker, hairdresser, office worker); however none of them was reported to be a software developer. The measurement instrument was a questionnaire with 5 points Likert items. The paper analyzes self-assessed skills, task difficulty, affective states triggered by the working task, and task performance. It is not uncommon in Psychology to let participants self-evaluate themselves, as self-assessed performance is consistent to objective measurements of performance [21]. Among the results of the study, it is shown that there is a strong positive correlation between positive affective states and task performance while there is a strong negative correlation between negative affective states and task performance. This paper encourages further research about real-time performance and emotions.

Shaw [31] observes that, although the role of affective states in the workplace is a subject of studies in management theory, Information Technology research ignores the role of affective states on Information Technology professionals. The study shows that the affective states of a software developer may dramatically change during a period of 48 hours. However, the study is a work-in-progress paper and no continuation is known. Nevertheless, the study calls for research on the affective states of software developers.

Khan et al. [16] echo the previously reported call and provide links from Psychology and Cognitive Science studies to software development studies. The authors construct a theoretical two-dimensional mapping framework in two steps. In the first step, programming tasks are linked to cognitive tasks. For example, the process of constructing a program – e.g. modeling and implementation – is mapped to the cognitive tasks of memory, reasoning, and induction. In the second step, the same cognitive tasks are linked to affective states. The authors show a correlation with cognitive processing abilities and software development. Two empirical studies on affective states and software development are then reported, which relate a developer's debugging performance to the affective states. In the first study, affective states were induced to software developers, who were then asked to complete a quiz on software debugging. The second study was a controlled experiment. The participants were asked to write a trace on paper of the execution of algorithms implemented in Java. The results suggest that when valence is kept high and the arousal related to the task varies, there is a positive correlation with the debugging performance. This study recommends more research on the topic.

The body of knowledge suggests that affective states are positively correlated to the productivity of individuals. Therefore, the research hypotheses of this study are on positive correlations between real-time affective states and the immediate productivity of software developers. The following are the research hypotheses of this study.

— H1: The real-time valence affective state of software developers is positively correlated to their self-assessed productivity.
— H2: The real-time arousal affective state of software developers is positively correlated to their self-assessed productivity.
— H3: The real-time dominance affective state of software developers is positively correlated to their self-assessed productivity.

3   Research Methodology

The research methodology of this study is a series of repeated measurements in the context of multiple case studies on software developers, in which quantitative and qualitative data is gathered. In this section, we describe the design of the empirical research, how the variables were measured, and how the data was analyzed.

3.1   Research Design

For a period of 90 minutes, the participant works on a software development tasks of a real software project. The researcher observes the behavior of the individual while programming. Each 10 minutes, the participant completes a short questionnaire on a tablet device. That is, valence, arousal, and dominance are measured for 9 times per participant. The same holds for the self-assessment of the productivity.

Each participant faces a pre-task interview in which basic demographic data, information about the project, tasks, and the developer's skills are obtained. Descriptive data is collected on the role of the participant (either "professional" or "student"), the experience with the programming language, and experience with the task (low, medium, and high).

After the completion of the working period, the researcher conducts a post-task interview. The instructions given to each participant are available in the on-line Appendix [12] of this paper. We wrote the instructions for the Self-Assessment Manikin (SAM) questionnaire following the technical manual by Lang et al. [18].

The researcher is present during the entire development period to observe the behavior of the participant without interfering. During the post-task interview, the observer and the participant look at a generated graph of the participant's productivity. If there are noticeable changes in the data trends, especially if these changes are in conflict with the observer's notes and predictions, the participant is asked to explain what happened in that interval. Complete anonymity is ensured to the participants.

The context of this study is natural settings (i.e., the working environment). Participants are obtained from the students of Computer Science of the Free University of Bozen-Bolzano and local IT companies. There are no restrictions in gender, age, or nationality. Participation is voluntary and not rewarded.

The only required instrument is a suitable device that implements the SAM questionnaire and the productivity item. We designed a website that implements SAM, and it is optimized for tablet devices. Since SAM is a pictorial questionnaire, the effort required for the questionnaire session is thus reduced to 4 touches to the screen.

All steps of the experiment are automatized.

3.2   Constructs and Measurements

The affective states dimensions - valence, arousal, dominance - describe differences in affective meanings among stimuli and are measured with the SAM pictorial questionnaire. The values of the affective state constructs range from 1 to 5. A value of 3 means "perfect balance" or "average" between the most negative (1) and the most positive value (5). For example, a value of 1 for the valence variable means "complete absence of attractiveness".

The task productivity is self-assessed by the participant, using a 5-point Likert item. The item is the sentence "My productivity is   ..." The participant ends the sentence, choosing the proper ending in the set {very low, below average, average, above average, very high}.

Each participant's data is converted to the individual's Z-score for the set of construct measurements, using the formula in (1):

$$z_{score}(x_{pc}) \frac{x_{pc} - \mu_{pc}}{\sigma_{pc}} \tag{1}$$

where x_{pc} represents the measured participant's construct, μ_{pc} is the average value of all the participant's construct measurements, and σ_{pc} is the standard deviation for the participant's construct measurements.

The measurements of each participant become dimensionless (strictly speaking, the unit is "number of standard deviations above or below the mean") and comparable, as they indicate how much the values spread. The range of the variables, while theoretically infinite, is practically the interval [-3, +3] due to the three-sigma rule [26].

3.3   Analysis Procedure

This study compares repeated measurements of individuals. The repeated measurements have a non-trivial impact on the analysis phase because 1) the data provided by each participant have dependencies among them, and 2) there might be time effects on the series of measurements per each participant. Thus, we have dependencies of the data at the participants' level and at the time level, grouped by the participant. Such dependencies present issues when employing Anova procedures, which are not designed for repeated measurements and multiple levels of dependency. Anova procedures are discouraged in favor of mixed-effects models, which are robust and specifically designed for repeated measurements and longitudinal data [14].

A linear mixed-effects model is a linear model that contains both fixed effects and random effects. The definition of a linear mixed-effects model given by Robinson [27] is given in (2):

$$y = X\beta + Zu + \varepsilon \tag{2}$$

where y is a vector of observable random variables, β is a vector of unknown parameters with fixed values (i.e., fixed effects), u is a vector of random variables (i.e., random effects) with mean $E(u) = 0$ and variance-covariance matrix $var(u) = G$, X and Z are known matrices of regressors relating the observations y to β and u, and ε is a vector of independent and identically distributed random error terms with mean $E(\varepsilon) = 0$ and variance $var(\varepsilon) = 0$.

The estimation of the significance of the effects for mixed models is an open debate. A convenient way to express the significance of the parameters is to provide upper and lower bound p-values[1]. We implement the model using the open-source statistical software R and the *lme4.lmer* function for linear mixed-effects models.

---

[1] We advise to read the technical manual by Tremblay et al.:
http://cran.r-project.org/web/packages/LMERConvenienceFunctions/

4   Results

The designed data collection process was fully followed. No deviations occurred. The participants were fully committed.

4.1   Descriptive Statistics

We obtained eight participants, for a total of 72 measurements. The mean of the participants' age was 23.75 (standard deviation=3.29). Seven of them were male. Four participants were first year B.Sc. Computer Science students and four of them were professional software developers. The Computer Science students worked on course-related projects. The four professional software developers developed their work-related projects.

Table 1. Participants and Projects Details

id	gender	age	role	project	task	p. lang.	p.lang exp.	task exp.
P1	M	25	PRO	Data collection for hydrological defense	Module for data displaying	Java	HIG	HIG
P2	M	26	PRO	Research Data Collection & Analysis	Script to analyze data	Python	LOW	HIG
P3	M	28	PRO	Human Re-sources Manag-er for a School	Retrieval and display of DB data	Java	HIG	HIG
P4	M	28	PRO	Metrics Ana-lyzer	Retrieval and sending of metrics	C++	HIG	HIG
P5	F	23	STU	Music Editor	Conversion of music score to pictures	C++	LOW	LOW
P6	M	20	STU	Code Editor	Analysis of Cyclomatic Complexity	C++	LOW	LOW
P7	M	20	STU	CAD	Single-lined labels on objects	C++	LOW	LOW
P8	M	20	STU	SVG Image Editor	Multiple ob-jects on a circle or ellipse	C++	HIG	HIG

The characteristics of the participants are summarized in Table 1. We notice that the roles do not always correspond to the experience. The professional participant P2 reported a LOW experience with the programming language while the student participant P8 reported a HIGH experience in both the programming language and the task type. Table 1 also contains the characteristics of the projects and the implemented task. There is high variety of project types and tasks. Five participants programmed using C++ while two of them with Java and the remaining one with Python. The participants' projects were non-trivial, regardless of their role. For example, participant P1 (a professional developer) was maintaining a complex software system to collect and analyze data from different sensors installed on hydrological defenses (e.g., dams). Participant P5 (a student) was implementing pictorial exports of music scores in an open-source software for composing music.

We provide in Fig. 1, in Fig. 2, and in Fig. 3, the charts representing the changes of the self-assessed productivity over time, with respect to the valence, the arousal, and the dominance dimensions respectively.

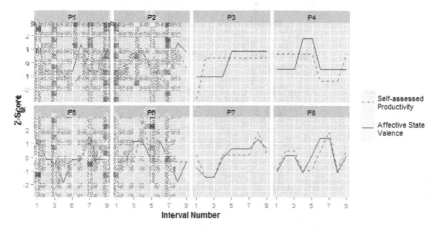

Fig. 1. Valence vs. Productivity over Time

As it can be seen in Fig. 1, there are cases in which the valence score provides strong predictions of the productivity (participants P2, P7, and P8). For the other participants, there are many matched intervals, e.g. P5 at interval 7, and P4 at intervals 4-7. Participant P1 is the only one for which the valence does not provide strong predictions. In few cases, the valence Z-score is more than a standard deviation apart from the productivity Z-score.

The arousal dimension in Fig. 2 looks less related to the productivity than the valence dimension. The behavior of the arousal line often deviates from the trend of the productivity line (e.g., all the points of participants P5 and P6). Nevertheless, there are intervals in which the arousal values are closely related to productivity, e.g., with participants P4 and P7.

The dominance dimension in Fig. 3 looks more correlated to the productivity than the arousal dimension. Participants P1, P5, and P7 provided close trends. For the other cases, there are intervals in which the correlation looks closer and stronger. However, it becomes weaker for the remaining intervals (e.g., with P4). The only exception was with participant P6, where a clear correlation between dominance and productivity cannot be spotted.

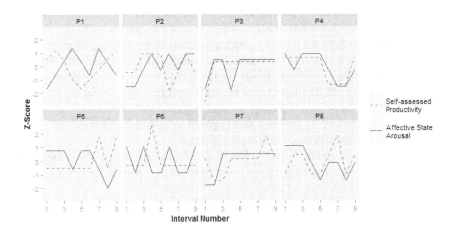

Fig. 2. Arousal vs. Productivity over Time

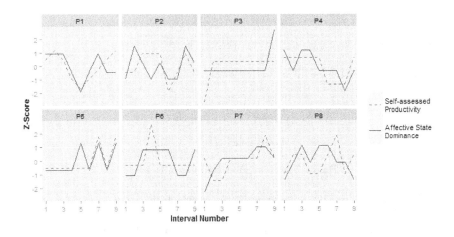

Fig. 3. Dominance vs. Productivity over Time

For all the participants, the Z-values of the variables show variations of about 2 units over time. That is, even for a working time of 90 minutes there are strong variations of both the affective states and the self-assessed productivity.

4.2 Hypotheses Testing

For the model construction, valence, arousal, dominance, and their interaction with time are modeled as fixed effects. The random effects are two: a scalar random effect for the participant grouping factor (i.e., each participant) and a random slope for the measurement time, indexed by each participant. In this way, the dependency of the measurements within the participants are taken into account: at the participant's level and at a time level. The final, full model[2] is given in (3) as a *lme4.lmer* formula.

productivity ~ (valence + arousal + dominance) * time + (1 | participant) + (0 + time | participant)   (3)

where *productivity* is the dependent variable; *valence, arousal, dominance,* and *time* are fixed effects; (1 | *participant*) is the scalar random effect for each participant, (0 + *time* | *participant*) is read as "no intercept and time by participant" and it is a random slope for the measurement time, grouped by each participant.

The full model in (3) significantly differs from the null model (4)

productivity ~ 1 + (1 | participant) + (0 + time | participant)   (4)

We checked for normality and homogeneity by visual inspections of a plot of the residuals against the fitted values, plus a Shapiro-Wilk test.

Table 2 provides the parameter estimation for the fixed effects (expressed in Z-scores), the significance of the parameter estimation, and the percentage of the deviance explained by each fixed effect. A single star (*) highlights the significant results (p-value less than 0.01). At a 0.01 significance level, valence and dominance are positively correlated with the self-assessed productivity of software developers.

Table 2. Parameter Estimation

Fixed Effect	Value	Sum Square	F-value	Upper p-value (64 d.f.)	Lower p-value (48 d.f.)	Deviance Explain. (%)
valence	0.10*	7.86	19.10	0.000	0.000	12.39
arousal	0.07	0.00	0.00	0.950	0.950	0.00
dominance	0.48*	7.44	18.07	0.000	0.000	11.71
time	0.00	0.11	0.26	0.614	0.615	0.17
valence:time	0.04	0.35	0.84	0.363	0.364	0.54
arousal:time	-0.03	0.45	1.09	0.300	0.301	0.71
dominance:time	-0.01	0.06	0.15	0.699	0.700	0.10

The scalar random effects values for the participants belonged to the interval [-0.48, 0.33]; the random effects for the time were estimated to 0.

There is significant evidence to support the hypotheses H1 and H3. There is a positive correlation between two affective states dimensions (valence, dominance) and the self-assessed productivity of software developers.

---

[2] Please note that if the intercept for the *time* parameter (i.e., (1+*time* | *participant*)) is not suppressed, the resulting model will be less valuable in terms of likelihood ratio tests (*anova* in R). Additionally, the value of the added random intercept would belong to the interval [-0.02, 0.03]. We thank an anonymous reviewer for the valuable feedback that let us improve this section.

Although we do not have evidence to support H2, regarding arousal, we will provide a possible explanation for this in the next section.

5   Discussion

In this section, we discuss the results and compare them with the related work. After the discussion of the results, we reflect on the limitations of the study.

5.1   Implications

The empirical results obtained in this study support the hypothesized positive correlation between the affective state dimensions of valence and dominance with the self-assessed productivity of software developers. No support was found for a positive correlation with the arousal affective state dimension and productivity. No evidence was found for a significant interaction between affective states and time.

The linear mixed-effects model provides an explanation power of 25.62% in terms of percentage of the deviance explained. Valence was estimated to 0.10 and dominance to 0.48, in terms of Z-scores. However, the percentage of the deviance explained by the two effects is almost the same: 12.39 for valence and 11.71 for dominance. In other words, high happiness with the task and the sensation of having adequate skills roughly have the same explanation power and provide almost the full explanation power of the model.

Regarding arousal, we suspect that the participants might have misunderstood its role in the questionnaire. All participants raised questions about the arousal dimension during the questionnaire explanations. A possible explanation of no significant interactions between the affective states dimensions and time is that each participant worked on different, independent projects. Also, the random effects related to time were estimated to 0, thus non-existing. It is worthy to report the full model with time as fixed and random effect because future experiments with a group of developers working on the same project will likely have significant interactions with time.

The results of this study are in line with the results of Khan et al. [16], where high valence resulted in the best performance on software debugging. However, the results are not in line with this study regarding the arousal dimension. The results of this study are also in line with those of Fisher and Noble [11], where positive affective states of different types of workers are found to be positively correlated with their productivity.

Although it is difficult to define productivity for software developers, all the participants had a clear idea about their productivity scores. None of them raised a question about how to self-rate their productivity. Nevertheless, in the post-task interviews, they were not able to explain how they defined their own productivity. The most common answer was related to the achievement of the expectation they set for the end of the 90 minutes of work. Again, this "expectation" was neither clearly definable nor quantifiable for them. Their approach was to express the sequent productivity value with respect to the previous one – as in "worse", "equal", or "better" than before.

The theoretical implication of this study is that the real-time affective states related to a software development task are positively correlated with the programmer's self-assessed productivity.

5.2   Limitations

In this section, we discuss the limitations of this study. We mitigated conclusion, internal, construct, and external validity threats while following the classification provided by Wohlin et al. [35].

Conclusion validity threats occur when the experimenters draw inaccurate inference from the data because of inadequate statistical tests. The employed linear mixed-effects models are robust to violations of Anova methods given by multiple dependencies of the data (see section 3.3). A threat lies in the limited number of participants (8) who worked for about 90 minutes each. However, the background and skills in the sample were balanced. Due to the peculiarity of the repeated measurements and the analysis method, all 72 measurements are valuable. It has been shown that repeated measures designs do not require more than seven measurements per individual [34]. We added two more measurements in order to be able to remove possible invalid data.

Internal validity threats are experimental issues that threaten the researcher's ability to draw inference from the data. Although the experiment was performed in natural settings, the fact the individuals were observed and the lack of knowledge about the experiment contents mitigated social threats to internal validity. A series of pilot studies with the measurement instrument showed that the minimum period to interrupt the participants was about 10 minutes if the case study was focused on a single task instead of longer periods of observations.

Construct validity refers to issues with the relation between theory and observation. A construct validity threat might come from the use of self-assessed productivity. In spite of the difficulty in using traditional software metrics (the project, the task, and the programming language were random for the researcher) and that measuring software productivity is still an open problem, self-assessed performance is commonly employed in Psychology studies [3, 11, 36] and it is consistent to objective measurements of performance [21]. We also carefully observed the participants during the programming task. Post-task interviews included questions on their choices for productivity levels, which resulted in remarkably honest and reliable answers, as expected.

External validity threats are issues related to improper inferences from the sample data to other persons, settings, and situations. Although half of the participants were students, it has been argued that students are the next generation of software professionals; they are remarkably close to the interested population if not even more updated on new technologies [17, 32]. Secondly, it can be questioned why we studied software developers working alone on their project. People working in group interact and trigger a complex, powerful network of affective states [2]. Thus, to better control the measurements, we chose individuals working alone. However, no participant was forced to limit social connections while working, and the experiment took place in natural settings.

6   Conclusions

For more than thirty years, it has been claimed that software developers are essential when considering how to improve the productivity of development process and the quality of delivered products. However, little research has been done on how human aspects of developers have an impact on software development activities. We echo a call on employing psychometrics in Software Engineering research by studying how the affective states of software developers - emotions, moods, and feelings - have an impact on their programming tasks.

This paper reports a repeated measures research on the correlation of affective states of software developers and their self-assessed productivity. We observed eight developers working on their individual projects. Their affective states and their self-assessed productivity were measured on intervals of ten minutes. A linear mixed-effects model was proposed in order to estimate the value of the correlation of the affective states of valence, arousal, and dominance, and the productivity of developers. The model was able to express about the 25% of the deviance of the self-assessed productivity. Valence and dominance, or the attractiveness perceived towards the development task and the perception of possessing adequate skills, were able to provide almost the whole explanation power of the model.

The understanding provided by this study is an important part of basic science in Software Engineering rather than leading to direct, applicable results: among Khan et al. [16] and Shaw [31], this is one of the first studies examining the role of affective states of software developers. We are providing basic theoretical building blocks on researching the human side of software construction. This work performs empirical validation of psychometrics and related measurement instruments in Software Engineering research. It proposes the employment of linear mixed-effects models, which have been proven to be effective in repeated measures designs instead of Anova. It is also stressed out that Anova should be avoided in such cases.

Are happy developers more productive? The empirical results in this study indicate towards a *"Yes, they are"* answer. However, a definite answer will be provided by future research characterized by the use of multidisciplinary theories, validated measurement instruments, and analysis tools as exemplified in this paper.

Experiments with a larger number of participants performing the same programming task will allow the use of traditional software productivity metrics and provide further explanations. Mood induction techniques should be employed to study causality effects of affective states on the productivity of software developers. Additionally, future studies on software teams with affective states measurements are required in order to understand the dynamics of affective states and the creative performance of software developers.

Software developers are unique human beings. By studying how they perceive the development life-cycle and how cognitive activities affect their performance, we will open up a different perspective and understanding of the creative activity of software development.

Acknowledgment. We would like to thank the participants of the experiment. We would also like to acknowledge Elena Borgogno, Ilenia Fronza, Cigdem Gencel, Nattakarn Phaphoom, and Juha Rikkilä for their kind help and support during this study. We are grateful for the insightful comments offered by three anonymous reviewers, who helped us to improve the paper.

References

1. Ashkanasy, N.M., Daus, C.S.: Emotion in the workplace: The new challenge for managers. The Academy of Management Executive 16(1), 76–86 (2002)
2. Barsade, S.G., Gibson, D.E.: Group emotion: A view from top and bottom. Research On Managing Groups And Teams 1(4), 81–102 (1998)
3. Beal, D.J., et al.: An episodic process model of affective influences on performance. Journal of Applied Psychology 90(6), 1054–1068 (2005)
4. Boehm, B.: Understanding and Controlling Software Costs. IEEE Transactions on Software Engineering 14(10), 1462–1477 (1990)
5. Bradley, L.: Measuring emotion: the self-assessment semantic differential. Journal of Behavior Therapy and Experimental Psychiatry 25(1), 49–59 (1994)
6. Cockburn, A., Highsmith, J.: Agile software development, the people factor. IEEE Computer 34(11), 131–133 (2001)
7. Csikszentmihalyi, M.: Finding flow. Psychology Today 30(4), 46 (1997)
8. Dow, J.: External and Internal Approaches to Emotion. Psycoloquy 3(1), 2 (1992)
9. Feldt, R., et al.: Towards individualized software engineering: empirical studies should collect psychometrics. In: International Workshop on Cooperative and Human Aspects of Software Engineering, pp. 49–52. ACM (2008)
10. Fischer, G.: Cognitive View of Reuse and Redesign. IEEE Software 4(4), 60–72 (1987)
11. Fisher, C.D., Noble, C.: A Within-Person Examination of Correlates of Performance and Emotions While Working. Human Performance 17(2), 145–168 (2004)
12. Graziotin, D., et al.: Appendix for "Are Happy Developers more Productive? The Correlation of Affective States of Software Developers and their self-assessed Productivity", http://figshare.com/articles/Appendix_for_Are_Happy_Developers_more_Productive_The_Correlation_of_Affective_States_of_Software_Developers_and_their_self_assessed_Productivity_/683885, doi:10.6084/m9.figshare.683885
13. Grimm, M., Kroschel, K.: Evaluation of natural emotions using self assessment manikins. In: 2005 IEEE Workshop on Automatic Speech Recognition and Understanding, pp. 381–385 (2005)
14. Gueorguieva, R., Krystal, J.H.: Move over ANOVA: progress in analyzing repeated-measures data and its reflection in papers published in the Archives of General Psychiatry. Archives of General Psychiatry 61(3), 310–317 (2004)
15. Ilies, R., Judge, T.: Understanding the dynamic relationships among personality, mood, and job satisfaction: A field experience sampling study. Organizational Behavior and Human Decision Processes 89(2), 1119–1139 (2002)
16. Khan, I.A., et al.: Do moods affect programmers' debug performance? Cognition, Technology & Work 13(4), 245–258 (2010)
17. Kitchenham, B.A., et al.: Preliminary guidelines for empirical research in software engineering. IEEE Transactions on Software Engineering 28(8), 721–734 (2002)

18. Lang, P.J., et al.: International affective picture system (IAPS): Technical manual and affective ratings. Gainesville FL NIMH Center for the study of emotion and attention University of Florida. Technical Report A–6 (1999)
19. Larson, R., Csikszentmihalyi, M.: The experience sampling method. New Directions for Methodology of Social and Behavioral Science 15(15), 41–56 (1983)
20. Lewin, K.: A dynamic theory of personality. McGraw-Hill, New York (1935)
21. Miner, A.G., Glomb, T.M.: State mood, task performance, and behavior at work: A within-persons approach. Organizational Behavior and Human Decision Processes 112(1), 43–57 (2010)
22. Ong, J.C., et al.: A two-dimensional approach to assessing affective states in good and poor sleepers. Journal of Sleep Research 20(2), 606–610 (2011)
23. Oswald, A.J., et al.: Happiness and productivity. The Warwick Economics Research Paper Series TWERPS 882, 1–44 (2008)
24. Parkinson, B., et al.: Changing moods: The psychology of mood and mood regulation. Addison-Wesley Longman, Amsterdam (1996)
25. Plutchik, R., Kellerman, H.: Emotion, theory, research, and experience. Academic Press, London (1980)
26. Pukelsheim, F.: The Three Sigma Rule. The American Statistician 48(2), 88–91 (1994)
27. Robinson, G.K.: That BLUP is a Good Thing: The Estimation of Random Effects. Statistical Science 6(1), 15–32 (1991)
28. Russell, J.: A Circumplex Model of Affect. Journal of Personality and Social Psychology 39(6), 1161–1178 (1980)
29. Sampaio, S.C.D.B., et al.: A Review of Productivity Factors and Strategies on Software Development. In: 2010 Fifth International Conference on Software Engineering Advances, pp. 196–204 (2010)
30. Scacchi, W.: Understanding Software Productivity. Advances in Software Engineering and Knowledge Engineering 4, 37–70 (1995)
31. Shaw, T.: The emotions of systems developers. In: Proceedings of the 2004 Conference on Computer Personnel Research Careers, Culture, and Ethics in a Networked Environment, SIGMIS CPR 2004, p. 124. ACM Press, New York (2004)
32. Tichy, W.: Hints for reviewing empirical work in software engineering. Empirical Software Engineering 5(4), 309–312 (2000)
33. Tsonos, D., et al.: Towards modeling of Readers' Emotional State response for the automated annotation of documents. In: 2008 IEEE International Joint Conference on Neural Networks IEEE World Congress on Computational Intelligence, pp. 3253–3260 (2008)
34. Vickers, A.J.: How many repeated measures in repeated measures designs? Statistical issues for comparative trials. BMC Medical Research Methodology 3(22), 1–9 (2003)
35. Wohlin, C., et al.: Experimentation in software engineering: an introduction. Kluwer Academic Publishers (2000)
36. Zelenski, J.M., et al.: The Happy-Productive Worker Thesis Revisited. Journal of Happiness Studies 9(4), 521–537 (2008)

A Model-Driven Approach to Specifying and Monitoring Controlled Experiments in Software Engineering

Marília Freire[1,2], Paola Accioly[3], Gustavo Sizílio[1,2], Edmilson Campos Neto[1,2], Uirá Kulesza[1], Eduardo Aranha[1], and Paulo Borba[3]

[1] Federal University of Rio Grande do Norte, Natal-RN, Brasil
{marilia.freire,gustavo.sizilio,edmilsoncampos}@ppgsc.ufrn.br,
{uira,eduardo}@dimap.ufrn.br
[2] Federal Institute of Rio Grande do Norte, Natal-RN, Brasil
[3] Federal University of Pernambuco, Recife-PE, Brasil
{prga,phmb}@cin.ufpe.br

Abstract. This paper presents a process-oriented model-driven approach that supports the conduction of controlled experiments in software engineering. The approach consists of: (i) a domain specific language (DSL) for process specification and statistical design of controlled experiments; (ii) model-driven transformations that allow workflow models generations specific to each experiment participant and according to the experiment statistical design; and (iii) a workflow execution environment that allows the monitoring of participant activities in the experiment, besides gathering participants feedback from the experiment. The paper also presents the results of an exploratory study that analyzes the feasibility of the approach and the expressivity of the DSLs in the modeling of a non-trivial software engineering experiment.

1 Introduction

The software engineering community has been increasingly demanding the conduction of more rigorous empirical studies to gather scientific based evidences about software technologies. In this context, hundreds of controlled experiments have been performed in the software engineering area [1]. A controlled experiment is a technique that allows scientists to test a research hypothesis and the cause and effect relationship between variables (dependent and independent) involved in the study environment. However, the planning, execution, analyzing and packaging of a controlled experiment are currently still complex, costly and error prone activities.

Over the last years, the software engineering community has proposed different approaches to reporting [2] and assisting the conduction of such experiments [3] [4] [5]. Although these approaches (environments, tools, infrastructure or frameworks) have brought support to many activities involved in a controlled experiment, they have a lot of limitations and potential for future improvements [15]. In general, they lack the following characteristics: (i) adaptability and extensibility according to the experimental study necessities; (ii) experiment execution automatic organization

J. Heidrich et al. (Eds.): PROFES 2013, LNCS 7983, pp. 65–79, 2013.
© Springer-Verlag Berlin Heidelberg 2013

according to its statistic design of experiment; (iii) automatic data collection for each participant; (iv) statistical data analysis; and (v) online monitoring.

In order to overcome these challenges, we have been developing a customizable model-driven environment for supporting and conducting controlled experiments. Our first aim has been to address the experiment planning and execution stages. Our approach is composed of: (i) a domain specific language (DSL) to modeling the domain of controlled experiments from different perspectives; (ii) model-driven transformations that map abstractions from our experiment DSL to workflow models for each experiment participant, where tasks are specified and metrics automatically collected; and (iii) a workflow execution environment that guides the experiment execution and monitoring.

To evaluate the feasibility of our approach, we applied it in the specification of a non-trivial experiment with statistical rigor. The modeled study was a controlled experiment in software engineering that compared two test techniques used in software product lines: (i) a Generic Technique (GT) that uses general specifications without variability representation; and (ii) a Specific Technique (ST) that uses product customized test suites. The experiment analyzed the benefits and drawbacks of these two techniques from the point of view of the test manager by measuring the execution effort of the resulting test cases [6].

The remainder of this paper is organized as follows. Section 2 presents existing research work on controlled experiment in software engineering by identifying several challenges when conducting this kind of empirical study. Section 3 gives an overview of the main stages of our approach. Section 4 presents the modeling of a controlled experiment [6] through an exploratory study. Section 5 discusses the results achieved and compare the usage of our approach to previous executions of the modeled experiment. Finally, Section 6 presents final conclusions and points out future work directions.

2   Modeling of Controlled Experiments in Software Engineering

The process of a controlled experiment is typically composed of the following phases: definition, planning, execution, analysis, and packaging [7]. Each one of these phases is associated with the execution of different activities that consume and produce artifacts related to the study in question. Controlled experiments require great care in planning so that they can provide useful and significant results [8]. In addition, planning, conducting and reporting the various tasks involved in a large-scale software engineering controlled experiment can be quite complex and time consuming without proper tool support [3].

This section describes five criteria taken into account for supporting the conduction of controlled experiments. These criteria have been identified from the experience reported by other researchers when conducting experiments in software engineering [15]. They are important to minimize costs and efforts, and to improve the data accuracy when conducting controlled experiments:

C1. *Support Multi-View Experiment Definition*: Controlled experiments are planned and documented in a multi-view fashion. In this context, defining an experiment manifests itself in different kinds of perspectives (e.g. researchers and participants) and structure view (e.g. different execution procedures involving several artifacts, different metrics, factor types and blocking variables, gathering of feedback). Each one of these views identifies multiple points of failure, thus requiring a large effort to organize and understand the experiment. Modeling the experiment using multiple views can improve the understanding of the involved team with their specific responsibilities, and it also specializes the involved knowledge minimizing the chance of misunderstanding. In addition, this is particularly important for the replication of experiments as it can encompass the remote execution of the experiment and a huge number of participants. Since replicate studies are necessary in order to build empirical knowledge with confidence, attention must also be taken to ensure that the produced artifacts and data collection protocols from the experiments are understandable and consistent.

C2. *Support online monitoring*: To control an experiment execution is a hard task. In the context of large-scale experiments, this task is even more complex. The care in which such data is reported and collected greatly affects the accuracy of the process. Consequently, the gathering of poor self-reported data can distort the results [3] and invalidate the experiment. Providing tools and mechanisms to help the early problem detection during the experiment execution can contribute to ensure the experiment validity. In addition, if the study is done at multiple sites in collaboration with other researchers, the use of online monitoring enables the remote researcher to assist the experiment monitoring. It also enables the researchers to register notes related to the execution thus contributing to maintain the experiment historical data and to share the knowledge with the research community. Furthermore, different process control techniques can be used for monitoring the experiment operation.

C3. *Provide process generation and execution according to the experimental design*: During the planning phase of the experiment, the researcher has to know how to deal with statistical skills needed to organize and analyze a controlled experiment. This is intrinsically linked with the choice of the statistical experiment design, since the kind of design constrains the analysis that can be performed and therefore the conclusions that can be drawn [8]. Although there are simple statistical experimental designs, it is not easy to a software engineer researcher that is unfamiliar with statistic to know how to set it up. This highlights the problem of abstraction mismatch and the need for a support environment that does not require additional statistical expertise. In the context of large-scale experiments, this task is even more complex and difficult;

C4. *Provide guidance and automatic data collection for each participant:* Whereas the skill required to define an experimental study is considerable and critical, the effort to run the experiment is even substantial. In this context, attentions and concerns are necessary, to minimize the time spent to run the experiment, and, consequently, to improve the data accuracy and quality. Providing a proper automated support environment is a key requirement in this context that can definitively contribute positively to achieve these aims.

C5. *Provide extension capability to integrate external tools:* Software engineering experimental environments have to deal with several empirical studies that pertain to different application domains and technologies. Some of the data necessary to perform such experimental studies may come from external tools as IDEs, testing tools, code analysis tools, modeling tools, and others. Therefore, it is important that these experimental environments provide extension points in order to support integration facilities. The integration with other external tools also contributes to give a unique and complete environment to the participants execute the experiment.

3 Approach Overview

In this section, we present an overview of our approach for automated support of controlled experiments in software engineering. It has been developed based on model-driven engineering and domain-specific languages. The five criteria described in Section 2 formed the basis for the design and implementation of our approach. Fig. 1 illustrates the main stages of our approach and their respective relationships. The three stages are implemented and they have been continuously improved. Next sections give an overview of the proposed approach.

3.1 Experiment Definition and Planning

The first stage of our approach is the experiment definition and planning using a domain specific language that allows specifying different perspectives from an experiment. The development of software systems using domain specific languages (DSLs) has increased over the last years. DSLs raise the abstraction level and bring facilities for generating models or source code. They can contribute to increase the development productivity and to facilitate a precise definition of concerns within a particular domain [9].

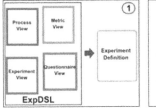 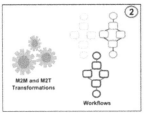 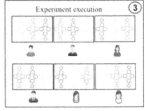

Fig. 1. Approach Overview

Our experimental DSL is called ExpDSL. It is a textual DSL developed using the xText[1]. ExpDSL is composed of four perspectives, as we can see in the box one from Fig. 1: (i) **the Process View** – allows defining the procedures of data collection from the experiment participants. It is similar to a software process language, where we can

---

[1] http://www.eclipse.org/Xtext/

define the activities, tasks, artifacts, and roles involved in the process; (ii) **the Metric View** – is used to define the metrics that have to be collected during the experiment execution. Each metric intercepts existing process activities or tasks in order to quantify observations of interest (dependent variables, etc.) in the study; (iii) **the Experimental Plan View** – is used to define the experimental plan. It allows setting the factors to be controlled (treatments, noisy variables, etc.), as well as a statistical design of experiment (DoE) used to organize treatment allocation and the experiment execution; and (iv) **the Questionnaire View** – allows defining questionnaires in order to collect quantitative and qualitative data from participants of the experiment. The questionnaires can be applied before or after all the experiment activities, or before or after procedures specified in the process view.

After specifying each view using the DSL, researchers obtain a complete experiment definition, which is used as an input artifact for the next step of our approach, the workflow generation.

3.2   Experiment Workflow Generation

The second stage of our approach is the model-driven transformations that receive as input the experiment definition specified in the ExpDSL (our textual DSL) and generates as output customized workflows for each experiment participant according to the specified statistical design. The workflows are responsible for guiding each participant through the activities and tasks needed to conduct the experiment and to extract data related to the specified metrics. Fig. 1, box 2 illustrates this approach stage.

Our approach defines two transformations to be executed in this stage: (i) a M2M (model-to-model) transformation that receives as input an Ecore model (generated from the ExpDSL specification) and generates as output the workflow model according to the defined processes related to the experiment factors and treatments, and the statistical design of experiment chosen by the researcher during the planning. The design of experiment is important to organize the participants and the experiment execution arrangement; and (ii) a M2T (model to text) transformation responsible for generating the web forms code and configuration files needed to execute the workflows of the experiment in a web engine.

The M2M transformation is implemented using QVTo (Operational QVT) language and the M2T transformation using the Acceleo template language. The workflow metamodel is based on the jBPM Process Definition Language (JPDL) schema, but it has more elements than the original one, which are specific to the experimental software engineering domain.

Table 1 presents the mapping between elements specified in ExpDSL, Workflow Model and Workflow Engine. The Process element from the ExpDSL is mapped to the process-definition elements in the workflow model, ending up as workflow instances in the workflow engine. The number of treatment applications is defined according to the attribute *internalReplication*. Each Activity in the process view is mapped to a task-node element in the workflow model, which is mapped to a web-form responsible to present the activities and their tasks to the participant during the experiment. Each attribute "next" from an Activity is mapped to a transition element in the workflow model and a transition button in the workflow engine.

The Metric element from the ExpDSL is mapped to a pair of elements in the workflow system: an Event element and an Action. They are mapped to actions implemented as Java methods in the workflow engine. The elements Artefact in and out are mapped to similar elements in the workflow model. The Artefact in represents a link to download in the corresponding Activity form, and the Artefact out represents an upload link in the corresponding Activity form.

Table 1. Elements Mapping

ExpDSL	Workflow Model	Web Application - engine
Process	process-definition	workflow instance*
Activity	task-node	web-form
Task	task	------
next (Activity)	transition	transition button
Metric (activity, task, artefact*)	(Event + action)	(java method)
Artefact in	artefact (type in)	link to download
Artefact out	artefact (type out)	upload form
artefact inout	artefact (type inout)	link to download + upload form
Participant	Role	users*

3.3   Experiment Execution

The third and last stage of our approach is the experiment execution in our web workflow engine (Fig. 1, box 3). It is performed as a web application in a workflow engine where each participant can follow the instructions for her/his tasks, and the researchers running the experiment can monitor these activities. Our research group has developed a workflow engine in order to support this approach stage. However, it is important to mention that our approach can be easily adapted to generate workflow specification, and code for other existing workflow engines. Indeed, we have previously evaluated our approach using the jBPM workflow engine [10] [11].

In order to execute an experiment, the researcher needs to upload the generated files (workflow specification, web forms and configuration files), which represents the whole experiment, in the web workflow engine environment. Then, they have to perform some simple configurations such as registering the participants and loading the input artifacts specified for the processes tasks. Finally, they can enable the experiment execution. From that point on, each participant can start the experiment execution following the activities described in his/her workflow. During the execution, the metrics will be collected according to the specification (we are initially collecting metrics related only to the time spent by the experiment) and the collected time will be available for the experiment analysis phase.

4   Approach in Action

In this section, we present an exploratory study performed in order to assess the expressivity of our approach and its elements. The main aims were: (i) to analyze the expressivity of the proposed DSL and model transformations of our approach; and (ii) to identify improvement points in our workflow engine. In order to address such aims, we model a controlled experiment previously executed [6], which used strong statistical design principles. The easy access to the responsible research team and the experiment results also contributed to the selection of this experiment. We have also simulated the experiment with the researchers that executed it with real subjects, aiming at collecting their feedback and impressions about our approach.

4.1   The Modelled Experiment: Investigating Black-Box Testing Techniques for SPL

In Software Product Lines (SPL), writing black-box test cases based on use case scenarios for derived products can be challenging due to the potential large number of products, and the variation points scattered through different SPL features scenarios. To deal with this problem, several techniques have been proposed. However, this research area still lacks empirical evidence about the real contribution of these approaches to improve both quality and productivity of the SPL test cycle. In this context, a controlled experiment [6] was designed to analyze the impact of the two black-box testing techniques (hereby called treatments) for SPL derived products (see Fig.2): (i) the Generic Technique (GT), which uses a general testing specification without variability representation, that is, a single test suite for all derived products; and (ii) the Specific Technique (ST), which uses product customized test suites, that is, one specific test suite for each derived product. The objective is to analyze these techniques by evaluating the time taken to execute the test suites and the numbers of invalid Change Requests (CRs) reported when using each testing technique. An invalid CR is an invalid indication of software defect, a consequence of an inaccuracy in a test case and not in the software under test.

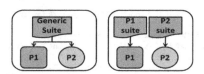

Fig. 2. Treatments investigated by the controlled experiment

The experiment has two factors to control: (i) the participants involved, since different background knowledge and testing skills usually impact test execution effort; and (ii) the number of existing variation points in the test cases, since test suites with more variation points may lead to more test case inconsistencies. These factors are controlled by a statistical experiment design called Latin square [12], which blocks the effect of two factors that are not of interest of the researcher. In fact, a 2x2 Latin square was used (two treatments to investigate) using participants (with their individual experiences) and features (with their different variations points) as blocking variables in the rows and columns of the Latin square.

4.2   Experiment Definition

During the experiment definition, we model the four views of our experimental study, which are detailed next.

The Process View. In the process perspective, we define four processes, one for each technique (ST and GT) and feature combination (features hereby called 1 and 2). Each process is composed of 12 activities, where each activity represents the execution of a different test case. We selected two test suites (each one with six tests cases) to be used in the experiment. Each process activity is composed of two tasks: one related to the test case execution, and another one related to the change request (CR) reporting, when faults are observed. The test case task has the test case itself as an input artifact, and the CR reporting task has the CR reporting as an output artifact.

Fig. 3 shows a partial fragment of the specification of the DSL for the process perspective that describes two activities from the process to execute the specific technique related to feature 1 (process "ST_F1"). The activity named "SP1_F1_1" has the description "Insert a new member – Product 1" whose responsible is the role "Subject". It also points the activity "SP1_F1_2" as the next activity to be executed. The activity "SP1_F1_1" has two tasks: the first one is named "Execute TC SP1_F1_1", with description "Execute the test case SP1_F1_1", with an input artifact named "Test case SP1_F1_1". The other tasks, activities and processes are similarly specified.

```
Experiment "Testing Strategies for SPL"

Process "ST_F1"{
    Activity "SP1_F1_1" "Insert a new member - Product 1" "SP1_F1_2" Role "Subject"; {
        Task "Execute TC SP1_F1_1" description "Execute the test case SP1_F1_1"
            artefacts
            artefact  "Teste case SP1_F1_1" description "Test case details SP1_F1_1" type input;;
        Task "Report CR SP1_F1_1" description "Describe TC SP1_F1_1 results"
            artefacts
            artefact "CR SP1_F1_1" description "Reporting the CR for Test Case SP1_F1_1" type output;;
    }
    Activity "SP1_F1_2" "Insert a new conference paper  - Product 1" "SP1_F1_3" Role "Subject";{
        Task "Execute TC SP1_F1_2" description "Execute the test case SP1_F1_2"
            artefacts
            artefact  "Test case SP1_F1_2" description "Test case details SP1_F1_2"  type input;;
        Task "Report CR SP1_F1_2" description "Describe  the test case TC SP1_F1_2 results"
            artefacts
            artefact "CR SP1_F1_2" description "Reporting the CR for Test Case SP1_F1_2" type output;;
    }
```

Fig. 3. Process View Fragment

The Experimental Plan View. The experiment view fragment of the DSL defines the experimental plan. It was used to define the factors and treatments, the parameters of the experiment, and the statistical design chosen for the controlled experiment from a list of three possibilities: (i) completely randomized design - CRD, (ii) randomized complete block design - RCBD, and (iii) Latin square - LS. Fig. 4 shows the DSL fragment to this specification. The Parameter element is used to specify any characteristic (qualitative or quantitative) of the experiment context that has to be invariable throughout the experimentation. In this case, we have the specification of parameters such as "Participants have to pause time for asking questions". The Factor "TestTechnique" is the element that represents the investigated techniques, therefore the attribute "isDesiredVariation" is "True". There are two treatments (levels or alternatives) specified for this factor, which are: (i) the Level "Generic" (Generic Technique); and (ii) the Level "Specific" (Specific Technique). The second Factor is " Feature" and the levels are named "F1" and "F2", representing each feature to be used in the experiment. The last factor specified is "Subject" with levels "Subject1" and "Subject2" (in our 2x2 Latin square, two subjects are required per replica of the square). Finally, the experimental design selected from the list of designs is the "LS – Latin Square".

During the experiment modeling, we have identified the necessity of two new elements required to improve the results of our model transformations. The first one was the "Internal Replication" element that is used to indicate the number of applications of each experiment treatment. This parameter has a different meaning according to the experimental design chosen. In a Latin square, it represents the number of square replicas. For our case, we indicate four internal replicas, which means to have eight subjects in the experiment. Each subject is responsible for running two workflow instances, according to the allocation defined by the Latin square technique.

The second new element identified during our assessment modeling study came from the need to link the data collection procedures to the related level of factors that they are associated. This information is needed to arrange the experiment execution order, mainly when applying the Latin square experimental design. So, in this study, the Link element is used to associate the Process element to the corresponding Levels

```
Experimental Plan Design "TestDesign"
    type LS - Latin Square  {
        Parameter "Participants have to pause time for asking questions"
        Parameter "The LPS complexity is low"
        Parameter "Artefacts are written in the participant source language"
        Parameter "Participants are undergraduating students"

        Factor "TestTechnique" isDesiredVariation True
            Level "Generic";
            Level "Specific";
            ;
        Factor "Feature" isDesiredVariation False
            Level "F1";
            Level "F2";
            ;
        Factor "Subject" isDesiredVariation False
            Level "Subject1";
            Level "Subject2";
            ;

        Internal Replication 4

        Link "ST_F1" to "TestTechnique.Specific" "Feature.F1"
        Link "ST_F2" to "TestTechnique.Specific" "Feature.F2"
        Link "GT_F1" to "TestTechnique.Generic" "Feature.F1"
        Link "GT-F2" to "TestTechnique.Generic" "Feature.F2"
}
```

Fig. 4. Experimental Plan Fragment

elements. In this experiment, the process name "*ST_F1*" is an abbreviation to Specific Technique and Feature 1. It is linked to the levels "*TestTechnique.Specific*" and "*Feature.F1*", meaning that this collection procedure is responsible per conducting the participants that are using the Specific test technique in order to test the feature F1. In a similar way, the process "*ST_F2*" is linked to the Level "*TestTechnique.Specific*" and "*Feature.F2*". Each defined process has to be linked to their associated levels (the source of variation).

The Metrics View. In this perspective, we specify the metrics that have to be collected during the experiment execution. These metrics are associated to the response variables of the studies. We model here two different metrics for each process. One metric is responsible to quantify the time spent to execute each test case execution task, and the other one is related to the time spent to reporting each CR

Fig. 5 shows a fragment of the DSL specification for the metrics perspective. It describes the two metrics modeled for the process "ST_F1". The first one is named "TimeExecutingTest_ST-F1-Product1" and it has the description "Test case execution time - F1 in P1". The collection form of this metric is defined as "continuous" meaning that the time will be collected for each task and for the total of tasks. The unit defined is *minutes*. All the tasks that have to be intercepted by this metric has their names listed in the *tasks* element, which are: "Execute TC SP1_F1_1", "Execute TC SP1_F1_2", "Execute TC SP1_F1_3", "Execute TC SP1_F1_4", "Execute TC SP1_F1_5", and "Execute TC SP1_F1_6". The second metric is "TimeReportingCR_ST-F1-Product1", which is modeled in a similar way that the previous metric.

```
Metric "TimeExecutingTest_ST-F1-Product1" relates "ST_F1" {
        description "Test case execution time - F1 in P1"
        form continuous
        unit minutes
        tasks "ST_F1.SP1_F1_1.Execute TC SP1_F1_1" "ST_F1.SP1_F1_2.Execute TC SP1_F1_2"
              "ST_F1.SP1_F1_3.Execute TC SP1_F1_3" "ST_F1.SP1_F1_4.Execute TC SP1_F1_4"
              "ST_F1.SP1_F1_5.Execute TC SP1_F1_5" "ST_F1.SP1_F1_6.Execute TC SP1_F1_6" }

Metric "TimeReportingCR_ST-F1-Product1" relates "ST_F1" {
        description "Reporting CR time - F1 in P1"
        form continuous
        unit minutes
        tasks "ST_F1.SP1_F1_1.Report CR SP1_F1_1" "ST_F1.SP1_F1_2.Report CR SP1_F1_2"
              "ST_F1.SP1_F1_3.Report CR SP1_F1_3" "ST_F1.SP2_F1_4.Report CR SP2_F1_4"
              "ST_F1.SP2_F1_5.Report CR SP2_F1_5" "ST_F1.SP2_F1_6.Report CR SP2_F1_6"}
```

Fig. 5. Metrics View Fragment

The Questionnaire View. Gathering feedback from the experiment participants is very important to support the qualitative analysis. We modeled two questionnaires for our experiment. The first one is applied before the experiment execution in order to collect the experience level of the participants. The second one is applied after the experiment execution to gathering subjects' feedback. A questionnaire is a set of questions where each question has a type to be selected according to the kind of question. Due to space restrictions, the Questionnaire specification is not presented in this paper, for additional details please refer to: http://bit.ly/11q4sM5.

4.3   Workflow Generation

The experiment specification using the DSL is the input artifact to the second step of our approach, which involved the workflow specification generation. This generation is supported by a M2M transformation where abstractions from the DSL are mapped to specific elements in the workflow model. The mapping is currently implemented through a QVTo transformation. Fig. 6 shows a fragment of the generated workflow file. The workflow metamodel is based on the JPDL schema.

The experimental design settled for this experiment was the Latin Square. Therefore, the four specified processes for the experiment in the DSL were associated to the treatments combination, and arranged as a square where the columns represented the SPL features, and the rows represented the subjects. Each square cell represents the factor under investigation (desired source of variation), which are the testing techniques. The information about the design is specified in a configuration file generated during the M2T transformation.

```
<expl:process-definition name="ST_F1" quantity="4">
    <expl:start-state name="Starting">
      <expl:transition name="startTransitionSP1_F1_1" to="SP1_F1_1"/>
    </expl:start-state>
    <expl:end-state name="End"/>
    <expl:swimlane>
      <expl:assignment name="Subject" actor-id="Subject"/>
    </expl:swimlane>
    <expl:task-node name="SP1_F1_1" description="Insert a new member - Product 1">
      <expl:transition name="SP1_F1_1_Transition" to="SP1_F1_2"/>
      <expl:event type="task-end">
        <expl:action class="ST-F1-Product1ActionHandler" name="TimeTesting-ST-F1-Product1" />
      </expl:event>
      <expl:task description="Execute the test case SP1_F1_1" name="Execute TC SP1_F1_1">
        <artefacts name="Teste case SP1_F1_1" type="input" description="Test case details SP1_F1_1"/>
        <expl:event type="task-end">
          <expl:action class="SP1_F1_1ActionHandler" name="Execute TC SP1_F1_1" />
        </expl:event>
      </expl:task>
      <expl:task description="Describe TC SP1_F1_1 results" name="Report CR SP1_F1_1">
        <artefacts name="CR SP1_F1_1" type="output" description="Reporting the CR for Test Case SP1_F1_1"/>
        <expl:event type="task-end">
          <expl:action class="SP1_F1_1ActionHandler" name="Report CR SP1_F1_1"/>
        </expl:event>
      </expl:task>
    </expl:task-node>
```

Fig. 6. Workflow Generated Fragment

4.4   Execution Environment

During this approach stage, we have deployed in our workflow engine: the XMI generated file that comprises the experiment workflows, and the configuration file that specifies the design of experiment. Each workflow is responsible for collecting data from each participant of the experiment. After the deployment of the workflows and configuration file, the researcher must upload all the needed input artifacts (such as the test suites) by using the environment configuration form. The researchers who are conducting the experiment are also responsible for registering the real subjects, so the execution environment can randomize participants to the treatments

Once the experiment workflow is specified and the subjects are informed in the workflow engine of our execution environment, the researchers can begin the experiment execution enabling the subjects to accomplish their respective workflows.

From this point, each subject is able to start the execution of his/her activities according to the experiment planning. They will be guided by the workflow specification. Our execution environment will be also responsible to collect time metrics before and after the execution of each workflow activity or task.

During the experiment execution, the researchers can monitor all the activities in progress as well as to see details about the executed activities for each experiment participant, such as the uploaded artifacts, time spent for different tasks and activities, and comments added. Thus, the researcher can get early information about the data accuracy and can detect misunderstanding by the participants. In addition, each web workflow form presents a pause button that must be used by the participant if she/he needs to shortly interrupt the current experiment activity to do some action that can affect the quantified time for that activity. This interruption can be to perform some extra activity (such as, to answer the cell phone or to go to the restroom) that can affect the activity time resulting, according to the experiment rules.

5   Discussions

In this section, we discuss several issues and lessons learned, after applying our approach to generate a customized environment to the controlled experiment of SPL testing. In our discussions, we focus on the criteria analysis for supporting controlled experiments presented in Section 2.

C1. *Support Multi-View Experiment Definition.* Each knowledge block in ExpDSL specifies the definition related to only one perspective from the controlled experiment knowledge. ExpDSL was initially designed to specify the information needed to enable the generation of automatic support to conduct the experiment, such as: (i) the process view that addresses the experiment procedure – activities and data collection – for subjects, and instructions to prepare the environment for the researcher; (ii) the metric view that allows defining the metrics related to the response variables; (iii) the planning view helps the choice of the experimental design; and (iv) the questionnaire view contributes to the gathering of feedback modeling. All this information is used to generate the experiment support environment, and it contributes to improve the understanding of the different views of the experiment (processes, metrics, experimental design and questionnaires). In addition, the specification of the DSL also contributes to explicitly document existing experiments, and consequently to keep the consistence during the experiment replication. Our current execution environment only supports the subject perspective, but it is also possible to define perspectives for the different processes and roles played by researchers involved in the study (environment configuration, recruiting subjects, training, dry run).

C2. *Support online monitoring*: our approach enables researchers to monitor the activities of the subjects and the data produced during the experiment execution. It contributes to the experiment control because the researchers can get early information about the data accuracy and can detect misunderstandings by the participants. During a previous manual execution of the SPL testing experiment reported [6], for example, a subject reported a CR in six seconds, which is very unlikely. However, the researchers, who conducted the experiment, could not be able to observe that fault during the experiment execution or before the data reporting in the experiment analysis phase. Because of that, it was necessary to invalidate this subject data, and as a consequence to increase the bias of the experiment. This online monitoring also allows researchers to take notes for the experiment and produce historical information that can be useful during the qualitative analysis.

C3. *Provide process generation and execution according to the experimental design*: although there are different kinds of statistical experimental design, as explained in Section 4.2, our approach currently supports three basic designs: (i) CRD, (ii) RCBD, and (iii) LS. These designs can cover a large number of kinds of experiments in software engineering. Moreover, it is important to consider that simple design help to make the experiment more practical as they can minimize the spent and usage of resources (time, money, people, and experimental features). Last but not least, simple designs are also easier to analyze [8]. Based on the chosen design and the specification of blocking variables or factors, our approach generates customized procedures to be executed in a workflow for each different subject according to the selected experimental design. In that way, our approach contributes to help the researchers in the application of statistical techniques by releasing them of the manual organization of the many combinations of alternatives unitary experiments that they have to deal with.

C4. *Provide guidance and automatic data collection for each participant:* Once specified the processes related to each treatment combination (the data collection procedure) as well as having specified the experimental plan, the approach is responsible for the workflow generation for each subject (Section 4.3). The generated workflows provide a step-by-step customized procedure for each different subject, helping the registering and storing of his/her activities. Every participant does not need to explicitly register and measure the time spent for each activity. This can directly contribute to minimize the overhead of collecting such data and increasing the accuracy of the collected data.

C5. *Provide extension capability to integrate external tools:* Currently, our workflow engine is implemented and executed as a web application, which does not provide extension capability to integrate with external tools. We are refining our environment support to offer extension points in the workflow execution to integrate external tools that are used or needed during the experiment execution. We also intend to provide expressivity to model this integration in our ExpDSL in order to keep the high abstraction level to the researcher who is modeling the controlled experiment.

6 Related Work

There are few approaches (environments, tools, infrastructures or frameworks) developed to support experiments conduction in software engineering [15]. Travassos et al. [5] present an experimentation environment to support large-scale experimentation (eSEE). It is an environment to manage several kinds of empirical software engineering studies. It works in three levels of knowledge organization about the experimentation process: (i) knowledge for any kind of experimental study (meta level), (ii) knowledge for each experimental study (configuration level), and (iii) knowledge for a specific experimental study (instance level). It has a prototype and an initial set of tools to populate the eSEE infrastructure. Sjøberg et al. [4] present a web-based tool that supports participants' management, capturing the time spent during the experiment, and enabling the work product collection, and monitoring participants' activities. The weakness of this approach is the data collection and analysis. Hochsteinet et al. [3] describe a framework as an integrated set of tools to support software engineering experiments, the Experiment Manager Framework. It was used only in high performance computing (HPC) experiments. It helps the subjects by applying heuristics to infer programmer activities.

Freire et al [15] present a systematic review of automated support for controlled experiments in software engineering. They have noticed that most of the existing approaches offer some kind of support to many activities involved in a controlled experiment, but they have a lot of limitations and potential for future improvements, such as: (i) they are not adaptable and extensible according to the experimental study necessities; (ii) they do not enable the experiment automatic execution organization according to the statistic design of experiment; and (iii) they offer weak analysis capabilities.

7   Conclusions and Future Work

This paper described a process-oriented model-driven approach that supports the conduction of controlled experiments in software engineering. In addition, it also presented an exploratory study performed to analyze the expressivity and feasibility of our approach. We have also applied the proposed DSL to model two other experimental studies [13] [14]. In this work, the approach was applied in the modeling of a controlled experiment with statistical rigor. The study confirmed the feasibility of the approach by allowing the adequate modeling of the selected study and the generation of the experiment workflow that supports its execution. Finally, the study also identified some improvement points related to the DSL and workflow engine of the approach to model different perspectives during the conduction of an experiment. As future work, we plan to incorporate the identified improvements in the approach, as well as to promote the conduction of several new experiments in software engineering in order to assessing the benefits and new possibilities for our automated environment.

Acknowledgments. This work was partially supported by the National Institute of Science and Technology for Software Engineering (INES), funded by CNPq, grants 573964/2008-4 and PDI – Great Challenges, 560256/2010-8, and by FAPERN and CAPES/PROAP.

References

1. Sjoeberg, D.I.K., Hannay, J.E., Hansen, O., Kampenes, V.B., Karahasanovic, A., Liborg, N.-K., Rekdal, A.C.: A survey of controlled experiments in software engineering. IEEE Transactions on Software Engineering 31(9), 733–753 (2005)

2. Jedlitschka, A., Ciolkowski, M., Pfahl, D.: Reporting Experiments in Software Engineering. In: Guide to Advanced Empirical Software Engineering. Springer Science+Business Media (2008)
3. Hochstein, L., Nakamura, T., Shull, F., Zazworka, N., Basili, V., Zelkowitz, M.: An Environment for Conducting Families of Software Engineering Experiments. Advances in Computers 74, 175–200 (2008)
4. Sjøberg, D., Anda, B., Arisholm, E., Dybå, T., Jørgensen, M., Karahasanovic, A., Koren, E., Vokác, M.: Conducting Realistic Experiments in Software Engineering. In: International Symposium on Empirical Software Engineering (2002)
5. Travassos, G., Santos, P., Mian, P., Dias Neto, A., Biolchini, J.: An environment to support large scale experimentation in software engineering. In: 13th IEEE International Conference on Engineering of Complex Computer Systems, pp. 193–202 (2008)
6. Accioly, Borba, P., Bonifácio, R.: Comparing Two Black-box Testing Strategies for Software Product Lines. In: Proceedings of SBCARS, Natal, Brazil (2012)
7. Wohlin, C., Runeson, P., Höst, M., Ohlsson, M., Regnell, B., Wesslén, A.: Experimentation in Software Engineering: An Introduction. Kluwer Academic Publishers, Boston (2000)
8. Pfleeger, S.: Experimental design and analysis in software engineering: Part 2: how to set up and experiment. SIGSOFT Softw. Eng. Notes 20, 22–26 (1995)
9. Lochmann, H., Bräuer, M.: Towards Semantic Integration of Multiple Domain-Specific Languages Using Ontological Foundations. In: ATEM on MoDELS, Nashville (2007)
10. Freire, M., Aleixo, F., Uira, K., Aranha, E., Coelho, R.: Automatic Deployment and Monitoring of Software Processes: A Model-Driven Approach. In: SEKE 2011, Mi/Fl (2011)
11. Freire, M., Alencar, D., Aranha, E., Kulesza, U.: Software Process Monitoring using Statistical Process Control Integrated in Workflow Systems. In: SEKE 2012, SF/CA (2012)
12. Juristo, N., Moreno, A.M.: Basics of Software Engineering Experimentation. Kluwer Academic Publisher, Madrid (2001)
13. Campos, E., Bezerra, A., Freire, M., Kulesza, U., Aranha, E.: Composição de Linguagens de Modelagem Específicas de Domínio: Um Estudo Exploratório. In: MDSD, pp. 41–48 (2012)
14. Campos, E., Freire, M., Kulesza, U., Bezerra, A., Aranha, E.: Composition of Domain Specific Modeling Languages: An Exploratory Study. In: MODELSWARD (2013)
15. Freire, M., Alencar, D., Campos, E., Medeiros, T., Kulesza, U., Aranha, E., Soares, S.: Automated Support for Controlled Experiments in Software Engineering: A Systematic Review. In: SEKE, Boston/USA (2013)

Beyond Herding Cats: Aligning Quantitative Technology Evaluation in Large-Scale Research Projects

Michael Kläs[1], Thomas Bauer[1], and Ubaldo Tiberi[2]

[1] Fraunhofer Institute for Experimental Software Engineering, Kaiserslautern, Germany
{michael.klaes,thomas.bauer}@iese.fraunhofer.de
[2] Volvo Group Trucks Technology, Advanced Technology & Research, Göteborg, Sweden
ubaldo.tiberi@volvo.com

Abstract. A large-scale research project involving many research and industry organizations working on a common goal should be an ideal basis for profound technology evaluations. The possibility for industrial case studies in multiple settings ought to enable reliable quantitative assessment of the performance of new technologies in various real-world settings. However, due to diverse challenges, such as internal agendas, implicit constraints, and unaligned objectives, leveraging this potential goes beyond the usual challenge of cat-herding in such projects. Based on our experience from coordinating technology evaluations in several research projects, this paper sketches the typical issues and outlines an approach for dealing with them. Although new in its composition, this approach brings together principles and techniques perceived to have been useful in earlier projects (e.g., cross-organizational alignment, abstract measures, and internal baselining). Moreover, as we are currently applying the approach in a large research project, this paper presents first insights into its applicability and usefulness.

Keywords: Empirical study, Multiple case studies, Baselines, GQM+Strategies.

1 Motivation

Besides bringing together specialists working on one specific topic, a key advantage of large-scale research projects is the availability of a large number of "customer" companies that provide an opportunity to perform empirical evaluations under real conditions.

In software engineering, *case studies* are a commonly used empirical method for investigating phenomena in such real-world settings. They contribute to a better understanding of software engineering technologies and their practical performance [9]. This is especially important when new software engineering technology is to be introduced in a company, because observations collected in vitro, for instance via controlled experiments, do not necessary scale up to realistic applications in a company setting, and introducing a new technology not sufficiently evaluated beforehand can have serious consequences [11].

J. Heidrich et al. (Eds.): PROFES 2013, LNCS 7983, pp. 80–92, 2013.

In recent years, a second term, action research, has been used increasingly in the context of software engineering studies investigating the effect of new technologies and process improvement activities. Runeson et al. use this term to separate (action research) studies investigating a process improvement activity from case studies investigating the current state before or after an improvement action [16]. However, based on their literature survey on action research, Santos et al. conclude that action research is rarely used in software engineering [17], which matches our observation that most studies conducted in the context of process improvement activities are published as (industrial) cases studies. In this paper, we therefore do not differentiate between action and case study research when talking about technology evaluation and subsume both methods under the more common term *case study* (CS).

We agree with Kitchenham et al. [9] that CSs are not only needed in software engineering to investigate "how" and "why" questions but also to check whether a new technology is better in a given real-world context and, if so, how strong this improvement effect is. However, some inherent characteristics of CSs [16] limit their validity in such applications. First of all, since most CSs represent only one 'case', statistical tests as a typical means for assuring *conclusion validity* can rarely be applied. Moreover, the fact that a CS is conducted in a real-world setting limits the degree to which potential confounding factors can be controlled (*internal validity*). Finally, since a CS usually considers one specific project in one company, it is difficult to determine the degree to which study findings can be generalized to other situations (*external validity*).

One solution for addressing these weaknesses, at least partially, is to *conduct multiple CSs*, which would provide more cases and a more diverse context. However, such multiple CS research – an example is presented by Mohagheghi and Conradi [13] – is still rare. Reasons that typically inhibit such studies are the limited number of available cases and the difficulty to get data measured consistently for available cases that can be aggregated into more general statements.

An alternative might be found in performing a *meta-analysis* for existing case studies; however, a "meta-analysis is seldom possible [...] because there are often insufficient primary studies" [8]. For instance, only four papers (5%) in the area of model-based testing (MBT) present industrial applications [15]. In consequence, Davis et al. (like many others) exclude CS results from their meta-analysis [4].

On the other hand, *large-scale research projects* seem to provide a good opportunity to perform a higher number of CSs addressing one topic. However, in reality, various reasons (which we will discuss in more detail in the following section) limit the practicability of getting combinable CS-based evaluation results in such projects. Therefore, the majority of projects provide survey-based summarizing results in the best case (e.g., [3][14]).

The aim of this paper is to support persons coordinating and setting up empirical technology evaluations in large research projects by presenting an approach that addresses the most common challenges we and other researchers have typically been faced with in the past. The intention of this paper is not to present a closed framework for CS-based research in the context of large-scale research projects. Rather, it contributes by highlighting major challenges that need attention, presents an approach based on a set of mutually supporting recommendations, illustrates its application in an ongoing large-scale research project, and reports on our experiences.

The remainder of this paper is structured as follows: First, existing work and guidelines in the area are discussed (Section 2), followed by challenges that make technology evaluation in large-scale projects difficult and which motivate our work (Section 3). The approach and its application are presented in Section 4 and the paper closes with a summary and an outlook on future work in Section 5.

2   Related Work

Available guidelines for conducting CSs in software engineering are scientifically elaborated and well detailed but focus mainly on qualitative research [12] and researchers planning to conduct a single CS [16]. Thus, they address the challenges occurring in large-scale research projects only insufficiently.

Only few papers report on multiple CSs [13]. Moreover, they focus on reporting their specific results and not on providing guidelines for conducting such studies.

Besides the general CS guidelines for technology evaluation provided by Kitchenham et al. [9], we are aware of only one contribution that explicitly deals with the challenges of industrially based multiple CSs [1]. In contrast to our objective of technology evaluation, their guidelines focus on and were applied to explorative studies. In explorative studies, however, the challenges addressed in this paper such as baselining are of less importance and are thus not elaborately discussed or evaluated.

In education and social science, designs for multiple CSs (more formally called *multiple site, structured case study designs*) were developed, for instance, by Greene and David as an extension to the more traditional research strategies [6]. As in our case, their major intention behind conducting multiple CSs in a structured way was to increase the generalizability of their results. However, in accordance with the social science understanding of CS research, their focus is on collecting and combining qualitative data (such as information extracted from interviews). In consequence, they do not deal with issues occurring when defining measures and determining baselines, which are essential for quantitative technology evaluation.

A research direction that is related to this work since it is also driven by the goal of supporting quantitative technology evaluation across multiple independent cases is presented by Williams et al. [20]. They propose the concept of technology-dependent frameworks for industrial case study research. They instantiated their concept idea by developing a framework for evaluating extreme programming, which comprises a core set of metrics and context factors [19]. Although defining a fixed set of metrics seems appealing, in large-scale research projects we have observed two major issues with such an approach: (1) Since the metrics are predefined, they cannot be simply substituted by other metrics that would be easier to collect or more appropriate in a specific case; (2) the proposed set of metrics comprises metrics demanding absolute numbers regarding defects and productivity, which most companies are not willing to reveal due to confidentiality issues (see also challenges discussed in the next section).

3   Observed Challenges

This section summarizes typical challenges that can be observed during quantitative technology evaluation and sketches how they are addressed in our approach.

In order to enrich and back up our own opinions, we conducted a focus group meeting [10] where we identified challenges observed by the participants in the context of quantitative technology evaluation. Eleven researchers with practical experience in empirical research participated; most of them also had experience in organizing its application in large-scale research projects. In total, 17 challenges were mentioned; 16 of them could be clustered into four major groups: *organizational issues* (5), *collecting the right data* (4), *providing combinable data* (3), and *defining a baseline* (4). Since organizational issues deal with scheduling, distribution of efforts, and empowerment of roles, they have to be addressed in the organization of the project. The remaining three groups are easier to target with methodological solutions and are therefore presented in more detail:

1. *Collecting (the right) data* to quantify the obtained improvements is often a major challenge for several reasons. We will focus on the most critical ones: (1) Data collection has to be well *motivated*, especially in a large research project where potential CS providers cannot be forced to collect data but have to be convinced that they will personally benefit from such data collection. In our approach, we address this issue by providing the means for aligning measurement activities not only with the objectives of the research project but also with company-specific businesses goals. (2) In order to be useful, the measures have to be clearly defined and address the goals of the research project. In our approach, we define what data are relevant by developing consolidated goal and strategy graphs for the project objectives with abstract measures. Additionally, we develop examples of suitable CS-specific measurement plans and conduct workshops to teach goal-oriented measurement.

2. *Providing (combinable) data:* In order to get more general statements on the effects of new technologies, CS-specific measurement results have to be provided and combined. In large-scale projects, this is usually difficult due to data confidentiality and the different environments in which these data were collected. To assure that such data can be *combined* (at least at a certain level of abstraction), we define in our approach a common set of general but abstract measures that quantify consolidated project goals but can be implemented with different strategies and measurement plans. The issue that certain types of data (e.g., defect numbers, productivity data, etc.) can be collected but not *provided* to persons outside the organization due to confidentiality reasons is addressed in the definition of measures, which call not for absolute but only for relative improvement numbers.

3. *Defining a baseline:* In order to evaluate improvements resulting from a new technology, we need a baseline for comparison. Identifying an appropriate source for collecting baseline data is one of the most essential but also challenging tasks, since in large projects with one or two dozen CSs, researchers with an empirical background are usually not involved deeply enough in each CS context to guide and support baseline data collection. On the other hand, for the people responsible

for a CS, it is typically not clear where baseline data can be obtained, what the advantages and limitations of the different sources of baseline data are, and how they can deal with confidentiality issues if sensitive company data are involved. In our approach, we support CS providers by introducing the concept of *internal baselines* to deal with sensible company data, providing dedicated guidelines for baselining that show possible *sources of baselines*, and explaining the specific *advantages and drawbacks* of different baselining solutions.

4   Approach and Application

In the following, we will first sketch the overall approach, then briefly introduce the context in which we are currently evaluating the approach, and finally present the three major components of the approach. In its general procedure, our approach follows the quality improvement paradigm [1] used (at least implicitly) in most CS research and refined by related guidelines: At the beginning, the overall project- and CS-specific goals are consolidated, documented, and quantified via measures (characterize and set goals); then, the studies design is concretized, sources of baseline data are defined, and measures are operationalized via measurement plans (plan); next, baselining is performed, the CSs are conducted, and measurement data is collected (execute); finally, the collected data is analyzed, aggregated, and reported (analyze and package).

4.1   Application Context: MBAT

We applied the approach to the ARTEMIS project MBAT[1] (Combined <u>M</u>odel-<u>b</u>ased <u>A</u>nalysis and <u>T</u>esting of Embedded Systems). MBAT aims at facilitating a new leading-edge Reference Technology Platform in the European Union for the efficient validation and verification of software-intensive technical systems by using model-based technologies, focusing primarily on the transportation domain. The 3-year project is supported by 38 European partners ranging from large companies from the automotive, rail, and aerospace domains, via innovative tool vendors to leading-edge research institutes. The project with its structure, tasks, and activities is industrially driven by more than 20 case studies.

4.2   Goal Alignment and Measurement Plans

In order to identify relevant measures in a goal-oriented way and assure that the collected measurement data can be interpreted and aggregated across the boundaries of a single evaluation, we adapted GQM+Strategies (GQM+) [2], which was originally developed for clarifying and harmonizing goals and strategies across different levels of an organization with goal and strategy graphs and support monitoring the success or failure of strategies and goals by means of goal-oriented measurement.

---

[1] MBAT project website: www.mbat-artemis.eu

In our case of multiple CSs, where we apply GQM+ to a large-scale research project, we introduce four major layers, one with the CS provider's high-level goals and strategies, one with the overall (research) project goals, one with refinements of these through sub-goals, including corresponding strategies, and one with the CS-specific implementation of the addressed strategies and measures. Fig.1 illustrates these layers.

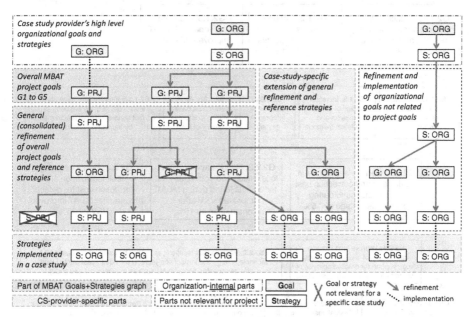

Fig. 1. Relationships between high-level organizational, general project, and case-study-specific goals and strategies

In the first step, the general overall goals are defined based on the project objectives, which can usually be extracted from the project proposal. However, these goals should be made more concrete with more specific sub-goals and strategies, which should obviously include the application of techniques or tools developed in the research project. This refinement needs to be done jointly between measurement and domain experts since the project proposal is usually not detailed enough and contains gaps and ambiguities regarding goals and strategies that need to be resolved. Typical cases are that strategies are mentioned without a clear link to the goal they address or vice versa – that goals are stated without any explanation of how exactly they are to be achieved.

Using a questionnaire, the initially refined goal and strategy graphs are evaluated by all CS providers to check for completeness, identify dispensable parts, and assure a common understanding in the consortium. The feedback is integrated into a consolidated version of the graphs. Fig. 2 presents an example of such a consolidated goal and strategy graph developed in MBAT.

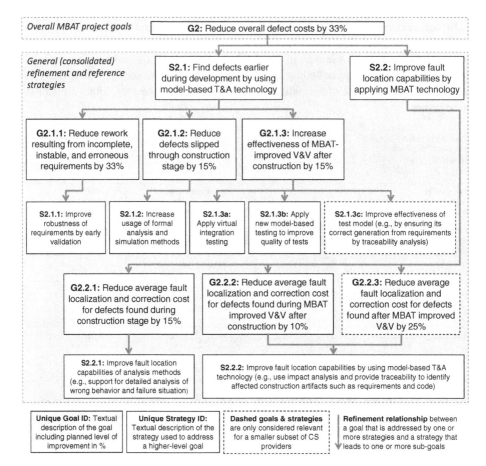

Fig. 2. General refinement of overall MBAT project goal G2

Not every general project goal has the same relevance for each CS provider. More-over, in different CSs, different combinations of strategies (e.g., selections of technol-ogies) can be used to reach the same project goal. Therefore, in the next step, the GQM+ approach is applied for each CS to identify a CS-specific subset of consolidat-ed goals and align them with the company's *high-level organizational goals*. This allows the CS providers to show the relevance of the general project goals internally and motivate the collection of data. It also means that a CS provider will typically not collect measurement data for all but only for a selection of goals defined in the gener-al Goals+Strategies graphs (which is illustrated in Fig. 1 by the crossed-out goals and strategies).

In the next step, specific measurement plans using abstract measures have to be de-fined for each CS. Fig. 3 illustrates the template used based on an actual measurement plan developed in the MBAT project.

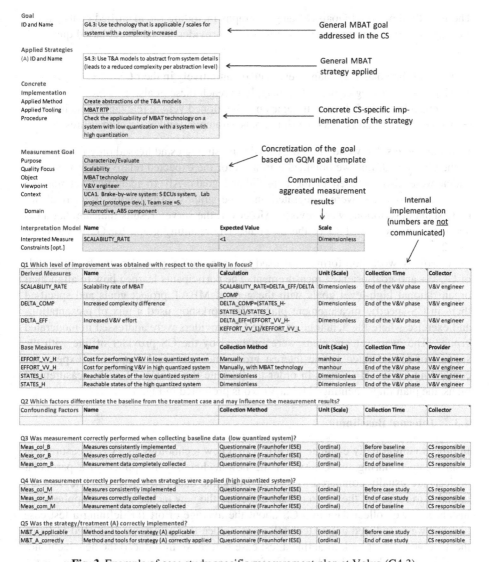

Fig. 3. Example of case study specific measurement plan at Volvo (G4.3)

Application Experience in MBAT: Based on the business needs and objectives stated in the project proposal, we extracted five overall project goals for MBAT and developed a Goals+Strategies graph refining them:

- **G1** Reduce overall verification and validation costs by 20%;
- **G2** Reduce overall defect costs by 33%;
- **G3** Reduce total cost of ownership for development platform by 15%;
- **G4** Provide high quality in the face of increased complexity by 30%;
- **G5** Reduce time to market for embedded systems products by 20%.

The initially developed Goals+Strategies graphs including the identified goals, strategies, and abstract measures were sent to all CS providers as an Excel-based questionnaire asking

— which of the goals they plan to evaluate quantitatively in their CS,
— which of the strategies they plan to apply to reach these goals,
— which additional goals and strategies not mentioned yet are relevant for their CS,
— open questions and issues regarding goals, strategies, and abstract measures.

Based on the results, we identified 21 goals and strategies addressed only few or none of the CS. In addition, we obtained estimates for the expected relative improvements, which were also included in the consolidated goals. All 16 identified yet missing goals and strategies were integrated into the graphs. Ambiguous or difficult-to-understand descriptions were revised. Moreover, the survey results indicate that a CS addresses an average of 14 of the 29 goals. The resulting graph for G2 is shown in Fig. 2.

A two-day workshop format was used to teach the CS providers the fundamentals of GQM+ and goal-oriented measurement. The participants learned how to align their organizational high-level goals with the general MBAT project goals and specified them in CS-specific measurement plans. The workshop used a mix of presentations and exercise where the actual goals of the CS providers were addressed in moderated groups. The measurement plans were finalized by the CS provider offline with the support of a moderated online interest group and individual support by experts for conducting empirical studies. In order to illustrate the content of such measurement plans, the plan implementing G4.3 at Volvo is presented in Fig. 3.

4.3   Internal Baselining

In order to empirically evaluate the effect of a new technology in a CS, measurement results gained during the CS (when the new technology is applied in a particular project) are usually compared to so-called baseline data [5]. These baseline data are intended to represent the "current" status before the new technology was applied. For instance, if we collect data in a CS about the average effort for defining a test case because we introduced a new technology to reduce this effort, we also need to know the average effort it took to define a test case before we introduced the new technology. If we do not have a baseline value for this measure, we cannot judge whether the new technology reduced the average effort or not.

The software engineering literature (e.g., [9][5][18]) commonly mentions three means to get baseline data: use data from a sister project, use historical company data, or split the studied project into components with and without application of the evaluated technology. These three options span the dimensions of time (sequential: historical project vs. concurrent: sister or split project) and locality (inside CS project: split project vs. outside CS project: historical or sister project). Therefore, we extend these three possibilities by a fourth option not mentioned before: taking data from an earlier release of the CS project for baselining (sequential/inside). In the following, we will discuss each baseline source regarding its strengths and weaknesses, taking as a basis the three baselining assumptions by Jung et al. [7], which we extended in this work with a fourth one that we called "comparable context" to get a total of *four properties of good baselines*[2]:

— *Absence of treatment:* Because we want to evaluate the effect of our treatment (i.e., the new or modified technology in our case study), we obviously need to collect baseline data in a situation where the new or modified technology does not affect the measurement results.
— *Consistent operationalization:* Baseline data should be collected using the same operationalization used to collect the data during the case study in which the new or modified technology is applied. Using a different kind of operationalization makes the data potentially incomparable (e.g., if effort numbers are collected for the baseline with overtime, but without overtime during the case study).
— *Comparable context:* Baseline data should be collected in a context as comparable as possible to the context in which the application of the new or modified technology takes place. The objective is to reduce the effect of confounding factors such as time pressure or experience that influence the measured performance.
— *Multiple measurements:* In the best case, a baseline should consist of more than one measurement point. The reason is that a natural and uncontrollable fluctuation in the measured value that is not the effect of the newly introduced or modified technology can only be determined if multiple measurement points are available.

Additionally, we discuss the baselines in the context of three potential obstacles hindering the usage of a specific baseline source: Differences regarding the *period needed* to collect the required data, whether an *intervention* in non-CS projects is required to collect the data, and on which *level of detail* data have to be collected (e.g., total effort vs. effort per module), which affects the effort and ease of data collection.

— *Historical project baseline:* One option for establishing a baseline is to use data collected for one or more past projects as a baseline. The advantage is that the data were typically collected in the past and must only be extracted in order to be used as a baseline. The major disadvantage is that past project data were usually not collected using the defined measures to be collected during the CS (*consistent operationalization*). Moreover, it is hard to assure that the projects for which the required data are available are sufficiently similar to the CS project to draw reliable conclusions (*comparable context*). The second point can be partially addressed by identifying potential confounding factors other than the new or modified technology that may influence the measured properties as well as analyzing the variation in the measured values for the different applications of the "current" baseline technology in the past projects.
— *Sister project baseline:* An option that addresses the most critical limitation of historical project baselines (i.e., having *consistent operationalization*) is to use one

---

[2] The comparability of baseline and treatment context was most likely not considered in Jung et al. since they assumed in their understanding of baselining a given stable context.

or more similar concurrent projects instead of past projects to get the required baseline data. Because a sister project runs in parallel to the CS, the same measures as in the CS can be collected, assuring consistent operationalization. However, this means additional measurement effort in the sister projects. A challenge kept from the historical project baseline is to identify one or more sister projects that are sufficiently similar to the CS project to allow drawing reliable conclusions (*comparable context*). As mentioned for the historical project baseline, this can be partially addressed by identifying and controlling influencing factors other than the new technology.

— *Inter-release baseline:* An inter-release baseline does not use historical or sister projects to define a baseline, but rather uses different releases of the same (longer running) project to first define the baseline and then conduct the CS. The major advantage is that the context in different releases of the same project is usually much more stable than between different projects (e.g., similar team, work environment, processes). Thus, inter-release baselines address the major challenge of sister project baselines (*comparable context*). Moreover, data only need to be collected in one project. On the other hand, sufficient time should be planned for collecting the baseline data and then conducting the CS, since these activities cannot be parallelized.

— *Split-project baseline:* A split-project baseline is the most elaborate way to evaluate the effect of a new technology in a real-world context. The activities affected by introducing the new technology are identified and the people who are to perform these activities are randomly assigned to one of two groups. The members of the baseline group apply the "current" baseline technology, whereas the members of the treatment group apply the new technology. For each group, performance is measured separately. For instance, if a new MBAT technique is to be evaluated against the existing manual derivation of test cases, it has to be possible to differentiate between defects found in the product parts tested in a model-based manner and the parts tested with manually defined test cases. Also, effort data has to be collected separately for the parts tested in a model-based manner and those tested manually (*granularity in data collection*).

Table 1 summarizes the discussion by presenting the result of a small survey conducted among six researchers with experience in technology evaluation. Each participant rated each baseline data source regarding each aspect on an ordinal scale (-,o,+,++). With the exception of "Granularity required in data collection", which had to be excluded from the analysis due to an ambiguous formulation in the survey, the table presents the median of their rating.

Our approach introduces the concept of *internal baselines*. This means that a baseline is defined individually for each CS provider. Baseline data stay inside the organization that applies the technology and collects the data, meaning that baseline data do not need to be communicated to other project partners nor to organizations outside the project. Instead of reporting that 2.5h (*baseline*) were needed with the old techniqueand 1.5h with the new one to write an average test case, for example, a CS provider only reports the 40% reduction in time (*relative improvement*) and potential confounding factors in the baseline and CS.

Table 1. Strengths and weaknesses of baseline data sources

Type of Baseline Data Source	Historical Project	Sister Project	Inter-Release	Split-Project
Feasibility of baseline data collection				
Period needed to collect required data	++	O	O	+
Intervention in non-case study projects	+	O	+	+
Granularity required in data collection	+	+	+	O
Accuracy of technology evaluation				
Absence of treatment	++	+	+	O
Consistent operationalization	-	+	+	++
Comparable context	-	O	+	++
Multiple measurements	++	O	+	++

Application Experience in MBAT: Based upon the feedback, CS providers in MBAT considered the overview of baseline sources including strengths and weaknesses as useful when selecting an appropriate baselining approach. However, it is difficult to evaluate whether this will ultimately also increase the availability of reliable baseline data.

5   Conclusion and Future Work

This paper motivates the need for more multiple case studies in the context of technology evaluation for which specific guidelines are still missing. *Major challenges* identified by a focus group were presented and an approach was proposed to address them. In particular, we showed how a simplified version of GQM+Strategies can be instrumented and applied to consolidate general project goals and align them with CS-specific goals. Moreover, we address typical confidentiality issues in our approach by communicating and aggregating only relative measurement results on the project level in combination with our concept of *internal baselines*. Finally, typical baseline approaches are extended by *inter-release baselines* and presented together with an evaluation of their advantages and disadvantages using expert-based evaluation.

Currently, we are applying the approach in a large-scale project with more than 20 CSs. In this paper, first but promising results regarding applicability and usefulness are reported; however, after project completion in 2014, we plan to provide more elaborate results.

Acknowledgments. The research leading to these results has received funding from the ARTEMIS Joint Undertaking under grant agreement n° 269335 and from the German Federal Ministry of Education and Research (BMBF). We would also like to thank all empirical experts for their survey and workshop participation and Andreas Jedlitschka, Adam Trendowicz, Liliana Guzman, and Sonnhild Namingha for their support and initial review of the paper.

References

1. Basili, V.: Quantitative Evaluation of Software Engineering Methodology. In: Proc. of 1st Conf. on Pan Pacific Computer (1984)
2. Basili, V., et al.: Linking Software Development and Business Strategy through Measurement. Computer 43, 57–65 (2010)
3. Ciolkowski, M., Heidrich, J., Simon, F., Radicke, M.: Empirical results from using custom-made software project control centers in industrial environments. In: Proc. of the 2nd Int. Symp. on Empirical Software Engineering and Measurement, pp. 243–252 (2008)
4. Davis, A., Dieste, O., Hickey, A., Juristo, N., Moreno, A.: Effectiveness of Requirements Elicitation Techniques: Empirical Results Derived from a Systematic Review. In: Proc. of 14th IEEE Int. Conf. on Requirements Engineering, pp. 179–188 (2006)
5. Fenton, N., Pfleeger, S.: Software metrics – a rigorous and practical approach, 2nd edn. PWS publishing group, Boston (1997)
6. Greene, D., David, J.: A research design for generalizing from multiple case studies. Evaluation and Program Planning 7, 73–85 (1984)
7. Jung, J., Nunnenmacher, S., Ciolkowski, M.: A Constructive Approach towards Defining Baselines in Empirical Software Engineering. Public Fraunhofer IESE report (2012)
8. Kitchenham, B., et al.: Systematic literature reviews in software engineering – A tertiary study. Information and Software Technology 52, 792–805 (2010)
9. Kitchenham, B., Pickard, L., Pfleeger, S.: Case studies for method and tool evaluation. IEEE Software 12, 52–62 (1995)
10. Kontio, J., Lehtola, L., Bragge, J.: Using the Focus Group Method in Software Engineering: Obtaining Practitioner and User Experiences. In: Proc. of the Int. Symp. on Empirical Software Engineering, pp. 271–280 (2004)
11. Lindstrom, D.: Five Ways to Destroy a Development Project. IEEE Software 10, 55–58 (1993)
12. McLeod, L., MacDonell, S., Doolin, B.: Qualitative research on software development: a longitudinal case study methodology. Empirical Software Engineering 16, 430–459 (2011)
13. Mohagheghi, P., Conradi, R.: Quality, productivity and economic benefits of software reuse: a review of industrial studies. Empirical Software Engineering 12, 471–516 (2007)
14. Mohagheghi, P., Gilani, W., Stefanescu, A., Fernandez, M.: An empirical study of the state of the practice and acceptance of model-driven engineering in four industrial cases. In: Empirical Software Engineering (2012) (online first)
15. Neto, A., et al.: Improving Evidence about Software Technologies: A Look at Model-Based Testing. IEEE Software 25, 10–13 (2008)
16. Runeson, P., Höst, M.: Guidelines for conducting and reporting case study research in software engineering. Empirical Software Engineering 14, 131–164 (2009)
17. Santos, P., Travassos, G.: Action research use in software engineering: An initial survey. In: Proc. of 3rd Int. Symp. on Empirical Software Engineering and Measurement, pp. 414–417 (2009)
18. Verner, J., et al.: Guidelines for industrially-based multiple case studies in software engineering. In: Proc. of 3rd Int. Conf. on Research Challenges in Information Science, pp. 313–324 (2009)
19. Williams, L., Krebs, W., Layman, L., Antón, A., Abrahamsson, P.: Toward a framework for evaluating extreme programming. In: Proc. of 8th Int. Conf. on Empirical Assessment in Software Engineering, pp. 11–20 (2004)
20. Williams, L., Layman, L., Abrahamsson, P.: On establishing the essential components of a technology-dependent framework: a strawman framework for industrial case study-based research. ACM SIGSOFT Software Engineering Notes 30, 1–5 (2005)

Software Process Improvement in Inter-departmental Development of Software-Intensive Automotive Systems – A Case Study

Joakim Pernstål[1,*], Tony Gorschek[2], Robert Feldt[3], and Dan Florén[1]

[1] Volvo Car Corporation, 405 31 Göteborg, Sweden
{jpernsta,dfloren}@volvocars.com
[2] Blekinge Institute of Technology, Karlskrona, 372 25, Sweden
tony.gorschek@bth.se
[3] Chalmers University of Technology, 412 96 Göteborg, Sweden
robert.feldt@chalmers.se

Abstract. This paper presents a software process improvement (SPI) initiative conducted at two automotive companies, focusing on the inter-departmental interplay between manufacturing and product development, which are central players in automotive development. In such a complex environment with multiple departments with varying challenges—the planning of improvement possibilities was considered as mission critical to get support for changes in the companies. This paper reports the results of the SPI efforts following the process assessment, namely specifically the improvement planning step, which is often overlooked in empirical reports. We also thoroughly describe and report on lessons learned from employing our tailored planning method involving 41 professionals.

We found that requirements engineering, early manufacturing involvement and roles and responsibilities were prioritized as main challenges to address. Furthermore, our and the involved professionals' experiences of the used SPI (planning) method, showed that it was useful, giving valuable decision support for the planning of the improvement.

Keywords: Empirical Software Engineering, Software Process Improvement, Case Study, Automotive, Process Improvement Planning.

1 Introduction

Software is becoming an increasingly important component and seen as the main enabler of innovations in a number of traditionally hardware-focused industries (e.g., automotive and aerospace) [1]. For example, the worldwide value of automotive software-intensive systems is expected to rise from 127 billion Euros in 2002 to 316 billion Euros in 2015 [2]. In these organizations, but generally in large organizations, the software-intensive

---

* Corresponding author.

J. Heidrich et al. (Eds.): PROFES 2013, LNCS 7983, pp. 93–107, 2013.

systems are commonly developed in the context of large-scale development, where software constitutes only one, but important, part of the whole [3, 4].

With the development of such systems follows many challenges, among which the needed interaction between different competencies and departments is critical [5, 6]. Using an automotive vehicle manufacturer as a case, coordination and communication between individuals and groups (e.g., system owners. architects and developers) within a department (intra-departmental issues) is critical. But also across departments (inter-departmental issues). In particular, the inter-departmental interaction between Product Development (PD) and Manufacturing (Man) has been recognized in research and industry as a key challenge [7-11].

For increasing efficiency and quality when creating software-intensive products, both industry and researchers have acknowledged the importance of software process improvement (SPI) by continuously assessing and improving processes and practices [12-14].

The work presented in this paper is part of a SPI project focusing on the inter-departmental interaction between PD and Man in large-scale development of software-intensive automotive systems. PD concerns development of software-intensive automotive systems (e.g., development of power train and chassis control systems for vehicles). Man concerns managing these systems when producing vehicles (e.g., vehicle manufacturing operations affected by power train and chassis control systems). The inter-departmental interaction in our definition includes all the phases of development, from concept (e.g., exploration of requirements and solutions) to design, implementation and validation, but also manufacturing involving pre-production verification and validation of the manufacturing processes cf. [11, 15, 16]. In a new car model project, these activities commonly span over three to four years [15], [16].

The SPI was undertaken at two Swedish automotive companies: Volvo Car Corporation (VCC) and Volvo Truck Corporation (VTC) utilizing the iFLAP framework (improvement Framework utilizing Light weight Assessment and improvement Planning) as described in [17]. This paper presents a study on the improvement planning (IP) of nine improvement issues identified in the prior process assessment (PA) step in iFLAP reported in [11]. The main purpose of this study is to establish a realistic planning of the development and implementation of improvements determined from priorities and dependencies between the nine issues, as well as risk and cost of implementation, and time to return on investment (TTROI).

The main contributions of this paper are twofold. First, even though the IP has only been performed within two automotive companies, we believe the results can be valuable for practitioners that want to improve the inter-departmental interaction, at least between PD and Man in the automotive domain. This because many of the characteristics of VCC and VTC are typical for automotive companies. Furthermore, to enhance the validity of the results, data were collected both in workshops and as a web survey, where professionals (subjects) at VCC and VTC gave priority to each issue and mapped their dependencies. In total 41 subjects participated. Of those, 80% had at least 6-10 years experience of development of software intensive automotive systems.

Second, no studies on SPI efforts targeting the process area of inter-departmental interaction in large-scale software development have been found. For helping researchers and practitioners to perform IP in such process areas, we thoroughly describe and demonstrate how the use of improvement issue packaging as a method for IP was applied in practice. We also report the results of a questionnaire-based evaluation of the method, our concrete lessons learned, and the required effort used.

The paper is organized as follows. Section 2 presents related work and motivations and needs. Section 3 describes the IP method used and how it was evaluated. The results of the IP step are presented and analyzed in Section 4 and Section 5 discusses lessons learned. Finally, conclusions are presented in Section 6.

2   Related Work and Motivation

There are a few empirical studies focusing on the PD/Man interface [18]. Vandevelde and Van Dierdonk [18] claim that formalization and empathy on the part of PD towards manufacturing are contributors to a smooth start of production. Formalization entails clear goals, roles and responsibilities. Empathy means that the product developers consider manufacturing aspects during the design stage through building a better understanding of each other's work in the different development stages. Similarly, Nihtilä [4] and Lakemond et al. [19] emphasize the need for formalization and empathy and observed that such as early and active Man involvement, balanced recruitment between PD and Man, and continuous communication are critical factors in the PD/Man interface. An interesting conclusion in [4] is that due to the increased amount of software in products, there is emerging need for integrating software development operations to the project as a whole, indicating an important direction in future research. Earlier work on large-scale software development projects also show that the success is largely depending on the effectiveness of communication and coordination in the company [6], especially when it comes to requirements engineering (RE) across organizational boundaries [5].

There are several studies on Lean Product Development (LPD) at Japanese automakers (e.g., [8-10]) that have had a strong influence on approaches that have been developed to reinforce communication and coordination across departments in the PD process. Several of them can be explicitly associated with inter-departmental interaction between PD and Man. For example, to accelerate the PD process, Wheelwright and Clark [10] emphasize the necessity of understanding how problem solving is carried out across PD and Man and Sobek et al. [9] present Set-Based Concurrent Engineering. Even though lean principles and practices have been translated to the context of software development [20] it is not clear to what extent they have been applied and studied in large-scale software development [21, 22].

Three main factors motivate the work presented in this paper. First, the rapid growth of software in vehicles and the increasing demands on effective launches of new vehicle programs in manufacturing indicate an industrial need of investigating the inter-departmental interaction between PD and Man in the development of software-intensive automotive systems. Second, empirical research addressing the PD/Man interface in PD is limited [18] and SPI initiatives performed in the industrial setting studied here, has not been found. Even though above mentioned literature is relevant, it is important to understand and adopt specific organizational needs in the search for solutions to industrial problems that have been identified [23].

Third, during the PA step we realized that there was an explicit need to enable planning, but also inherently building a consensus on an inter-departmental level. That is, when we knew what parts needed to be improved (results from the PA step) we needed not only to establish changes yielding most potential benefit, but also the rationale of the improvement order and priority needed to be conveyed and anchored in the organizations.

3   Methodology

This section presents the improvement packaging method used for the IP. We also present the design for evaluating this method and validating its results

The SPI methodology used in this study is based on iFLAP [17] and its predecessor [12, 13]. IFLAP was chosen mainly because of two factors: (1) iFLAP and its predecessors have been proven to be scalable and useful in industry, especially in the automotive domain [17, 23], and (2) concerns the studied organizations' limitations in allocating the necessary resources for the SPI project. Commencing top-down SPI effort such as CMMI [24] or Automotive SPICE [25] would not have been possible due to the large amount of resources required [26].

The underlying research strategy when employing iFLAP is case research [27, 28]. IFLAP takes a bottom-up approach and its process consists of three main consecutive steps (see Fig. 1): (1) Selection—includes selection of relevant cases, such as organizations, projects, roles and subjects for the PA, (2) PA—embodies data collection and analysis by using multiple data sources such as interviews and documents that are triangulated, yielding a set of confirmed improvement issues, and (3) IP—involves prioritization and dependency mapping of the established improvement issues that generate packages of improvement issues, and aims to establish a road map that describes an appropriate way of developing and implementing improvements on the basis of specific organizational needs.

Fig. 1 shows the overall process for the SPI project, and the sub-steps used in this study for the IP in Step 3, each detailed below. The selection and PA (Steps 1 and 2) are reported in [11].

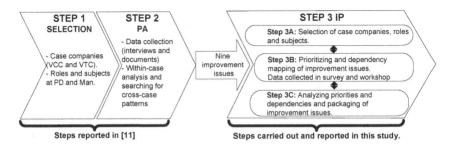

Fig. 1. Overall process overview for the SPI project (note Step 3 IP is reported in this paper)

The main output from the PA (Step 2) to the IP (Step 3, in Fig. 1) were the nine improvement issues identified (see Appendix A[1]), but also such as practical restrictions and cost limitations, and important roles and subjects, and documents (e.g., process descriptions) relevant to the process area assessed. As methods for collecting data in Step 3 and the evaluation, we used self-completion questionnaires in a web survey and workshops (see Appendix B[1] and C[1], and Table 2 in Section 4.2) The workshops and the survey were carried out during the period of January 2010 to June 2010. The duration of each workshop varied between two and four hours. How each of the sub-steps of Step 3 (see Fig. 1) were used to plan the improvements in the SPI-project is detailed below, as this is the focus of this paper.

3.1   Step 3A – Selection

The strategy for selecting case companies and subjects participating was based on a non-probability quota sampling, mainly because the underlying purpose of the inquiry presented in this paper is to set the baseline for subsequent development and implementation of improvements in the companies assessed. Consequently, subjects from VTC and VCC were selected based on the roles identified in the previous steps (Step 1 and 2).

VCC is a premium car manufacturing company and has approximately 22,000 employees all over the world and produces roughly 450,000 cars per year (2011) [29] VTC is a global automotive company that focuses on the development and production of medium and heavy-duty trucks. The number of employees is about 17,000 and approximately 75,000 trucks are produced in 16 countries (2010) [30]. Both companies are organized as matrix organizations and uses a traditional plan-based approach including a stage gate model for governing the development of the complete car and the V-model to present an overview of design and verification of inherent software-intensive systems [11, 15]. Currently, this approach is commonly used in the automotive industry [3, 31] and thus should strengthen the possibility to generalize some of the findings reported in this paper, at least to the automotive domain.

A central concern underlying the selection of subjects was to cover all the roles and competences that are involved in the assessed area. The subjects' experiences of development of software-intensive automotive systems were also considered.

Special considerations were taken regarding the team set-up in the workshops. To save time (selecting and introducing the subjects to the improvement initiative at each workshop) and obtain continuity and commitment, the intention was to use the same workshop team throughout the improvement work. Consequently, the selected subjects had to be available for the workshop series. Furthermore, putting together managers, who were identified as having an important role, and subordinates was another concern, since there is a risk that subjects in a superior position become dominant and suppress everyone else's voice in the group.

---

[1] This can be downloaded via the URL:
http://www.cse.chalmers.se/~pernstal/
publications/2012Pernstal_IP/pernstal_2012_iFLAP_IP.html

To obtain the right team set-up in the workshops and ensure the subjects' availability, senior management at the companies were informed about the purpose and planning of the workshop series and involved in the selection of the subjects. Some of the senior managers were also members of the steering group of the SPI project, ensuring that management was involved and committed. Table 1 in Section 4.1 shows the main characteristics of the subjects.

3.2   Step 3B – Prioritizing and Dependency Mapping

The data for prioritization and dependency mapping were collected through a web survey and in a workshop. Combining these two data sources provided a broader set of data from a larger sample size, which increases the analysis possibilities, especially in relation to be able to do statistical tests (e.g., [32, 33]). Using two methods for measuring the priorities and identifying dependencies also alleviated the risk for measurement bias as data can be analyzed across methods [34].

A major challenge in the creation of the survey and workshop instruments (self-completion questionnaires) was the choice of prioritization techniques. The choice of technique for the workshop and the survey was mainly based on the capability of each technique to fulfill desired granularity, scalability and applicability to different analysis methods. Most of the analysis methods, such as disagreement and satisfaction charts [35], and principal component analysis (PCA) [36] are possible to utilize when the relative prioritization techniques, cumulative voting (CV) [37] and Analytical Hierarchy Process (AHP) [38], are used, while the techniques based on an absolute grading poorly support the analysis methods [35, 36].

In AHP, the validity of the resulting priorities can be checked by calculating the consistency ratio (CR) for each subject, which makes AHP less sensitive to judgment errors compared to the CV technique. On the other hand, a common criticism of AHP is its limitations regarding scalability, since the number of comparisons increases dramatically with the number of elements. Prioritizing the nine improvement issues in this study gave 36 comparisons. In comparison to AHP, CV is a more straightforward and easy prioritization technique, and its scalability is better [17, 37]. As AHP brings the benefits of consistency checking but with limited scalability it was chosen for the workshop while CV (100$-test) was chosen for the survey due to the fact that simplicity and completion time are critical factors for the response rate on survey questionnaires [39].

Owing to the deviating interests of PD and Man, it was specifically important to agree upon the criteria of what to base the prioritizing on. As the underlying goal of the improvement initiative was to improve the interaction between Man and PD, it was agreed that the priorities should be assigned regarding how the subjects perceive the importance of each improvement issue for the interaction between PD and Man in development of software-intensive automotive systems.

The dependency mapping aims at establishing a scheme for the interdependencies between the improvement issues, where the dependencies between the issues are identified by a sample of subjects. It is preferable to allow the same subjects as were involved in the prioritizing also to identify the dependencies between the improvement issues, because other factors (e.g., practical restrictions and costs) than the priorities of the improvement issues that influence the order in which improvements are best implemented can be better uncovered. Thus, the dependency mapping was carried out in conjunction with the prioritizing in both the workshop and the survey.

To ensure that the survey and workshop instruments were comprehensible and unambiguous, and could be completed relatively quickly (one hour or less was the target for the survey instrument), drafts of them were iteratively reviewed and piloted several times. The workshop and survey instruments are shown in Appendix B[1] and C[1].

3.3   Step 3C – Analyzing and Packaging

The data from the prioritizing and identification of dependencies were analyzed within each, but also across the workshop and survey. The analysis of the prioritizing consisted of three main parts: (1) ordering of priority of the improvement issues based on the assigned priorities (2) visualizing the dispersion of priorities (disagreement) among the subjects for each improvement issue in disagreement charts, and (3) displaying how well each subject's or subject group's ranking of the improvement issues corresponds to the resulting priority order of the improvement issues in satisfaction charts. To further analyze discovered disagreements, PCA and statistical tests were used to reveal whether there are groups of subjects (e.g., PD and Man, and roles) that have opinions deviating from the rest of the subjects.

Each of the assigned dependencies were listed and given a relative weight in order to identify dependencies. We calculated the weight by dividing the number of subjects that had identified the dependency by the total number of subjects. Next, a threshold was set and the dependencies with a lower weight than the threshold were removed, the others above the threshold were considered as 'confirmed'. The threshold for the workshop and the survey was set to 3, that is three independent subjects had to have identified the same dependency. Furthermore, to discern valid and invalid relationships (e.g., due to misinterpretations or too vague motivation), each dependency was scrutinized to assure that the rational specified in relation to the dependency was nontrivial and corresponded between the subjects.

The overall idea of the packaging of the improvement issues is to enable the organizations to focus their improvement efforts on the most critical issues first, while taking priorities and dependencies into account. In addition, we considered the subjects' and senior company representatives' view on importance and dependencies utilizing their knowledge of critical aspects in the IP. For example, their views on risks and costs of implementing too many improvements at once and the TTROI.

3.4   Evaluation

The evaluation process consisted of three main activities. First, the research team gathered in follow-up meetings where their shared experiences were discussed and recorded after applying each of the IP Steps 3A, 3B and 3C. During the execution of each step required effort in terms of time spent was also measured.

Second, to ensure the quality of the packaging, it was presented in a second workshop, where the workshop subjects and the research team reviewed and evaluated the results. Furthermore, the subjects were asked to evaluate the IP method used with regard to their perception of some of the main concerns in SPI (commitment, and involvement), reliability, usefulness of the method, and validity of the results [13, 17]. For this we developed and used a self-completion questionnaire (see Table 2 in section 4.2). The self-completion questionnaire used a five-point Likert scale, representing levels of agreement from "do not agree at all" to agree completely, and usefulness from "useless" to "very useful".

Third, we reviewed and evaluated the results also among senior company representatives at a steering group meeting. The results of the evaluation are reported in terms of lessons learned from using improvement packaging as a method for IP (see Section 5).

4   Results

This section presents the main results of the IP (Steps 3A, 3B and 3C) of the nine improvement issues and the evaluation.

4.1   Results of the IP (Steps 3A, 3B and 3C)

In total, the sample consisted of 77 subjects from VCC and VTC. The survey was sent to 64 subjects, of whom 28 responded (response rate 44%), and the workshop involved 13 subjects, yielding 41 responses in total. Of these, 16 subjects belonged to Man (39%) and 25 were organized in PD (61%). Unfortunately, only four responses were received from VTC. This mainly because the sample of VTC (11 subjects) was lower than that of VCC due to lack of resources for identifying and selecting representative subjects at VTC. Table 1 summarizes the main characteristics of the subjects in the survey and the workshops. Furthermore, 80% (33 out of 41) of the subjects had at least 6-10 years experience from development of software-intensive automotive systems, and 40 of the subjects had been working at the companies for more than six years.

Table 1. Characteristics of the subjects

Characteristic	Survey (Number of subjects)	Workshop (Number of subjects)
Company	VCC (26); VTC(2)	VCC(11); VTC(2)
Function	PD(18); Man (10)	PD(7); Man (6)
Role	Line Manager(10);Program Manager (1)	Line Manager (0);Program Manager (2);
	Design Engineer (6);Manufacturing	Design Engineer (4); Manufacturing
	Engineer (9);Process Developer (2)	Engineer (4);Process Developer (3)

The consistency of the collected data from the workshop was checked by calculating the subjects' CR values. Following the recommendation by [38] of 0.10 would have excluded all of the subjects except one, which was not practical. Therefore, a CR of 0.3 or less was judged to be a practical compromise, as it on one hand forms a relatively large group (eight out of 13 subjects) that is balanced between Man and PD, and on the other hand it sorts out results with very high inconsistency. Moreover, the group covers all the roles included in the workshop.

The aggregated results of the prioritizing of the nine improvement issues identified in the PA (Step 2) from the workshop (eight subjects) and survey (28 subjects) are given in Fig. 2. The issues are sorted from left to right with respect to their assigned priorities (normalized priorities). It also visualizes the dispersion of priorities (disagreement) among all subjects in the workshop and the survey for each issue.

Fig. 2 shows that Issue 1 (Requirement Engineering) has the highest priority (0.173) and Issue 8 (Adoption of New Technologies) was given the lowest priority (0.076). There are disagreements among the subjects for all of the issues and the level of disagreement varies. For example, the subjects disagree more on the resulting priority for Issue 7 (77%) than on Issue 1 (57%). However, the level of disagreement is quite uniform, varying between 50% and 77%, and there is no indication that those issues with high priority are related to a high level of disagreement.

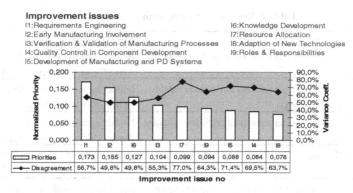

Fig. 2. Aggregated priorities and disagreements

Furthermore, the satisfaction charts (not included in this paper due to space limitations) showed that a majority of the subjects (37 out of 41) were satisfied with the resulting ranking of the issues (spearman rank-order correlation >0). This indicates a possibility to reach consensus on the planning of improvements.

Differences in assigned priorities between PD and Man were also analyzed. There were relatively small differences between these two groups of subjects and a Mann-Whitney test (data did not have normal distribution) showed that there were no significant differences at a significance level of 0.05.

The nine improvement issues were packaged (according to dependencies and priorities, risks and costs, and TTROI) into four separate improvement packages. The resulting packaging is presented and motivated in Appendix D[1]. Improvement package 1 were deemed most critical and should be addressed first in the further improvement work, and consisted of three improvement issues: Issue 1—Requirements Engineering, Issue 2—Early Manufacturing Involvement, and Issue 9—Roles and Responsibilities.

4.2   Results of the Evaluation

During the second workshop 11 of the 13 invited subjects attended. Of these, six subjects represented PD and five belonged to Man. Apart from the manager role, all the other roles were covered. Overall, the subjects agreed upon that the issues in Improvement package 1 are the most critical and must be dealt with first.

In Table 2, the questions and answers of the questionnaire based evaluation are given (levels given zero answers are not shown). For example, 73% (eight out of 11) of the subjects agreed and 18% (two out of 11) of them agreed completely to Q1, whereas 9% neither agreed nor disagreed (one out of 11), 0% disagreed, and 0% did not agreed at all.

In the steering group meeting, eight senior company representatives participated. There was no disagreement on the results, since the overall view among them was that the results closely reflected their 'gut feeling' of what was most important and beneficial to improve. However, in order to identify causes for the issues in Improvement package 1, it was suggested to decompose them into smaller and more targeted problems.

Table 2. Results from evaluation questionnaire

Question	Answer format
Q1: The method makes you feel involved in the development work.	Neither agree nor disagree (9%) Agree (73%) Agree completely (18%)
Q2: The method gives you the possibility to influence the improvement development work.	Neither agree nor disagree(18%) Agree(64%) Agree completely(18%)
Q3: The method makes you feel committed to the improvement development work.	Neither agree nor disagree (27%) Agree (55%) Agree completely (18%)
Q4. The method is reliable.	Neither agree nor disagree (36%) Agree (45%) Agree completely (18%)
Q5: The method is capable of finding out what need to be improved.	Neither agree nor disagree (9%) Agree (45%) Agree completely (45%)
Q6: Do you agree with the resulting list of what needs to be improved?	Neither agree nor disagree (9%) Agree (55%) Agree completely (36%)
Q7: What is your overall opinion of the usefulness of the used method to achieve efficient improvement development?	Useful (73%) Very useful (27%)

The effort (time spent), for the steps of the IP and for the evaluation was in total 196 man-hours. Of those, 24 hours were used in Step 3A, 110 hours were used in Step 3B, 22 hours were used in Step 3C, and 40 hours were used in the evaluation.

The effort of the research team was 72 hours and the company effort was 124 hours where the company hours used was mainly dependent on the number of participating subjects in the workshop and the survey. Roughly, 40 % (30 out of 72 hours) of the research team effort was spent on developing the instruments where a major part (~25 hours was used for elaborating the web layout of the survey instrument.

5   Lessons Learned

5.1   Results of Using the IP

Overall, our study indicates that there is an agreed view among staff and managers in the organizations about what the most critical issues are, and what their improvement efforts should focus on. The results of the prioritizing show that the level of disagreement among all the subjects for the issues with high priorities is not higher than for those issues with low priorities. There are also no significant differences for the assigned priorities given by the groups of subjects belonging to PD and Man. In addition, the answers to Q4, Q5 and Q6 in Table 2 indicate a good confidence in the method for producing reliable and valid results among the subjects. Despite the consistently positive attitude toward the method, any conclusions from the answers should be drawn with a great deal of caution mainly because of the relatively small sample representing the organizations investigated and since the answers might have been biased by the agree/disagree questions, as some people tend to agree regardless of their real opinion [39].

The packaging of the nine improvement issues resulted in four improvement packages among which Improvement package 1 includes the three issues that were found most important to deal with first in the SPI project: Issue 1—Requirements Engineering, Issue 2—Early Manufacturing Involvement, and Issue 9—Roles and Responsibilities. This is much in line with earlier studies even though these studies have other focus than our study and have been performed in other contextual settings. In requirements engineering, Curtis et al. [5] found that requirements communication is a crucial part in enabling stable requirements and a correct understanding of them, but that for large software systems development organizational boundaries impede the communication. Active involvement of Man in early phases of the development has in previous work been identified as one of the most critical factors for achieving flawless launches as well as cost efficient and quality assured production [4, 7-11, 19]. For example, Daetz [7] shows that 75% of the production costs are determined early in the development of products. Earlier field studies on the PD/Man interface point out the importance of establishing clear roles and responsibilities, which become more critical in later development phases [18, 19].

5.2   Results of the Evaluation

Using expert judgment by relying on industrial representatives showed out to be an efficient way to perform the selection of subjects. However, relying on the judgment of industrial representatives, and not be able to critically evaluate the selection can introduce bias (e.g., the subjects have been selected so they conform to a specific view). It is difficult to avoid this but it can be alleviated by discussing and anchoring the selected subjects among the managers in the project steering group. Furthermore, the research team should have done their homework by scrutinizing the results of the PA (Steps 1 and 2 in Fig.1), and collecting and analyzing additional information that is accessible and needed. This in turn may disclose the originators who could be excellent candidates for further participation.

When selecting the subjects, the overall strategy was to cover all the roles identified in the assessed process area. The experience of the identification of roles is that the results of the prior PA must be considered. For example, in the IP (Step 3), the process developer role was added to obtain a better coverage. Furthermore, including managers in the workshops was, however, deemed a risk factor as it could threaten the goal of allowing everyone to contribute their experiences and ideas in the improvement work. Here the survey made it possible to capture the views of the managers with regard to priorities and dependencies of the improvement issues without jeopardizing further improvement development carried out by the team selected for the workshops. In order to involve management, the most concerned senior managers were also represented in the project steering group.

Using also the survey as data collection method, increased the sample size of the workshop from 13 to 41 subjects. This made it possible to perform further analysis through PCA and statistical tests, revealing whether there were significant differences between groups of subjects (e.g., Man and PD, see Section 4).

A disadvantage of collecting data through both workshop and survey was the relative increase in effort of the research team mainly because of elaborating the survey instrument. Furthermore, online questionnaires limit the possibilities to discuss and clarify obscurities in the instrument. This was reflected on when discussing the results and the IP method in the second workshop. The subjects found it difficult to carry out the prioritization and dependency mapping mainly because of difficulties in getting an overview of the improvement issues and interpreting them. These difficulties are probably related to the fact that it is hard to describe the issues only through written text. The value of discussing and clarifying the improvement issues before letting the subjects prioritize and identify dependencies is pointed out in [13, 17]. Thus, the aim of obtaining validity between the workshop and survey by not providing additional information about the improvement issues in the workshop can be questioned.

Applying AHP in industrial settings commonly results in CR higher than 0.1 [40]. Apostolou and Hassell [41] suggest that it is possible to use responses with CR >0.1 without affecting the overall results. For example, Gorshek and Wohlin [13] included subjects having a CR of 0.2 or less and showed that if subjects with CR>0.2 also were included the priority of the improvement issues did not substantially change. When analyzing the impact of excluding the five subjects with a CR of 0.3 or more, it could be observed that there were minor differences except for Issue 3, which showed a moderate change where the ranking dropped from fourth to seventh place.

Attaining commitment is one of the most important success factors in any improvement initiative [42, 43]. The answers to Q1, Q2, and Q3 in Table 2 indicate that a majority of the subjects felt committed to the SPI effort according to. However, as mentioned above the answers might have been biased. On the other hand, as the IP was done jointly, there was a larger joint commitment to perform improvements, thus enabling the continuation of the SPI project.

Finally, according to the answers to Q7 in Table 2, all of the 11 subjects perceived the method to be either useful (73%) or very useful (27%), which indicates a strong support for its usefulness.

6   Conclusions

SPI is an important enabler for effectively developing software-intensive products with competitive edge. Many of these products are complex and developed in large organizations where inter-departmental communication and coordination are critical.

This paper reports on a study focusing on improvement issue packaging as method for IP, which was applied to an SPI project performed at two Swedish automotive companies. The SPI project focuses on the inter-departmental interaction between PD and Man in large-scale development of software-intensive automotive systems. The overall aim was to establish decision support, based on organizational needs, for the further planning of the improvement work at the companies.

This study makes two main contributions. First, we believe there is an industrial value of the results of the IP for practitioners aiming at improving in similar industrial setting. In total 41 subjects at the companies, assigned priorities and dependencies in both a survey and a workshop. Based on the outcome of the packaging three issues were deemed most important: Issue 1—Requirements Engineering, Issue 2—Early Manufacturing Involvement, and Issue 9—Roles and Responsibilities.

Second, we tailored and applied IP to inter-departmental interaction in large-scale software development, which differs from earlier studies on SPI. We provide a detailed description and demonstration of using improvement packaging as an IP method and report our lessons learned and feedback from professionals on its industrial usefulness. This information is most likely helpful for practitioners wanting to conduct SPI in similar industrial settings as investigated here.

An overall conclusion related to the use of our IP method is that it is useful and has the capability of identifying the most critical issues and sorting them into feasible packages. However, the benefits of extending iFLAP by using a survey can be questioned mainly due to increase of resources and higher risk of misinterpretations among the participating subjects.

The companies presented in this paper intend to continue the improvements based on the results presented here, which includes using iFLAP and the IP method.

Acknowledgements. The authors would like to express their gratitude to all those somehow involved in this study and especially the participants at VCC and VTC.

References

1. Venkatesh Prasad, K., Broy, M., Kreuger, I.: Scanning Advances in Aerospace & Automobile Software Technology. Proc. of the IEEE 98, 510–514 (2010)
2. Dannenberg, J., Kleinhans, C.: The coming age of collaboration in the automotive industry. Mercer Manage. J. 18, 88–94 (2004)
3. Broy, M., Kruger, I.H., Pretschner, A., Salzmann, C.: Engineering Automotive Software. Proc. of the IEEE 95, 356–373 (2007)
4. Nihtilä, J.: R&D–Production integration in the early phases of new product development projects. Journal of Engineering and Technology Management 16, 55–81 (1999)
5. Curtis, B., Krasner, H., Iscoe, N.: A field study of the software design process for large systems. Communications of the ACM 31, 11 (1988)
6. Kraut, R.E., Streeter, L.A.: Coordination in software development. Communications of the ACM 38, 69–81 (1995)
7. Daetz, D.: The Effect of Product Design on Product Quality and Product Cost. Quality Progress 20, 6 (1987)

8. Morgan, J.M., Liker, J.K.: The Toyota Product Development System: Integrating People, Process, and Technology. Productivity Press, New York (2006)

9. Sobek, D.K., Ward, A.C., Liker, J.K.: Toyota's Principles of Set-Based Concurrent Engineering. Sloan Management Review 40, 2 (1999)

10. Wheelwright, S.C., Clark, K.B.: Accelerating the design-build-test cycle for effective product development. International Marketing Review 11, 32–46 (1994)

11. Pernstal, J., Magazinius, A., Gorschek, T.: A Study Investigating Challenges in the Interface between Product Development and Manufacturing in the Development of Software Intensive Automotive Systems. Int. Journal of Software Engineering and Knowledge Engineering 22(2), 965–1004 (2012)

12. Gorschek, T., Wohlin, C.: Identification of Improvement Issues Using a Lightweight Triangulation Approach. In: The European Software Process Improvement Conf., Graz, Austria (2003)

13. Gorschek, T., Wohlin, C.: Packaging Software Process Improvement Issues—A Method and a Case Study. Software: Practice & Experience 4, 1311–1344 (2004)

14. Humphrey, W.S.: Managing the Software Process. Addison Wesley, Reading (1989)

15. Almefelt, L., Berglund, F., Nilsson, P., Malmqvist, J.: Requirement management in practice: findings from an empirical study in the autmotive industry. Research in Engineering Design 17, 3 (2006)

16. Sumantran, V.: Accelerating product development in the automobile industry. Int. Journal of Manufacturing Technology and Management 6(3/4) (2004)

17. Pettersson, F., Ivarsson, M., Gorschek, T., Öhman, P.: A practitioner's guide to light weight software process assessment and improvement planning. The Journal of Systems and Software 81, 972–995 (2008)

18. Vandevelde, A., Van Dierdonk, R.: Managing the design-manufacturing interface. Int. Journal of Operations & Production Management 23, 1326–1348 (2003)

19. Lakemond, N., Johansson, G., Magnusson, T., Safsten, K.: Interfaces between technology development, product development and production: critical factors and a conceptual model. Int. Journal of Technology Intelligence and Planning 3, 317–330 (2007)

20. Poppendieck, M., Poppendieck, T.: Lean software development: an agile toolkit. Addison-Wesley, Boston (2003)

21. Dybå, T., Dingsøyr, T.: Empirical Studies of Agile Software Development: a Systematic Review. Journal of Information and Software Technology 50, 833–859 (2008)

22. Wang, X., Conboy, K., Cawley, O.: Leagile software development: An experience report analysis of the application of lean approaches in agile software development. J. of Systems and Software 85, 1287–1299 (2012)

23. Gorschek, T., Garre, P., Larsson, S., Wohlin, C.: A Model for Technology Transfer in Practice. IEEE Softw. 23, 88–95 (2006)

24. CMMI.: Capability Maturity Model Integration Version 1.3. Technical Report CMU/SEI-2010-TR-033. Software Engineering Institute, SEI (2010),
http://www.sei.cmu.edu/cmmi/

25. Automotive SIG.: The SPICE User Group, Automotive SPICE Process Assessment Model v2.5 and Process Reference Model v4.5 (2010),
http://www.automotivespice.com

26. Zahran, S.: Software Process Improvement: Practical Guidelines for Business Success. Addison-Wesley, Reading (1998)

27. Yin, R.: Case study research: design and methods, 3rd edn. SAGE Publications, Inc., Thousand Oaks (2003)

28. Runesson, P., Host, M.: Guidelines for conducting and reporting case study research in software engineering. Empirical Software Engineering 14, 131–164 (2009)
29. Volvo Car Corporation (2011),
    https://www.media.volvocars.com/global/enhanced/
    en-gb/Media/Preview.aspx?mediaid=41678
30. Volvo Truck Corporation. Quick facts about Volvo Trucks (2010),
    http://www.volvotrucks.com/trucks/global/
    en-gb/newsmedia/quick_facts_about_volvo_trucks/pages/
    quick_facts_about_volvo_trucks.aspx
31. Charfi, F., Sellami, F.: Overview on Dependable Embedded Systems in Modern Automotive. In: Proc.of the 2004 IEEE Int. Conference on Industrial Technology (2004)
32. Cohen, J.: Statistical Power Analysis for the Behavioral Sciences, 2nd edn. Laurence Erlbaum, Hillsdale (1988)
33. Wohlin, C., Runeson, P., Höst, M., Ohlson, M.C., Regnell, B., Wesslén, A.: Experimentation in Software Engineering: An Introduction. Kluwer Academic, Boston (2000)
34. Mingers, J.: Combining IS Research Methods: Towards a Pluralist Methodology. Information Systems Research 12, 240–259 (2001)
35. Regnell, B., Host, M., Nattoch Dag, J., Hjelm, T.: An Industrial Case Study on Distributed Prioritisation in Market-Driven Requirements Engineering for Packaged Software. Requirements Engineering 6, 251–262 (2001)
36. Kashigan, S.K.: Statistical Analysis—an Interdisciplinary Introduction to Univariate and Multivariate Methods. Radius Press, New York (1986)
37. Berander, P., Andrews, A.: Requirements Prioritization. In: Aurum, A., Wohlin, C. (eds.) Engineering and Managing Software Requirements. Springer (2005)
38. Saaty, T.L.: The Analytic Hierarchy Process: Planning, Priority Setting, Resource Allocation. McGraw-Hill, London (1980)
39. Robson, C.: Real World Research: A Resource for Social Scientists and Practitioners-Researchers, 2nd edn. Blackwell (2002)
40. Karlsson, J.: Software requirements prioritizing. In: Proc. of 2nd IEEE Int. Conf. on Requirements Eng., pp. 110–116 (1996)
41. Apostolou, J.M., Hassell, J.M.: An empirical examination of the sensitivity of the analytic hierarchy process to departures from recommended consistency ratios. Mathematical and Computer Modelling 17, 163–170 (1993)
42. El Emam, K.D., Goldenson, D.J., McCurley, J., Herbsleb, J.: Modeling the Likelihood of Software Process Improvement: An Exploratory Study. Empirical Software Engineering 6, 207–229 (2001)
43. Conradi, R., Fugetta, A.: Improving Software Process Improvement. IEEE Softw. 19, 92–100 (2002)

Improving Requirements Engineering by Artefact Orientation

Daniel Méndez Fernández[1] and Roel Wieringa[2]

[1] Technische Universität München, Germany
http://www4.in.tum.de/~mendezfe
[2] University of Twente, Netherlands
http://www.cs.utwente.nl/~roelw

Abstract. The importance of continuously improving requirements engineering (RE) has been recognised for many years. Similar to available software process improvement approaches, most RE improvement approaches focus on a normative and solution-driven assessment of companies rather than on a problem-driven RE improvement. The approaches dictate the implementation of a one-size-fits-all reference model without doing a proper problem investigation first, whereas the notion of quality factually depends on whether RE achieves company-specific goals. The approaches furthermore propagate process areas and methods, without proper awareness of the quality in the created artefacts on which the quality of many development phases rely. Little knowledge exists about how to conduct a problem-driven RE improvement that gives attention to the improvement of the artefacts. A promising solution is to start an improvement with an empirical investigation of the RE stakeholders, goals, and artefacts in the company to identify problems while abstracting from inherently complex processes. The RE improvement is then defined and implemented in joint action research workshops with the stakeholders to validate potential solutions while again concentrating on the artefacts. In this paper, we contribute an artefact-based, problem-driven RE improvement approach that emerged from a series of completed RE improvements. We discuss lessons learnt and present first result from an ongoing empirical evaluation at a German company. Our results suggest that our approach supports process engineers in a problem-driven RE improvement, but we need deeper examination of the resulting RE company standard, which is in scope of the final evaluation.

Keywords: Requirements Engineering, Artefact Orientation, Empirical Design Science, Software Process Improvement.

1 Introduction

Requirements engineering (RE) constitutes an important success factor for software development projects, since stakeholder-appropriate requirements are important determinants of quality. Incorrect or missing requirements can greatly add to the implementation or maintenance effort later. At the same time, RE is an interdisciplinary area in a software development process that is driven by

J. Heidrich et al. (Eds.): PROFES 2013, LNCS 7983, pp. 108–122, 2013.

uncertainty and is therefore highly volatile and complex. The first step for companies towards good RE is to establish an *RE reference model*, i.e. a company-wide definition of activities and modelling methods to be applied, roles to be assigned, and artefacts to be created. Once an RE reference model is established, it should be continuously improved to reflect, e.g. project experiences and the continuously evolving organisational culture.

To improve RE in industrial contexts, process engineers have to decide on whether to opt for a problem-driven improvement according to individual problems and needs or for a normative improvement, e.g. as part of an assessment in which companies are benchmarked against an existing norm [1]. Although we understand, especially in small companies, the reluctance against normative improvements [2,3], the high number of available RE improvement approaches still remains normative, solution-driven, or at least process-oriented. They are normative, because a pre-defined standard is taken to be the norm for RE processes; they are solution-driven, because the improvement skips a profound problem analysis and starts with a standard process definition that pretends to be a one-size fits-all solution and against which companies are too often blindly assessed [4]; they are process-oriented, because problems are assumed to consist of flaws in the current process and in the methods used for creating RE artefacts.

As a result, those RE improvement approaches encounter problems in practice [2]. RE is complex by nature and hardly standardisable with a norm, and the notion of RE quality depends, inter alia, on whether an RE reference model contributes to project-specific goals of a company. Starting with a predefined universal solution and attempting to analyse the gap with current practice may not lead to an improvement, because methods, related artefacts, and roles are added without regard for stakeholder-specific goals and problems of a company [5]. Therefore, improvements cannot be meaningfully implemented without a qualitative problem investigation that reveals which goals must be achieved [1,4] and which artefacts should be created in which way [5].

Problem. Although the importance of continuously improving RE in companies is recognised for many years, available approaches are either normative focussing on assessing and benchmarking companies against given norms, or they are at least process-driven. Yet missing is an approach to effectively guide a problem-driven analysis and improvement of RE while giving attention to the improvement of the RE artefacts in response to stakeholder goals.

Principal Idea. We propose to use a problem-driven approach that starts with an empirical study of the improvement problem, and that focusses on artefacts rather than on processes. We use the term "problem-driven" to indicate that we start with stakeholder goals and an empirical study of the improvement problem before initiating the improvement implementation. In our experience, the focus on RE artefacts benefits furthermore the analysis and the improvement of RE processes as it allows to objectively reproduce and analyse RE processes without having to take into account the variability of the RE processes reflected in the different projects of a company [6]. Our problem-driven approach implies that we start from understanding the practice of modelling and documentation in a company, rather than from a normative view of how artefacts should be developed and structured in an ideal world. The RE improvement proposals based on this are more likely to consist of small, feasible steps jointly implemented with the stakeholders as part of a series of action research workshops, rather than of large, impractical leaps that will be not be implemented, because they are, for example, too risky or simply do not fit their project demands [3,4].

Contribution. We contribute an *artefact-based RE improvement approach*, which has been developed over the last five years based on a series of completed bilateral research cooperations with industrial partners. We first introduce the underlying principles of an empirical engineering cycle used to steer problem-driven research, and the principles of artefact orientation. We present the RE improvement approach as a specialisation of the engineering cycle that aims at a problem-driven RE analysis and an improvement implementation by the use of artefact models. Finally, we discuss lessons learnt and first results from an initial empirical evaluation we are performing at a German company.

2   Fundamentals and Related Work

Software process improvement (SPI) is iterative by nature. Having its seeds in the known plan-do-check-act (PDCA) paradigm, it aims at continuously analysing problems/the current situation in processes as part of an appraisal, planning an improvement, implementing the improvement, and evaluating the improvement, before initiating the next iteration. In general, we can distinguish normative approaches and problem-driven approaches. Following the definition of Pettersson et al. [4], normative approaches are based on a prescriptive "collection of best practices [...] to be adhered by all organizations [...]" while "no special consideration is taken to an organisation's situation and needs, other than how the development process compares to the one offered by the framework". In contrast, problem-driven approaches are based on a "thorough understanding of the current situation [...]" whereas the choice of solutions is done according to problems identified in the organisation's projects.

For requirements engineering process improvement (REPI), there exist mostly normative contributions [1] of which a prominent and representative one is R-CMM, a CMMI-based RE process improvement model by Beecham at al. [7]. Approaches of this category focus on a prescriptive benchmarking of the maturity of RE according to a specific norm. As they follow the process-oriented paradigm [8], they propagate a norm that consists of a set of activities and best practices (see [4]), each indicating to the need of producing some artefacts. Those artefacts, however, remain underspecified, i.e. companies have to define those artefacts in personal responsibility without any guidance or blueprint. The guidance on the actual implementation of the improvement is, in general, not in scope of those approaches as they focus on comparable benchmarking and the adaptation of a company-specific RE to that given norm by adding potentially missing processes, methods, or other resources. Although approaches of this category are frequently applied in practice and empirically evaluated in different contexts [9], current studies do not provide evidence for the general benefits of normative approaches for the actual quality of a company-specific RE [2]. Those normative approaches often neglect company-specific goals and problems [3], whereas these goals determine the notion of quality, i.e. the extent to which a solution achieves a goal from a company's perspective [5].

In response to this shortcoming, current approaches focus on problem-driven RE improvement. They follow the evaluation and tailoring of solutions according to the particularities of single companies due to the sensitivity of RE to stakeholder goals and context phenomena. An example for approaches of this category is the iFLAP approach by Pettersson et al. [4]. They propose to conduct a process assessment and improvement by means of a specific set of empirical qualitative methods, such as interviews. In fact, qualitative methods are gaining much attention to investigate the sensitive contexts of organisations, their processes, and the people involved [10]. However, although there exist first valuable contributions that apply such methods in the area of SPI, they still do not rigorously cover the overall improvement life cycle and, thus, they do not close the gap left open by solution-driven REPI approaches. Furthermore, to the best of our knowledge, there exist no REPI approach that gives any attention on how to conduct an improvement taking into account the quality of the RE artefacts.

Previously Published Material. In [5], we presented first results on how to perform problem-driven RE analyses with a particular focus on artefacts to plan the implementation of an RE improvement in a problem-driven manner. However, we left open an understanding on how to apply empirical research to the whole improvement life cycle. In this paper, we will add these stages to define an approach to conduct a seamless artefact-based RE improvement covering the problem investigation and its implementation.

3   Artefact-Based Requirements Engineering Improvement

In the following, we show the principles of design science and artefact orientation, before contributing our conceptual framework for problem-driven, artefact-based RE improvement.

3.1   Design Science Principles

Design science is the design and investigation of artefacts for useful purposes. As illustrated in Fig. 1 (middle part), it consists of two activities, practical problem solving and knowledge question investigation, each with their own context [11].

By a practical problem, we mean a problem to change real world phenomena so as to achieve stakeholder goals; for example, to improve RE. We will call a solution proposal to a practical problem a *treatment* to emphasise that problem solvers treat a problem without guarantee of a complete solution. The treatment is designed and validated by the design scientist and will consist of a modelling technique, notation, or an artefact that helps stakeholders to achieve their goals. In design science context, the socio-economic context (left-hand side of Fig. 1) is, e.g. a software engineering department that wants to improve RE performed at the various projects of a company.

Problem solving may lead to knowledge questions, such as the question what the problematic phenomena are, or what the properties of a proposed solution should be. This leads to the other design science activity, answering knowledge questions (right-hand side of Fig. 1). To answer these questions, we use a knowledge base of published knowledge, in our case SPI knowledge.

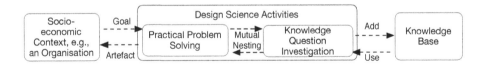

Fig. 1. Design science framework

Conversely, validated answers to our knowledge questions, to the extent they are not confidential, can be published and added to the public knowledge base. In some cases, answering a knowledge question generates a new practical problem, such as the problem to build observation instruments, or to run a pilot project to test an artefact. In this way, the design scientist may jump between the two main design science activities of Fig. 1.

We postulate that any rational improvement attempt requires problem investigation, treatment design and validation, implementation, and evaluation. We call this the *engineering cycle* (Fig. 2), which can be considered as a specialisation of the PDCA cycle (see Sect. 2) and which logically structures the practical problem solving task shown in Fig. 1. During *problem investigation*, the design scientists ask who the stakeholders are and what goals they have, what problematic phenomena there exist and what their effects are, and what this means for the goal contribution. All these questions are of empirical nature and no treatment design is done.

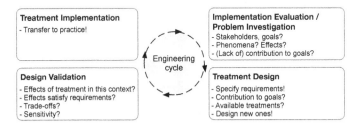

Fig. 2. The engineering cycle

Treatment design consists of two sets of design choices, indicated by exclamation marks, and two knowledge questions, indicated by question marks. The first design choice to be made is the specification of requirements for a treatment. These could be, for example, requirements for artefacts used in the treatment. The difference with the goal analysis is that requirements are desired properties of the treatment, whereas goals are states of the world that stakeholders want to achieve. The design scientist thus infers sets of requirements that could achieve the elaborated stakeholder goals. The contribution question asks for an argument why a treatment that satisfies these requirements would contribute to the satisfaction of the stakeholder goals. Once we are sure enough about the requirements for a treatment, we can make an inventory of available treatments that satisfy these requirements. With this information, the design scientist designs a treatment for the case. This is an integration of elements of available treatments, possibly with newly designed elements expected to be effective for the case.

In *design validation*, the design must be investigated to see what its effects will be in the case, and whether this will satisfy the requirements. A comparison with alternative treatments must be made (trade-off analysis) and sensitivity to changes in the problem context must be investigated. *Treatment implementation* in the engineering cycle is the transfer to practice after which the treatment has been realised and is outside the control of the designer of the treatment. Implementation can be followed by an evaluation of experience, which may lead to a new iteration through the cycle.

3.2   Principles of Artefact Orientation

In artefact-based RE improvement, we focus on a specialisation of the previously introduced engineering cycle where the treatments focus on artefacts and artefact models. As artefact orientation comes with a plethora of interpretations, we rely on a meta model we developed for artefact-based RE [12]. This meta model defines the constructs and rules for artefact-based RE, i.e. the basic notion of artefacts and how they relate to further process elements like roles.

We define an *artefact* as any document or data set required by an RE process in its intermediate or final form, e.g. models and specification documents. Each artefact has structure, usually captured in a taxonomy (comparable to a document outline), a particular content that defines a blueprint of the modelling concepts, and it is formulated in some syntax agreed by stakeholders. During artefact-based RE improvement, our process-agnostic focus on artefacts allows us to abstract from the variability in the processes, because the actual creation of artefacts by the use of particular methods in a particular sequence is reduced to the created artefacts, their contents, and their dependencies. During analysis, the focus on what has been produced rather than on how it has been produced results in an empirical understanding about how RE specifications are created and used in practice, and in a proposal to improve RE in a problem-specific way. The subsequent problem-driven implementation of an *artefact-based RE reference model*, i.e. the RE reference model including the artefacts, their structures, and their dependencies, as well as roles and responsibilities, supports the project-specific flexible creation of consistent result structures in contrast to when concentrating on methods and dependencies [12,13].

3.3   Artefact-Based RE Improvement Approach

Our artefact-based requirements engineering improvement approach emerges from experiences we gathered in a series of research projects with German companies. Table 1 summarises an excerpt of completed projects where we followed the principles of design science introduced in the foregoing section and where we applied the same empirical methods to conduct an artefact-based RE improvement. Details on the empirical methods applied during problem investigation and design validation in those projects can be taken from [5].

Table 1. Research projects that served as basis for the RE improvement approach .

Project	Company	Objective	Results
A	Capgemini TS (Germany)	Exploratory study on organisational and project-specific needs and RE improvement leading to the company standard for RE.	Study: [6], RE standard on demand
B	Siemens	Feasibility study on application of requirements engineering approach to qualitatively compare legacy approach with new approach	Study: [13]
C	Deutsche Lufthansa	Study to analyse requirements engineering process definition and exemplary development project	Confidential

The resulting overall artefact-based RE improvement approach is illustrated in Fig. 3 and incorporates the commonalities and experiences of all previously conducted action research projects.

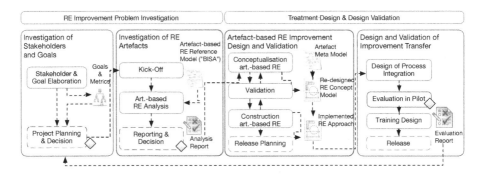

Fig. 3. One iteration through the artefact-based RE improvement life cycle

The approach contains a set of tasks of the engineering cycle (marked with solid shapes) and a set of management tasks (marked with dashed shapes). Milestones indicate decision points about the initiation of the next phase. In the following, we introduce each phase in detail.

Investigation of Stakeholders and Goals. In the first phase, we identify the stakeholders and their RE goals, and potential measurements to evaluate whether the improvement (given treatments) has achieved those goals at the end of an iteration. We then decide together with the stakeholders on whether to initiate an artefact-based improvement at all in dependency to the stated goals and available experiences about how well artefact orientation is generally suited to satisfy those goals. Those experiences arise from experimental research where we investigated to which extent particular goals such as "increase the syntactic consistency in the RE artefacts and support traceability" are supported by arte-fact orientation. An exemplary study that indicates to different goals supported by artefact orientation is provided in [13]. We create a project plan that includes which cases and subjects are necessary and when they will be involved, e.g. as part of workshop sessions or interviews. The plan is then put into a schedule with an appointment for a kick-off workshop clarifying also contractual issues like confidentiality (see, e.g. [14]).

Investigation of RE Artefacts. The investigation of RE artefacts considers the analysis which phenomena can be observed when applying the company-specific RE reference model in projects and what effects the application has. The analysis serves the identification of relevant RE artefacts and potential shortcomings. To conduct this analysis in an artefact-based manner, we define three research questions:

RQ1 Which artefacts are created in which syntactic quality?
RQ2 What is the artefacts' semantic quality?
RQ3 What is the quality of RE from the perspective of project participants?

The data collection procedure begins with a preparation phase in which we col-lect information about the definition of the RE process (i.e. artefacts, processes, milestones, and roles and responsibilities) and conduct one knowledge transfer workshop on artefact orientation. This supports us in creating a big picture of the overall RE process, its dependencies to surrounding processes, as well as the def-inition of the scope for the analysis. The subsequent data collection and analysis procedure then concentrates on manual and tool-supported document analyses and interviews; both serve the purpose of identifying an RE artefact model as it is lived in current company practice and which stakeholder-appropriate mea-sures can be taken to improve that model. The results are then documented in a report, which we structure following the guideline proposed by Runeson et al. [14] and which we discuss in a concluding joint workshop. We identify follow-ing techniques to be useful to conduct the analysis procedures for answering our research questions.

Syntactic Document Analysis (RQ 1). We analyse provided documents from a series of representative company-specific development projects in which the current RE reference model is applied. The comparison with the company-wide process definition serves to harmonise potential terminological deviations in the projects. During a document analysis, we induce an ("as-is") artefact model from the project documentation. To this end, we define a structure model that defines which general content items are created in the projects. In an in-depth analysis, we enrich this structure model with a content model that abstracts from the modelling concepts used in the projects to create the requirements specifications; for instance, we define which elements and relations are used to create the use case models and how they relate to other concepts such as the ones of acceptance testing. In a second step, we perform a gap analysis and compare the created artefact model to an artefact-based RE reference model we have developed over the last years based on current best practices and the state of the art, namely the BISA model ("Business Information Systems Analysis") [15], see also Fig. 3. We use deviations from the current artefact model to the BISA model to discover (1) potential fields of improvement, which we (2) validate in the interviews (RQ 3) to ensure the problem-driven nature of our analysis.

Semantic Document Analysis (RQ 2). For each class of requirements defined in the project-specific specifications, we take random samples and manually analyse them for semantic inconsistencies, ambiguities, linguistic defects (amortisations or generalisations), and redundancies; for instance, we identify inconsistencies by conducting a walkthrough through the documents following the references provided in the corresponding specification sections. The semantic document analysis serves in addition to the syntactic analysis to identify which modelling techniques and textual artefact templates could help to avoid potential problems.

Qualitative Analysis of Expert Interviews (RQ 3). Having investigated the documents in isolation, we conduct interviews with representatives from the corresponding projects. Those interviews aim at encouraging the participants to reflect on their current practice and help us to get a better understanding of the project backgrounds. To this end, we define open and closed questions and ask for potential improvement fields in the company-wide RE reference model and for decisions taken in the projects that have lead to the analysed documents. The latter is structured according to the content items in the artefact model, which took our attention during the syntactic document analysis. We ask, for example, for artefacts being incomplete or missing in comparison to the BISA model and why they have been specified in this particular way. This helps us to validate the current practice and to understand contemporary needs in the project environments, as well as to adopt the treatment to the organisational context; for instance, by defining under which circumstances to create specific RE contents recommended in practice, i.e. to prepare tailoring profiles for the new improved RE reference model.

Artefact-Based RE Improvement Design and Validation. The actual RE improvement considers the practical problem solving in design science and is conducted over three engineering steps performed in iterations. We begin the conceptualisation of the new ("to-be") artefact-based RE reference model by conducting a series of action research workshops. In those workshops, we begin with a simplified view on an artefact model and sketch their currently used artefact model using whiteboards and paper cards. We begin the design of the artefact model on basis of the artefact model created during the analysis with RQ 1 and validated with RQ 3, i.e. we use the artefact model abstracting from their project documentation and extend it step-by-step with those content items proposed by the BISA and found useful by the stakeholders to support for their goals. Where reasonable, we annotate project-specific situations in which to omit the creation of the content items to infer, in the end, a tailoring profile. We enrich the artefact model with milestones, roles and to which further development artefacts the content items relate (e.g. acceptance testing) for the subsequent process integration. Between those workshops, we build the improved RE reference model by conceptualising the artefacts, roles, and milestones in isolation without direct stakeholder involvement with, e.g. UML class diagrams, before discussing resulting concepts again in joint workshops. After validating the proposed concepts and their effects on the organisational context and whether the concepts help to overcome the shortcomings identified in the analysed projects, we implement the concepts in a tool-supported manner, which itself is considered as a technical validation [16]. This implementation considers, for example, the design of UML profiles and their implementation as part of CASE tool plugins.

Design and Validation of Improvement Transfer. Once the RE reference model is conceptualised and constructed, it is disseminated. This dissemination itself must be designed. This includes the design of the process integration, i.e. the integration of the RE reference model into existing organisational practice by defining the dependencies between the elements in the new approach and elements in the overall development process model (e.g. the dependencies between the new RE artefacts and further existing architectural design or testing artefacts). After evaluating the new approach in a pilot project, we need to carefully design its training and release. The evaluation itself needs to investigate whether we eventually improved RE in dependency to the initially stated goals and the problems discovered during the analysis. To this end, we apply the new RE reference model in a pilot project and compare the conducted RE process as well as the created artefacts with the previously used approaches using interviews, both used to evaluate potential improvements of the variables investigated with the previously stated research questions. An exemplary evaluation investigating the improvement of the syntactic and semantic quality of the RE artefacts and of the flexibility in the RE process is shown in [13]. If the improvement is accepted, we design training material and release the model, before initiating, where reasonable, the improvement life cycle again. At the example of project A in Tab. 1, we conducted three iterations over 2 years, before the resulting artefact-based RE reference model was declared as the company standard.

4   Preliminary Results from Ongoing Evaluation

The introduced approach has been developed based on experiences we gained in fundamental and applied research projects in the area of artefact orientation [12] and the application of developed concepts in different research projects to solve industrially relevant problems (see Tab. 1). So far, the resulting problem-driven approach is successful, because up to now the concepts of artefact-based RE improvement have resulted in an successful RE improvement leading, e.g. to new company-specific RE standards (see, e.g. project A). We have, however, reached the point where we need to empirically evaluate our approach in different socio-economic contexts. Also, it yet has to be shown whether our approach can be used by others if we are not involved at all.

Our current evaluation, described next, is one step in this direction. Currently, we are conducting two research projects, each of them with a duration of one year. One project is performed with Wacker Chemie (Munich, Germany). The company works in the chemical business and develops, inter alia, custom software for their operation processes and their production sites. We are applying our approach to improve their RE reference model. At the time of writing the paper, we finalised the improvement design and validation phase and are currently evaluating the resulting artefact-based RE reference model of the company in a series of pilot projects (Fig. 3, phase 4). In the following, we first discuss lessons learnt gathered from applying our approach, before summarising the results from an intermediate evaluation we performed with the involved process engineers.

Lessons Learnt. The most remarkable observation we have done so far considers the artefact-based RE improvement design and validation phase. We observed that we are shifting the approach from a classical action research paradigm to a *canonical action research* paradigm [17]. This means that we, as researchers, are not taking the exclusive role anymore, in which we do process consultation by proposing different solutions, which are then discussed with all technical details in workshops. Instead, the approach is now strongly iterative and collaborative in which the researchers take a more observational perspective.

We have used this observational role for two purposes: The first purpose is to generate new knowledge, i.e. to draw further conclusions about artefact orientation itself and how it manifests in practical settings as the paradigm still comes with various practical interpretations and implications [12]. We consider this also to be the main reason for the shift to a canonical action research. The second purpose is to guide the solution finding process between the stakeholders rather than proposing different solutions and risking to miss company-specific (hidden) requirements. To this end, we begin with the results of the analysis and encourage them to design their new artefact-based RE model on their own on a white board while we actively aim at knowledge transfer regarding possible implications of their design decisions. Figure 4 briefly sketches the role of the workshops.

In the centre of the figure, we illustrate the whiteboard and the paper cards used at Wacker as a means for the improvement design and validation workshops. Each card symbolises a content item identified during the investigation of RE artefacts. The structuring and colour coding of the cards results from the gap analysis: red cards (left part of the photo) illustrate content items that were missing in comparison to the BISA model, yellow cards illustrate incomplete content items, and green cards (right part of the photo) illustrate content items that were specified in full. During the improvement workshops, we further abstract from technical details of artefact orientation to not interrupt discussions between the stakeholders, i.e. instead of focussing on models and their technical details, we focus on paper cards and keep technicalities away from the discussions. We still continuously ensure the conformance of the new model sketched during the workshops to the underlying meta models (see Sect. 3.2) to ensure the feasibility during implementation.

Although we have experienced a generally high effort for the RE improvement, we believe this procedure to be the more effective one, because we expect it to pay off in reduced rework later. We have already observed a high communication between the stakeholder focus groups while backing their decisions in their

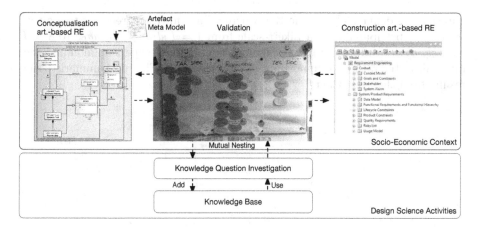

Fig. 4. Continuous knowledge transfer during validation workshops while abstracting from realisation details (re-design concept model, meta models, and construction)

project environments. Over and above all, we believe that this procedure best reveals the problem-driven nature of our approach. These observations, however, need a deeper empirical evaluation, which we are currently performing.

Intermediate Evaluation. Currently, we are performing an empirical evaluation of our artefact-based improvement approach where we evaluate it in comparison to previously used process-oriented and solution-driven approaches taking into account resulting RE reference models, i.e. we evaluate our improvement approach and its results. This evaluation considers the overall artefact-based RE improvement undertaking at Wacker Chemie involving 4 researchers and 5 process engineers of the company with an estimated effort of 8 person months including in total 13 workshops (each with a duration of 4 hours).

In the following, we briefly summarise the results from an intermediate evaluation we performed with the process engineering group involved in the workshops and remaining anonymous. The initial evaluation serves to detect first trends and validate the study design itself. Since this is a preliminary evaluation, we do not go into details and refrain from a rigorous study design and interpretations of the results. The evaluation will be completed after finishing the research project to allow for more precise and generalisable results taking also into account the expert opinion of project participants that apply the resulting artefact-based RE reference model. The overall evaluation is steered by two research questions:

RQ1 How well are process engineers supported in their RE improvement tasks?
RQ2 How well are project participants supported by the RE reference model?

The first question directly evaluates our improvement approach for applicability and usability, and the second question evaluates the appropriateness of the resulting RE reference model from the perspective of project participants. During the intermediate evaluation, we conduct an assessment where the lead of the process engineering group answers a questionnaire (jointly discussed with the group). The questionnaire includes 8 criteria for assessing the improvement approach and 8 criteria for assessing the resulting RE reference model. For each criterion, we define a closed question where we ask for the agreement to a given statement distributed over a Likert-scale from 1 = *I strongly disagree* to 8 = *I strongly agree*, and we ask in an open question for their expert opinion and the rationale of the rating to support a reproducible result. Figure 5 summarises the results from the evaluation.

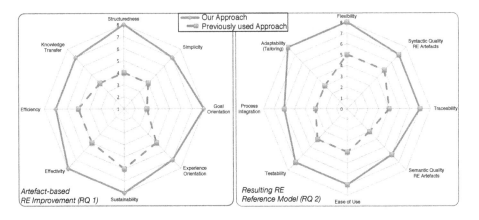

Fig. 5. Results from an intermediate comparative evaluation of the improvement approach (left side) and of the resulting RE reference model (right side)

In general, our improvement approach was overly rated to be better suited for a problem-driven RE improvement in comparison to previously used process-oriented and solution-driven RE improvement approaches. The overall rating already indicates to confirm our perceived support for the aforementioned problem-orientation and, in particular, to support for knowledge transfer. Our approach is stated to be problem-driven whereas previously experienced undertakings "disregard [company-specific] main objectives [...]" and the "[...] integration of quality management aspects into RE [...]", which was a major improvement goal. In contrast to our observation of the lower efficiency due to our effort spent in the preparation of the workshops, the workshops were perceived as efficient. Previous undertakings were rated to be "less efficient [having a] longer time period for the conception phase with more workshops needed". Similarly, the structuredness was rated high due to the "logical and continuous approach". The simplicity was rated to be high in comparison to previously used approaches, because those where focussing on "method-based approaches, which imply process models [leading to] more complexity both the projects and for quality management". Finally, the effectivity was rated to be high due to the "conception of content items structures, their relationships and dependencies, and an overall traceability", i.e. the artefact-based nature of the new RE reference model.

The resulting artefact-based RE reference model (RQ 2) is thus perceived to be an improvement in comparison to the previously used RE reference model. In particular, the flexibility and the adaptability is rated to be of high quality due to the artefact-based nature and the inferred tailoring profiles. The artefact-based nature also indicates to reveal the benefits in supporting a higher quality in the RE artefacts when applying the model in project settings. This is reflected in the rating of the syntactic quality of the artefacts w.r.t. consistency and completeness and in the aforementioned traceability. As we profoundly took into account the interfaces of the artefacts to further development tasks, the reference model is rated to be well integrated into the overall software development process.

These preliminary results suggest that our artefact-based RE improvement approach is well suited for a problem-driven improvement, but cannot be taken as definitive in any sense. The evaluation needs deeper examination and the participation of all project participants of the currently ongoing pilot phase. This should reveal more insights into benefits and any negative, unforeseen phenomena that would motivate further development of our RE improvement approach.

5 Conclusion

In this paper, we contributed a problem-driven, artefact-based RE improvement approach and made explicit the steps we successfully applied in different research co-operations where we developed artefact-based RE reference models for companies in a problem-driven manner over the last 5 years. We introduced the basic concepts of our artefact-based RE improvement approach and discussed preliminary experiences from an ongoing evaluation, which needs, however, deeper examination as well as replications to increase the validity of our results.

Our problem-driven improvement approach already seems to avoid the pitfalls of solution-driven process improvement approaches, in which ways of working alien to an organisation, and not relevant for its problems, may be introduced. The artefact-based nature of our approach increases the freedom for process improvement as the focus lies on the RE artefacts rather than on strict, inflexible processes used to create and modify the artefacts. The artefact models abstract from processes, methods, and description techniques. This supports a structured analysis and improvement of RE in joint action research workshops with stakeholder focus groups without having to take into account the inherent complexity of the RE processes in their individual project environments.

We thus made first steps in closing a gap in current improvement research that is often solution-driven and process-oriented, focussing on assessments of processes of a company against a pre-defined solution that is propagated to be per se of high quality. We do not claim that our approach suits every situation in which to improve an RE process of a company. In fact, we discussed that we need further understanding about the general benefits and limitations of artefact orientation by relating it to business domain characteristics. Furthermore, the success of every improvement endeavour in a socio-economic context depends on many soft factors that hardly can be formalised in a procedure. Consequently, we encourage researchers and practitioners to critically discuss our approach and to join us to empirically evaluate artefact-based RE improvement.

Acknowledgements. We thank S. Eder, B. Penzenstadler, J. Eckhardt, and K. Wnuk for their valuable feedback on previous versions of this paper. We are also grateful to the employees at Wacker for their participation and support.

References

1. Napier, N., Mathiassen, L., Johnson, R.: Combining Perceptions and Prescriptions in Requirements Engineering Process Assessment: An Industrial Case Study. IEEE Transactions on Software Engineering 35(5), 593–606 (2009)
2. Méndez Fernández, D., Wagner, S.: Naming the Pain in Requirements Engineering: Design of a global Family of Surveys and first Results from Germany. In: EASE 2013, pp. 183–194. ACM (2013)
3. Staples, M., Niazi, M., Jeffery, R., Abrahams, A., Byatt, P., Murphy, R.: An Exploratory Study of why Organizations do not adopt CMMI. Journal of Systems and Software 80(6), 883–895 (2007)
4. Pettersson, F., Ivarsson, M., Gorschek, T., Öhman, P.: A practitioner's Guide to light weight Software Process Assessment and Improvement Planning. Journal of Systems and Software 81(6), 972–995 (2008)
5. Méndez Fernández, D., Penzenstadler, B., Kuhrmann, M.: Pattern-based Guideline to Empirically Analyse Software Development Processes. In: EASE 2012, pp. 136–145. IET (2012)
6. Méndez Fernández, D., Wagner, S., Lochmann, K., Baumann, A., de Carne, H.: Field Study on Requirements Engineering: Investigation of Artefacts, Project Parameters, and Execution Strategies. Information and Software Technology 54(2), 162–178 (2012)
7. Beecham, S., Hall, T., Rainer, A.: Defining a Requirements Process Improvement Model. Software Quality Journal 13(3), 247–279 (2005)
8. Brinkkemper, S., van de Weerd, I., Saeki, M., Versendaal, J.: Process Improvement in Requirements Management: A Method Engineering Approach. In: Rolland, C. (ed.) REFSQ 2008. LNCS, vol. 5025, pp. 6–22. Springer, Heidelberg (2008)
9. Beecham, S., Hall, T., Britton, C., Cottee, M., Austen, R.: Using an Expert Panel to Validate A Requirements Process Improvement Model. Journal of Systems and Software 76, 251–275 (2005)
10. Seaman, C.: Qualitative Methods in Empirical Studies of Software Engineering. IEEE Transactions on Software Engineering 25(4), 557–572 (1999)
11. Wieringa, R.: Relevance and problem choice in design science. In: Winter, R., Zhao, J.L., Aier, S. (eds.) DESRIST 2010. LNCS, vol. 6105, pp. 61–76. Springer, Heidelberg (2010)
12. Méndez Fernández, D., Penzenstadler, B., Kuhrmann, M., Broy, M.: A Meta Model for Artefact-Orientation: Fundamentals and Lessons Learned in Requirements Engineering. In: Petriu, D.C., Rouquette, N., Haugen, Ø. (eds.) MODELS 2010, Part II. LNCS, vol. 6395, pp. 183–197. Springer, Heidelberg (2010)
13. Méndez Fernández, D., Lochmann, K., Penzenstadler, B., Wagner, S.: A Case Study on the Application of an Artefact-Based Requirements Engineering Approach. In: EASE 2011, pp. 104–113. IET (2011)
14. Runeson, P., Höst, M.: Guidelines for Conducting and Reporting Case Study Research in Software Engineering. Empirical Software Engineering 14(2), 131–164 (2009)
15. Méndez Fernández, D., Kuhrmann, M.: Artefact-Based Requirements Engineering and its Integration into a Process Framework. Technical Report TUM-I0929, Technische Universität München (2009)
16. Wieringa, R., Aycse, M.: Technical Action Research as a Validation Method in Information Systems Design Science. In: Peffers, K., Rothenberger, M., Kuechler, B. (eds.) DESRIST 2012. LNCS, vol. 7286, pp. 220–238. Springer, Heidelberg (2012)
17. Davison, R., Martinsons, M.G., Kock, N.: Principles of Canonical Action Research. Information Systems Journal 14(1), 65–86 (2004)

Managing Constant Flow of Requirements: Screening Challenges in Very Large-Scale Requirements Engineering

Sanja Aaramaa[1], Tuomo Kinnunen[2], Jari Lehto[3], and Nebojša Taušan[1]

[1] University of Oulu, Department of Information Processing Science, M-Group,
P.O. Box 3000, 90014 Oulu, Finland
[2] University of Oulu, Department of Industrial Engineering and Management,
P.O. Box 4610, 90014 Oulu, Finland
{Sanja.Aaramaa,Tuomo.Kinnunen,Nebojsa.Tausan}@Oulu.fi
[3]Nokia Siemens Networks Oy, P.O. Box 1, 02022 Nokia Siemens Networks
Jari.Lehto@nsn.com

Abstract. Market-driven software development has been the dominant context in Very Large-Scale Requirements Engineering (VLSRE) research. This case reveals screening as a VLSRE practice in the development context which has characteristics both of market- and customer-driven software development. Requirements are received as a continuous high rate flow. The exploratory industrial case study was conducted to clarify a current practice to manage the inflow of requirements. As a result, a description of the requirement screening process (RS) is provided and practical management challenges related to the process are analysed. This case study provides insight into the requirement screening practice beyond the market-driven software development domain and thus extends the current VLSRE literature.

Keywords: Very Large-Scale Requirements Engineering, VLSRE, product management, industrial case, requirement screening.

1 Introduction

Requirements Engineering (RE) enables the success of product development effort [1]. An efficient RE process is needed in any large organisation where the number of new requirements increases while the management resources cannot be increased accordingly. The importance of RE is further emphasized in incremental software development since each increment should optimize the value to the stakeholders [2]. The concept of Very Large-Scale Requirements Engineering (VLSRE) emerged from the research conducted in the context of market-driven software development (MDSWD) [3]. Typically, MDSWD aims at developing products for a large market in contrast to customer-driven software development (CDSWD), which creates software for a specific customer [4], [5]. Requirements originate from a variety of sources like end users, sponsors, technology, markets, standards and government and they come constantly at a high rate [6], [7]. Screening has been proposed as a means to quickly assess the value of new requirements [7].

J. Heidrich et al. (Eds.): PROFES 2013, LNCS 7983, pp. 123–137, 2013.

Problem Statement. Published studies on VLSRE have focused on MDSWD [3], [8], [9], [10] and the research lacks empirical evidence of other types of software development approaches. This case study extends current VLSRE literature since it looks into the screening of new requirements in feature-oriented release-based software development [11], which has the characteristics of both MDSWD [12], [13], [14] and of CDSWD [13], [15].

The case company had learned that the requirement screening process (RS) is not functioning in an optimal way towards elicitation and release planning (RP). In terms of elicitation, it fails to meet the expectation of fast screening and to provide feedback quickly enough to the stakeholders. In terms of RP [11], the shortcoming is that screening is not effective enough since too many feature proposals get through and the priorities of the proposed features change too often. The case company identified the need to improve their current process and they decided to co-operate with researchers to tackle the shortcomings on their existing process.

Research Objectives. Our motivation to carry out this study was to understand current practice for managing a constant high rate inflow of new requirements. This objective was divided into two more detailed research questions:

RQ1: How to process a constant high rate inflow of new requirements?

RQ2: What challenges does product management have during requirement screening?

The aim is to answer the questions by reviewing the relevant literature and conducting an industrial case study in the VLSRE context. The case study analyses the challenges that product management (PM) faces in feature-oriented release-based software development in a large ICT company.

Case Context. The case company is a global business-to-business operator in the ICT industry. The company has an extensive product portfolio and most of the products are considered as software-intensive systems. A software development process of the company can be described as having the following characteristics: a) RE process meets the criteria of VLSRE b) RE is carried out as a parallel and interconnected set of processes run by different stakeholders c) the processes include product-specific RS processes d) RS processes are feature-oriented e) software is delivered in releases [16], where each release is a collection of new and/or enhanced features f) the served market is large but the number of customers is measured in hundreds and the customers are a significant source of requirements inflow.

In this case study, the unit of analysis is the RS process. The RS process has an important role in feature-oriented release-based software development, which the company applies. The RS process is a link between elicitation and RP [11]. By its definition, the RS process ought to filter out any requirements that are considered out of scope or that do not bring value to stakeholders. Therefore, the RS process may also be characterized as a feature selection, decision-making and prioritisation process [16].

The paper is structured according to the guidelines presented in [17]. The following Section 2 summarises work related to this case study. Section 3 then describes the chosen research approach. The gathered empirical evidence is explained in Section 4. Conclusion and future work are outlined in Section 5.

2   Related Work

The starting point for the literature study was the article by Regnell & al. in which the concept of VLSRE was introduced [3]. The existing VLSRE literature was reviewed excluding non-English sources (24 publications). Another remarkable article was Barney, Aurum and Wohlin paper [16]. These articles formed the basis for the literature study, which highlighted a gap in the body of knowledge: the empirical studies did not cover the industrial setting beyond MDSWD. In addition to the aforementioned publications, other relevant articles that address RE, RS and RP issues related to the topic of the paper were studied. The search techniques like key word search (e.g. title words; product management, Requirements Engineering) and snowballing [18] were applied to find relevant publications. All the researchers had access to the literature, since all the articles were stored into NVivo.

Very Large-Scale Requirements Engineering. A company operates in VLSRE 'mode' if the number of requirements in a database to be processed is greater than 10,000 items [3]. The concept of VLSRE was born in the context of MDSWD based on the research and experience gained through empirical studies on large industry aimed at global markets. A large number of requirements cause numerous interdependencies between requirements and it also implies a high number of internal and external stakeholders [3].

Bjarnason & al. [19], [8] studied causes and root causes for the over-scoping of product releases and the effects it has on development. They finally identified eight causes, several root causes for over-scoping, and nine possible effects on software-release planning. They found out that scoping poses a challenge to RE and is a project management risk. The results indicate that a risk of over-scoping is mainly caused by the market-driven domain and the management of a continuous inflow of requirements. Bjarnason & al. [20] suggest that a combination of low involvement of development-related roles in the early phases of project development and a lack of awareness of project goals may lead to over-scoping. Quality issues, delays and customer dissatisfaction are examples of the negative and somewhat expensive effects of over-scoping. Worse yet is that an organisation may end up being stuck with the 'never-ending' cause-root-cause cycle of over-scoping. Agile practices has been proposed to ease the challenge of over-scoping, however, this case showed that over-scoping remains a PM issue even if agile RE practices are applied [20].

Screening Process. The idea of a screening process is to quickly assess each new requirement to decide whether it is worth spending more time on it or not [7]. An efficient screening process ensures that resources are mainly used for those requirements that should be finally implemented [9]. A corresponding approach to screening is requirement triage [21] which has been adopted from the medical discipline.

Ebert [22] divides product development processes into two main categories; 1) upstream processes, which include phases prior to a project launch and 2) downstream processes, which cover the definition and execution of development projects. The RE process is seen to last throughout the project lifecycle.

Currently, there are several RE process models described in the literature [9], [23]. It has been drawn parallels between RE and RP and processes including similar tasks has been differently renamed. However, it has been reported that there is a gap between scientific the view on RE and the one actually used in practice [23].

Release Planning. The purpose of the software RP process is to select and assign features to be delivered in a sequence of consecutive product releases, while ensuring that constraints such as resources and budget are met. A good release plan should 1) provide maximum business value through the best possible set of features implemented in the right sequence of releases, 2) satisfy the most important stakeholders, 3) be feasible in terms of available resources and 4) reflect existing dependencies between features. [24] RE and RP are decision-rich processes that play a critical role in the success of software projects [1]. Typically, there are too many requirements proposed compared with what can be reasonably included in a release [25], therefore requirements need to be prioritised. Deciding which requirements should get high priority is not a straightforward task, since requirements are often incomplete at the beginning of their life cycle and relevant stakeholders have divergent expectations and priorities in terms of requirements. In addition, it is not clear to managers what the relationship between the set of requirements is and that effort the implementation would take. [26]

3   Research Process – Case Study Design

The case study was designed as a collaborative effort between researchers and a representative from the case company. The objective of the company was to improve the efficiency of the RS process in a VLSRE context. Since theoretical contributions on VLSRE are scarce, an exploratory study was initiated. The objective of the case was to understand the root of the identified shortcomings relating to the RS process and to discover the means for improving the RS process. To accomplish the objective, it was agreed that a state-of-the-practice description would be provided along with the challenges faced by practitioners during the RS process. Naturally, any empirical findings ought to be discussed in relation to the existing scientific literature. To reach the objective, two goals were defined: first, aim was to describe how the case company carries out the RS process to manage the large number of incoming requirements efficiently; and second, to explore and define the challenges facing PM during the RS process.

The case study was chosen as an applicable research method for studying the process as a contemporary phenomenon in a real-life context. In addition, interviewing was chosen as a primary data collection method as it provides direct contact with informants and lends control over data collection to the researchers. [17]

Case and Subjects Selection. The RS process is run by PM in the case company. Four PMs, who had an extensive knowledge about the RS process and experience of different roles in the company, were chosen to be interviewed. In addition, the chosen interviewees covered the most business critical products in the company. The voluntary interviewees were located in three different European countries (cf.Table 1). The interviews were conducted over the phone and they lasted from 85 to 110 minutes.

Data Collection Procedures. The data were collected using semi-structured thematic interviews [27]. The chosen interview themes were 1) the RS process in general, 2) information handled during the RS process, 3) requirement analysis procedures and 4) decision-making practices. Interviews were carried out confidentially and they mainly followed the structure of the questionnaire. The interviewers also asked additional questions to get a more in-depth understanding and the interviewees were allowed to thoroughly explain issues related to the themes. Researchers worked under a non-disclosure agreement (NDA) and the data were handled anonymously to ensure rich authentic data. In addition to the interviews, other data sources were used. Moreover, company's internal documents (such as process descriptions and example requirements, and workshop notes) were used to complement the interview data and studied the literature.

Table 1. Interview background data

Int.	Position	Role in RS process	RS tasks
A1	Senior system specialist	Requirement analyst (mainly technical role)	Analysing and issuing requirements; Answering customers' technical questions; Creating documentation for decision-making
A2	PM	Release PM; Requirement analyst	Analysing requirements; Release planning; Tool support
A3	Product specialist	Local RS process coordinator; Requirements management	Coordinating requirements management; Administrating SW licensing
A4	System PM	Local RS process coordinator; System manager; Tool support	Issuing requirements; Works on feasibility of the features; Acts as an interface between two business lines

Analysis Procedures. Interviews were transcribed by third party professionals and subjected to analysis. The analysis implied coding of interview transcripts and drawing conclusions which reflect the research objectives. A software tool (NVivo) for qualitative research was utilized during the data analysis.

Validity Procedures. The validity of the results was considered throughout the study by utilizing the several approaches to ensure solid bases for analysis and for drawing a conclusion. The evaluation of validity is further discussed in 4.3.

4   Data Analysis and Results – RS Process and Challenges

This chapter provides a rich view of the RS process and lists challenges in the case company based on analysis of the interview data, company confidential documentation and workshop notes. The RS process is characterized in subsection 4.1 as a case company-specific practice for processing requirements in the context of VLSRE. The challenges are presented in the subsection 4.2. The results are explained including quotes from transcripts and interpretations from coding and analysis. Due to the limited number of interviewees, the quotes are not identified in any way to protect the integrity of the interviewees.

4.1   RS Process Description

Over the years, the RS scale has changed, the number of products and requirements per requirement screening team (RST) has multiplied and the number of requirement engineers has increased. For example, one product specific RS process receives about 1,100 completely new requirements per year and its database contains around 7,000 requirements. Another RS process example:

'Earlier we had two main products, half less requirements engineers in product management and a process coordinator. But now we have in reality six products, half more people, a process coordinator and the number of requirements has been doubled.'

The RS process is a globally-defined company-specific methodological response to requirements processing challenges in the context of VLSRE. The RS process is one of several interconnected processes that together cover the RE process phases in the case company. Compared to the process definition presented in [22], the RS process starts from the upstream process side, but does not cover all of its activities. On the other hand, the RS process still continues in the downstream process side, but again does not cover all of the activities there. The RS process interacts as a daily practice with processes related to customer, market, development, etc. The process illustration shown in Fig. 1 is based on the company's process documentation and data received from the interviews.

The RS process is supported with a common tool (cf. Fig. 1), which corresponds to the process. The tool is used for initiating new requirements, storing requirement data, managing the status of decisions and tracking process performance. The tool is a commercial tool, but its installation is very much tailored according to company specific needs. Furthermore, the process and the tool have been slightly tailored for most of the products. The RS process follows a step-by-step approach and consists of three analysis phases and one follow-up phase. Each analysis phase is described as a list of tasks and criteria for the subsequent decision points (DP1, DP2 and DP3) of each phase.

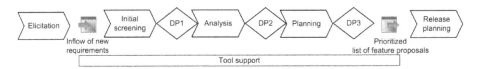

Fig. 1. The case company's RS process

Some RSTs consider that the task lists are too long to be followed and that the process is too complex for their needs. Thus, RSTs may not follow the process precisely for every requirement. Practically, initial screening and analysis phases may be partly or totally bypassed. For example, high-priority customer requirements are often processed using an informal fast track. In the fast track, the requirements are quickly assigned to a release for implementation. R&D teams utilize agile methodologies and some of the RSTs have started to follow R&D's example. However, the agile methodologies are not supported by the defined RS process. From the agile perspective, multiple analysis phases create waste because new requirements are just kept in the system waiting for the next analysis phase. Although the RS process is globally well-defined, we identified several challenges both concerning the process as a whole and its core activities. These challenges shall be further discussed in the subsequent sections.

4.2   The Identified Challenges in RS Process

The identified challenges are explained in relation to the RS process phases starting from the vast number of new incoming requirements and ending up with global tool issues.

C1 – A Large Number of New Requirements. New requirements ought to be communicated to the RS process from the elicitation step using the common tool. In practice, very often new requirements and further clarifications are communicated in an informal manner such as e-mails, phone calls and offline discussions.

'We are gathering these requirements and receiving this information practically just via e-mails.'
'... it is quite a lot coffee, phone and e-mail.'

Informal communication is one of the factors that cause shortcomings in the quality of requirement information content. For example e-mail discussions may last for several weeks, parts of discussions may be lost, and thing are forgotten, all of which can lead to incomplete data and pose challenges to traceability.

Usually, the stakeholders who elicit customer requirements are not technical experts and their strength is in understanding customer relationships and the market situation. For this reason, it cannot be expected that they could provide detailed technical argumentation when a new requirements are issued.

According to the interviewees, new requirements are quite often issued based on a customer's claim that a competitor is offering certain functionality. In such cases, a PM needs to contact the requirement initiator to start discussions with the customer team in order to understand the technical details of the requirement and to verify that the claim is justified.

The common tool provides a standardized form to issue new requirements. However, the form is considered too complicated since customer contact teams are not able to deliver all of the information required by the form.

The case company may consider implementation of new customer-specific requirements, if the customer is committed to purchasing the functionality. However, ensuring customer commitment is rather challenging for PM in spite of activities under taken to improve the situation?

C2 – Initial Screening. The principal idea behind initial screening is that each incoming requirement is assessed within a few hours. Based on this quick evaluation, only the most promising requirements which provide value for the company and its customers should pass the DP1. More effort should be put into analysis only if a value potential is identified. If value is not identified, the requirement is rejected for the time being. However, most of the time, decisions need further clarification with customer teams.

The starting point for the RS process is always gaining a correct understanding of what a customer really wishes for. Reaching consensus requires a lot of communication between the PM, the customer team and the customer since information on a new requirement is never complete and it may even be unreliable. The requirements quite often change during customer communications. In addition, discussions may conclude that it is not reasonable to implement the required functionalities. Some of the bottlenecks during initial screening are due to the lack of information about a world market, the impact of rejecting the requirement and potential alternatives to offer.

There are several sources providing necessary data and various places to seek it. The customer teams ought to have the best understanding about the customers' business, the criticality of the requirement for the customer and the market situation in the area. Thus, customer teams are the primary source for customer specific data. A considerable amount of material is available for internal use, mainly free-form MS Office documents. However, it is rather time-consuming to find what is needed from the huge databases. Even though a great number of reports are prepared, some are not accessible. For example, a competitor assessment is done regularly, but not delivered for PM use. According to interviewees, some of the material is considered highly sensitive. Thus, strict access control of the material is necessary in order to avoid the risk of leaking material to competitors.

C3 – Analysis. In addition to understanding the customer's needs, requirements need to be analysed to determine their impact on implementation from a technical perspective and their value from a business perspective. The analysis includes clarifying technical uncertainties and finding the best implementation alternative, estimating cost and effort required, defining the added value for the customer or market, and business value for the case company. Clearly, in order to complete this analysis, a great deal of information needs to be gathered.

Value Analysis. The feasibility of a requirement is defined by comparing the market situation and business value with what is necessary in order to implement the requirement.

> '...to put it shortly, the RS process starts with the value analysis, that is what is the value for a customer and for us.'

The company prices its features based on the cost and the added value it ought to bring for customers. In most cases it is not easy to assess the added value even if the case is clear in a technical sense including some kind of cost analysis. The main challenge is that implementation and business benefits will only be finally realized years after the requirements' initiation. In addition, the PM may never see the final business performance for each release. Financial data is not available on feature level at all.

Technical Analysis. The starting point for analysis is a technical description of the problem, that the customer wants to solve, and a specification for the customer's installation. For example, does the customer require completely new functionality or is it a change to an existing installation, and how is the customer's system configured?

> 'Of course when you receive a new requirement, just because of our experience, I think in one or two hours you are able to categorize it into three categories: it's just some kind of customization so it is a minor work, it's a medium one, or you know that there are several interworkings and it will really require detailed specification.'

R&D prepares a detailed technical analysis for PM use. The analysis is not a trivial task, since in most cases there are many different implementation alternatives that could fulfill the customer's requirement. Certain alternatives might be flexible, but they would cost more while others might be less flexible but cheaper to develop. PMs find it challenging that it takes such a long time to get the detailed technical analysis and effort estimations from R&D.

Dependencies. Managing product dependencies is considered a demanding task. Typically, in the case of mature products, new requirements have more dependencies on other products as well as impacts on other elements of a product. PMs are not always able to identify the dependencies that the changes in the product would cause to other interrelated products.

The current RS process does not support the documentation and management of product dependencies across business lines as PM would like. Thus, several varying practices for different products have emerged. As an example, an interviewee has personally consolidated information about all dependencies between two business lines and maintains the list of requirements issued by business line A to business line B. Another more detailed approach that is applied is to list the dependencies of a product against products from other business lines. The challenge is that all these documents are offline documents and a business line-specific approach is not covered by the process. According to interviewees, exchanging information between products in different business lines is a complex issue.

Time Constraint. One major issue is that one PM has many requirements to process concurrently. Thus, the time that may be spent on analysing individual requirement is a significant limitation to screening. According to the interviews, it is hard to find the time necessary for thorough value analysis since much of the daily working time is spent on 'running the business' (meetings, e-mails, phone calls, etc.) and other similar tasks.

> *'I too receive inquisitive e-mails; those are more technical questions such as how a feature could be activated. These I receive quite a lot.'*

The restricted time per requirement also affects the quality of the data fed into the tool. PMs collect, use and have information, but they do not necessarily record it into the tool, even though it is dictated by the process description that all requirement information should be held in one defined place.

> *Usually it happens so that shade shortcuts are taken and proper care is not taken that the quality of the data is constantly valid in the tool'*

C4 – Planning, Decision-Making and Prioritisation. In principle, DP1 and DP2 decisions are either accept, reject/ postpone or clarify. If a requirement fulfills the accept criteria, it goes to the next phase for further analysis. The decision 'clarify' means that the requirement is sent back to the previous handler to be elaborated or to provide additional information. In case a requirement does not get high priority, it will either be rejected or postponed to be implemented in some future release. Rejection reasons for the requirement are, for example, 'out of the scope of product' and 'requires years of implementation to be fulfilled'. The criteria for priority-setting during the RS process are based, for example, on customer size, monetary value, business value for the company, known risks and generic priority based on the priority feedback from customer teams. PM faces three major challenges related to decision-making and prioritisation:

Negotiation. If the PM decides to reject the requirement, the negotiation challenge may be to reach consensus between the customer and the company. Negotiations are difficult, since the customer is usually disappointed with a negative decision and they might be frustrated after waiting for months to receive the decision. During this phase, considerable communication skills are required to seek alternative solutions or to maintain a good customer relationship in spite of the negative decision. In some cases, common understanding about the situation is not reached which leads to a situation where the PM has no other choice but to keep the requirement in the tool, even though they see no point of fulfilling it in the near future.

Priorities. At first, a major challenge is to define priorities for each requirement during the RS process since the goal is to send the most valuable set of requirements for RP. Second, the priorities for requirements that have been planned for implementation need to be managed. The priority of candidates is checked once again during RP, taking into account available release resources and the urgency of the selected requirements.

Decision Rationale. Core activity for PMs during the RS process is using and producing information. Currently, a considerable amount of time is used seeking missing pieces of information to complete analysis. On the other hand, product PM has to follow tight decision schedules. Together, these two issues mean that the PM (under heavy time pressure) sometimes has to make decisions based on incomplete information even though valuable information could be available.

C5 – Overloaded Releases. Initial screening and analysis could be done quickly. However, the interviews indicate that the planning phase and implementation are not able to keep the schedule accordingly. During the planning phase, defining the business value of a requirement, as well as (re-)prioritisation, takes way too long compared with the first two phases. In addition the implementation queue of features for the forthcoming releases is so full that a new requirement may be in waiting mode for months or even years in the worst cases.

> *'...once we piloted the case by putting small, similar implementation existing and obvious implementation requirements in the front of the queue, but there was no sense in continuing since the following phases failed to perform equally.'*

After feature proposals have been chosen during the RS process, an RP process starts. In the case company, RS and RP processes are separated, but in practice the processes are often intertwined at the terminological, task and mental level. PM, which has responsibility for the RS process, also participates in RP.

> *'At the very beginning, new requirements are often assigned for realization in an appropriate release. This is a kind of release planning done during the RS.*

C6 – Tool Support. Interviewees indicate that the RS process descriptions and tool installations are not necessarily kept up-to-date which poses a challenge. In addition, the tool is considered more as a common place to store requirement information than a tool to facilitate the process. Despite expectations, the challenge remains that the tool does not adequately support actual requirement analysis, identification and management of requirements' dependencies as well as information content evolvement during the RS process. From a technical viewpoint, the tool is considered not reliable enough, unbearably slow and not well-integrated into the overall process landscape of the case company. In addition, the tool is not as straightforward as it had been prior to recent changes. The work efficiency of RS has suffered considerably since a restructured tool has increased the need for manual feeding of requirement data from one place to another.

4.3   Discussion

The following table summarises the findings of the conducted exploratory case study connecting them with the empirical data and the studied literature.

Table 2. Data synthesis

Ch	Conjecture
C1 A Number of New Reqs.	Previous studies [8], [9] have shown that continuous inflow of an immense number of requirements is mainly caused by MDSWD. It has been reported that an increasing number of requirements stress PM in RE and RP tasks [19] and new ways to manage requirement databases are needed [10]. The case study presented in the paper also shows that a large organisation, which applies a feature-oriented release-based approach when developing features for individual customers or global markets, has challenges in managing the constant inflow of requirements. The case company uses the globally well-defined RS process and the PMs have a clear understanding of the objectives of the RS process. In addition, R&D experts are engaged early in the process, and yet the case company has not been able to fully tackle the over-scoping issue. This finding is contradictory to that reported in [20]. The conjecture is that C1 leading to over-scoping should be addressed from the very beginning of the RS process by developing a standardized form for eliciting requirements systematically from all stakeholders. Thus, the template should provide the appropriate requirements architecture [10] for each phase of the RS process. It should tackle the challenge of too much 'wrong' information versus the lack of 'right' information.
C2 Init.Screen.	The RS process should work by following the principles of requirement triage [21]. However, the information received rarely enables fast screening and typically, a lot of time is lost looking for missing information (C2). The time could be shortened, e.g., by providing market relevance information already along the requirement, and by implementing a proper template for initiating requirements [28] so that it covers the information PM needs at least in the initial screening and it explicitly differentiates between mandatory and optional fields.
C3 Analysis	Maximizing the value that is gained through implementation of a software release is essential for an ICT organisation in the current competitive market situation. How successful an organisation is in value creation greatly depends on PMs' ability to understand the relationships between technical and business aspects. The task is by far not an easy one and the alignment of product, project and business decisions has been seen as a major challenge in the software industry. [16] In the case PMs clearly struggle with defining potential value in relation to market and investment costs (C3). The situation could be improved by providing a means to get the necessary effort estimations earlier for PM use. The estimations could be used as screening-out or prioritisation criteria. Another great improvement would be systematically collecting data on the financial performance of each release. This information could then be utilized when planning future releases. However, the effects of such a practice are not visible in the short term.
C4 Plan.,Decisions,Priorit.	There are two key factors what comes to setting priorities for requirements during the RS process: 1) the content of requirements is not comparable as such and 2) performing all pairwise comparisons is practically impossible due to the number of requirements (C4). The issue of combinatorial explosions has been reported earlier in relation to quality predictions [3], but based on the case study presented, it is clearly an issue for any type of requirement. RE is seen on the one hand as an organisational activity since it should dictate what requirements will be implemented in products and on the other hand it is considered as a project activity when implementation takes place [1]. This dualism of RE is also visible in the RS process, but it concerns requirement prioritisation; during the RS process, requirements are set in order as a preferred list, but RP and implementation will ultimately set the implementation order.

Table 2. (*continued*)

C5 Overl.Releases	As a result of insufficient screening out of requirements, releases are heavily overloaded, the planned 30 per cent buffer for urgent high priority requirements is not realized and implementation is delayed (C5). Similar challenges, as well as root causes for them, have also been reported in [8], [19], [20]. Based on the case at hand, it is concluded that a double role for PM in the RS process and RP may jeopardize the goal of the RS process, since there is a temptation to trim the edges of the process. This issue is evident in the case of urgent customer requirements which bypass the RS process and go directly to release. In urgent cases analysis is rather light or even skipped, so it is possible that impacts on other requirements are realized as late as during RP or even during implementation.
C6 T.S.	The utilized tool(s) should be one of the major enablers for communication during RE. The current configuration of the global tool does not meet PM needs (C6). The means to enhance the tool could include adding services such as those proposed in [28], [29], [30].

Evaluation of Validity. *Trustworthiness* of the results was addressed from the beginning of the study using several methods. For *construct validity*, the questionnaire was developed *iteratively*. The first draft of the questionnaire was developed based on notes from a workshop with the case company representatives. This version was later updated based on comments from senior researchers and the company's feedback. Senior researchers were also present during the first interview to observe whether the interviewee understood the questions as they were intended. As a result, minor change in the wording of one question was made.

For *reliability*, strategies like representativeness, researcher effects, triangulation, and feedback from informants were considered [31]. For *representativeness* the interviewees worked in the RS process, acting in different roles, which covered the main roles in the RS process. A technical report about the findings of the case was sent for confirmation to the company representatives. The *researchers' effect* was mitigated by ensuring transparency; the interviewees were familiar with the topic and reasons of the study, as well as methods of the data collection and handling. In addition, the researchers had a long history of cooperation with the case company and thus had a solid understanding about the context of the case. Throughout the case, *different data sources* were used. Data triangulation was applied to verify the findings against several sources.

Since the study was exploratory in nature, the aim was not to examine or explain any causal relationships, *internal validity* aspects were not considered. Applying qualitative methods in a single case study has a weak generalization potential. Therefore, *external validity* is very restrictive and thus not considered.

The biggest *validity threat* in the case was the scarce number of interviews. That fact has been mitigated through above mentioned means and it can be stated with confidence the data and findings indeed represented the phenomenon under investigation.

5   Conclusion and Future Work

This industrial case study aimed to clarify a current practice for managing a constant high rate inflow of new requirements. The case study was conducted in a large globally operating systems provider which deals with software development in VLSRE. As a result of the study, the case description of the RS process is provided and those challenges faced by PM during the process are identified and analysed. The RS process consists of initial screening, analysis and planning phases to provide a prioritised list of feature proposals for RP. Major challenges in the RS process were: 1) the informal communication practices at the beginning of the process, which led to incomplete information;2) hindrance of efficient screening (often as a result of the first challenge); and 3) defining the value and priority for each requirement.

A constant high rate inflow of new requirements has been reported to be typical in the context of VLSRE. Previous studies have focused mainly on MDSWD, thus this case study provided insights to the developmental context, having characteristics of both MDSWS and CDSWD. Based on the results it can be stated that in the context of the case, PM faces both the phenomena of the constant inflow of new requirements and similar challenges to those reported earlier in MDSWD.

The biggest limitation in the case was the low number of interviewees. However, the interviewees were carefully chosen and their collective experience was more than sufficient to describe the phenomena studied. Therefore, the case should provide implications for any large ICT organisation which faces a constant high rate inflow of new requirements and wishes to investigate their relationship to other companies.

Future Work. As stated above, in conjunction with the identified challenges, some improvement possibilities have also been identified. Future research should investigate the means for a smoother transition from elicitation to the RS process and from RS to RP. An important challenge that PM faces during the RS process, is the management of requirement dependencies. In this case, the challenge is addressed by creating offline documents by individual PMs. Thus, future research should look for solutions to enable more efficient solutions to handle these issues. In addition, future studies should develop the information content of requirements in order to increase the efficiency of initial screening. This should tackle the challenge of overloaded releases, known also over-scoping.

Acknowledgements. The authors would like to thank the interviewees and the case company for their time and effort. This research has been supported by ITEA2 and TEKES – the Finnish funding agency for technology and innovation.

References

1. Aurum, A., Wohlin, C.: The Fundamental Nature of Requirements Engineering Activities as a Decision Making Process. Information and Software Technology 45, 945–954 (2003)
2. Carlshamre, P.: Release Planning in Market-Driven Software Product Development: Provoking an Understanding. Requirements Engineering 7(3), 139–151 (2002)

3. Regnell, B., Svensson, R.B., Wnuk, K.: Can we beat the Complexity of Very Large-Scale Requirements Engineering? In: Paech, B., Rolland, C. (eds.) REFSQ 2008. LNCS, vol. 5025, pp. 123–128. Springer, Heidelberg (2008)
4. Nattoch Dag, J., Regnell, B., Carlshamre, P., Andersson, M., Karlsson, J.: A Feasibility Study of Automated Natural Language Requirements Analysis in Market-Driven Development. Requirements Engineering 7(1), 20–33 (2002)
5. Bjarnason, E., Wnuk, K., Regnell, B.: Requirements are slipping through the gaps — A case study on causes & effects of communication gaps in large-scale software development. In: 19th IEEE International Requirements Engineering Conference (RE), pp. 37–46 (2011)
6. Regnell, B., Beremark, P., Eklundh, O.: A market-driven requirements engineering process: Results from an industrial process improvement programme. Requirements Engineering 3(2), 121–129 (1998)
7. Regnell, B., Karlsson, L., Höst, M.: An Analytical Model for Requirements Selection Quality Evaluation in Product Development. In: 11th IEEE International Requirements Engineering Conference, pp. 254–263 (2003)
8. Bjarnason, E., Wnuk, K., Regnell, B.: Are you biting off more you can chew? A case study on causes and effects of overscoping in large-scale software engineering. Information and Software Technology 54(10), 1107–1124 (2012)
9. Gorschek, T., Gomes, A., Pettersson, A., Torkar, R.: Introduction of a process maturity model for market-driven product management and requirements engineering. J. of Softw. Evol. and Proc. 24(1), 83–113 (2012)
10. Wnuk, K., Regnell, B., Schrewelius, C.: Architecting and Coordinating Thousands of Requirements – An Industrial Case Study. In: Glinz, M., Heymans, P. (eds.) REFSQ 2009 Amsterdam. LNCS, vol. 5512, pp. 118–123. Springer, Heidelberg (2009)
11. Soffer, P., Leah, G., Tsvi, K.: A Unified RE Approach for Software Product Evolution: Challenges and research agenda. In: Ralyté, Å.P.J., Kraiem, N. (eds.) Proceedings of Situational Requirements Engineering Processes, Paris (2005)
12. Potts, C.: Invented Requirements and Imagined Customers: Requirements Engineering for Off-The-Shelf Software. In: Proceedings of the Second IEEE International Symposium on Requirements Engineering (1995)
13. Wieringa, R.: Requirements engineering: frameworks for understanding. John Wiley & Sons (1996)
14. Sawyer, P., Sommerville, I., Kotonya, G.: Improving market-driven RE process. In: Oivo, M., Kuvaja, P. (eds.) International Conference on Product Focused Software Process Improvement, Oulu, vol. 195, pp. 222–236 (1999)
15. Bray, I.: An Introduction to Requirements Engineering, 1st edn. Addison Wesley (2002)
16. Barneya, S., Aurum, A., Wohlin, C.: A product management challenge: Creating software product value through requirements selection. Journal of Systems Architecture 5(6) (2008)
17. Runeson, P., Höst, M.: Guidelines for conducting and reporting case study method in software engineering. Empirical Software Engineering 14(22), 131–164 (2009)
18. Skoglund, M., Runeson, P.: Reference-based search strategies in systematic reviews. In: Proceedings of the 13th International Conference on Evaluation and Assessment in Software Engineering, pp. 31–40 (2009)
19. Bjarnason, E., Wnuk, K., Regnell, B.: Overscoping: Reasons and consequences — A case study on decision making in software product management. In: Fourth International Workshop on Software Product Management (IWSPM), pp. 30–39 (2010)

20. Bjarnason, E., Wnuk, K., Regnell, B.: A case study on benefits and side-effects of agile practices in large-scale requirements engineering. In: Proceedings of the 1st Workshop on Agile Requirements Engineering, New York (2011)
21. Davis, A.: The art of requirements triage. Computer 36(3), 42–49 (2003)
22. Ebert, C.: Requirements before the requirements: understanding the upstream impacts. In: 13th IEEE International Conference on Requirements Engineering, pp. 117–124 (2005)
23. Martin, S., Aurum, A., Jeffery, R., Paech, B.: Requirements engineering process models in practice. In: Proceedings of the Seventh Australian Workshop in Requirements Engineering, Melbourne (2002)
24. Ruhe, G., Saliu, M.: The Art and Science of Software Release Planning. Software 22, 47–53 (2005)
25. Karlsson, L., Thelin, T., Regnell, B., Berander, P., Wohlin, C.: Pair-wise comparisons versus planning game partitioning—experiments on requirements prioritisation techniques. Empirical Software Engineering 12(1), 3–33 (2007)
26. Ruhe, G., Eberlein, A., Pfahl, D.: Trade-Off Analysis for Requirements Selection. International Journal of Software Engineering and Knowledge Engineering 13(4), 345–366 (2004)
27. Gubrium, J., Holstein, J.: Handbook of Interview Research. Context & Method. Sage Publications, Thousand Oaks (2002)
28. Kelanti, M., Lehto, J., Aaramaa, S., Kuvaja, P.: A Practice for Recording Problem and Solution Domain Requirements in VLSRE. In: 38th EUROMICRO Conference on Software Engineering and Advanced Applications (SEAA), pp. 323–326 (2012)
29. Liang, P., Avgeriou, P., He, K., Xu, L.: From collective knowledge to intelligence: pre-requirements analysis of large and complex systems. In: Proceedings of the 1st Workshop on Web 2.0 for Software Engineering, Cape Town, pp. 26–30 (2010)
30. Boutkova, E.: Experience with Variability Management in Requirement Specifications. In: 15th International Software Product Line Conference (SPLC), pp. 303–312 (2011)
31. Miles, M., Huberman, M.: Qualitative data analysis: a sourcebook of new methods. Sage Publications (1984)

Who Cares About Software Process Modelling?
A First Investigation About the Perceived Value
of Process Engineering and Process Consumption

Marco Kuhrmann[1], Daniel Méndez Fernández[1], and Alexander Knapp[2]

[1] Technische Universität München, Faculty of Informatics, 85748 Garching, Germany
{kuhrmann,mendezfe}@in.tum.de
[2] Universität Augsburg, Institute of Informatics, 86159 Augsburg, Germany
knapp@informatik.uni-augsburg.de

Abstract. When it comes to designing a software process, we have experienced two major strategies. Process engineers can either opt for the strategy in which they focus on designing a process using an artefact model as backbone or, on the other hand, they can design it around activities and methods. So far, we have first studies that directly analyse benefits and shortcomings of both approaches in direct comparison to each other, without addressing the questions relevant to process engineers and which implications the selection of a particular design strategy has on the process consumption. We contribute a first controlled investigation on the perceived value of both strategies from the perspectives of process engineers and process consumers. While our results underpin the artefact-oriented design strategy to be an advantageous instrument for process engineers, process consumers do not evidently care about the selected design strategy. Furthermore, our first investigation performed in an academic environment provides a suitable empirical basis, which we can use to steer further replications and investigations in practical environments.

Keywords: Software processes, Software process modelling, Action research.

1 Introduction

Software process models are the glue that holds organisations, projects, and people together. They provide a blueprint of all relevant artefacts, activities, roles, and supporting entities necessary to implement a company-specific software process. The way of operating projects of different complexities, including its distribution, people, different cultures and application domains, is reflected in the complexity of today's software processes. This increases the demand to structure and implement software processes in a systematic manner, and to make the resulting process descriptions easily accessible and understandable to project participants. Consequently, one has to consider two basic perspectives on software processes: their design and their consumption.

To design a software process, process engineers face the choice between two major strategies: the *activity-oriented* strategy and the *artefact-oriented* one. The activity-oriented strategy concentrates on analysing the activities and methods applied in projects, and defining a software process on basis of the behaviour of project teams [17].

J. Heidrich et al. (Eds.): PROFES 2013, LNCS 7983, pp. 138–152, 2013.

The basic idea of artefact orientation, in turn, consists of concentrating on what has to be done rather than on how something has to be done. A software process is designed on the basis of an artefact model that defines a blueprint of the results to be created and, thus, it abstracts from the activities for creating the results by using particular methods and modelling notations.

For the last decade, we are investigating the shortcomings and the benefits of the two introduced strategies in direct comparison to each other [11]. Our findings indicate to the benefits of artefact orientation in order to support flexibility in the process, precision in the results, a standardised terminology among different project participants, or a systematic quality assurance. However, the industrial context of those case studies was always characterised by a given process defined and probably lived for years. People had certain expectations and needs regarding the instantiation of a process to efficiently organise and run a project, and to give guidance on how to create precise result structures during operations.

The still unsolved question remains whether the initial choice of a certain strategy matters for the process design and the process consumption if no expectations are present and which implications the choice has.

Problem Statement. Although we have deep knowledge on specific benefits and shortcomings of different software process models and the underlying paradigms when applying them at selected socio-economic contexts, we have still no knowledge which implications the choice of a particular strategy has for process engineers and process consumers independently of given expectations and experiences in same or similar contexts. The decision for one strategy or the other is, however, of critical importance as the maintenance and a re-design of a process model as part of a software process improvement initiative is a cost- and time-intensive endeavour.

Research Objective. We aim at investigating which implications the choice for a particular software process design strategy has for process engineers and process consumers. Our expectation is that the selection of a strategy does not affect the consumers' perceived value. To lay the foundation for a systematic investigation of this expectation, we describe a first controlled experiment to be further replicated in different contexts. In this experiment proposal, we compare the design strategies from the perspective of a process engineer and furthermore we investigate the users understanding of the particular outcomes. In summary, we define the research objective as follows:

We analyse	the selection of software process design strategies
for the purpose of	evaluation
with respect to	the perceived values
from the point of view of the	process engineers and the process consumers
in the context of	the process life cycle

Contribution. We contribute a controlled student experiment in which we analyse the perceived value of a given software process w.r.t. the strategy followed when designing and implementing it, as well as when consuming its deployed descriptions from the perspective of process consumers. The context of the study is the lecture "Software Engineering Processes", given at the Technische Universität München.

Our experiment compares one process and two representative software process frameworks (incl. software process meta models, authoring tools, and deployment infrastructures). We use both frameworks to analyse, conceptualise, and implement the given process in a tool-supported manner. We finally evaluate the deployed process documentations according to a fixed set of criteria by simulating an appraisal. We opt for the Eclipse Process Framework [4] as a representative of the activity-oriented paradigm and for the V-Modell XT framework [6] as a representative of the artefact-oriented paradigm. Inherited from the nature of a controlled experiment, we have to avoid any side effects to distort the aforementioned procedure, such as organisational cultures, the integration of the constructed process into an organisational structure and further aspects of process maintenance.

Outline. The paper is organised as follows. Section 2 introduces the fundamentals necessary for the study environment. We furthermore discuss related work, which gaps are left open, and how our contribution intends to close the gaps. In Sect. 3, we introduce the study design, and we present the results in Sect. 4. In Sect. 5, finally, we give a summary of conclusions, discuss the relation to existing evidence, the impact and limitations of the study, and planned future work.

2   Fundamentals and Related Work

In the following, we briefly discuss the fundamentals in terms of engineering software processes, and related work in the context of our investigation.

Software Process Design Strategies. For the context of this paper, we distinguish between two design strategies: activity orientation and artefact orientation. The activity-oriented strategy relies on the idea of defining a concrete process by a set of methods to be performed in a particular order by a specific set of roles. Each of the methods provides a construction procedure to combine description techniques [13]. The activity-oriented strategy is especially favoured in the area of (Situational) Method Engineering. For instance, Ralyté and Rolland [15] discuss an assembly-based approach in which pre-fabricated method chunks are combined. Method chunks shall comprise activities as well as artefacts. Since method engineering is still in the phase of discussing and consolidating the basic concepts, first proposals are made to introduce systematic modelling approaches, e.g. Brinkkemper and Saeki [2]. However, method engineering in general pays little attention to artefacts, which is reflected by the summary of method engineering concepts by Henderson-Sellers and Ralyté [7]. Beyond method engineering, current software process metamodels lay the foundation to develop arbitrary software processes. Prominent examples are software processes, which are based on the Software & Systems Process Engineering Metamodel (SPEM; [14]), such as the Rational Unified Process (RUP; [8]) or Hermes [3]. Still, although the importance of a well-defined artefact model is recognised in this area [5], artefacts are not in scope in available approaches. Braun et al. [1] mention that only 50% of the analysed approaches include an artefact description at all, while approaches that include an artefact description often reduce the artefacts to an optional outcome of the methods.

The activity-oriented strategy thereby does not provide assistance in the creation of precise result structures. In response to this situation, a new design strategy arose baptised as artefact orientation. The idea of the artefact-oriented strategy consists of defining a blueprint of all artefacts that are an (intermediate) result of a project. At project level, the actual process is then defined by agreeing on a set of artefacts to be created by particular roles and to be delivered when reaching particular milestones. The diversity in the process definitions is thereby reduced to the dependencies among the artefacts themselves without having to take into account the complexity of differing processes and detailed workflows. Artefact-oriented approaches are thereby meant to guide in the creation of precise results while offering the necessary flexibility during their creation by avoiding to dictate concrete methods. A detailed discussion on both strategies can be taken from [12].

Comparative Evaluations and Studies. There exist, to the best of our knowledge, barely studies that empirically evaluate both previously introduced strategies to design and implement a software process in direct comparison. We conducted such a study on the application of an artefact-based requirements engineering approach in direct comparison to an activity-based approach previously used in an industrial environment [11]. We could show, for example, an increase in the flexibility of the process and the syntactic quality of the created artefacts when relying on artefact orientation. However, as stated in Sect. 1, our focus lied on an industrial context with practitioners' expectations and experiences shaped for years in that context. So far, we could gain data that shows advantages of the artefact-oriented design strategy when narrowing down the context to a particular discipline, but at the cost of analysing the overall software process life cycle.

To investigate the perceived value of a particular strategy taking into account the overall life cycle of a process while controlling potential side-effects given by aforementioned expectations and experiences, a controlled experiment is yet necessary. The paper at hand reduces this gap by contributing the design for such a controlled experiment as well as first results.

3   Research Design

We organise the experiment's design according to [16]. After defining the goal and the research questions, we describe the case and subject selection. Finally, we describe how we collect and analyse the data, before discussing the validity procedures.

3.1   Research Questions

As stated in Sect. 1, we investigate which implications the choice of a particular software process design strategy has for process engineers and for consumers. To this end, we formulate a working hypothesis in accordance with our expectation that the selection of a particular design strategy has no impact on the consumers' perceived value:

WH: *The selection of a design strategy for establishing an effective process management does not affect its actual consumption.*

Since we initiate experimentation on this hypothesis, we opt for a case-study-like action research approach to capture the domain of interest and to get initial data. To this end, we formulate two research questions that shall investigate the perceived value of the artefact-oriented and the activity-oriented strategy taking first the perspective of a process engineer into account and then taking the perspective of a process consumer.

RQ 1: *How suitable is the used design strategy to cover the needs of process engineers when analysing, designing, and implementing a process?*
    The first research question considers the analysis of the strengths of one strategy to another when constructing a process. This construction covers the analysis of a process, its conceptual design, and its tool-supported implementation.

RQ 2: *To what extent does the used strategy matter for process consumers when interpreting the resulting process documentation?*
    Once we constructed a process (and rated the strategies for their support during the construction), we want to know which strategy better supports the application of the generated process documentation from a consumer's perspective.

3.2 Case and Subject Selection

The choice of the software process frameworks is opportunistic. We need, however, to ensure that the following prerequisites are fulfilled:

1. The software process framework has to be based on a metamodel representing either the activity-based strategy or the artefact-based one.
2. The software process framework has to offer a tool infrastructure that allows for the implementation and export of a process.

As example process to be implemented with the framework, we opt for a process that reflects the complexity of a "real life" process and that offers enough information for the process engineers to realise the process.
    Regarding the subjects involved in the study, we define two groups. The *process engineer* is responsible for realising the process and to rate the realisation. The *process consumer* is exclusively responsible for evaluating the created process documentation without any insights into the construction of the process.

3.3 Data Collection Procedure

Figure 1 depicts an overview of the data collection procedure. We set up the study as part of our lecture "Software Engineering Processes" [9] in the winter term 2011/2012. Two groups of students of roughly the same size were assigned to the particular strategy (artefact or activity orientation). Each student group then conducted three workshops with fixed time frames for analysing, for conceptualising, and for implementing the process in a tool-supported manner. The last session of the lecture considered the evaluation of the results where the students changed their role to the one of a process consumer for evaluating also the process documentation created by the other team. In the following, we explain each step of the data collection in detail.

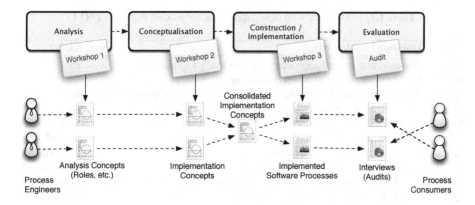

Fig. 1. Overview of data collection procedure

Analysis Workshop. The analysis comprehends two sessions in which a given scenario is analysed. The scenario is a real-life process model of a special interest group of the German Computer Society[1]. In the first session, two student groups analyse the particular sources for stakeholders to infer the basic roles. The roles are collected, structured, and prepared for discussion. In the second session, the students analyse either the process elements or the artefacts, depending on the group assignments.

Conceptualisation Workshop. In the second workshop, the two student groups discuss the analysis results; one group gets the material for the artefacts as input, the other group gets the overall process, including milestone structures and an assignment to a set of activities, as input. The students then switch to the conceptualisation and create first platform-independent artefact and process models.

The outcome of the analysis and conceptualisation workshops are synthesised into an integrated concept. This step is done by the supervisors to get consistent conditions during the construction workshop supporting for comparable outcomes during the evaluation. To this end, the students are provided with a set of consolidated spread sheets and a requirements document for the realisation. Furthermore, the supervisors prepare the technical infrastructure in terms of creating (Subversion) repositories and bare process templates for the students to start with.

Construction Workshop. In the construction workshop, the students are initially introduced into the consolidated concept. Two implementation groups are formed and in

---

[1] Available at: http://www.vorgehensmodelle.de (in German).

each group one student takes the lead. The first group uses the Eclipse Process Framework to implement the process and the second group uses the V-Modell XT framework, respectively. During the construction, the supervisors assist the students with discussion w.r.t. modelling techniques, in general, and concrete design decisions, in particular. Presentations of the groups' outcomes conclude the construction workshop.

Table 1. Questionnaire with closed questions for process engineers (RQ 1)

No.	Question (condensed)	Aspect
Q1-2	The used tool and the approach were intuitively applicable.	Tool
Q1-3	I got familiar with the tool and could implement all process elements.	Tool
Q1-5	The tool was suitable to implement the process with minimal overhead.	Tool
Q1-6	I was aware of every decision and its consequences.	Tool
Q1-7	The process documentation could be created appropriately.	Tool
Q1-8	I could implement all process elements.	Methodology
Q1-9	I could implement all designed roles.	Methodology
Q1-10	I could implement all designed artefacts.	Methodology
Q1-11	I could implement all designed relationships among roles and artefacts.	Methodology
Q1-12	I could implement all designed activities.	Methodology
Q1-13	I could implement the designed overall process.	Methodology
Q1-14	I could always create an export of the model (process documentation).	Tool
Q1-15	I could perform all required tasks for the implementation.	Tool
Q1-16	I was always able to identify and check the model consistency.	Tool

Table 2. Quewith closed questions for process consumers (RQ 2). Considered aspect is the process documentation only.

No.	Question (condensed)
Q2-1	The information in the export is easy to access.
Q2-2	The information in the export is easy to access for non-familar users.
Q2-3	The overall process is clearly presented and provides a good overview of all elements.
Q2-4	The export supports the analysis of consistency.
Q2-5	All expectations were met and all designed concepts were appropriately implemented.
Q2-6	All designed roles were implemented.
Q2-7	All designed artefacts were implemented.
Q2-8	All designed relationships between roles and artefacts were implemented.
Q2-9	All designed activities were implemented.
Q2-10	The designed overall process was adequately implemented.
Q2-11	The process model is consistent.

Evaluation Session. The final step of the experiment considers the evaluation of the designed and implemented processes. The evaluation consists of two steps, both using a given questionnaire:

1. Self-assessment of the produced process documentation taking the perspective of a process engineer (Table 1)
2. Audit of the process documentation of the other group taking the perspective of a process consumer (Table 2)

In the self-assessment, the students rate their own work with a particular focus on the used tool and followed methodology. For the assessment and the audit, questionnaires with closed and open questions are made available (see Table 1 with the condensed, closed questions for the assessment and Table 2 for the audit). We are especially interested in the closed questions to rate and compare given strategies. Each of the closed questions considers the rating of one particular criterion against a given statement in a scale ranging from 0 ("I strongly disagree") to 7 ("I strongly agree").

3.4   Analysis Procedure

Due to the low number of samples (8 students), statistical (hypothesis) testing is not suitable. After collecting the data, we thus plot radar charts with the rankings given in the closed questions to qualitatively analyse the results and directly compare the results of the groups with each other.

4   Study Results

We first give a description of the case and the subjects and summarise, as a second step, the results w.r.t. the single research questions.

4.1   Case and Subject Description

Case – Process Frameworks. Since one part of the study is to implement a selected process, we select two software process frameworks and the corresponding authoring tools. The first chosen framework is the *Eclipse Process Framework* (EPF; [4]), the second framework is the German V-Modell XT [6]. Both frameworks are based on a metamodel supporting process modelling and structuring, as well as providing support for publishing processes to make the process accessible for the process users, and are of a maturity [10] that allows for using these frameworks in an experimentation setting. EPF is based on SPEM [14], an OMG specification, which is basically an UML profile for process engineering. The V-Modell XT is based on the *V-Modell XT Metamodel* [18], a metamodel that was specifically developed to create artefact-oriented processes.

Case – Process Model. The selected case is a process model given by the special interest group "Software Development Processes" of the German Computer Society. The process under consideration describes how the annual special interest group workshops are organised (including roles, activities, and milestones). Since the process was originally defined in the late 1990's, it evolved and got into an inconsistent state. Summarised, the process consists of a 20-page word document, an (incomplete) project plan of about 200 (hierarchal) activities, a set of templates, and a couple of Excel spreadsheets that contain checklists and further detailed information for certain tasks.

Subjects. The subjects are 8 students of the lecture "Software Engineering Processes" (winter term 2011/2012). As shown in Fig. 1, for each workshop the students are divided into two groups at the beginning of the particular workshops. For the analysis and conceptualisation workshops, the groups are formed at random. At the beginning of the construction workshop, the students are allowed to select a process framework themselves, which, in consequence, also defines the groups for the self-assessments and the audits.

The goals of the selected grouping procedure are that (1) each student should have the same basic knowledge about the considered process model, and that (2) each student should act in different roles—in the role *Process Engineer* during the analysis, conceptualisation, construction and self-assessment, and in the role *Process Consumer* during the audit.

4.2 Workshops

Three workshops are performed to analyse, conceptualise, and construct the process models (see Fig. 1). In this section, we show the results of each particular workshop.

Analysis Workshop. In the analysis sessions, the students analyse the given material to gather information about roles, artefacts, activities, and the basic process structure (i.e. artefact-role assignments). For those sessions, the students use creativity techniques for the elaboration (see Fig. 2) and are provided with pre-defined templates by the supervisors to structure the information. The outcomes of the analysis workshop are:

 – An unordered set of 37 roles and stakeholders
 – An unordered set of 32 artefacts
 – A list of more than 50 activities (partially inferred from the artefacts)

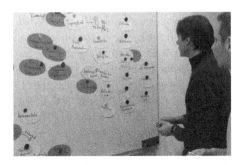

Fig. 2. Photo of the analysis workshop (elaboration of artefacts)

Fig. 3. Photos of the conceptualisation workshop (artefact and process structures)

Conceptualisation Workshop. The last analysis workshop session fades into the conceptualisation workshop in which the students need to aggregate all information. One group concentrates on artefacts and roles, structures and dependencies (Fig. 3, upper part), and the number of artefacts of a certain type being created. The second group focusses on the overall process structure that needs to be inferred from the activity structure, and the milestones (see Fig. 3, lower part). Since both groups exchange information, the second group also includes core artefacts to prepare a first mapping between the process elements leading to an overall process and its core workflows.

Since the outcomes are complex and heterogeneous, the supervisors boil down the outcomes to an integrated realisation concept that is the input for the construction workshop. The realisation concept is a 20-slide Powerpoint presentation that contains:

- The overall process, including the phases and top-level work packages
- A breakdown structure for each of the top-level work packages, including the core artefacts, fine-grained activities/workflows, and possible execution orders of the activities/workflows
- Information w.r.t. the dependency structure (between activities and roles, artefacts and roles, and so on)
- A consolidated set of 33 roles and stakeholders
- Consolidated artefact and activity sets
- Refined requirements for the construction

Construction Workshop. The construction workshop is a full-day event in which the students are at first introduced to the realisation concept. Afterwards, the two implementation groups are formed. To ensure that all groups have the same starting conditions, the supervisors prepare the coarse process template the students can start with. As outcomes, the students create:

- An EPF-based implementation of the process (5 students)
- A V-Modell-XT-based implementation of the process (3 students)

4.3 Evaluation (Audit)

The evaluation consists of two parts, according to our research questions. Figures 4 and 5 show the results of the self-assessment w.r.t. RQ 1 considering the two aspects *methodology* and *tool*. Figure 6 shows the results of the audit covering RQ 2. For the second evaluation, a questionnaire is used that requires the students to change their perspectives form the *Process Engineer* view to the *Process Consumer* view.

RQ 1:   Research question 1 considers the analysis of the strengths and limitations of one strategy compared with the other when constructing a process. This construction covers the analysis of a process, its conceptual design, and its tool-supported implementation. For the evaluation, we distinguish between the aspects *methodology* and *tool*. The first aspect thereby covers the approach to transfer an analysed process and to implement an analysed process in a given process framework. The ratings for the first aspect are shown in Tab. 3 and Fig. 4.

The ratings show that the artefact-oriented strategy behind the V-Modell XT provides better support for the transfer and implementation of its proclaimed basic process elements, i.e. roles, artefacts (work products), and relations/dependencies between the process elements. The questions Q1-9 (completeness of roles), Q1-10 (completeness of artefacts), and Q1-11 (completeness of relationships) have the maximum rating of 7, while the EPF framework especially suffers in the area of relations/dependencies (Q1-11: 6.2). Regarding the activity parts and the overall process, both frameworks provide comparable support for process engineers. Since EPF is basically built on the activity-oriented strategy, the framework better supports the implementation of activities and workflows and, in consequence, shows a higher rating for Q1-12 (completeness of activities), while the V-Modell XT only allows the implementation of one activity per work product, but does not support the design of workflows.

Regarding the overall process design, both frameworks do not allow for a straight-forward implementation, but require the process engineer to select one of the possible approaches to model the process (e.g., copied vs. referred capability pattern in EPF, or non-/hierarchical procedure modules in the V-Modell XT). The question whether the designed process could be easily implemented in general, is undecided with a slightly better rating for EPF (Q1-8, overall completeness: 6.2, to 6.0 for the V-Modell XT).

Table 3. Results for closed questions for process engineers (RQ 1, methodology)

No.	Rating EPF	Rating V-Modell XT
Q1-8	6.2	6.0
Q1-9	6.8	7.0
Q1-10	6.7	7.0
Q1-11	6.2	7.0
Q1-12	6.6	6.5
Q1-13	6.4	6.5

Table 4. Results for closed questions for process engineers (RQ 1, tool)

No.	Rating EPF	Rating V-Modell XT
Q1-2	4.4	5.5
Q1-3	4.8	4.0
Q1-5	4.8	3.5
Q1-6	4.6	6.0
Q1-7	6.6	4.0
Q1-14	5.4	6.5
Q1-15	5.8	6.0
Q1-16	5.0	2.5

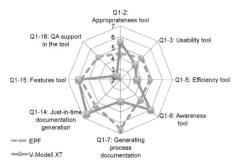

Fig. 4. Radar chart with the results for research question 1 (aspect: methodology)

Fig. 5. Radar chart with the results for research question 1 (aspect: tool)

The second aspect covers the appropriateness of the tool environment used for the realisation. The results are shown in Tab. 4 and Fig. 5. The results for the second aspect show that the EPF tool was easier to use for the process design in terms of usability (Q1-3), efficiency (Q1-5), generating process documentation (configurability, Q1-7), and quality assurance (Q1-16). While most of the subjects were familiar with the Eclipse platform and, thus, had a steeper learning curve w.r.t. technical details, the editor for the V-Modell XT is an expert tool on a fairly basic (technical) level. In consequence, the usability of the EPF tool is better, but the appropriateness (Q1-2) and the awareness

(Q1-6) are, due to the direct implementation, better. The data also shows that the just-in-time export of a process (Q1-14) was better rated for the V-Modell XT, while the flexibility of the export (Q1-7) was better rated for EPF.

RQ 2: Once the process is constructed, we want to know to which extent the design strategies support the usage of the generated process (documentation) from the consumers' perspective. The ratings of the second questionnaire are shown in Tab. 5 and Fig. 6.

Table 5. Results for closed questions for process user (RQ 2)

Question	Q2-1	Q2-2	Q2-2	Q2-4	Q2-5	Q2-6	Q2-7	Q2-8	Q2-9	Q2-10	Q2-11
Rating EPF	4.67	5.00	6.00	6.33	7.00	7.00	6.67	5.67	6.33	6.67	6.00
Rating V-Modell XT	4.20	3.80	3.00	4.00	5.20	6.00	6.20	4.40	3.80	4.75	4.67

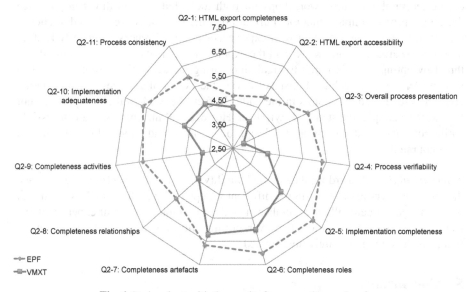

Fig. 6. Radar chart with the results for research question 2

The data show that for all questions the EPF-based process is better rated than the V-Modell-XT-based process. Significant questions are Q2-3 (overall process presentation – EPF: 6.0, V-Modell XT: 3.0) and Q2-9 (completeness of activities – EPF: 6.33, V-Modell XT: 3.80). Even regarding the completeness of the artefacts (Q2-7), the EPF-based process is better rated than the V-Modell-XT-based process (EPF: 6.67, V-Modell XT: 6.20). Referring to RQ 1, where the implementation capabilities w.r.t. artefacts and dependencies were rated better for the V-Modell XT (Q1-9 – Q1-11), the data does not underpin similar effects for the users of the process.

4.4   Evaluation of Validity

In this section, we evaluate our findings and critically review our study w.r.t. threats to validity.

Construct Validity. Regarding the construct validity, we cannot guarantee that the assessment criteria chosen in the questionnaire are complete enough to answer our research questions. The chosen criteria, however, rely on our experiences in the analysed design strategies (see, e.g. [12]) and were narrowly defined, whereby we consider this threat as a minor one. Regarding the process chosen as a case, we believe that it sufficiently covers the complexity of real-life processes.

Internal Validity. There are different threats to the internal validity we are aware of. For instance, the authors themselves have deep knowledge about the technical infrastructure of the V-Modell XT as they directly participated in its development. We minimised this threat by giving introductory talks about both infrastructures and serving as coaches during the implementation workshops for both tools, but without direct interference during the process implementation. Furthermore, the students were allowed to choose the framework on basis of their own experiences and preferences potentially leading to a bias towards the frameworks and the exported documentation. We minimised this threat by opting for a research triangulation during the evaluation. Another threat to be considered is that technical mistakes during the export of a process documentation could have distorted the results in the audit. In fact, the V-Modell XT export did not follow, for example, the standard stylesheet. However, all information were accessible while non-functional aspects in the design of the tools and exported documentation were not rated.

External Validity. Regarding the external validity, one major concern is that we have differing numbers of students in the different groups (EPF: 5 students, V-Modell XT: 3 students) and a generally low number of analysed samples. With our experiment, we cannot allow for generalisation. However, our intention was to get first insights into a field, which is, by now, barely investigated.

5   Conclusions

We conducted a controlled experiment in which a group of students analysed, conceptualised, implemented, and assessed a software process in a comparative manner. To investigate the perceived value of process modelling and process consumption, we selected two process frameworks covering the artefact-oriented and the activity-oriented strategy to design and implement the given process. Both process frameworks support the deployment of a designed process into the html-format, which we used to investigate the value from the perspective of process consumers. Our results indicate that the artefact-oriented strategy, implemented with the V-Modell XT framework, seems to be perceived of high value to serve process engineers. For example, the tool-supported realisation of an artefact model, role model, and explicitly defined relationships among those models is better supported by the artefact-oriented strategy. Still, our results do not show similar effects from the perspective of the process consumers. Even the artefacts' completeness and especially the responsibilities, e.g. relationships to roles, were rated to be better accessible using the activity-oriented framework.

Our findings imply that the assessment of a process design strategy in process crafting needs not to coincide with the perceived value of the resulting process (documentation) from the viewpoint of a process consumer. It may well be that the artefact-oriented approach accommodates better the request of process engineers for declarative goal-driven design—to "have something to talk about"—whereas process consumers prefer clear cut procedures.

Impact/Implications. We opted for a controlled experiment to explicitly simulate a context where, on the one hand, a pre-defined process was given, and, on the other hand, this given process was not implemented and maintained at all. That is, no particular strategy existed as it is often the case in industrial environments. This gave us the possibility to investigate the perceived value of a strategy without any distortion by given expectations and experiences. Inherited from the nature of a controlled experiment with a limited scope is the need to further replicate the study in other contexts.

The replication should further proof the current working hypothesis that the selection of a strategy for establishing an effective process management does not affect its actual consumption.

This will put us in the situation to empirically infer improvement goals, not only for software process meta models, but also for the process development environments, even already established ones such as EPF (see, e.g. Q1-15 and Q1-16).

Limitations. The experiment has several limitations that arise from the particular setting in which we performed the experiment without any side effects. The setting was characterised by limited time, a small number of participants and the choice of two representative process frameworks. Also, we did not cover all features provided by the frameworks that could have impacted the consumers' opinion, e.g., tailoring capabilities and project set-up. Hence, this first controlled experiment does not yet allow for generalisations of our results, but reflects our experiences in practical software process improvement endeavours and is therefore a first step into this direction.

Future Work. As future work, we plan to extend our experiment with further empirical studies to support for a long-term generalisation of the results. To this end, we (1) will conduct a survey to determine a taxonomy of characteristics important to process engineers and users, and (2) plan to perform further experiments with student groups involving several meta model-based frameworks to ground our data, before (3) extending our experiments to industrially hosted environments. Besides covering the engineering level, we need further investigation at the application level.

References

1. Braun, C., Wortmann, F., Hafner, M., Winter, R.: Method Construction — A Core Approach to Organizational Engineering. In: Proc. 20th ACM Symp. Applied Computing (SAC 2005), pp. 1295–1299. ACM (2005)

2. Brinkkemper, S., Saeki, M.: Meta-Modelling Based Assembly Techniques for Situational Method Engineering. Inf. Syst. 24(3), 209–228 (1999)
3. Confédération Suisse. The HERMES Method (2011), http://www.hermes.admin.ch
4. Eclipse Foundation. Eclipse Process Framework (EPF) (2010), http://www.eclipse.org/epf
5. Foorthuis, R., Brinkkemper, S., Bos, R.: An Artifact Model for Projects Conforming to Enterprise Architecture. In: Stirna, J., Persson, A. (eds.) PoEM 2008. LNBIP, vol. 15, pp. 30–46. Springer, Heidelberg (2009)
6. German Federal Ministry of the Interior. V-Modell XT. Definition and Documentation on the Web, http://www.v-modell-xt.de.
7. Henderson-Sellers, B., Ralyte, J.: Situational method Engineering: State-of-the-Art Review. J. Univ. Comp. Sci. 16(3), 424–478 (2010)
8. Kroll, P., Kruchten, P.B.: The Rational Unified Process Made Easy: A Practitioner's Guide to the RUP. Addison-Wesley (2003)
9. Kuhrmann, M., Méndez Fernández, D., Münch, J.: Teaching Software Process Modeling. In: Proc. 35th Int. Conf. Software Engineering (ICSE 2013), pp. 1138–1147. IEEE Computer Society (2013)
10. Kuhrmann, M., Méndez Fernández, D., Steenweg, R.: Systematic Software Process Development: Where Do We Stand Today? In: Proc. Int. Conf. Software and Systems Process (ICSSP 2013). ACM Press (in print, 2013)
11. Méndez Fernández D., Lochmann, K., Penzenstadler, B., Wagner, S.: A Case Study on the Application of an Artefact-Based Requirements Engineering Approach. In: Proc. 15th Ann. Conf. Evaluation and Assessment in Software Engineering (EASE 2011), pp. 104–113. IET (2011)
12. Méndez Fernández, D., Penzenstadler, B., Kuhrmann, M., Broy, M.: A Meta Model for Artefact-Orientation: Fundamentals and Lessons Learned in Requirements Engineering. In: Petriu, D.C., Rouquette, N., Haugen, Ø. (eds.) MODELS 2010, Part II. LNCS, vol. 6395, pp. 183–197. Springer, Heidelberg (2010)
13. Nuseibeh, B., Easterbrook, S.: Requirements Engineering: A Roadmap. In: Proc. 22nd Int. Conf. Software Engineering (ICSE 2000) — Future of Software Engineering Track, pp. 35–46. ACM (2000)
14. Object Management Group. Software and Systems Process Engineering Metamodel (SPEM) Specification v2.0. Technical Standard formal/2008-04-01, OMG (2008)
15. Ralyté, J., Rolland, C.: An Assembly Process Model for Method Engineering. In: Dittrich, K.R., Geppert, A., Norrie, M. (eds.) CAiSE 2001. LNCS, vol. 2068, pp. 267–283. Springer, Heidelberg (2001)
16. Runeson, P., Höst, M.: Guidelines for Conducting and Reporting Case Study Research in Software Engineering. Emp. Softw. Eng. 14(2), 131–164 (2009)
17. Tell, P., Babar, M.: Activity Theory Applied to Global Software Engineering: Theoretical Foundations and Implications for Tool Builders. In: Proc. 7th Int. Conf. Global Software Engineering (ICGSE 2012), pp. 21–30. IEEE Computer Society (2012)
18. Ternité, T., Kuhrmann, M.: Das V-Modell XT 1.3. Metamodell. Technical Report TUM-I0905, Technische Universität München (2009) (in German)

Modeling Variabilities from Software Process Lines with Compositional and Annotative Techniques: A Quantitative Study

Fellipe A. Aleixo[1], Uirá Kulesza[1], and Edson A. Oliveira Junior[2]

[1] Federal University of Rio Grande do Norte (UFRN),
Department of Computer Science and Applied Mathematics (DIMAP), Natal, RN, Brazil
uira@dimap.ufrn.br, fellipe.aleixo@ppgsc.ufrn.br
[2] State University of Maringá (UEM), Informatics Department (DIN),
Maringá, PR, Brazil
edson@din.uem.br

Abstract. A software process line (SPrL) represents a set of software process that share a common base of roles, practices, activities, and artifacts. Various individual approaches have been proposed to modeling software process lines. The majority of these approaches can be characterized as compositional or annotative approaches. This work presents a quantitative comparative study of the EPF Composer compositional approach, and the GenArch-P annotative approach. Our study has considered internal attributes of the specification of SPrLs, such as modularity, size and complexity. Our study has found that the GenArch-P approach presented better results in terms of size and complexity attributes, while the EPF Composer improve the modularity of SPrL specifications. We also envisioned a possible integration of the two approaches.

Keywords: Software process variabilities, Software process lines, Compositional and annotative approaches.

1 Introduction

A software process line represents a set of software processes that share a common base of roles, practices, activities, and artifacts. Each SPrL is structured to represent the similarities and variabilities across the instances of a family of related software processes [1]. The variabilities in SPrLs are related to high-level process features, such as [2] [3]: (i) the choice of a given level of a maturity model for software processes; (ii) the choice of a given technique for requirements specification; (iii) the choice of a style for software architecture documentation; or (iv) the choice for a given programming language or technology. Recent research work has explored the use and adaptation of consolidated software product lines techniques with the main aims of: (i) promoting the variability management of a software process family, and (ii) customizing and deriving a specific software process to answer the specialized demands of a given software development project.

J. Heidrich et al. (Eds.): PROFES 2013, LNCS 7983, pp. 153–168, 2013.

Many approaches have been proposed to the modeling of SPrLs [4] [5] [6] [7] [8] [9] [10]. These individual approaches can be grouped in terms of the modularization techniques used to organize the process elements. The compositional and the annotative approaches are the most outstanding. Since there are different approaches with the aim of specifying and modularizing variabilities in SPrLs, there is a strong need of development of empirical studies to evaluate these approaches and reveal their strengths and weaknesses.

This work is aimed at realizing a quantitative comparative study to evaluate both the compositional and the annotative approaches for modeling SPrLs. Similar studies have been conducted in the context of software product lines [11] [12] [13] [14]. In order to achieve this aim, we have modeled a large SPrL using the EPF Composer [15] and GenArch-P [8] [16] approaches, which represent the compositional and annotative techniques, respectively. After that, we quantified a metric suite to evaluate relevant attributes – such as, modularity, size and complexity – regarding the specification of the SPrL. Finally, we present the results obtained for each of the metrics, and discuss and confront them with the results of a previous qualitative study [2] [3].

The remainder of this document is organized as follows. Section 2 presents the study settings of our comparative study. Section 3 presents details on the modeling procedures of the target process line by the EPF Composer compositional approach, and the GenArch-P annotative approach. Section 4 presents the study results, with the analysis of each selected attribute for the study. Section 5 presents additional discussions about the results. Section 6 discusses the threats to study validity, and how they were treated. Section 7 discusses related work. Section 8 presents some conclusions and future work.

2   Study Settings

This section presents the study settings, in terms of: its main goal and research questions, its phases and assessment procedures, the adopted metrics suite, the modeling approaches of SPrLs, and the target process line to be modeled.

2.1   Study Goal and Research Questions

The GQM methodology [17] was used to structure our study. The main goal of the study was to compare (*purpose*) compositional and annotative techniques (*issue*) in the modeling of variabilities from software process lines (*process*), in the perspective of the users of these approaches (*viewpoint*). To achieve this goal, three research questions (RQ) were defined:

(i) RQ1 – which of the investigated techniques – compositional or annotative – provide better support to the modularization of SPrLs?

(ii) RQ2 – which of the investigated techniques can produce more concise SPrL specifications with respect to the number of process elements?

(iii) RQ3 – which of the investigated techniques can generate more complex SPrL specifications with respect to the amount of variability management mechanisms and the number of applications of these mechanisms in the modeling of a SPrL?

In order to provide answers for these research questions, we have adopted metrics to quantify the modularity, size and complexity internal attributes, respectively. The modularity attribute is measured through the amount of subsequent process elements associated with a specific process feature. The size attribute, on the other hand, is quantified by measuring the number of process elements used to specify a SPrL. Finally, the complexity attribute is measured through the number of the variability management mechanisms, and the amount of applications of these mechanisms in the modeling of a SPrL. These metrics are discussed in the Section 2.3.

2.2   Study Phases and Assessment Procedures

The study was realized in three main phases: (i) implementation of the target process line with the investigated approaches; (ii) the quantification of the metrics; and (iii) the analysis, discussions and conclusions about the metrics results. The definition of the target process line considered a previous study realized by our research group [2]. The modeling of the same SPrL with the investigated approaches was considered an evolution of the results made in our previous qualitative study [2]. To the assessment of the obtained results, each selected metric was quantified in order to identify: (i) which approach obtained better and inferior results considering the attributes under evaluation; and (ii) which were the identified causes and reasons for the obtained results. Finally, the obtained results and their conclusions were compared and confronted with the results of the previous study.

2.3   The Metrics Adopted in Our Study

After the completion of a previous comparative qualitative study [2], we feel the lack of quantitative results to improve the confidence of our conclusions. This was the main motivation for the development of this comparative quantitative study. We have adapted some metrics previously used in the context of empirical studies related to the design and implementation of software product lines [11] [12] [13] [14] to the context of SPrLs. They are based on three relevant attributes of the modeling of SPrLs: (i) modularity, (ii) size, and (iii) complexity.

The modularity attribute is concerned about the use of modular structures to isolate the process elements associated with a specific software process feature. The modularity of a SPrL is relevant because it can make easier the variability management. If an approach can modularize features with a reduced number of modular structures than other approach, it represents a better modular solution. A reduced number of modules can facilitate the understanding and management of them, and the access to the process elements specified in these modules.

The size attribute is concerned about the number of process elements involved in the modeling of a SPrL. It is important because large SPrL specifications are more difficult to understand and to manage. A high number of process elements increases the work of process engineers during the modeling of SPrLs.

The complexity attribute is related to the mechanisms used to specify software process variabilities. The usage of different kinds of mechanisms can bring difficulties to the comprehension and management of the specification. The usage of different mechanisms and the amount of individual application of these mechanisms during the modeling of SPrLs can contribute to increase the management of their complexity during their specification and maintenance. The Table 1 presents the defined metrics for each investigated attribute and a brief explaining of each metric.

Table 1. Adopted Metrics

Attribute	Metric	Meaning
Modularity	(1) Number of groupings of process elements associated with a specific feature	It counts the number of adjacent groups of process elements associated with a specific feature
Size	(2) Number of process elements	It counts the total number of process elements used to model the SPrL
Complexity	(3) Kinds of mechanisms used to specify software process variabilities	It counts the kinds of different mechanisms from each approach used to model software process lines
	(4) Number of usages of the software process variability mechanisms	It counts the number of usages of the variabilities mechanisms on the modeling of the SPrL

To evaluate the modularity of the investigated approaches, we have adapted a metric of separation of concerns [11] [18], previously used in several empirical studies in the context of software product lines and software systems, to be applied to SPrL specifications. It focuses on the interchange of group of process elements associated with a specific feature. A high number of alternated groups of process elements associated with different features becomes more difficult their management, due to the scattering of the process elements associated with a given feature.

The size of SPrL is quantified through the total number of process elements in the investigated specifications. Similar to the modularity metric, a high number of process elements in the SPrL specification also bring difficulties to specify and evolve it. Thus, the approach that presents the lowest result in this metric it is considered the best according to this criterion.

Two metrics were defined to evaluate the complexity of the modeling of a given SPrL: (i) the number of different mechanisms to model process variabilities; and (ii) the number of usage of these mechanisms during the modeling of the SPrL. Higher is the number of variability modeling mechanisms and the number of usage of these mechanisms higher is the time necessary to understand each one and to choose the most appropriate in each application.

2.4   Modeling Approaches for Software Process Lines

In the context of SPrLs, two techniques stand out the compositional and annotative approaches. As representatives from these two approaches, we have chosen the EPF composer [15] and the GenArch-P [8] [16], respectively. The EPF Composer was chosen because is a consolidated authoring environment for software processes that enables the definition of content variability. On the other hand, GenArch-P was chosen because it represents an approach that promotes the usage of annotative techniques in the context of software process lines. These two approaches were selected based on the following arguments: (i) both approaches have available tooling support; (ii) both approaches provide accessible documentation; and (iii) considering the experience of the team responsible for the study using the two approaches.

The compositional approach is characterized by the reuse of part of the content of base process elements, and the refinement of part of their content with a variant content related with a specific process feature. The annotative approach is characterized by the annotation of process elements with feature expressions. A product derivation tool is responsible to process and interpret these annotations based on the chosen features, and it produces as output a process instance with the content associated to these features.

The EPF Composer is a tool provided by the Eclipse Process Framework Initiative from the Eclipse Foundation. This initiative provides open source tools and open source process content to be used and refined by the software process community. The EPF Composer allows the refinement of process elements with variant content through a mechanism named content variability. With this mechanism the content of a specialized process element can: (i) contribute, (ii) extend, (iii) replace, or (iv) extend and replace, the content of a base process element.

The adaptation of the annotative approach for the context of SPrLs is a recent proposal [8]. In the context of software product lines, the annotative approach is already consolidated, and various tools are available, such as: CIDE, pure::variants, and GenArch. In our study, we have used the GenArch for Process, or simply GenArch-P, which represents an adaptation of the GenArch tool for the context of software processes The GenArch-P allows the annotation of process elements in order to associate them to specific features. The annotations are made inside an abstract representation of the software process model, and are the base for the generation of a correspondent feature model. After the features selection in a feature model instance, the tool uses this information to generate a software process specification that addresses the features selected.

2.5   The Target Software Process Line

We have chosen a SPrL based on OpenUP to be modeled in our empirical study. Three processes used in research and development projects from our institution were modeled as a SPrL, which are: (i) the development of a software system for auditing the telephony networks; (ii) the development of a module of a distributed system responsible for the gathering and the storage of the information related to the federal institutions of professional and technological education in Brazil; and (iii) the implementation of an integrated academic and administrative management system for the federal institutions of professional and technological education in Brazil. The same SPrL was used in a previous work of our group [2].

During the specification of the SPrL, the extractive technique [19] was used. We have analyzed the commonalities and variabilities between the chosen software process instances, as members of the software process family. This task demanded an expert software process engineer that was responsible for analyzing the documentation and records of the members of the software process family. In this task, it was elicited the similarities and variabilities in the practices and activities of the studied software process instances, in a work analogous to domain engineering. The commonalities and variabilities of the software process line were then registered and associated with software process features. Table 2 presents the identified features for the process line and the number of associated process elements. The identified features were classified according to the process disciplines or practices that they belong. We have identified 76 process elements as part of the core of the process line. Regarding the variabilities, it was found 9 optional features (14-22), 9 alternative features (1-9), and 4 OR-features (10-13).

During our analysis, we have also found constraints between features from the process line. For example, the features representing the usage of JavaEE and JUnit frameworks require the selection of the feature that represents the use of Java as the programming language. Further information about the specification of the SPrL using the different approaches can be found here [20].

Table 2. Features identified for the target software process line

Feature	Alternative features
Requirements techniques and technologies	
Specification techniques	(1) Use cases
	(2) Users stories
	(3) Product backlog
Specification tools	(4) Asta Community
	(5) Rational Software Architect
	(6) Borland Together
	(7) ArgoUML
Design techniques and technologies	
Architecture documentation	(8) Agile design
	(9) Well documented architecture
Implementation techniques and technologies	
Used language	(10) Java
	(11) C#
	(12) Ruby
	(13) Phyton
(14) Usage of JavaEE framework	
(15) Usage of Eclipse IDE	
(16) Usage of JUnit framework	
Others processes influences	
(17) Additional elements from the Scrum Process	
Continuous integration techniques and technologies	
(18) Usage of Hudson tool	
Metrics techniques and technologies	
(19) Usage of Maven tool (code metrics – SVN mined)	
(20) Metric for assessing the activities progress	
(21) Metric for assessing the deadlines fulfillment	
(22) Metric for assessing the duration of main activities	

3 Modeling of the Target Software Process Line

In this section, we present the results of the modeling of the OpenUP based SPrL using the EPF Composer (Section 3.1) and GenArch-P (Section 3.2).

3.1 Compositional Approach: EPF Composer

The modeling of the target SPrL with the EPF Composer [15] was conducted using the original OpenUP method plugin provided by the EPF. The first step was the creation of a new method plugin to represent the SPrL, based on the original OpenUP method plugin. Next we specified the mandatory process elements. These process elements were grouped in a content package named "core". The other process elements, associated with specific variabilities, were organized in content packages structures representing these process variable features. To group the alternative features, we have created a content package to group the content packages associated with each alternative. To clarify the purpose of each of them, the names of the features were used in the content packages containing the related process elements.

If a specific process feature has implied a change in the core workflow of the process line, the additional behavior was modeled and isolated in a capability pattern structure. The core workflow of the SPrL only refers to the mandatory process elements. The capability patterns were named with the names of the correspondent features. Each content package that represents a specific feature aggregates: (i) additional process elements; (ii) a link to the mandatory elements that will be extended by content variabilities; and (iii) the process elements representing the variants and that will apply changes to the content of the mandatory elements. Figure 1 presents an overview of the content packages created to model the target SPrL using the EPF Composer.

Content Packages:
- optional_agile-scrum (21-8-8)
- alternative_requirements-specification
    - alternative1_use-cases (16-7-7)
    - alternative2_user-stories (11-7-7)
    - alternative3_product-backlog (11-7-7)
- alternative_requirements-specification-tool
    - alternative1_asta-community (4-9-12)
    - alternative2_rational-software-architect (4-9-12)
    - alternative3_borland-together (4-9-12)
    - alternative4_argo-uml (4-9-12)
- alternative_architecture-design
    - alternative1_agile-design (22-11-22)
    - alternative2_well-documented (18-7-5)
- alternative_implementation-language
    - alternative1_java (1-9-3)
    - alternative2_c-sharp (1-9-3)
    - alternative3_phyton (1-9-3)
    - alternative4_ruby (1-9-3)
- optional_jee-framework (1-4-0)
- optional_eclipse-ide (2-3-1)
- optional_junit-framework (2-12-5)
- optional_hudson-continuos-integration-tool (2-8-2)
- optional_maven-svn-mining-tool (2-8-1)
- optional_metric-activities-progress (2-8-1)
- optional_metric-deadlines-fulfillment (2-8-1)
- optional_metric-activities-duration (2-8-1)

Fig. 1. Organization of the process elements in the EPF Composer

For each content package illustrated in Figure 1, it is also illustrated the number of elements grouped inside of them. The quantity of process elements is presented between parentheses with three numbers separated by a hyphen. The (2-3-1) sequence of numbers for the Eclipse IDE optional feature, for example, represents: 2 specific process elements for this feature; 3 elements with content variability; and 1 element associated with other feature. The specific elements are: the "Using Eclipse Plugins" guideline and the "How to Create Applications on Eclipse" roadmap. The elements with content variability are: the concept of "Coding Standard", the activity of the elaboration phase instructing to "Develop a Solution Increment", and the activity of the construction phase instructing to "Develop a Solution Increment". The element associated with other features is the concept of "Refactoring".

3.2   Annotative Approach: GenArch-P

The modeling of the SPrL using GenArch-P [8] [16] involved initially the definition of a specification of a software process corresponding to the SPrL. In this definition, it was created all the necessary software process elements, the mandatory and the variant ones. The organization of these process elements in the process specification is not fundamental to GenArch-P, because the user only interacts with an abstract representation of the process specification. The second step is the analysis of the resultant software process specification, and the automatic generation of an abstract visualization of it using the tool, where the process elements appear grouped by the respective types. Figure 2 presents an illustration of a group of process elements, that represent work products, and how they were annotated.

Work Products:

- **Mandatory Process Elements**
  - o Implementation
  - o Build
  - o Iteration Plan
  - o Project Plan
  - o Vision

- **Specific Process Elements Representing a Variable Content**
  - o Implementation_Ruby [alt4_ruby]
  - o Build_Ruby [alt4_ruby]
  - o Implementation_Phyton [alt3_phyton]
  - o Build_Phyton [alt3_phyton]
  - o Implementation_C# [alt2_c-sharp]
  - o Build_C# [alt2_c-sharp]
  - o Implementation_Java [alt1_java]
  - o Build_Java [alt1_java]
  - o Build_Hudson [optional_hudson-tool]
  - o Build_Agile Design [alt1_agile-design]
  - o Developer Test_JUnit [optional_junit-framework]
  - o Vision_Product Backlog [alt3_product-backlog]
  - o Vision_User Stories [alt2_user-stories]
  - o Vision_Use Cases [alt1_use-cases]
  - o Use Case Model_ArgoUML [alt4_argo-uml]
  - o Use Case Model_Borland Together [alt3_borland-together]
  - o Use Case Model_RSA [alt2_rational-software-architect]
  - o Use Case Model_Astah Community [alt1_asta-community]

- **Generic Process Elements Representing a Variable Content**
  - o Architecture Notebook [alt2_well-documented]
  - o Developer Test [alt1_asta-design] [optional_junit-framework]
  - o Design [alt1_asta-community] [alt2_rational-software-architect] [alt3_borland-together] [alt4_argo-uml] [alt2_well-documented]
  - o Risk List [opt_agile-scrum]
  - o Work Items List [opt_agile-scrum] [alt2_user-stories] [alt3_product-backlog]
  - o Product Backlog [alt3_product-backlog]
  - o User Stories Book [alt2_user-stories]
  - o Use-Case Model [alt1_use-cases] [alt1_asta-community] [alt2_rational-software-architect]
  - o Use Case [alt1_use-cases]
  - o Test Case [alt1_agile-design]
  - o Test Script [alt1_agile-design]
  - o Test Log [alt1_agile-design]

Fig. 2. Example of process elements annotated with GenArch-P

To associate a process element with specific process features in GenArch-P, each element must be annotated with a feature expression. These annotations are the specification of the configuration knowledge – mapping of features to the process line assets (process elements). The features are identified by a name, and defined as optional or alternatives. One process element can be associated with more than one feature, using logical operators – "OR" and "AND" (dependencies between features). During the specification of the SPrL other constraints can also be specified.

The process elements illustrated in Figure 2 are work products from the target SPrL modeled with GenArch-P. These process elements are presented in three groups: (i) mandatory elements; (ii) specific elements with variable content; and (iii) generic elements with variable content. One example of a mandatory work product is the "Implementation", which indicates that there is always an implementation, independently of how the process varies. The main difference between a specific and a generic process element is that the specific element is created to add content relative to a particular feature. For example: "Implementation_Java" and "Build_Java" determines the implementation and the build process using the Java language. The same generic process elements could be associated with more than one feature, if necessary.

4   Study Results

After the modeling of the same SPrL by the two investigated approaches, we have applied and quantified the metrics for each of them. Table 3 presents the obtained results for all the metrics. Next sections discuss the results to each research question.

Table 3. Quantitative Results for the Metrics Suite

		SPrL Approaches	
Attribute	Metric	Compositional	Annotative
Modularity	Alternations of group of process elements associated with a specific feature	21	161
Size	Number of process elements	516	303
Complexity	Number of mechanisms to model software process variabilities	6	2
	Number of usages of the mechanisms to model software process variabilities	463	368

4.1   Modularity Analysis

To answer the first research question (RQ1), it was analyzed the degree of separation of concerns of the investigated approaches. In the EPF Composer, the separation of concerns is quantified by the alternations between content packages. The number of alternations quantified was 21. On the other hand, in the GenArch-P, modular structures cannot be created; only annotations can be added to one process element. In order to relate the process elements associated with the same feature, the annotations of the same feature were colored with the same color. In addition, the elements annotated with the same feature can be organized in different groups of process elements. Thus, in the GenArch-P annotative approach, we have counted the alternation of colors in the process specification. The number of alternations for GenArch-P was 161.

With these results, we concluded that the EPF Composer compositional approach presents better results than the GenArch-P annotative approach when considering the modularity metric. It shows that EPF Composer has provided a better separation of concerns/features compared to GenArch-P. As a general conclusion, we have observed that modularity is a relevant weakness for the annotative approach.

4.2   Size Analysis

To answer the second research question (RQ2), it was analyzed the number of process elements in the SPrLs modeled with the two investigated approaches. As the process models of both approaches are based on SPEM, they represent the smaller units that can be specified in process, such as: task, activity, role, artifact, guide, guidance, and their respective relationships. In the two investigated approaches, the number of process elements was bigger than the software process model used as basis to the modeling of the SPrL. In the GenArch-P this is justified by the need of modeling the variant process elements. However, the EPF Composer led to a higher number of process elements. This great number of process elements was caused, beyond the variant of process elements, by the necessity of duplication of certain core process elements, to enable the application of the content variability in these elements. Considering these results, we have observed that the GenArch-P annotative approach has presented a reduced number of process elements in the SPrL specification.

4.3   Complexity Analysis

To answer the third research question (RQ3), it was analyzed the necessary knowledge and the amount of work to manage the variabilities in the target process line. The EPF Composer compositional approach introduced the concepts of (i) content packages, (ii) content variability, and other four specific mechanisms of content variability – (iii) contributes, (iv) extends, (v) replace, and (vi) extends and replace. The GenArch-P annotative approach allowed the modeling of the software process variabilities by annotating the process elements related to (i) optional and (ii) alternative features. This means that EPF Composer presented a total of 6 variability management mechanisms, and the GenArch-P has only introduced 2 mechanisms.

The second metric of the complexity attribute counts the usage of these mechanisms to model the software process variabilities. The EPF Composer compositional approach modeled the OpenUP based SPrL variabilities using 22 content packages that group 440 process elements, with the total of 462 modeled elements. It is important to mention that in 173 of the 440 process elements, we have applied the content variability mechanism. The GenArch-P annotative approach models the variabilities of the SPrL using 368 annotations of features expressions. It is also important to mention that the 368 annotations were made in 150 process elements, because some process elements were annotated with more than one feature. Considering these results, GenArch-P annotative approach obtained better results when considering the complexity metrics.

5   Discussions

The GenArch-P annotative approach has obtained better results in two of the three attributes analyzed in this study, which are: size and complexity. On the other hand, the EPF Composer compositional approach obtained better results considering the modularity attribute. In a previous study [3] the EPF Composer and GenArch-P approaches were qualitative compared according to several criteria, such as: modularity, granularity and adoption. With the quantitative results of this work, we can revisit and discuss the conclusions about these criteria presented in this previous study.

The modularity criterion in our previous study was related to the isolation of the process elements associated with specific process features. It concluded that compositional approach has a good support for the modularity criterion and the annotative approach has a partial support for this criterion. According to the quantitative results for modularity criterion of the investigated approaches (compositional = 21 and annotative = 165), we can reinforce that the compositional approach had a better support for modularity than the annotative approach.

The granularity criterion in the previous study was related to the support of the approach for modeling variabilities in different granularities (fine or coarse grained). It concluded that compositional approach has a good support for granularity criterion, and the annotative approach has a partial support for it. The quantitative results for the complexity metrics presented in this paper have revealed the use of 22 content packages (coarse grained) that group 440 process elements and 173 process elements with content variability (fine grained) in the compositional approach. On other hand, the annotative approach used 368 annotations (fine grained mechanism) to model the variabilities. Thus, we have observed that the variety of mechanism of EPF Composer compositional approach for modeling fine and coarse grained variabilities has not contributed to reduce the complexity of the SPrL modeling compared to GenArch-P.

The adoption criterion in the previous study cared about how easy is the adoption of the investigated approaches. It concluded that compositional approach has a weak or no support, and the annotative approach has a good support for this criterion. The quantitative results of this work revealed that the compositional approach produced a specification with 516 process elements. On the other hand, the annotative approach produced a specification with 303 process elements. The quantitative results also presented that the compositional approach provides 6 mechanisms to model the process variabilities, while the annotative approach provides only 2 kinds of annotations. As the annotative approach produced a smaller specification and provided fewer mechanisms to model the process variability, we can reinforce the conclusion that the annotative approach has a better support for the adoption criterion.

These considerations about some of the results of the previous study do not affect the general conclusion that the annotative approach obtained better results than the compositional approach. The quantitative results found in this work also point in the same direction. On the other hand, we have also observed that considering the modularity and granularity criteria, the EPF Composer had even better results than the GenArch-P. These strengths of the EPF Composer compositional approach and the overall better results of the GenArch-P annotative approach leaded us to consider the integration of them.

This integrated approach could be mainly based on the characteristics of the annotative approach, to take advantage of: (i) the use of annotations may render the approach independent of the used software process model; (ii) the abstraction of some details of the used software process model; (iii) a simpler specification of a SPrL; and (iv) the ability to explicitly defining and modeling the process features. On the other hand, some characteristics of the compositional approach should be considered, which are: (i) the ability to define and visualize the modular structures provided by the software process model used, besides allowing the annotation of these structures; and (ii) the ability to define fine-grained variability mechanisms to be applied to the refinement of process elements, such as the content variability mechanism provided by EPF Composer.

6   Threats to Validity

Threats to the study validity were analyzed in accordance with the following taxonomies: construct validity, internal validity and external validity.

The construct validity concerns to establish the relationship between the theory behind the study, and the observations. One threat to construct validity was the way that the representatives of the investigated approaches were used. The usage and choice of the best mechanisms of each approach were discussed between different researchers during reviews of the modeling using each approach. Another threat to construct validity is related to the metrics defined for the study. They have been adapted from a previous study from the context of software product lines. When choosing the metrics to evaluate the investigated approaches, we avoid defining new metrics from the scratch. Our objective was to adapt some previous used metrics to the context of SPrLs. The results of the metric suite allowed the analysis of the selected attributes and to answer our research questions. However, a deeper validation of the metric suite is planned as future work.

The internal validity concerns to define causal relationships, where certain conditions lead to other conditions. One threat to the internal validity is that same team was responsible to model the SPrL with the two investigated approaches. The choice of the team responsible to conduct this study was made to address this threat; preference was given to the researchers that demonstrated good knowledge in the two approaches under study. The research team responsible for executing the study also contributes in the development of the GenArch-P tool, and had a good experience using this approach. On other hand, the EPF Composer is a consolidated initiative in the software processes community. Several guides, instructions and examples are available for download, which were also fundamental to guarantee a better understanding of the approach advantages and drawbacks. The research team responsible for the study execution also had a good experience in the use of the EPF Composer, because this tool has been used in other previous studies.

The external validity is interested to establish the context in which the results of a study can be generalized. One threat to the external validity it is the academic nature of the projects used as basis to the definition of the SPrL defined as the target for the study. Even if they have been developed in an academic institution, the demands and schedule for each project were quite similar to a project developed in the industry. To reduce this threat, it is planned the replication of the study using a SPrL extracted from an institution devoted to software development. Another threat to external validity is that the study conclusions are restricted to the context of EPF Composer and GenArch-P approaches in the modeling of software process lines. The results can only serve as initial evidence to hypotheses formulation related to the compositional and annotative approaches.

7   Related Work

Bendraou et al [21] draw a comparison of six UML-based languages for software process modeling. The study investigated how these approaches fulfill important requirements from process modeling, namely: semantic richness, modularity, executability, conformity to the UML standard, and formality. It concluded that each of the investigated approaches presented advantages and drawbacks, and that is up to the projects managers based on the results of the evaluation, to choose the proper approach for answering their demands. The main difference from our work is that we focused on the assessment of modeling techniques for software process variabilities.

Martínez-Ruiz et al [22] present the results of an empirical study evaluating two software process modeling notations, which are: SPEM and vSPEM. The aim of this work was to present an empirical validation to check if the variability constructs of the vSPEM are more appropriate than the SPEM to modeling software process variability. They have analyzed: (i) the understandability of the variability mechanisms, and (ii) the understandability of the notation as a whole. The work concluded that the understandability of the variability mechanisms of vSPEM was 126.99% higher than for SPEM. On the other hand, the understandability of the diagrams of vSPEM was 34.87% lower than for SPEM. In our study, we have not considered the understandability attribute. We plan to conduct more controlled experiments using EPF Composer and GenArch-P to also observe the understandability from the perspective of the users of the modeling language.

Simmonds et al [23] present the results of an investigation of the appropriateness of different approaches for modeling software variability, such as: (i) SPEM 2.0, (ii) vSPEM, (iii) OVM, and (iv) feature models. It was analyzed the expressiveness of each notation, as well as the understandability of the specification. It was also made an evaluation of the tool support for variability modeling in processes. The authors recognized the power of general-purpose languages (OVM and feature models) in expressing the properties of the variabilities. Finally, considering the definition of a tool chain for implementing automatic process tailoring, the best choice was the feature model and the SPLOT tool for modeling the software process variabilities. In our comparative quantitative study we focused on internal attributes related to the modeling mechanisms of the SPrL, which are: modularity, size and complexity. On the other hand, the cited work focused on usability aspects, exploring the users point of view by only providing a discussion of the mechanisms not supported by a more rigorous quantitative or qualitative analysis with the modeling of a non-trivial SPrL, as we have conducted in our work.

In a previous research work [2], we have presented a qualitative comparative study between the EPF Composer and GenArch-P approaches. They were compared according to seven different criteria, which are: (i) modularity, (ii) traceability, (iii) error detection, (iv) granularity, (v) uniformity, (vi) adoption, and (vii) systematic variability management. The results of the modeling of the same SPrL using EPF Composer and GenArch-P were analyzed and discussed against these criteria. We concluded that the annotative approach obtained the better results in five of seven criteria, but the compositional approach presented some strength that must be considered. The main drawback of that work is that are missing quantitative results to better support the work conclusions. The quantitative study presented in this paper aimed complementing the qualitative analysis results obtained for this previous work. We have also discussed and confronted the results of both studies in Section 5.

8   Conclusions and Future Work

After analyzing and discussing the results of the study, we provided answers for the research questions defined for this work. The answer for the first research question was that the EPF Composer compositional approach obtained better results considering the modularization metric than the annotative approach. This is a strong characteristic of the compositional approach that motivates its integration with annotative techniques for the modeling of SPrLs. The answer for the second research question was that the GenArch-P annotative approach could produce a SPrL with a smaller size. A reduced number of process elements during the SPrL modeling can assist the process engineer in the management of its complexity. Finally, the answer for the third research question was that the GenArch-P approach obtained better results in terms of complexity metrics. This happened because the EPF Composer approach has a greater number of mechanisms to the modeling of the software process variabilities, and a greater number of usages of these mechanisms in the modeling of the SPrL.

In general terms, the study bring preliminary evidences that based on the selected attributes for the study and the specific context of the target SPrL modeled for the two approaches, the GenArch-P annotative approach obtained better results. The analysis of the strengths and weaknesses of the approaches showed us that the integration of the characteristics of the compositional and annotative approaches could produce a better solution to the modeling of SPrLs. As future work, we can summarize the following topics: (i) to provide a more deep validation of the proposed metrics suite; (ii) to replicate this study in the context of an industrial SPrL; (iii) to include more representatives of the compositional and annotative approaches; and (iv) to design, implement and evaluate an annotative and compositional integrated approach.

Acknowledgments. This work was partially supported by the National Institute of Science and Technology for Software Engineering (INES), funded by CNPq, grants 573964/2008-4 and PDI – Great Challenges, 560256/2010-8, and by FAPERN and CAPES/PROAP.

References

1. Rombach, H.: Integrated Software Process and Product Lines. In: Li, M., Boehm, B., Osterweil, L.J. (eds.) SPW 2005. LNCS, vol. 3840, pp. 83–90. Springer, Heidelberg (2006)
2. Aleixo, F., Kulesza, U., Freire, M., Costa, D., Campos Neto, E.: Modularizing Software Process Lines using Model-driven Approaches: A Comparative Study. In: 14th International Conference on Enterprise Information Systems (ICEIS), Wroclaw, Poland, vol. 2 (2012)
3. Aleixo, F., Freire, M., Alencar, D., Campos, E., Kulesza, U.: A Comparative Study of Compositional and Annotative Modelling Approaches for Software Process Lines A Comparative Study of Compositional and Annotative Modelling Approaches for Software Process Lines. In: 26th Brazilian Symposium on Software Engineering (SBES), Natal, RN, Brazil (2012)
4. Washizaki, H.: Building Software Process Line Architectures from Bottom Up. In: Münch, J., Vierimaa, M. (eds.) PROFES 2006. LNCS, vol. 4034, pp. 415–421. Springer, Heidelberg (2006)
5. Armbrust, O., Katahira, M., Miyamoto, Y., Münch, J., Nakao, H., Ocampo, A.: Scoping software process lines. Software Process: Improvement and Practice 14(3), 181–197 (2009)
6. Ternité, T.: Process Lines: A Product Line Approach Designed for Process Model Development. In: 35th EUROMICRO Conference on Software Engineering and Advanced Applications, Patras, Greece, pp. 173–180 (2009)
7. Martínez-Ruiz, T., García, F., Piattini, M.: Process Institutionalization using Software Process Lines. In: 11th International Conference on Enterprise Information Systems (ICEIS), Milan, Italy (2009)
8. Aleixo, F.A., Freire, M.A., dos Santos, W.C., Kulesza, U.: Automating the Variability Management, Customization and Deployment of Software Processes: A Model-Driven Approach. In: Filipe, J., Cordeiro, J. (eds.) ICEIS 2010. Lecture Notes in Business Information Processing, vol. 73, pp. 372–387. Springer, Heidelberg (2011)
9. Freire, M., Aleixo, F., Kulesza, U., Aranha, E., Coelho, R.: Automatic Deployment and Monitoring of Software Processes: A Model-Driven Approach. In: 23rd International Conference on Software Engineering & Knowledge Engineering (SEKE), Miami Beach, USA, pp. 42–47 (2011)
10. Alegria, J., Bastarrica, M.: Building software process lines with CASPER. In: International Conference on Software and System Process (ICSSP), Zurich, Switzerland, pp. 170–179 (2012)
11. Figueiredo, E., et al.: Evolving Software Product Lines with Aspects: An Empirical Study on Design Stability. In ACM, (ed.) International Conference on Software Engineering (ICSE), Leipzig, Germany, pp.261–270 (2008)
12. Kästner, C., Apel, S.: Integrating Compositional and Annotative Approaches for Product Line Engineering. In: GPCE Workshop on Modularization, Composition and Generative Techniques for Product Line Engineering (McGPLE), Passau, Germany (2008)

13. Kästner, C.: Virtual Separation of Concerns: Toward Preprocessors 2.0. Dissertation, Otto-von-Guericke-Universität, Magdeburg, Germany (2010)
14. Bonifácio, R., Borba, P.: Modeling Scenario Variability as Crosscutting Mechanisms. In ACM (ed.) International Conference on Aspect-Oriented Software Development (AOSD), Charlottesville, Virginia, USA, pp.125–136 (2009)
15. Eclipse Foundation: Eclipse Process Framework Project (EPF), http://www.eclipse.org/epf/ (accessed 2012)
16. Aleixo, F., Freire, M., Santos, W., Kulesza, U.: A Model-driven Approach to Managing and Customizing Software Process Variabilities. In: 12th International Conference on Enterprise Information Systems (ICEIS), Funchal, Madeira, Portugal, vol. 3, pp. 92–100 (2010)
17. Basili, V., Caldiera, G., Rombach, H.: The Goal Question Metric Approach. In: Encyclopedia of Software Engineering. Wiley (1994)
18. Garcia, A., Sant'Anna, C., Figueiredo, E., Kulesza, U., Lucena, C., von Staa, A.: Modularizing design patterns with aspects: a quantitative study. In: Press, A. (ed.) Aspect-Oriented Software Development Conference (AOSD), Chicago, USA, pp. 3–14 (2005)
19. Linden, F., Schmid, K., Rommes, E.: Software Product Lines in Action: The Best Industrial Practice in Product Line Engineering. Springer (2007)
20. Aleixo, F.: Software Process Lines, https://sites.google.com/site/softwareprocesslines/ (accessed 2013)
21. Bendraou, R., Jézéquel, J.-M., Gervais, M.-P., Blanc, X.: A Comparison of Six UML-Based Languages for Software Process Modeling. Transactions on Software Engineering 36(5), 662–675 (2010)
22. Martínez-Ruiz, T., García, F., Piattini, M., Münch, J.: Modelling Software Process Variability: an Empirical Study. IET Software 5(2), 172–187 (2011)
23. Simmonds, J., Bastarrica, M., Silvestre, L., Quispe, A.: Analyzing Methodologies and Tools for Specifying Variability in Software Processes, Universidad de Chile, Santiago, Chile (2011)

SMartySPEM: A SPEM-Based Approach
for Variability Management
in Software Process Lines

Edson A. Oliveira Junior[1], Maicon G. Pazin[1], Itana M.S. Gimenes[1],
Uirá Kulesza[2], and Fellipe A. Aleixo[2]

[1] State University of Maringá (UEM), Informatics Department (DIN)
Maringá-PR, Brazil
{edson,itana}@din.uem.br, maiconpazin@gmail.com
[2] Federal University of Rio Grande do Norte (UFRN),
Department of Computer Science and Applied Mathematics (DIMAP)
Natal-RN, Brazil
uira@dimap.ufrn.br, fellipe.aleixo@ifrn.edu.br

Abstract. The definition of customized software processes can lead to improve the quality of software products and increasing the productivity. The Software Process Line (SPrL) approach might be taken into consideration to improve the establishment of customized processes for a given domain. The specific processes are derived in a systematic way, based on the resolution of variabilities explicitly represented in process notations, such as SPEM. SPEM has an UML 2 profile used to model software process elements. Therefore, this paper presents the SMartySPEM approach, which extends the SPEM profile for representing variabilities in SPrLs taking into consideration the SMarty approach for variability management. SMartySPEM is composed of an UML profile (SMartySPEM-Profile) for representing variabilities and guidelines that suggest how to identify variabilities in a SPrL. A SMartySPEM application example is presented in an excerpt of a SPrL designed based on the Unified Process.

1 Introduction

Industry is currently experiencing a constant demand for improving software products and reducing respective production costs. These products must have a reduced time to market [1]. Companies have been engaged on improving their software processes as a means to both increase the quality of their products and accelerate their development. Therefore, such companies demand a faster and effective software process customization which takes into account a diversity of existing scenarios, technologies, and cultures [2]. Thus, it is important to have tools and technology to support quick process adaptation based on established knowledge in specific domains.

Research related to Software Process Lines (SPrL[1]) [1,14,15,9,3,4] have been developed and evolved over the last years. SPrL is a family of processes that

---

[1] Note that in this paper we use SPrL as an acronym for Software Process Line, whereas the term "product line" is used for Software Product Line.

J. Heidrich et al. (Eds.): PROFES 2013, LNCS 7983, pp. 169–183, 2013.

has a set of managed features that satisfy specific needs of an organization and are developed from a set of basic common processes [3]. Therefore, based on concepts and techniques from the software product line approach [8], the SPrL research area aims to provide techniques and mechanisms for: (i) modeling existing similarities and variabilities in a family of software processes; and (ii) support the customization of software processes according to specific needs of software process domain.

Amongst the existing notations for software process modeling in the current literature is the Software & Systems Process Engineering Metamodel (SPEM) [11], which is standardized by the Object Management Group (OMG). Several related work, discussed in Section 5, take into consideration SPEM, which is a UML profile composed of stereotypes and tagged values. The SMarty [10,6] approach is composed of an UML profile and a set of guidelines. It has been developed to support variability management in software product lines. As SPEM does not take into consideration variabilities, SMarty can support SPEM on variability identification and representation. This paper presents the Stereotype-based Variability Management for SPEM (SMartySPEM) that aims to support both the identification and the representation of variabilities in SPEM-based software process elements.

The rest of this paper is organized as follows: Section 2 discusses essential concepts with regard to software processes modelling using the SPEM meta-model, software process lines, and the SMarty approach; Section 3 presents the proposed approach, SMartySPEM; Section 4 illustrates the modeling of a software process line based on the Unified Process using SMartySPEM; Section 5 discusses related work; and Section 6 concludes our work and presents directions for future work.

2 Background

2.1 Software Processes Modelling with SPEM

Software & Systems Process Engineering Metamodel (SPEM) [11] is an OMG specification. It is a metamodel to support the modeling, representation, and managing software processes [11]. It reuses the UML 2 infrastructure library by means of a metamodel specified as a Meta-Object Facility (MOF). The SPEM 2.0 specification is composed of: (i) the SPEM meta-model, which defines the structural rules specified as a MOF model and reuses essential classes of the UML 2.0; it defines diagrams for modeling specific processes; and (ii) the SPEM profile, which defines a set of UML 2.0 stereotypes.

SPEM also provides, as an optional feature, a set of icons for representing the elements defined in its metamodel. SPEM uses such icons for representing its stereotypes. Table 1 presents such icons and respective stereotypes and descriptions.

Figure 1 presents an excerpt of the Analysis Workflow of the the Unified Process modeled in SPEM. There are four tasks: `Architectural Analysis`, `Analyze a Use Case`, `Analyze a Class`, and `Analyze a Package`. Each of these tasks has an associated role. For instance, the task `Analyze a Use Case` has the `Use-Case`

Table 1. Main Icons of SPEM

Icon	Stereotype	Description
	Activity	Represents a grouping of elements, such as, instances of an Activity, Task Use, Role Use and Work Product Use.
	TaskUse	Represents a task which is being realized by a Role in an Activity context.
	Step	Represents necessary steps to realize a Task.
	WorkProductUse	Represents an artifact that is used or produced in the context of a specific Activity.
	RoleUse	Represents a Role responsible for one or more specific Tasks.

Engineer role which is responsible for performing such a task. Several artifacts are represented by means of a WorkProductUse as, for instance, Analysis Class, Use-Case Model and Architecture Description.

2.2   Software Process Lines Concepts and History

Software process line (SPrL) [1,2,14] refers to the application of product line principles and techniques to the context of software processes. It aims to provide techniques and mechanisms to: (i) the modeling of existing commonalities and variabilities of a software process family; and (ii) the automatic derivation of customized software processes that address specific needs of a given software development project.

Variability is the general term used to refer to the variable aspects of the products of a SPrL. It is described through variation points and variants. A variation point is the specific place in a product line artifact to which a design decision is connected. Each variation point is associated with a set of variants that corresponds to design alternatives to resolve the variability [8], [13].

A SPrL represents commonalities and variabilities associated with process elements such as activities, artifacts, roles, and actions. Examples of variabilities that can be modeled in a SPrL are: (i) to represent a specific level of software process maturity model: (ii) to represent alternatives for the usage of a specific technique for specifying the requirements, modeling the software design or executing testing activities; (iii) to represent the choice for a style of documenting the software architecture; and (iv) to represent the choice for a specific programming language. These variabilities represent points where the process elements can be extended or refined. Existing research works propose modeling techniques that are used to promote an adequate management of these variabilities and the automatic process customization.

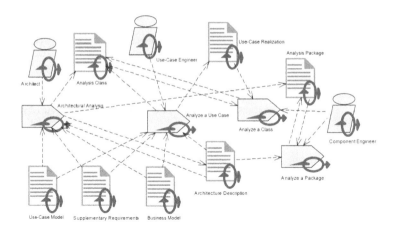

Fig. 1. Excerpt of the Unified Process Analysis Workflow in SPEM

In 2005, Rombach [14] brought the discussion about the integration of software process and product lines. Rombach observed that the software processes vary across projects, but they are not still managed in a similar systematic way than the software products in a product line. Some of these challenges were: how to define variabilities in software process specifications, and how to define theoretical and engineering foundations for process lines.

In 2006, Washizaki [15] presented a technique for establishing process lines, called process lines architectures. Process lines architectures incorporate the commonalities and variabilities of a process family. The technique presented by Washizaki include some extensions to the Software Process Engineering Meta-model, to enable the definition of commonalities and variabilities in process workflows described as UML activities diagrams.

In 2008, Martínez-Ruiz et al. [9] proposed an extension to SPEM v2.0 to define process line variability mechanisms. In such work the authors conclude that the SPEM meta-model - the OMG pattern to software processes specification - does not include the appropriate mechanisms to model such variabilities. The proposed extensions are based on the definition of variation points and variants, which are necessary to the process line representation. They also pointed the necessity to further empirical validations for the proposed approach.

In 2009, Armbrust et al. [3] proposed an approach to developing software process lines. The proposed approach was based on three main steps, which are: (i) scoping, (ii) modeling and (iii) architecting the software process line. The work presented some aspects of the application of the proposed approach in a study case in the Japan Aerospace Explorations Agency. The authors conclude that the application of the proposed approach does not prove its general applicability, and are necessary further empirical works to evaluate its applicability.

In 2010, Barreto et al. [4] described the application of a software process line to support the definition of software processes in a consulting organization. In such a work the authors describe the concept of software process component, as an encapsulation of information and behavior at a certain granularity level. The authors conclude that some benefits could be achieved by the proposed approach, which are: (i) experienced process engineers can make knowledge explicit; (ii) less experienced process engineers will be able to define processes more easily and learn from it; and (iii) client organizations will be able to more easily tailor processes for each project; but these benefits need to be evaluated in practice.

In 2011, Aleixo et al. [2] proposed an approach for the definition of software process lines through the adaptation of a product derivation tool, allowing the automatic derivation of software process instances of a software process line. With this approach a process engineer could specify a software process line through the annotation of variabilities in a software process model. The annotations made are recognized by the used tool and mapped in a feature model for the software process line. The feature selections in a feature model instance could be used by the tool to derivate a correspondent software process instance. The authors also concluded that it is needed more empirical and evaluation studies to attest the applicability of the proposed approach.

In 2012, Alegria and Bastarrica [1] proposed the definition of a meta-process, called CASPER, which allows the definition of adaptable software process models. According to CASPER the software processes are modeled in SPEM, and the variability is represented by the variation points in the kernel process (common to all instances) and the process variants. The process variants could be represented as plug-ins, process components, process patterns, processes, activities, method elements and managed content elements. In the adaptation process in CASPER the project manager provides the characteristics of the project, and a project-adapted process is automatically generated. The tailoring decisions are encapsulated as auxiliary rules.

Even with all these results, this research field still presents challenges to be pursued. All the works that presented approaches for dealing with the conception, modeling and implementation of software process lines, make it clear the need for more empirical studies and evaluations of their proposals.

2.3   The SMarty Approach for UML-Based Variability Management

SMarty is an approach for UML Stereotype-based Management of Variability in product line. It is composed of a UML 2 profile, the *SMartyProfile*, and a process, the *SMartyProcess*. **SMartyProfile** contains a set of stereotypes and tagged values to represent variability in product line models. Basically, *SMartyProfile* uses a standard object-oriented notation and its profiling mechanism [12] both to provide an extension of UML and to allow graphical representation of variability concepts. Thus, there is no need to change the system design structure to comply with the product line approach. **SMartyProcess** is a systematic process that guides the user through the identification, delimitation, representation, and tracing of variabilities in product line models. It is supported by a set of application guidelines as well as by the *SMartyProfile* to represent variabilities [10].

The *SMartyProfile* represents the relationship of major product line concepts with respect to variability management. There are four main concepts: variability [5], variation point [13], variant [13], and variant constraints [5].

Based on these variability management concepts, the SMartyProfile is composed of the following stereotypes and respective tagged values:

≪**variability**≫ represents the concept of product line variability and is an extension of the metaclass `Comment`. This stereotype has the following tagged values: `name`, the given name by which a variability is referred to; `minSelection`, represents the minimum number of variants to be selected to resolve a variation point or a variability; `maxSelection`, represents the maximum number of variants to be selected in order to resolve a variation point or a variability; `bindingTime`, the moment at which a variability must be resolved, represented by the enumeration class `BindingTime`; `allowsAddingVar`, indicates whether it is possible or not to include new variants in the product line development; `variants`, represents the collection of variant instances associated with a variability; and `realizes`, a collection of lower-level model variabilities that realize this variability.

≪**variationPoint**≫ represents the concept of product line variation point and is an extension of the metaclasses `Actor`, `UseCase`, `Interface`, and `Class`. This stereotype has the following tagged values: `numberOfVariants`, indicates the number of associated variants that can be selected to resolve this variation point; `bindingTime`, the moment at which a variation point must be resolved, represented by the enumeration class `BindingTime`; `variants`, represents the collection of variant instances associated with this variation point; and `variabilities`, represents the collection of associated variabilities.

≪*variant*≫ represents the concept of product line variant and is an abstract extension of the metaclasses `Actor`, `UseCase`, `Interface`, and *Class*. This stereotype is specialized in four other non-abstract stereotypes which are: ≪mandatory≫, ≪optional≫, ≪alternative_OR≫, and ≪alternative_XOR≫. The stereotype ≪variant≫ has the following tagged values: `rootVP`, represents the variation point with which this variant is associated; and `variabilities`, the collection of variabilities with which this variant is associated.

≪**mandatory**≫ represents a compulsory variant that is part of every product line product.

≪**optional**≫ represents a variant that may be selected to resolve a variation point or a variability;

≪**alternative_OR**≫ represents a variant that is part of a group of alternative inclusive variants. Different combinations of this kind of variants may resolve variation points or variabilities in different ways.

≪**alternative_XOR**≫ represents a variant that is part of a group of alternative exclusive variants. This means that only one variant of the group can be selected to resolve a variation point or variability;

≪**variable**≫ is an extension of the metaclass `Component`. It indicates that a component has a set of classes with explicit variabilities. This stereotype has the tagged value `classSet` which is the collection of class instances that form a component.

The Arcade Game Maker (AGM), used to illustrate the application of SMarty, is a pedagogical and exemplary product line created by the Software Engineering Institute (SEI) to support learning and experimenting based on product line concepts. It has a complete set of documents and UML models, as well as a set of tested classes and the source code for three different games: Pong, Bowling, and Brickles. Although AGM is not a commercial product line, it has been used to illustrate the concepts of several different product line approaches, as well as product line and architecture evaluation case studies.

The essential AGM UML models include [10] the use case model (Figure 2). Such a model has two actors, `GamePlayer` and `GameInstaller` which trigger several use cases such as `Save Game`, `Exit Game`, and `Play Selected Game`. The use cases `Check Previous Best Score` and `Save Score` are triggered by the `GamePlayer` actor, whereas `Install Game` is triggered by `GameInstaller`.

The use case `Play Selected Game` is the most important use case. It has two extension points: `initialization_ext_point` and `animation_ext_point`. The former is responsible for allowing specific actions from the use case `Initialization`, whereas the latter is responsible for specific actions from `Animation Loop` which can be realized by different games.

3   The SMartySPEM Approach for Process-Line Variability Management

The Stereotype-based Variability Management for the SPEM meta-model (SMartySPEM) approach is aimed at supporting one to identify and represent variability in SPEM-based software process elements. In addition, SMartySPEM supports the derivation of specific processes by resolving variabilities. Currently, SMartySPEM does not support automatic derivation of specific processes.

SMartySPEM is composed of an UML profile, the SMartySPEMProfile, and a set of guidelines which provides directions to identify and represent variabilities. Figure 3 depicts the activities that need to be carried out to model SPrL and deriving specific processes based on SMartySPEM. The `Apply SMartySPEM Guidelines` activity takes as input `SPEM-based Process Models`. These models are previously created for a given software process based on the SPEM meta-model. Thus, SMartySPEM guidelines (presented next) contain directions to identify and represent variabilities in such process models. As an output of this activity, `SMartySPEM-based Process Models` are generated. These models contain variabilities represented and are taken as input for the next activity, `Resolve Variabilities/Derive Specific Process`. In this activity, several specific processes (`Process 1`, `Process 2` ... `Process n`) are derived.

The SMartySPEM guidelines basically provide directions on how to identify variabilities and model them into SPEM-based process elements by applying UML stereotypes from the SMartySPEMProfile. Figure 4 provides an overall view of the SMartySPEMProfile and its related packages. Note that the SMartySPEMProfile (first bottom-up) stereotypes extend UML metaclasses or are

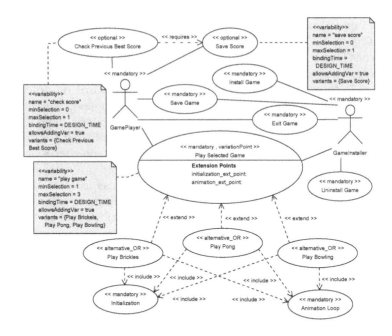

Fig. 2. Arcade Game Maker Use Case Model According to SMarty [10]

extensions of the SPEM metamodel. Therefore, one can apply such stereotypes directly to UML elements or SPEM elements.

Figure 4 depicts the SMartySPEMProfile (first package bottom-up) and the extended stereotypes from the SPEM 2.0 UML 2 Profile and the UML 2 Metamodel. SMartySPEMProfile takes into account the following SPEM stereotypes: ≪Step≫, ≪Activity≫, ≪RoleUse≫, ≪TaskUse≫ and ≪WorkProductUse≫. Such stereotypes represent the elements Activity, Role Use, Task Use, and Work Product Step and Use, respectively, which are taken into consideration for modeling software processes. Thus, only a specific subset of the UML metaclasses is extended by the SPEM and SMartySPEM profiles.

The stereotypes that form the SMartySPEMProfile are as follows:

- ≪variability≫ - represents the concept of variability in LPS and it is an extension of the metaclass Comment;
- ≪variationPoint≫ - represents specific places at which process elements variation occurs. It is an extension of the DecisionNode and Class metaclasses and it specializes the following SPEM 2.0 profile stereotypes RoleUse, TaskUse, and WorkProductUse;
- ≪variant≫ - represents the concept of a variant process element in a SPrL and it is an abstract extension of the Class and Action, and a specialization of the SPEM stereotypes ≪Activity≫, ≪RoleUse≫, ≪TaskUse≫, ≪Step≫ and ≪WorkProductUse≫;

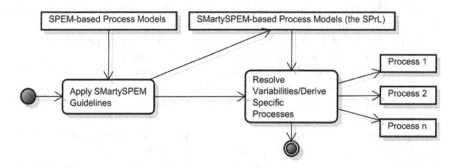

Fig. 3. Modelling LPS and Deriving Specific Processes based on the SMartySPEM Approach

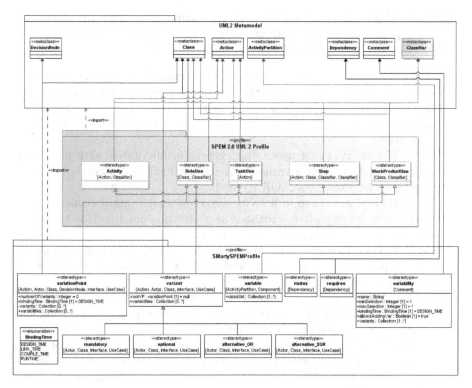

Fig. 4. The SMartySPEMProfile and its Stereotypes

- ≪mandatory≫ - represents mandatory process elements that must be present in all specific derived processes of a SPrL;
- ≪optional≫ - represents optional process elements that might be part of an instantiated process;

- ≪alternative_OR≫ - represents different possible combinations of elements for resolving a variation point or a variability;
- ≪alternative_XOR≫ - represents the selection of only one process element from a set for resolving a variation point or a variability;
- ≪mutex≫ - represents the concept of variant constraint and it is a mutually exclusive relationship between two variant process elements. It means that the selection of a variant requires the deselection of another variant for a specific process;
- ≪requires≫ - represents the concept in which the selection of a variant implies the selection of another variant for a specific process; and
- ≪variable≫ - it is an extension of the metaclass `ActivityPartition`. It indicates that a partition in an activity diagram contains a set of process elements with explicit variabilities.

SMartySPEM provides the following set of guidelines to support the identification and representation variability in modeled process elements by taking into consideration the SMartySPEMProfile stereotypes:

- **G1.** `DecisionNode` elements in activity diagrams suggest variation points tagged as ≪variationPoint≫ as they explicitly represent different paths;
- **G2.** SPEM `Activity` elements in activity diagrams might be defined as mandatory or optional variants tagged as ≪mandatory≫ and ≪optional≫, respectively;
- **G3.** SPEM `Activity` elements which represent alternative path flows of a ≪DecisionNode≫ suggest variant activities inclusive (≪alternative_OR≫) or exclusive (≪alternative_XOR≫); and
- **G4.** `ActivityPartition` in activity diagrams that contain elements with associated variability - `DecisionNode` as a variation point and/or `Activity` as a variant - must be tagged as ≪variable≫;
- **G5.** Role Use, Task Use and Work Product Use SPEM elements suggest variation points tagged as ≪variationPoint≫ as they might be selected for different specific processes;
- **G6.** Role Use, Task Use, Step and Work Product Use SPEM elements might be tagged as mandatory or optional variants, respectively, by applying the stereotypes ≪mandatory≫ and ≪optional≫;
- **G7.** Role Use, Task Use, Step and Work Product Use SPEM elements that specialize or are composition/aggregation of ≪variationPoint≫ elements, suggest inclusive (≪alternative_OR≫) or exclusive (≪alternative_XOR≫) variant elements;
- **G8.** selected variant elements which require the presence of another element must have a dependency relationship tagged as ≪requires≫; and
- **G9.** mutually exclusive variant elements for a specific process must have a dependency relationship tagged as ≪mutex≫.

The SMartySPEM approach provides the same set of icons of the SPEM meta-model (Table 1). However, each SPEM icon has several variant icons tagged with one of the following acronyms (see Figure 5 for an example): MDT for mandatory,

OPT for optional, OR for inclusive variants, XOR for exclusive variants, and VP for variation points. It means that each SPEM icon receives one of these acronyms to improve the readability of a SMartySPEM-based SPrL model.

4   SMartySPEM Application Example

In order to illustrate the application of the SMartySPEM approach, we have designed a hypothetical SPrL based on the Analysis Workflow of the Unified Process [7]. Such a workflow was adapted to represent the realization of activities related to component-based development.

Figure 5 presents an activity diagram of the designed SPrL according to SMartySPEM. Such a model uses the element Activity for representing the respective SPrL activities. Each element is tagged with SMartySPEMProfile (Figure 4) stereotypes/icons. The first activity is Architectural Analysis, which is mandatory according to guideline G2. It means that for every derived process, such an activity must be realized. The first decision node is tagged as a variation point, according to guideline G1. A variability named Analyse Type Select is associated to such a decision node, providing details on name, min and max selection and binding time. There are two Activity elements that are exclusive variants and represent the variation point alternatives. For instance, for a specific process, if one is interested on classes and/or packages, but not interested on component specifications, the Analyze a Use Case activity must be selected. Note that activity Analyze a Package is optional, according to guideline G2. For another specific process, if one is interested on analyzing interfaces and, then, creating the initial component specifications and architecture, as well as discovering business operations for such interfaces, the Analyze Interfaces activity must be selected. Classes and packages are then discovered in the next activities after Analyze Interfaces.

Figure 6 presents the modeling of the Architectural Analysis activity (first activity of Figure 5), as well as its related process elements. The Architectural Analysis element represents a variation point with three step elements which are inclusive variants: Identifying Obvious Entity Classes, Identifying Common Special Requirements and Develop Business Type Model. The Architect role element is identified as a mandatory variant as it is responsible for realizing the Architectural Analysis activity. The Analysis Class element is a variation point, which has three inclusive variants: Control Class, Entity Class and Boundary Class.

Figure 7 presents an example of a derived Architectural Analysis activity for a specific process from the hypothetical SPrL. Note that the mandatory elements in Figure 6 are in such a derived process activity (Figure 7). Furthermore, optional elements as Suplementary Requirements and Business Type Model, were not selected to compose the derived activity. For resolving the variation point Architectural Analysis Task, the element Identifying Obvious Entity Classes was selected. In addition, the following elements were selected to resolve the Analysis Class variation point: Entity Class and Boundary Class.

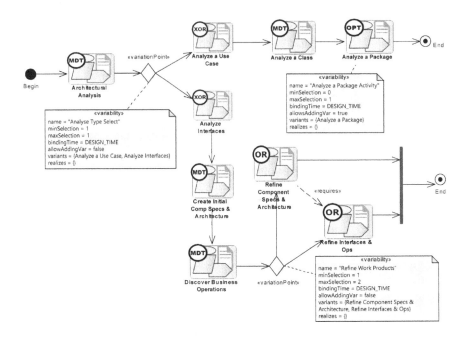

Fig. 5. Excerpt of a Hypothetical LPS According to SMartySPEM

5   Related Work

Variability representation in SPEM elements is also taking into account in vSPEM [9] in which it defines variation points and variants, making it possible the generic definition of a process and respective activities. The variability mechanism was introduced in the vSPEM metamodel by adding new elements in the ProcessLineComponents SPEM package. Alternatively, SMartySPEM adds its variability mechanism directly to the SPEM UML profile by extending some of its stereotypes based on the SMarty approach. Therefore, SMartySPEM does not modify the standard structure of the SPEM 2.0. On the contrary, it introduces new stereotypes to the original elements.

Several limitations of the vSPEM approach were taken into consideration for proposing SMartySPEM. Concepts as inclusive and exclusive variants and constraints between variants are not specified by the vSPEM approach. In addition, it was not defined the concept of optional elements and the possibility of associating more than one variant to a given variation point.

Differently of existing SPrL variability approaches, SMartySPEM also provides a set of guidelines to support the application of the SMartySPEMProfile to the identification and the representation of variability in SPEM-based software process elements.

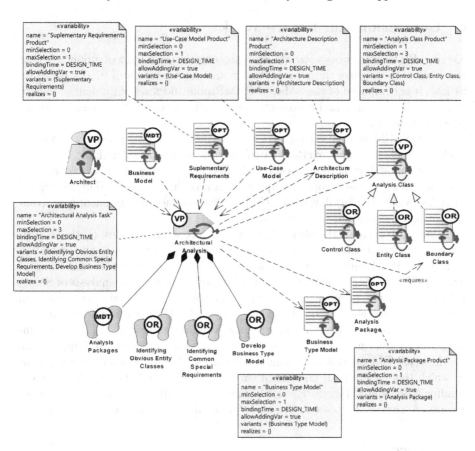

Fig. 6. Architectural Analysis Activity Model According to SMartySPEM

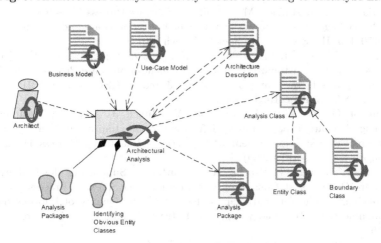

Fig. 7. Specific Architectural Analysis Activity Model Derived from the Hypothetical LPS

6   Conclusion and Future Work

SMartySPEM introduces a variability representation and a set of guidelines that contributes to improve the representation and configuration of SPrLs based on SPEM. It is composed of the SMartySPEMProfile and a set of guidelines to support the identification and representation of variability in SPEM-based software process elements.

SMartySPEM is focused on providing a mechanism to precisely represent optional, inclusive, and exclusive variant process elements making the SPrL variability modeling activity easier and effectiveness compared to existing approaches. The proposed approach application was illustrated based on a designed SPrL for Analysis Workflow of the Unified Process, modified to encompass component based development activities.

Taking into account the obtained results, future work includes: (i) the investigation of different software process elements that might be vary and the adding of SMartySPEM support to such elements; (ii) the investigation and using of existing SPrLs for improving the application and effectiveness analysis of SMartySPEM; (iii) the proposition of a SPrL for component based development in a reactive way based on the Unified Process, the UML Components and the Catalysis approaches; (iv) the experimental validation of SMartySPEM by planning and conducting a set of experiments; (v) the investigation and application of SMartySPEM for different domains, such as, Web and mobile development in which there are a high number of variabilities; and (vi) the possibility of extending/adapting SMartySPEM for business process diagrams elements, such as, Events, Activities, Gateways, Sequence Flow, Message Flow, and Association.

References

1. Alegria, J.A.H., Bastarrica, M.C.: Building Software Process Lines with CASPER. In: Proceedings of the International Conference on Software and System Process, pp. 170–179. IEEE Computer Society, Zurich (2012)
2. Aleixo, F.A., Freire, M.A., dos Santos, W.C., Kulesza, U.: Automating the Variability Management, Customization and Deployment of Software Processes: A Model-Driven Approach. In: Filipe, J., Cordeiro, J. (eds.) ICEIS 2010. LNBIP, vol. 73, pp. 372–387. Springer, Heidelberg (2011)
3. Armbrust, O., Katahira, M., Miyamoto, Y., Münch, J., Nakao, H., Ocampo, A.: Scoping Software Process Lines. Software Process: Improvement and Practice. Software Process: Improvement and Practice - Examining Process Design and Change 14(3), 181–197 (2009)
4. Barreto, A., Duarte, E., Rocha, A.R., Murta, L.: Supporting the Definition of Software Processes at Consulting Organizations via Software Process Lines. In: Proceedings of the International Conference on the Quality of Information and Communications Technology, pp. 15–24. IEEE Computer Society Press, Porto (2010)
5. Bosch, J.: Preface. In: Proceedings of the 2nd Groningen Workshop on Software Variability Management: Software Product Families and Populations, pp. 1–2. University of Groningen, Groningen (2004)

6. Fiori, D.R., Gimenes, I.M.S., Maldonado, J.C., Oliveira Junior, E.A.: Variability Management in Software Product Line Activity Diagrams. In: International Conference on Distributed Multimedia Systems, pp. 89–94 (2012)
7. Jacobson, I., Griss, M.L., Jonsson, P.: Software Reuse: Architecture, Process, and Organization for Business Success. Addison-Wesley Professional, Boston (1997)
8. Linden, F.J., Schmid, K.V.D., Rommes, E.: Software Product Lines in Action: The Best Industrial Practice in Product Line Engineering. Springer, New York (2007)
9. Martínez-Ruiz, T., García, F., Piattini, M.: Towards a SPEM v2.0 Extension to Define Process Lines Variability Mechanisms. Software Engineering Research, Management and Applications 150(1), 115–130 (2008)
10. Oliveira Junior, E.A., Gimenes, I.M.S., Maldonado, J.C.: Systematic Management of Variability in UML-based Software Product Lines. Journal of Universal Computer Science 16(17), 2374–2393 (2010)
11. OMG: Software & Systems Process Engineering Metamodel (SPEM) (2010), http://www.omg.org/spec/SPEM
12. OMG: Unified Modeling Language (UML) - Superstructure v.2.2 (2010), http://www.omg.org/spec/UML/2.2
13. Pohl, K., Böckle, G., Linden, F.J.V.D.: Software Product Line Engineering: Foundations, Principles and Techniques. Springer, New York (2005)
14. Rombach, H.D.: Integrated Software Process and Product Lines. In: Li, M., Boehm, B., Osterweil, L.J. (eds.) SPW 2005. LNCS, vol. 3840, pp. 83–90. Springer, Heidelberg (2006)
15. Washizaki, H.: Building Software Process Line Architectures from Bottom Up. In: Münch, J., Vierimaa, M. (eds.) PROFES 2006. LNCS, vol. 4034, pp. 415–421. Springer, Heidelberg (2006)

Aligning Corporate and IT Goals and Strategies in the Oil and Gas Industry

Victor Basili[1], Constanza Lampasona[2], and Alexis Eduardo Ocampo Ramírez[3]

[1] Fraunhofer Center for Experimental Software Engineering,
University of Maryland, and King Abdulaziz University
College Park, MD, USA
basili@fc-md.umd.edu
[2] Fraunhofer Institute for Experimental Software Engineering
Kaiserslautern, Germany
constanza.lampasona@iese.fraunhofer.de
[3] ECOPETROL S.A.
Bogotá, Colombia
alexis.ocampo@ecopetrol.com.co

Abstract. Companies increasingly recognize that IT plays a significant role in their current and future business strategies, and IT departments increasingly need to justify their role in terms of contributions to business goals. Currently, little experience exists on how to effectively create this missing business-IT link. In 2010, ECOPETROL, a global player in the oil and gas industry, launched an initiative to align their IT activities with their overall business goals. IT is becoming a key information provider for making business-oriented decisions and achieving business success. Consequently, the view of IT is from that of a support organization to that of a value-creating information provider. This article describes how ECOPETROL is utilizing IT services to improve their competitiveness in the marketplace. They are applying the GQM⁺Strategies® approach for measurement-based IT-business alignment.

Keywords: D.2.8 Metrics/Measurement, D.2.9 Management.

1 Introduction

IT and software are becoming central drivers for innovation and growth for many organizations, and business success increasingly depends on IT and software-related strategies.

In 2010, ECOPETROL, a global player in the oil and gas industry ranked 12 among the top 50 energy companies according to the PIW ranking [6], launched an initiative to better align their IT software development activities with their overall business goals. This changed the role of IT software development from a simple service provider to a central information provider to support decision-making at the highest levels of the organization and thus become a tool for achieving business success. The information orientation [13] concept characterizes the change from classical IT service departments to providers of high-quality information. As a consequence, IT

J. Heidrich et al. (Eds.): PROFES 2013, LNCS 7983, pp. 184–198, 2013.
© Springer-Verlag Berlin Heidelberg 2013

software applications have to provide high-quality information. As a result, software development is affected by a lot of implications on how applications should be designed and how they should interact with each other and which architectural patterns should be used in order to enhance information quality and promote effective information usage.

For the implementation of this paradigm shift, it was necessary to link the goals and strategies of the IT department to the overall goals and strategies of ECOPETROL, creating a hierarchy of aligned goals from the top level business goals to the IT project goals making sure that the entire organization is moving in the same direction and demonstrating the value of IT-related activities to the overall organization.

In order to make the goals operational at all levels, it was necessary to establish a measurement system for quantifying the IT contribution and provide a mechanism for monitoring the attainment of goals and the success/failure of the strategies followed.

This article discusses how ECOPETROL is evolving their IT services to improve their competitiveness in the market utilizing the GQM⁺Strategies® approach. The GQM⁺Strategies® approach supports companies in aligning IT/software-related strategies with business goals across the entire organization through measurement [2]. It is being applied in several organizations in a variety of domains at various levels of depth. This article will briefly sketch the approach and illustrate how it is being utilized by ECOPETROL for creating an alignment model.

2   Related Work

In the past, a variety of approaches have been developed covering different aspects of linking activities related to IT services and software development to the upper-level goals of an organization and demonstrating their business value [4]. The aim of the GQM⁺Strategies® approach applied in this paper is not meant to replace these approaches, but rather to close the existing gaps with respect to the linking of goals, their implementation, and the measurement data needed to evaluate goal attainment.

The Business Motivation Model [14] (BMM) describes a model and terminology for defining so-called Ends and Means on different levels of an organization. The GQM⁺Strategies® model follows a similar idea, but explicitly links Ends (called "goals" in the GQM⁺Strategies® terminology) and Means (called "strategies") on multiple levels by specifying rationales for all linkages.

One issue not explicitly addressed by classical software measurement approaches, such as the Goal Question Metric approach [3] (GQM) or Practical Software and Systems Measurement [16] (PSM), is the connection between the data collected and the organizational goals of the company this data contributes to. GQM⁺Strategies® adds the capability to integrate all measurement data with organization-wide goals and strategies, thus demonstrating the business value generated by the collection of these data. It is based upon the GQM approach, but goes beyond it by making various implicit concepts, such as context and assumptions, explicit and formalizing the concept of a goal hierarchy leading to and derived from strategies.

When it comes to the higher-level goals of an organization, the Balanced Scorecard [8] (BSC) is a common tool for defining Key Performance Indicators (KPIs). Strategy maps are used to link strategies to corresponding goals and perspectives. However, alignment between different organizational levels and integration of the measurement data are not explicitly addressed. The GQM+Strategies® approach helps establish this link by taking the defined strategy maps and KPIs as input and offering a comprehensive model from the business level down to the project level.

For classical IT services and processes, such as those described by ITIL [15], more elaborate structures addressing business value already exist in the form of an information technology infrastructure library. CoBIT [7] offers an approach for IT governance that addresses multiple organizational levels, but is solely focused on the classical set of IT services. Addressing the change from classical IT service departments to providers of high-quality information requires a more open-ended capability geared to the business goals of the specific organization. GQM+Strategies® extends these predefined governance structures and focuses on alignment of the hierarchy of organizational goals. ITIL and CoBIT are basic underlying frameworks for classical IT services and governance, but which do not focus on helping an organization achieve its specific business goals.

3   GQM+Strategies® in a Nutshell

GQM+Strategies® is an approach for linking operational organizational goals and strategies from the top management level to the project level and back up, aligning the business at all levels of the organization in a seamless way and providing a mechanism for monitoring the success and failure of goals and strategies through measurement. The process consists of (1) generating a grid which represents the hierarchy of operational, strategies, measures and interpretations models, (2) planning and executing the strategies, and (3) analyzing and evaluating the successes and failures of the various strategies with recommendations for improvement. The *grid generation phase* provides a framework and notation to help organizations develop/package their operational, measureable business goals, select strategies for implementing them, communicate those goals and strategies throughout the organization, and translate those goals into an aligned set of lower-level goals and strategies. The *planning and execution phase* consists of planning for the implementation of the strategies and executing them as defined. The *analysis and evaluation phase* helps organizations assess the effectiveness of their strategies at all levels of the organization and recognize the achievement of their business goals over time.

The grid generation activities include learning about the organization and its objectives, specifying the scope of the application, i.e., those parts of the organization that will apply GQM+Strategies®, and educating and training the organization in the approach. The output of the planning phase is a detailed and comprehensive model, called the *grid*, which provides the organization with an aligned set of operational goals and strategies and defines all the elements necessary for a measurement program [2]. The grid allows *all* parts of the organization to recognize their role in achieving the organization's top-level goals, lets them see what is important, how it can be measured, and how those measures will be interpreted. This grid for the organization allows them to make their goals operational, see and achieve consensus on the alignment of the goals, understand what needs to be done to achieve their goals, and realize what measurement needs to take place. Grid generation maybe an end in itself as it clarifies the organization's thinking and can be used in a variety of ways, e.g., providing recognition of what needs to be done, letting the organization select projects that support the organization and eliminate those that do not.

The planning and executing phase and the analysis and evaluation activities involve the use of the measurement program to assess over time the effectiveness of the strategies, the achievement of the goals, and recognition of the need to change both strategies and goals based upon the collection of the prescribed data.

This paper is related with the grid generation phase of GQM⁺Strategies® at ECOPETROL.

The basic concepts of the approach, represented in the partial grid in Fig. 1, are:

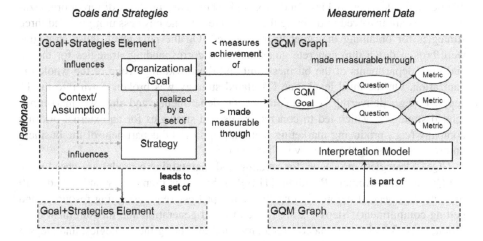

Fig. 1. The GQM⁺Strategies® Model Structure

- **Organizational Goals:** states that the organization wishes to achieve in order to accomplish its objectives. Their scope can be various parts of the organization (e.g., the management is interested in improved customer satisfaction, or the IT department is interested in reduced rework costs). They define a target state the organization wants to accomplish within a given time frame.
- **Strategies:** possible approaches for achieving a goal within the environment of the organization. The number of goal/strategy levels depends on the (internal) structure of an organization.
- **Context Factors:** the external and internal organizational environment, e.g., the business environment, the company's position in the market, or the resources available for innovation.

- **Assumptions:** estimated unknowns, i.e., what is believed to be true but needs to be re-evaluated over time. The relevant context factors and assumptions define the **rationale** for choosing specific goals and strategies.
- **GQM Graphs:** the definition of how to measure whether a goal was accomplished and whether a strategy was successful. Following the classical GQM approach, GQM goals are defined and broken down into concrete metrics. Interpretation models are used for objectively evaluating goals and strategies.

The entire model provides an organization with a mechanism for not only defining measurement consistent with larger, upper-level organizational concerns, but also for interpreting and rolling up the resulting measurement data at each level. Fig. 2 illustrates the relationship between different organizational units involved in defining a strategic measurement program and the GQM$^+$Strategies$^®$ grid. Obtaining a certain goal and applying a certain strategy are the responsibilities of different units in the organization. The grid documents the relationships between the different goals and strategies of the organizational units and explains how to use the collected measurement data for decision making. In the example shown in Fig. 2, six different organizational units are involved in defining the grid. Overall, one business unit goal and three strategies for obtaining that goal were modeled. On the next level, these strategies were broken down into concrete goals and their corresponding strategies for the IT and sales departments of the business unit and the marketing group of the whole organization. On the third level, one IT-related strategy was broken down into the IT supplier (e.g., delivering software to the IT department), and the two marketing-related strategies, which led to concrete goals and strategies for an external printing company (e.g., producing marketing material) and the IT department of the business unit (e.g., supporting the strategy with the IT).

GQM$^+$Strategies$^®$ processes for creating and maintaining a model are based upon the Quality Improvement Paradigm [1] (QIP). Step 0 is preparatory and includes all the activities needed before starting the actual process (e.g., assigning resources and getting commitment). Steps 1-2 are related to grid generation and measurement definition, steps 3 and 4 are related to planning and executing the strategies, and steps 5 and 6 are related to analyzing the outcomes of strategic measurement programs:

1. **Characterizing:** Defining the scope for creating a model, characterizing the external and internal environment, i.e., the context to which the approach will be applied, and determining responsibilities for carrying out the approach.
2. **Setting Goals:** Developing the model structure, grid, measurement and interpretations based upon existing objectives within the defined scope, a gap analysis, interviews, and goal and strategy elicitation workshops.
3. **Choosing Process:** Planning the processes for implementing the strategies and collecting the data.
4. **Executing Model:** Applying the strategies, collecting the data, and starting to analyze the data to make adjustments, where necessary and possible in real time.
5. **Analyzing Results:** Interpreting the measurement results, assessing the success and failure of the strategies and the achievement of the goals.

6. **Packaging and Improving:** Improving the model and measurement plan as well as reworking the goals and strategies over time.

The overall process defines a continuous improvement cycle. The defined goals and strategies are evaluated using the collected measurement data and decisions for improvement are made. These decisions result in removed, adapted, new goals and strategies, or extensions of the GQM⁺Strategies® grid.

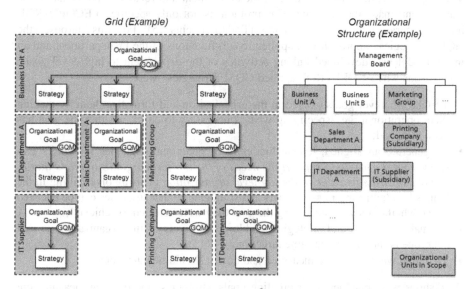

Fig. 2. Relationship between the GQM⁺Strategies® Grid and the Organizational Structure

4   Business Alignment at ECOPETROL

The following section gives an overview of the application of GQM⁺Strategies® in building a partial goal/strategy grid at ECOPETROL following the steps sketched above. The major activity applied and evaluated is the *grid generation phase*, so the emphasis is on the earlier steps in the process (characterize and set goals) and the effects of the grid development on the organization will be what is analyzed. The preparatory step 0 (initialize) is finished, i.e., initialization activities, such as planning and assigning resources and obtaining commitment, have taken place.

4.1   Characterizing

ECOPETROL is one of the top 50 oil and gas companies in the world and the largest company in Colombia. The IT function has roughly 140 employees and consists of several sub-groups addressing different IT-related tasks, including classical IT services as well as services related to information provision, software and system security, and Enterprise Architecture. A Software Factory (composed of external software development companies) is responsible for maintaining and integrating existing systems as well as for developing new IT-based software systems.

4.2   Setting Goals and Measures

In the context of evolving the department from a classical IT department to an information provider, the business value of the department and related activities had to be clarified and made measureable. This problem is not only specific to ECOPETROL but is generally an issue for many IT departments [5]. For this purpose, the GQM$^+$Strategies$^®$ approach was applied to sub-functions of the IT department and an initial model was developed linking activities of the department to high-level goals. The reasons why ECOPETROL applied GQM$^+$Strategies$^®$ were:

- To take whatever goals existed in the organization and formalize them by making them operational, i.e., specifying what is necessary to check whether the goal has been achieved;
- To generate an aligned, logical hierarchy of goals and strategies *so that IT can know what it must do to support the needs of the top-level organization and that IT can demonstrate its value to the top-level organization* (This involves filling in the blanks by identifying missing goals and strategies so that strategies can be checked to see whether they are achieving the goal they were selected to achieve.);
- To make all goals and strategies visible at all levels of the organization so that everyone is moving in the same direction;
- To define what should be measured and how it should be interpreted.

Workshops were conducted for eliciting goals, strategies, and existing measurement data in order to gain a common understanding. Mainly group and project leaders as well as SEPG (Software Engineering Process Group) people participated in those meetings. An initial gap analysis revealed that even though a set of high-level business-level goals (and corresponding strategies for implementing these goals) was available, it was hard to define the relationships among those goals and, most important, their impact on IT-level goals and activities. Fig. 3 shows excerpts from the initial GQM$^+$Strategies$^®$ model. It focuses on connecting goals (G1 to G5) and strategies (S1 to S5) from the business level down to the IT level. It also documents the major rationales for linking the goals and strategies in terms of context factors (C1) and assumptions (A1 to A6). At the business level, three goals and corresponding strategies were defined, starting with the very high-level goal of being among the top 30 companies in terms of oil and gas reserves down to the lower-level goal (G3) of decreasing the analysis time for finding oil and gas reserves. At this stage, a strategy was defined to improve the quality of the information, because providing high-quality data will quickly support the decision-making process by decreasing the time needed to find new oil and gas reserves.

So, one central goal on the IT level is to improve and maintain information quality, which corresponds to strategy S3. Table 1 defines the goal for improving and maintaining information quality (G4) using the GQM$^+$Strategies$^®$ goal template for

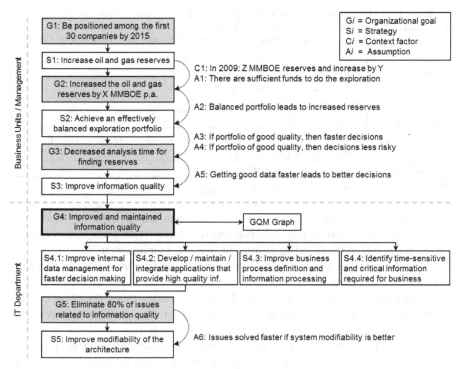

Fig. 3. Excerpt of the GQM⁺Strategies® Model

organizational goals. Information quality is broken down into five ECOPETROL-specific sub-concepts, which are representatives of common characteristics in the oil and gas industry [9] (Uniqueness, Completeness, Consistency, Timeliness, and Confidentiality). The IT department provides and manages several information units (pieces of critical information, such as information about wells or oil and gas reserves) for other ECOPETROL business units, covering the information needs of different business processes. The major goal on the IT level is to improve the quality of these information units by having 10% fewer critical information units (defined as status "red") and 10% fewer medium-critical units (defined as status "yellow").

Although the model in Fig. 3 offers four different strategies addressing and operationalizing this goal, only one of them (S4.2) is shown as broken down to the level of improving the modifiability of the software architecture (S5). The others are not shown here.

The measurement goal here focuses on the achievement of the information quality improvement goal. For that purpose, GQM interviews were conducted with selected stakeholders from the IT department. As part of a first brainstorming session of these interviews, potential measurement goals related to information quality were identified. For each goal, a GQM abstraction sheet was defined. Table 2 gives an example abstraction sheet for analyzing the uniqueness of information units at ECOPETROL.

Table 1. IT Organizational Goal "G4: Improved and maintained information quality"

Focus	Information quality (with attributes: Uniqueness, Completeness, Consistency, Timeliness, and Confidentiality)
Object	Information units of all business processes
Magnitude	10% decrease of #reds for each attribute 10% decrease of #yellows for each attribute
Timeframe	Every 3 months
Scope	Information division for the upstream (related to exploration and production of oil and gas reserves)
Constraints	Use of resources for other activities
Relations	Budget needs to be checked against revenue-related goals

A GQM abstraction sheet helps elicit and structure information during GQM interviews and assists in constructing, refining, and reviewing GQM goals, questions, and metrics. It consists of the GQM measurement goal and four quadrants.

During the planning phase, a prototype tool was used to store and access the grid. A spreadsheet was used for documenting all organizational goals, strategies, context factors, and assumptions, as well as the relationships among them. Based on that documentation, a simple tool generated visualizations of the specified structure, also enabling the user to browse through the different relationships.

Aligning and communicating all the goals, strategies, and measurement opportunities provides ECOPETROL with an integrated vision so that all elements of the organization can move in the same direction.

Based on the GQM⁺Strategies® model, an MS Excel-based questionnaire was developed for collecting data to analyze the achievement of the "improving and maintaining information quality" goal (Fig. 4). The questionnaire includes five different sections covering general information and the five attributes considered for information quality (uniqueness, completeness, consistency, timeliness, and confidentiality). The questionnaire was developed to ask representatives of both business and IT to provide their assessment of information quality. The opinions of both groups of representatives were critical, as some questions can only be answered if the knowledge and experience of business and IT come together.

Since it was critical to make the questionnaire understandable, and effective and efficient in gathering the appropriate information, it was piloted in a three-stage process. The first stage was conducted in a laboratory setting where influencing and environmental factors could be controlled (e.g., noise, distraction). During this stage, a sample group filled out the questionnaire in an artificial environment without disturbing influences. One purpose of this stage was to improve the understandability of the questionnaire based on the results of the laboratory study. During the second stage, the approach was piloted for a sample group that filled out the improved questionnaire in their real-life work setting. The results of this field study were used to analyze the information quality provided by individual business units and to do some final adaptation to the questionnaire before broadening the scope of users.

During the third stage, the approach was applied in 13 different areas of the company (such as Financial, IT, Petrochemicals, and Communication). 86 information unit owners used the approach to assess 184 information units as part of interviews conducted together with measurement experts (Fig. 5). The experts supported the interviewees in answering the questions and collected feedback about the understandability and applicability of the questionnaire in practice. The average time needed for an interview was approx. 20 minutes. This time is expected to be reduced by at least 50% when the approach is fully rolled out.

Table 2. GQM Abstraction Sheet Excerpt

Object	Purpose	Quality Aspect	Viewpoint	Context
Information unit	*Characterize / Evaluate*	*Uniqueness*	*Business / IT*	*X*

A. Quality Focus	**Variation Factors**

Uniqueness: An information unit has a named unique source and every representation of that information unit has the same value. For each information unit (relevant for the decisions to be made):
 	
Q1.1: Is there one defined unique source specified?
    M1.1: (yes/no/don't know)
Q1.2: Do you know about all replications of this information unit?
    M1.2.1: (yes/no)
    M1.2.2: Estimated # of known replications
Q1.3: Does every representation of that information unit have the same value (check a representative sample, 10% of # of known replications)?
    M1.3.1: (yes/no/don't know)
    M1.3.2: Estimated # of non-duplicates
	V1: Update Rate
	    VM1.1: Time between updates in minutes

Baseline Hypotheses	**Impact**
(confidential information)	(was not filled in during workshop)

Interpretation Model			
M1.1	*M1.2.1*	*M1.3.1*	*Assessment*
(all values)	(all values)	no / don't know	red
no / don't know	(all values)	(all values)	red
yes	no	yes	yellow
yes	yes	yes	green

	Information Quality Questionnaire (Information Unit Owner)
	This questionnaire will focus on some attributes for all information units of all business processes. With the information of this questionnaire, we want to characterize and improve the uniqueness, completeness, consistency, and timeliness of information units.
	The questionnaire is structured in five steps according to general information and relevant attributes for information quality. Please answer all questions in terms of your own information unit.
	Please use only the yellow cells for your answers. If you have any further comments, please do not hesitate and use the comment column. In the first step, we want to survey some general information about you and the information unit under investigation. The next steps focus on characterizing the uniqueness, completeness, consistency, timeliness, and confidentiality of the information unit.
	For your information: An Information Unit is a piece of critical information at EcoPetrol (like information about wells or oil and gas reserves) used in one or more business processes. Each information unit has one owner who maintains the information unit and is responsible for providing this piece of information at an appropriate level of quality. For a single information unit, there may be multiple users who make use of an information unit as part of a business process that has this information unit as input.

General

	General Information	Your answer:
G1.1	Name of your information unit	
G1.2	Names of the business processes	
G1.3	Your name	
G1.4	Reporting time (year/month)	
G1.5	Current date (year/month/day)	

Uniqueness

This part of the questionnaire deals with uniqueness issues related to information quality.

Definition of Uniqueness: An information unit has a named unique source and every representation of that information unit has the same value.

	Questions:	Your answer:	Comments:
M1.1.1	In the context of your information unit: Is one defined unique source of the information unit specified?		
M1.1.2	What is the name of the unique source? If you don't know the name, please write "I don't know".		
M1.2.1	In the context of all replications of your information unit: Do you know about all replications?		
M1.2.2	Please estimate the number of known replications.		
M1.3.1	What do you think: Does every representation (textual or in databases) of that information unit have the same value? Please check a representative sample of 10% to answer the question.		
M1.3.2	Please estimate the number of non-duplicates in your information unit.		
VF1.1	Thinking about all replications of an information unit that are not replicated automatically: Do all replications have a time-stamp indicating the expiration date?		
VF1.1a	Thinking about all replications of an information unit that are not replicated automatically: How often do replications have a time-stamp indicating the expiration date?		Alternative to VF1.1 using a different scale for answering (not in evaluation model)
VF1.2	Are all replications that are not replicated automatically assured to be valid for the time-stamped period only?		
VF1.3	Do you agree with the following statement: Replications should be updated as often as possible.		

Fig. 4. Implementation of an IQ Questionnaire

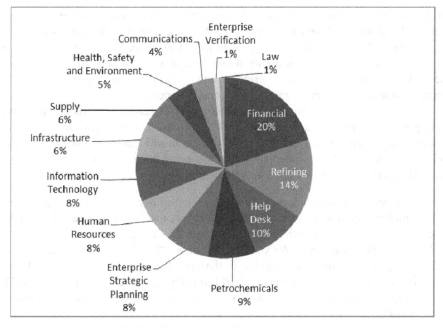

Fig. 5. Coverage of Business Areas

5   An Initial Evaluation

The evaluation of the application of the grid generation phase of GQM⁺Strategies® is an ongoing effort. Initial results are presented here.

First, an objective of the GQM+Strategies® developers was to assess how well the approach was communicated to the principal players at ECOPETROL so that they could apply the approach themselves. To this end, a form was used to evaluate the expertise of ECOPETROL personnel, which was filled out after the training and workshop sessions. The results of the evaluation support the belief that the training and workshops (two three-day sessions) provided sufficient expertise for ECOPETROL personnel to carry out the effort of grid development and implementation independently. More specifically, responders who participated in the tutorial and workshops said they understood the grid, could update and compare the strengths and weaknesses of variations in the grid, and could develop a grid for another part of the organization, but might want their results checked by an expert.

Second, the achievement of the specified Ecopetrol objectives was supported by the approach as seen by the example in this paper and the results of a second questionnaire. These objectives included: (1) taking existing implicit and explicit goals and formalizing them to make them operational, (2) generating an aligned, logical hierarchy of goals and strategies so that IT knows what it must do to support the needs of the top-level organization and can demonstrate its value to the top-level organization, (3) making all goals and strategies visible at all levels of the organization so that everyone is moving in the same direction, and (4) defining what should be measured and how it should be interpreted. The achievement of these objectives can be seen from the sample subset of goals in the paper as well as the responses to a second evaluation form, which revolved around assessing the benefits derived from the development of the grid. Both forms can be found at http://www.iese.fraunhofer.de/en/products/gqm/gqm_publications.html.

The resulting responses from both business and IT stakeholders were very positive. Both pointed out that it clarified their roles and goals, making it easy to see all the relationships (alignment) in order to communicate unambiguously with the business units (transparency). More specifically, the following comments were made by the evaluation participants, based upon interview questions:

- *Was the process of building the grid helpful for your organization?* "The grid really helped as a communication tool and a discovery tool, to gain more focus, and to explicitly link the goals of the organization with the IT organization."
- *Is the resulting grid helpful for your organization?* "Many of the IT services we're providing are not 100% represented in the grid. But we can show this grid to a business user and he/she can understand it quickly. [It is] really helpful for the IT organization because everyone should [think] about how his/her project supports the goals."
- *What part of the grid is most helpful?* "The explicit connections between the goals and the strategies."
- *How has building the grid and the resulting grid impacted your way of thinking about your business and daily work?* "The big cultural change we're [experiencing] right now is that you can use the grid to figure out where the new project should fit [in]."
- *How well did the grid help you to quantify your organization's goals and strategies?* "Before, we didn't have a measurement schema to deal with all the information. But the grid really helped us to define a formal way to ensure the quality of the data and the goals regarding what we want to do with the data."

The negative comments were related to tool support and the mental effort involved:

- The support tool for GQM⁺Strategies® is still a work in progress and is hard to use and not robust enough to deal with the full set of IT activities, much less the entire corporate grid; e.g., "We understand the methodology [and] can define and extend the grid. But we are not using the tool right now. The tool needs to be enhanced; especially the user interface." It should be noted that the tool used during this stage of the project has been replaced by a new tool with an interactive editor that allows specifying and browsing all elements of a GQM⁺Strategies® grid.
- The development of the grid requires the collaboration of several people representing different levels of the organization and is a non-trivial mental activity; e.g., "The people don't expect such intensive mental work [and] they should be prepared for that."

Although the goal of this paper was to discuss and evaluate the results of the grid generation phase at ECOPETROL, one sign of success is that the questionnaire is currently being used as a measurement instrument by 72 information unit owners who are responsible for 808 information units. A tool that semi-automates the process and supports the information unit owners in completing the questionnaire has been developed and is being used [11]. This tool generates reports, which allow the information quality indicator to be calculated automatically. This information is being used in several ways, e.g., for building/updating the Ecopetrol IT roadmap and demonstrating the value of IT to the top-level organization. It can also be used as a baseline for new projects in the company's IT department, or as a basis for discussions on information governance.

Current data shows that measuring the quality of information units has helped some departments support their claims with empirical evidence and identify gaps such as the need for specific tool support for concrete activities, and it has helped identify highly effective processes and tools.

6   Conclusions

The application of GQM+Strategies® is a work in progress. There is evidence that the grid generation process seamlessly aligned the business at several levels of the organization. It has created a thread that links one major top level management goal down to the IT level, providing a rationale for each intermediate goal selection, and a means for assessing the success/failure of the collection of goals and strategies through measurement.

ECOPETROL continues to extend the model and collect and analyze data based upon the questionnaire. Data on information quality is being collected via various measurement instruments and is being used to assess the data. One extension already in progress is a measurement model for architectural maintainability, which is especially important on the level of integrating various IT projects. The planning and execution phase is now in progress and early indications are that the strategies are working well.

Current work on the GQM+Strategies® approach is aimed at broadening the user base of the approach in order to gain more insights into the structure of goals and strategies, identifying common patterns that may be applicable in predefined environments, and   creating an experience base of goals, strategies, and measurement data. Research activities include the integration of the work on Value-Based Software Engineering to deal with evaluating the ROI of various strategies [12].

Acknowledgments. We thank Jens Heidrich, Jürgen Münch, and Sabine Nunnenmacher for contributions to former versions of this paper, Vladimir Mandic for developing the evaluation forms and participating in the interviews, and Sonnhild Namingha for reviewing the article.

References

1. Basili, V., Caldiera, G.: Improve software quality by reusing knowledge and experience. Sloan Management Review 37(1), 55–64 (1995)
2. Basili, V.R., Heidrich, J., Lindvall, M., Münch, J., Regardie, M., Rombach, D., Seaman, C., Trendowicz, A.: Linking software development and business strategy through measurement. IEEE Computer 43(4), 57–65 (2010)
3. Basili, V., Caldiera, G., Rombach, D.: Goal, question metric paradigm. Encyclopedia of Software Engineering, vol. 1, pp. 528–532. John Wiley and Sons (1994)
4. Carr, N.G.: IT doesn't matter. Harvard Business Review, 5–12 (May 2003)
5. CiGREF and Capgemini. Information: the next big challenge for business. White paper (December 2009)
6. Energy Intelligence. Petroleum Intelligence Weekly Newsletter (December 8, 2011)
7. ISACA, Control objectives for information and related technology (CoBIT®) (December 2007), http://www.isaca.org
8. Kaplan, R., Norton, D.: The balanced scorecard - measures that drive performance. Harvard Business Review 71 (January-February 1992)
9. Kozman, J., Ripley, T.: Sustainable spatial architecture for geo engineering data and workflows. In: Proceedings of the SPE Annual Technical Conference and Exhibition, Denver, Colorado, USA, September 21-24 (2008); paper no. SPE-116709.G
10. Lampasona, C., Heidrich, J., Basili, V., Ocampo, A.: Software quality modeling experiences at an oil company. In: ESEM 2012 Proceedings of the 2012 ACM-IEEE International Symposium on Empirical Software Engineering and Measurement, pp. 243–246 (2012)
11. Ocampo, A., Basili, V., Heidrich, J., Lampasona, C.: ECO-MAPS: An Information-Centered Approach for Enterprise Modeling. In: SATURN 2012: 8th SEI Architecture Technology User Network (SATURN) Conference (2012)
12. Mandic, V., Basili, V., Harjumaa, L., Oivo, M., Markkula, J.: Utilizing GQM+Strategies for business value analysis: an approach for evaluating business goals. In: Proceedings of the 2010 ACM-IEEE International Symposium on Empirical Software Engineering and Measurement (ESEM 2010), Article 20. ACM, New York (2010)
13. Marchand, D.A., Kettinger, W.J., Rollins, J.D.: Information orientation (IO): the link to business performance. Oxford University Press (2001)
14. Object Management Group (OMG), The business motivation model (BMM) v.1.1 (August 2010), http://www.omg.org
15. Office of Government Commerce (OGC). The IT infrastructure library (ITIL) service delivery, The Stationary Office London (2002)
16. US Department of Defense and US Army (DoD), Practical software and systems measurement: a foundation for objective project management, v.4.0c (March 2003), http://www.psmsc.com

Evaluating Maintainability
of MDA Software Process Models

Bruno C. da Silva[1], Rita Suzana Pitangueira Maciel[1], and Franklin Ramalho[2]

[1]Federal University of Bahia – UFBA
Salvador - Bahia, Brazil
[2]Federal University of Campina Grande – UFCG
Campina Grande – Paraíba, Brazil
{brunocs,ritasuzana}@dcc.ufba.br, franklin@dsc.ufcg.edu.br

Abstract. The description of a software process is called a process model. As well as traditional software processes/methods (e.g. RUP, XP, OSDP, etc.) an MDA software process requires the selection of metamodels and mapping rules for the generation of the transformation chain that produces models and application code. Before software process enactment, process models should be evaluated in order to improve some quality attributes and maintainability is one of the main factors for software process reuse and improvement. This paper presents a conceptual framework including a metrics suite to evaluate maintainability of MDA process models. We also describe an empirical assessment involving three case studies where the metrics suite was applied to over five MDA process models. We compared the results indicated by the measurements with software engineer opinions surveyed by an online questionnaire. We found that the results from the metrics-based conceptual framework application match software engineers' perceptions.

Keywords: MDA, MDA processes, process maintainability, process reuse.

1 Introduction

The wide conceptual gap between the problem and the implementation domains is a significant and well-known factor behind the difficulty of developing software systems [1]. The intrinsic and growing complexity of software is the motivation behind work on industrializing software development. In particular, Model Driven Development (MDD) is primarily concerned with this conceptual gap through the use of approaches and technologies that support systematic transformation of problem-level abstractions (models) for software implementations.

One of the most recognized initiatives in this scenario is the Model-Driven Architecture (MDA) standard [2] that defines a conceptual framework concerning the realization of MDD. MDA shifts the focus of development activities to models and transformations leading to code generation. It separates subject matters so that application-oriented models are independently reusable across multiple implementations through the construction

J. Heidrich et al. (Eds.): PROFES 2013, LNCS 7983, pp. 199–213, 2013.

of three categories of models: CIM – Computational Independent Model, PIM – Platform Independent Model and PSM – Platform Specific Model.

The use of MDA requires the definition of a software process that guides developers in the elaboration and generation of software models [1]. In contrast to traditional processes such as RUP (Rational Unified Process) and OSDP (Open Source Development Process), an MDA software process (called hereafter as MDA process) requires the selection of metamodels and mapping rules for the generation of the transformation chain that produces models and application code [3]. Several MDA processes have been proposed for Middleware Services [3], Web Applications [4], E-learning [5] and a version of the Open Unified Process for MDD [6]. However, there is a lack of consistent terminology since there is no unified language to specify MDA processes: each one adopts ad hoc notations and different concepts are used to define the activities and artifacts for the software development life cycle.

In order to provide a more flexible and extensible way to model and specify (instantiate) MDA process, an approach using MDA process concepts at the metamodel level according to SPEM 2[1] and OMG[2] standards was presented in [7]. To verify the feasibility and applicability of this approach some case studies were performed [8]. The initial analysis of these case studies was based on the information collected through questionnaires. The results indicated that the proposed approach was applicable, comprehensible and positively impressed the participants.

However, besides being comprehensible and applicable it is also desired that MDA processes be easy to maintain and reuse. There is an intrinsic risk of applying a process specification in an industrial scenario without information about its quality. However, this risk can be mitigated by assessing some properties of the process definitions. Thus, the process elements and models can be analyzed and evaluated in order to be certified in terms of quality properties such as maintainability.

In spite of several proposals that evaluate different aspects of software process enactment, there are few proposals for software process models [9]. Within this scenario we have worked on empirical evaluations of MDA process specifications in order to build a body of knowledge concerning the assessment of such a software process. Firstly, in previous work [7] [8] we evaluated the feasibility of specifying MDA process models and their enactment by using the SPEM/MDA approach for Process Specification and Enactment [8] and the MoDErNe tool [17]. However, there are other quality aspects that must be assessed when applying process models specified using the SPEM/MDA approach.

In this work, we propose a framework for evaluating the maintainability of MDA processes, i.e. how easy it is to understand, analyze and manage changes for process improvement and evolution. It is based on GQM (Goal Question Metric) [10] and extends the work presented by [11]. This framework is composed of a set of metrics to be applied in MDA process models concerning their maintainability. Furthermore, two steps were performed in order to evaluate the framework proposed. Initially three

---

[1] Software & Systems Process Engineering Metamodel specification (SPEM) Version 2.0 - www.omg.org/spec/spem2

[2] Object Management Group – www.omg.org

case studies were used to apply the proposed metrics and tool in five MDA process models. After that, through a questionnaire, software engineers assessed MDA process models by observing the process structure and workflow, and gave their opinion regarding process properties related to maintainability. The questionnaire responses were then compared to the results obtained in the first step.

Several related work have recognized the importance of measuring maintainability of software models at different levels, such as high/low level design, software architectures, code, and so on [12] [13] [14]. However, while many of them concentrate on assessment of software products representations, few works are dedicated to quantitative assessment of process models representations [11], the focus of this work.

This paper is organized as follows. Section 2 presents the SPEM/MDA approach, while Section 3 presents the evaluation framework comprising a metrics suite for MDA processes models. Section 4 presents the three case studies that illustrate and discuss the application of the framework, and finally Section 5 shows the conclusions.

2   SPEM/MDA Approach

The SPEM/MDA approach for Process Specification and Enactment [8] defines metamodel covering MDA concepts, which is important to provide a meaningful way to design software processes with characteristics of an MDA process.

Figure 1 shows the proposed metamodel extending some SPEM 2.0 concepts for the MDA context in order to allow a more explicit and precise semantic definition of process elements following the MDA approach.

The process specification is divided into two dimensions: the static concepts comprising disciplines, tasks, steps, roles and workproducts, called *Method Content* presented in the first box (top) of Figure 1; and the dynamic concepts comprising phases, iterations and taskUse, called *Process* showed in the second box (bottom) of Figure 1. Some concepts were specialized for the MDA context and are highlighted in gray.

During process enactment workproducts can be produced and consumed as input and output artifacts. A workproduct can be specialized into: UML model, transformed / generated in the process execution; transformation rule, that contains the rules for automatic model transformation and code generation; extra model, textual specifications or supplementary notation for documenting a project; profile, which gives the semantic for modeling a system; and code, that will become executable.

A process may comprise many phases specialized into CIM, PIM, PSM Modeling and Codification Phases,. The latter phase is considered to complement the source code generated by the transformation rules as not all MDA processes are supposed to generate 100% of system code. Furthermore, an ExtraPhase can be specified representing an additional stage apart from modeling and codification. The modeling phases can be associated to profiles to give the semantic of a specific domain.

In addition, the approach suggests different kinds of UML diagrams to be used as the concrete syntax to specify MDA processes. Class diagrams are recommended to model all the concepts (as classes) and their relations to be used as the base for other diagrams, use case diagrams to assign process roles to   tasks and activity diagrams to model the process workflow (behavior) for guiding the process enactment. These diagrams are omitted in this paper due to the lack of space, though more information can be found in [8].

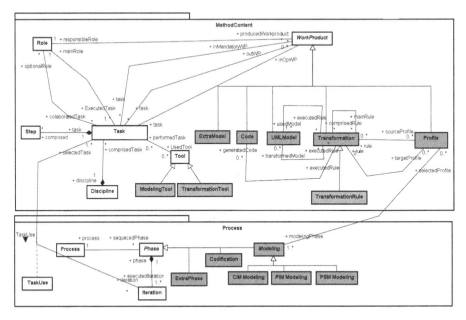

Fig. 1. SPEM/MDA Metamodel (Adapted from [8])

We have developed a support environment called MoDErNe (Model Driven Process Centered Software Engineering Environment) [17] taking into consideration the SPEM/MDA metamodel illustrated in Figure 1. MoDErNe provides a tool environment for the specification of MDA process models according to our SPEM/MDA metamodel and it also includes support for process enactment based on previously specified process models.

3   Evaluation Framework

In order to evaluate the maintainability of MDA processes, we have defined an evaluation framework which serves as a basis for assessing internal and external process model quality attributes concerning the maintainability quality characteristic. Figure 2 illustrates the structure of our framework, which was extended from [11]. Our previous work [7] concentrated on the evaluation of the construction aspects of MDA process specification, i.e. we aimed to verify the applicability of our SPEM/MDA approach and tool by assessing qualitative aspects (Figure 2 - Modeling Process). This is what we call our first dimension of evaluation. However, in the context of this paper, in a second dimension of evaluation, we consider another characteristic as an indicator of quality in the MDA process models (Figure 2 – Process Models

Maintainability), now assessing the MDA process models as a product to be maintained. An MDA process, as every software process, should be as maintainable as possible, i.e. easy to understand, analyze and manage changes for process improvement.

For *Maintainability*, we have used the relationships presented by [11]. This work defined that maintainability is divided into three external quality attributes (*Analyzability*, *Understandability* and *Modifiability*). According to [11] these *external* attributes can be explained as follows: (i) *Analyzability* is related to the ease with which the model discovers errors or deficiencies and guesses the parts that should be modified or reused; (ii) *Understandability* concerns the facility with which the model can be understood; and (iii) *Modifiability* is the ease with which the model can be modified due to possible errors, specific modification request, new requirements or the need to adapt it for reuse. Moreover, these three external attributes are influenced to some extent by *internal* quality attributes, referred to as *Size*, *Complexity* and *Coupling* [15]. Thus, in order to verify the maintainability level of an MDA process we should measure these internal quality attributes.

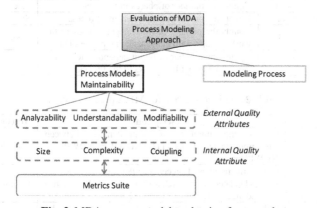

Fig. 2. MDA process model evaluation framework

We used the GQM (Goal Question Metric) approach [10] to evaluate process attributes by defining a goal and decomposing it into questions and metrics, as follows: *Goal*: Verify the maintainability of the MDA process model. *Question 1*: What size is the MDA process? *Question 2*: How complex is the MDA process?, *Question 3*: How easy is it to understand the MDA process?, *Question 4*: How complex is the transformation chain within the process? The corresponding metrics for those questions are presented in the next section.

3.1   Metrics Suite for MDA Process Models

The set of metrics that comprises the maintainability evaluation framework is based on the metrics used by [11], and also on other metrics which we defined for conventional processes and also for the specific context of MDA processes.

In [11], the authors defined metrics for software process models according to SPEM 1.0 concepts. Firstly, in order to update to SPEM 2.0, we modified the metrics terminology, such as the NoT (Number of Tasks) and NoR (Number of Rules) (Table I). Secondly, new metrics were defined, such as NoP (Number of Phases) and NoI (Number of Iterations). Finally, we defined some metrics specific to the MDA context, such as NoTR (Number of Transformation Rules).

Table 1. Direct metrics for MDA process models

Metric	Description	Internal Attribute
NoT (Number of Tasks)	Counts the number of tasks. Updated from NA (Number of Activities) [11]	Size
NoR (Number of Roles)	Counts the number of roles. Terminology updatd from NPR (Number of Process Roles) [11]	Size
NWP (Number of WorkProducts)	Counts the number of workproducts involved workproducts [11]	Size
NoUML (Number of UML Models)	Counts the number of workproducts defined as UML Models	Size
NoTR (Number of Transformation Rules)	Counts the number of workproducts defined as Transformation Rules	Size
NoP (Number of Phases)	Counts the number of phases in a process	Size
NoI (Number of Iterations)	Counts the number of iterations in a process	Size
NDWPIn	Counts the number of input dependencies of the workproducts with the tasks in the process [11]	Size
NDWPOut	Counts the number of ouput dependencies of the workproducts with the tasks in the process [11]	Size

Table 2. Derived metrics for MDA process models

Metric	Description	Internal Attribute
NDWP	Counts the number of dependencies between workproducts and tasks [11] NDWP = NDWPIn + NDWPOut	Complexity
NDT	Counts the number of precedence dependences between tasks. Updated from NDA (Number of Precedence Dependences between Activities) [11]	Coupling
NCT	Calculates the task coupling in the process model by dividing NoT by NDT. Updates from NCA [11]. NCT = NoT / NDT	Coupling
RDWPIn	The ratio between input dependences of workproducts with tasks and total number of dependences of workproducts with tasks [11]. RDWPIn = NDWPIn / NDWP	Size and Complexity
RDWPOut	The ratio between output dependences of workproducts with tasks and total number of dependences of workproducts with tasks [11]. RDWPOut = NDWPOut / NDWP	Size and Complexity
RWPT	Ratio of workproducts and tasks. Updated from RWPA [11]. RWPT = NWP / NoT	Size
DM (Density of UML Models)	Divides the number of UML models workproducts by the total number of workproducs. DM = NoUML / NWP	Size
DTR (Density of Transformation Rules)	Divides the number of transformation rules workproducts by the total number of workprodutcs. DTR = NoTR / NWP	Size

The metrics suite is composed of direct metrics (Table I) and derived metrics (Table II). The former are those metrics designed to count the number of process elements (tasks, roles, workproducts, UML models, transformation rules, phases and iterations). The latter are those whose value is calculated from the former. For instance, DM (Density of UML Models) and DTR (Density of Transformation Rules) integrate the metrics suite corresponding to NoUML and NoTR, respectively. When a metric is defined to just count the number of elements or to find a ratio between such numbers it is categorized as a size metric. Metrics related to calculating dependencies among workproducts and tasks are categorized as complexity metrics as they give the degree of interrelation of the workproducts and tasks within a process. Finally, coupling metrics are the ones which calculate the degree of relatedness among tasks. Process tasks give shape to the process behavior and so the more task connections a process has, the more coupling it has in terms of its internal behavior. In both tables, each line describes the metric acronym (column 1), its description (column 2) and the corresponding internal attribute to which the metric is associated   (column 3).

4   Empirical Evaluation

Our empirical evaluation aims to observe the maintainability of MDA process models assessed by means of the proposed evaluation framework. Thus, the overarching question addressed is: *Is the proposed evaluation framework feasible for quantitatively assessing maintainability of MDA processes?* For this, the evaluation involves two steps: (i) applying the proposed framework to the MDA processes models resulting from the   three case studies we have performed using our approach for MDA process specification and enactment; (ii) applying a questionnaire where selected process models were analyzed by software engineers regarding maintainability aspects. Therefore, we can compare the results obtained from the application of the proposed metrics with those provided by the engineers.

The resulting process models from these three case studies are the target of this current empirical evaluation. They are described as follows: (i) The first case study concerns an MDA process for specific middleware service development, (ii) The second case study, performed in conjunction with the Data Process Company of the State of Bahia (PRODEB),   concerned the building of web applications using MDA approaches; and (iii) the third case study involved participants from a post graduate course who elaborated three MDA process models based on their industry experience. The results from the application of the assessment framework are described and analyzed in Sections 4.1 and 4.2. In Section 4.3 we present the second step of our evaluation which consists of the application of the questionnaire and an analysis comparing the questionnaire responses with process measurements.

4.1   Maintainability Measurements from the First and Second Case Studies

Our first case study targeted the specification of an MDA process for the development of specific middleware services [7]. This process has evolved over the research and is divided into 3 stages: (i) initially, the process was defined without a specific notation; (ii) then the process was improved adjusting some definitions and separating the computational independent modeling phase from the platform independent modeling; (iii) and finally this process was specified using our SPEM/MDA approach and tool. We took the latest version of this MDA process and applied the metrics suite to obtain quantitative data about size, complexity and coupling attributes.

The second case study was conducted with PRODEB company. This experience has been previously described in [8]. However, the empirical data (especially those concerned maintainability aspect) is now presented in this paper. This study involved the specification of the PRODEB process for the development of web applications using our SPEM/MDA approach and tool. Before our study, PRODEB had a previous experience using the AndroMDA tool. However, they encountered limitations related to the tool environment particularly because the process definitions (phases, activities, artifacts, roles, transformations, etc.) were not specified and documented. Therefore the process knowledge had not been registered, just in the minds of the developers. Furthermore, as MDA is an emerging technology, not all professionals are familiar with it. In this context, we worked together with the professionals from PRODEB team for a couple of months in order to model the PRODEB process using our approach and also there was discussion and reasoning about what could be done to improve the modeled process they were carrying out.

Size Measurements

Figure 3 depicts the size measurements from the first two case studies. In terms of workproducts (NWP, NDWPIn, NDWPOut), roles (NoR) and phases (NoP) the MDA process for web applications (P1) is bigger than the MDA process for middleware services (P2). However, the latter has more tasks (NoT). The number of iterations (NoI) is equal for both processes. The ratio between workproducts and tasks (RWPT) is less than 2 for both, while RWPT for P1 has more workproducts and fewer tasks than P2. Figure 3 (b) and (c) show the size measurements concerning the workproducts of the type transformation rules and UML models. P2 deals more with UML models than P1. In terms of transformation rules, P2 has 3 rules corresponding to the transformation of CIMtoPIM, PIMtoPSM and PSMtoCode. As a consequence the derived metrics (DM - Density of Models and DTR- Density of Transformation Rules) is bigger in P2 than P1. P1 has no explicit transformation rules defined in the process model because the AndroMDA tool was used to handle transformations. This tool brings pre-defined transformations called transformation cartridges which make the execution of transformations transparent. Prodeb staff decided to define tasks representing the use of the AndroMDA tool. For this reason the MDA characteristics are more evident in process P2.

Therefore, we can conclude that P2 is bigger than P1, even though P1 has a bigger number of roles and workproducts. The metrics that reveal the MDA process characteristics in P2 (NoUML and NoTR) are bigger than the other ones. P2 is an MDA process which uses transformation rules defined explicitly as workproducts, while in P1 the transformations are pre-defined in the transformation supporting tool that forces the process to adapt to its environment and constraints.

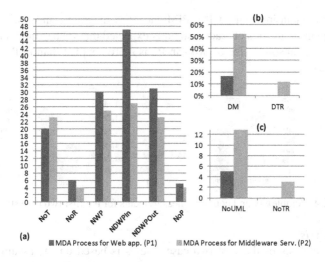

(a)

■ MDA Process for Web app. (P1)   ▨ MDA Process for Middleware Serv. (P2)

Fig. 3. Size measurements for the first two case studies

Complexity Measurements

The complexity measurements are shown in the first two charts of Figure 4. P1 has more dependencies between workproducts and tasks (NDWP) than P2, i.e. the process P2 is less complex in terms of relationships among workproducts and tasks. The second chart in Figure 4 illustrates the RDWPIn and RDWPOut, where we can observe that both processes P1 and P2 have more input dependences than output ones. It is expected that in an MDA process we find these characteristics because the tasks for automatic generation of models and code need four or more input workproducts in general (e.g. models, metamodels, profiles and transformation rules), and thus the output artifacts number is usually smaller than the input one. However, RDWPIn indicates that P1 is more complex, while RDWPOut states that P2 is more complex. This can be explained by the fact that P1 is a process defined in a real environment (PRODEB company) which involves managerial and contractual artifacts for administrative control, not necessarily associated with model transformations. By these measurements, the overall results for complexity indicate that process P1 is more complex than P2 (mainly due to the NDWP values because the RDWPIn and RDWPOut are balanced).

Coupling Measurements

Regarding the coupling measurements, the data presented in the last two charts of Figure 4 indicate that process P2 is more coupled, in the sense that it has more precedence dependences between tasks (NDT) and also more task coupling (NCT) in the process model. Although the difference between coupling measurements for both processes is not as high, the results indicate that the tasks of the MDA process for middleware services development (P2) are more coupled with each other, and therefore the MDA process for web applications from PRODEB company (P1) is simpler in terms of task coupling. It can be explained by analyzing the transformation chain and related tasks. In the case of process P1 we encountered only PIM for code transformations (again, due to the adoption of AndroMDA), while in P2 we have a

transformation chain involving CIM, PIM and PSM diagrams, and also code generation. Consequently, for this characteristic it is expected that P2 has more task coupling
than P1 (also the absolute size of tasks in P2 is more coupled than in P1, as depicted
in Figure 3 (a)).

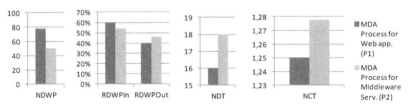

Fig. 4. Complexity and coupling measurements for the first two case studies

Overall Analysis
Our overall analysis of the first two case studies is based on the assumption that a
given process that is large, very complex and coupled makes it less maintainable.
Although P1 is more complex than P2, P2 is more coupled and also bigger than P1,
i.e. P1 has been shown more maintainable than P2 concerning two of the three internal attributes: size and coupling. Therefore, we can conclude that process P1 is more
maintainable than P2. In fact this result can be explained by the fact that process P2
was modeled in a research laboratory evolving over recent years and its model transformation strategy is based on transformation programming languages (ATL and
MofScript). Moreover, P1 uses a transformation engine, AndroMDA, as its model
transformation strategy, which encapsulates several transformation rules.

4.2   Maintainability Measurements from the Third Case Study

We have carried out two case studies with students of a post graduate software engineering course. Their participation was considered important because as well as being
students, many are also professionals with job positions in the software industry.

Initially some lectures about MDA concepts, technologies and also training on our
approach and tool were given to them, a total of 16 hours divided into 4 days in one
week (4h/day) . Then, they were organized into 4 groups and each group was given
the MoDErNE tool and asked to specify an MDA process motivated from their organizational needs and reality. However, each process should have all phases (CIM,
PIM and PSM modeling, and Codification) and the Java platform because transformations for this platform were available. Based on our approach, processes were modeled through UML use case and class diagrams.

Figures 5 and 6 show the measurement results obtained from this third case study.
Initially we had 4 groups working on process specification and so we analyzed 4
(four) process models. One of them was not well-formed and we decided to exclude it
from the data analysis, resulting thus in three software process models, which we
named P1, P2 and P3.

Size Measurements

The size measurements for the third case study are depicted in Figure 5. As can be observed, the 3 processes in terms of size are very similar. P1 is the biggest by two metrics (NoR e NWP). P2 is the biggest by another two metrics (NDWPIn e NWP). And P3 is the biggest by three metrics (NoT, NDWPOut and NoI).

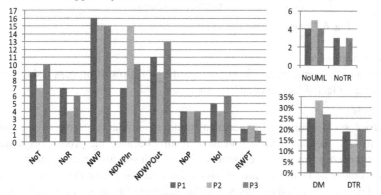

Fig. 5. Size measurement for the third case study

Concerning the kinds of workproducts we verified that P2 handles more UML arti-facts than the others. It is valid by the absolute counting of UML models (NoUML) and also by observing the number of UML models by the total number of workpro-ducts (see NoUML and DM in Figure 5). P1 and P3 come next with the same number (NoUML) and density of UML models (DM). In terms of transformations, P1 and P3 have more transformations as workproducts (NoTR). Also, both processes handle more with transformations in relation to the total number of workproducts (DTR). It means that in P2, the UML workproducts are involved in fewer transformations than in P1 and P3.The transformation chain is certainly bigger in P1 and P3 than in P2, although these processes involve fewer UML models than P2.

Complexity Measurements

By analyzing the complexity measurements (Figure 6), we verified that process P1 has a smaller number of dependences (NDWP) between workproducts and tasks (as input or output), while P2 and P3 have almost the same number. P1 also seems less complex by the ratio between input dependences of workproducts with tasks and total number of dependences of workproducts with tasks (RDWPIn). The numbers for process P3 are very similar to the P1 ones. On the other hand, concerning the isolated RDWPOut, the result indicates that P1 is more complex, i.e. there is a high number of workproduct dependences with tasks as outputs. In general, the analysis indicates that P1 is less complex by considering 2 of the 3 metrics (NDWP and RDWPIn), P2 is less complex if only observing the RDWPOut, while P3 stays in second position in the three complexity measurements. Therefore, we can conclude that by these measure-ments process P2 is the most complex, while P1 is the least.

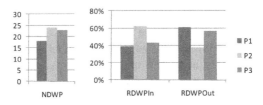

Fig. 6. Complexity measurements for the third case study

Coupling Measurements
For this case study the participants did not design the workflow of process tasks so we do not have data collected for the coupling attribute.

Overall Analysis
The three processes of this third experiment are very similar in terms of size and complexity. In fact, we expected to find these results because the groups of participants are homogeneous in terms of experience in the industry and in computing background. The number of tasks has proven to be the decisive factor in the analysis of their size analysis. As P3 has more tasks, and the number of phases and workproducts are almost the same, we consider that P3 is bigger than the others. Moreover, P2 and P3 are more complex than P1. Thus, we can conclude that P1 is more maintainable than the others, while P3 is the least maintainable.

4.3   Questionnaire Application and Analysis

After applying the proposed framework, the second step in our evaluation was the application of a questionnaire to professionals who were invited to analyze the MDA process models and answer questions about the properties of the processes. The goal of this step was to make a comparison between participant answers and the resulting application of the metrics suite over the first two case studies (Section 4.1). The questionnaire was applied to the MDA process for web applications (P1) and MDA process for middleware services (P2) because these are real processes that were used in the organizations for which they were specified. The questionnaire is available at http://softwareprocessevaluation.blogspot.com.br/. It is divided into three parts: (i) participant profiles; (ii) MDA process models presentation through class and activity diagrams, and (iii) questions and answers about the process models.

A request for questionnaire responses was sent by e-mail to about ninety software engineers, but only twenty-seven of them answered. None of them had participated in the specification of the processes mentioned in the questionnaire. Among them 27% worked in industry and had more than seven years of experience. Of all participants 33% worked with software processes, 22% had previous experience in process specification in their organization or academic work. Furthermore, 57% were familiar with the MDA approach. The questions were made very similar to those presented in Section 3. *Question 1:* Which one is the largest process? *Question 2:* Which process is more complex? *Question 3:* Which process is easier to understand? *Question 4:* Which process has a more complex transformation chain?

In Questions 2 and 3 participants had to justify their answers regarding some MDA process aspects (e.g., tasks, artifacts, transformation rules, etc).

Concerning the largest process, 75% answered that P2 the MDA process for middleware services is larger than P1 (*Question 1*). 88% considered P2 more complex than P1 because it has a higher number of tasks and transformation rules than P2 (*Question 2*).78% considered P1 easier to understand because it had fewer artifacts and transformation rules (*Question 3*). Finally, participants considered that P2 had a more complex transformation chain than P1.Because P2 was perceived as bigger, more complex, more difficult to understand and having a more complex transformation chain than P1, it can be considered as more maintainable than P2.

As the measurements guided by the framework give results about process maintainability on a quantitative basis and the questionnaire provided a qualitative evaluation of the process models, we could not apply quantitative analysis nor statistical tests to the measurements and questionnaire answers. However, the process maintainability perceived by the respondents was observed and compared against the framework measurements. Except for question two, the results of the framework metrics application were very similar to those obtained in the questionnaire answers and led to the same overall conclusion (P1 is more maintainable than P2). Ultimately, as the measurements from the framework application and the participants' perception indicated that P1 is more maintainable than P2, we conclude that in the context in which they were applied, the evaluation framework proposed metrics to measure the maintainability of MDA process models.

4.4   Threats to Validity

The case studies that we have carried out enable us to make useful observations about whether quantitative evaluation of MDA process models using metrics is worth studying further. We address the threats to validity that we have identified as well as explain how we tried to control or mitigate their effects on the observations below.

Conclusion Validity: The main goal of the study has been to observe the feasibility of the proposed evaluation framework. Therefore, a case study rather than a rigorous experiment was a more suitable choice. The results from the study are limited and we do not have statistical evidence to support general conclusions.

Internal Validity: Empirical assessment usually takes into account the amount of data collected from the subjects. However, in the case of an activity of process specification it is difficult to involve a great number of people in the case studies. There are few professionals in organizations involved in this kind of work. In general, many people enact on processes, but few of them specify or model a software process. This observation has already been made in our previous studies. Therefore, the amount and maturity of the subjects who have demonstrated different levels of expertise appear as a threat to the internal validity. To control this factor, training and a tutorial about MDA process models was provided. Additionally, subjects were grouped according to their experience and background in MDA artifacts, including process models.

Construct Validity: We made the assumption that a given process when large, complex and coupled is also less maintainable. It is common thinking for software product artifacts, but we believe it is a reasonable assumption for software process models as they are also software artifacts. Other authors have observed the same [11]. It is also worth emphasizing that in this study we consider equal weights for the three internal attributes: size, complexity and coupling. In addition, most of the proposed metrics are designed to measure the size aspect. This scenario can influence the results because the size aspect is more precisely measured than the coupling and complexity aspects. Regarding the application of the questionnaire, participants may have distinct mental models and make qualitative and quantitative analysis at the same time and to different extents. Therefore, people may observe other aspects of the questionnaire in parallel to the process aspect, such as granularity and type of tasks. This may have influenced the questionnaire answers. However, we did not make fine-grained comparison between the observations from participants and the measurements from the evaluation framework. Rather, we compared the overall classification about the most/less maintainable among the questionnaire results and the measurement results. Therefore, we believe that small variations concerning the participants' reasoning and how well their answers reflect what they really think about process properties did not affect the overall comparison we made.

External Validity: The two processes from the first case study are MDA processes specific for a certain context: one for the development of web applications using the AndroMDA tool; and the other one for the development of domain-specific middleware services and components. Such processes are not generic enough to be customized in different scenarios other than those they were defined for.

5   Conclusion and Future Work

This work presented an evaluation framework for MDA processes. To verify our framework feasibility, three case studies covering five processes models were applied. Then, to evaluate the framework results we applied a questionnaire for developers to evaluate two models, previously evaluated by the framework, and then we compared the results of these two distinct forms of assessment. The results were very similar therefore affirming that our proposal, in this context, was feasible. However, it is important to highlight that our evaluation considered the three internal attributes, i.e. the size, complexity and coupling aspects, as each having a uniform weight.. They were attributed with the same relevance as a factor indicating how maintainable the evaluated processes are, regardless of the number and relevance of the metrics of each of these attributes.

As future work, we aim to (i) conduct new empirical studies which may point out threshold values as references for good/bad maintainability indicators of MDA processes and also to compare measurements with respect to the performance of engineers when conducting modification tasks over the process models; (ii) extend our framework targeting new external and internal quality attributes; and (iii) investigate how the metrics suite deals with different weights assigned to each attribute and each group of attributes.

References

1. France, R., Rumpe, B.: Model-driven Development of Complex Software: A Research Roadmap. In: Proc. of Future of Software Engineering, pp. 37–54. IEEE Press (2007)
2. OMG – Object Management Group. MDA Guide. Version 1.0.1 (omg/2003-06-01) (2003)
3. Maciel, R., Silva, B.C., Mascarenhas, L.: An Edoc-based Approach for Specific Middleware Services Development. In: Proc. of 4th Workshop on MBD of Computer Based Systems, Postdam, Germany, pp. 135–143. IEEE Press (2006)
4. Koch, N.: Transformation Techniques in the Model-Driven Development Process of UWE. In: Workshop Proc. of the 6th Intl. Conference on Web Engineering, California. ACM, NY (2006)
5. Wang, H., Zhang, D.: MDA-based Development of E-Learning System. In: Proc. of 27th International Computer Software and Applications Conference, Texas, p. 684. IEEE Press, California (2003)
6. OpenUP Component – MDD, http://www.eclipse.org/epf/ openup_ /mdd.php
7. Maciel, R., Silva, B., Magalhães, A., Rosa, N.: An Approach for Model-Driven Development Process Specification. In: Proc. of the 11th Intl. Conf. on Enterprise Information Systems, Milan, Italy (2009)
8. Maciel, R., Silva, B., Magalhães, A., Rosa, N.: An Integrated Approach for Model Driven Process Modeling and Enactment. In: Proc. of the 23th Brazilian Symp. on Software Eng., Fortaleza (2009)
9. Monteiro, L.F., de Oliveira, K.M.: Defining a catalog of indicators to support process performance analysis. In: Software Process: Improvement and Practice. John Wiley & Sons (2009)
10. Basili, V., Caldiera, G., Rombach, H.D.: Goal Question Metric Approach. In: Encyclopedia of Software Engineering, pp. 528–532. John Wiley & Sons, Inc. (1994)
11. Canfora, G., García, F., Piattini, M., Ruiz, F., Visaggio, C.A.: A family of experiments to validate metrics for software process models. J. of System and Software 77(2), 113–129 (2005)
12. Alagar, V.S., Li, Q., Ormandjieva, O.S.: Assessment of Maintainability in Object-Oriented Software. In: 39th International Conference and Exhibition on Technology of Object-Oriented Languages and Systems, TOOLS39 (2001)
13. Bosch, J., Bengtsson, P.: Assessing Optimal Software Architecture Maintainability. In: Proceedings of the 5th European Conference on Software Maintenance and Reengineering, CSMR, IEEE Computer Society, Washington, DC (2001)
14. Briand, L.C., Morasca, S., Basili, V.R.: Measuring and Assessing Maintainability at the End of High Level Design. In: Card, D.N. (ed.) Proceedings of the Conference on Software Maintenance, pp. 88–97. IEEE Computer Society, Washington, DC (1993)
15. Briand, L., Morasca, S., Basili, V.: Property-based Software Engineering Measurement. IEEE Transactions on Software Engineering 22(1), 68–86 (1996)
16. Maciel, R., Silva, B., Magalhães, A.: Applying and Evaluating an MDA Process Modeling Approach. In: Proc. of the 12th Intl. Conf. on Enterprise Information Systems, Madeira, Portugal (2010)
17. Maciel, R.S.P., Gomes, R.A., Magalhães, A.P., Silva, B.C., da Queiroz, J.P.B.: Supporting model-driven development using a process-centered software engineering environment. In: MobiCASE 2012. LNCS, vol. 1, p. 1 (2013)

The Evaluation of Weighted Moving Windows for Software Effort Estimation

Sousuke Amasaki[1] and Chris Lokan[2]

[1] Okayama Prefectural University,
Department of Systems Engineering
amasaki@cse.oka-pu.ac.jp
[2] UNSW Canberra,
School of Engineering and Information Technology
c.lokan@adfa.edu.au

Abstract. In construction of an effort estimation model, it seems effective to use a window of training data so that the model is trained with only recent projects. Considering the chronological order of projects within the window, and weighting projects according to their order within the window, may also affect estimation accuracy. In this study, we examined the effects of weighted moving windows on effort estimation accuracy. We compared weighted and non-weighted moving windows under the same experimental settings. We confirmed that weighting methods significantly improved estimation accuracy in larger windows, though the methods also significantly worsened accuracy in smaller windows. This result contributes to understanding properties of moving windows.

1 Introduction

Software effort estimation is an important activity in software development. Its accuracy has a significant effect on project success. Research on the topic has studied two types of effort estimation approach: non-model-based methods (e.g. "expert judgment"), and model-based approaches (e.g. COCOMO, CART, etc.) [1]. A systematic review revealed that model-based software effort estimation models have been popular [2].

A software effort estimation model is developed from training data. Evaluation of the accuracy of the model is based on estimated efforts for testing data. Most studies split project data into training data and testing data randomly, or used a cross-validation approach.

In a practical sense, software projects can be ordered chronologically. Predicting the effort of future projects based on past projects, instead of forming training and testing sets, is more reasonable. Furthermore, it also seems appropriate to use recent projects as a basis of effort estimation. This is because old projects might be less representative of an organization's current practices.

Lokan and Mendes [3] examined whether using only recent projects improves estimation accuracy. They used a window to limit the size of training data so that an effort estimation model uses only recently finished projects. As new projects

J. Heidrich et al. (Eds.): PROFES 2013, LNCS 7983, pp. 214–228, 2013.
© Springer-Verlag Berlin Heidelberg 2013

are completed, old projects drop out of the window. They found that estimation accuracy could increase by using the window.

Their view of a moving window assumes that old projects that are no longer in the window are not included have no value as training data, and projects within the window all have the same weight as training data. This does not take into account the chronological order of projects within the window. Projects within the window could be given different weights, according to their relative age to a target project. Weighting projects according to the order within a window may also affect estimation accuracy.

This study explored the effects of weighted moving windows for software effort estimation. The weighted moving windows generalizes the original moving windows. Recent projects receive higher importance than older projects. Linear regression models can consider different importance with *case weights*. The case weights can make a window have gradual weights.

In this paper, we addressed the following questions:

RQ1. Is there a difference in the accuracy of estimates between moving windows and weighted moving windows?

RQ2. If there is a difference, are there any insights with regards to trends with the use of different weighting functions?

2   Related Work

Research in software effort estimation models has a long history. However, few software effort estimation models were evaluated with consideration of the chronological order of projects.

Auer and Biffl [4] evaluated dimension weighting for analogy-based effort estimation, considering the effect of a growing data set. However, the authors used datasets having no date information. Thus, this evaluation method did not consider chronological order. Mendes and Lokan [5] compared estimates based on a growing portfolio with estimates based on leave-one-out cross-validation, using two different data sets. In both cases, cross-validation estimates showed significantly superior accuracy.

Some studies such as [6,7] used a project year in software effort estimation model construction. However, these studies did not consider chronological order in evaluation. Maxwell [8] demonstrated the construction and evaluation of software estimation model with the consideration of chronology. A candidate effort estimation model selected a year predictor. She also separated project data into training and test data according to a year.

To the best of our knowledge, Kitchenham et al. [9] first mentioned the use of moving windows. As a result of an experiment, they argued that old projects should be removed from the data set as new ones were added, so that the size of the dataset remained constant.

MacDonell and Shepperd [10] investigated moving windows as part of a study of how well data from prior phases in a project could be used to estimate later phases. They found that accuracy was better when a moving window of the 5 most recent projects was used as training data, rather than using all completed projects as training data.

Lokan and Mendes [3] studied the use of moving windows with linear regression models and a single-company dataset from the ISBSG repository. Training sets were defined to be the N most recently completed projects. They found the following insights: the use of a window could affect accuracy significantly; predictive accuracy was better with larger windows; some window sizes were 'sweet spots'.

Later they also investigated the effect on accuracy when using moving windows of various durations to form training sets on which to base effort estimates [11]. They showed that the use of windows based on duration can affect the accuracy of estimates, but to a lesser extent than windows based on a fixed number of projects.

This study is similar to [3] in that the same data set is investigated, using the same range of window sizes. It differs in that one additional independent variable is considered here, and models were based on variables selected with Lasso[12] instead of stepwise regression. In addition, this study differs from [3], and all other previous studies, by investigating different weights for projects of different ages: the main point of the paper.

3   Research Method

3.1   Dataset Description

The data set used in this paper is the same one analyzed in [3]. This data set is sourced from Release 10 of the ISBSG Repository. Release 10 contains data for 4106 projects; however, not all projects provided the chronological data we needed (i.e. known duration and completion date, from which we could calculate start date), and those that did varied in data quality and definitions. To form a data set in which all projects provided the necessary data for size, effort and chronology, defined size and effort similarly, and had high quality data, we removed projects according to the following criteria:

- The projects are rated by ISBSG as a high data quality (A or B).
- Implementation date and overall project elapsed time are known.
- Size is measured in IFPUG 4.0 or later (because size measured with an older version is not directly comparable with size measured with IFPUG version 4.0 or later). We also removed projects that measured size with an unspecified version of function points, and whose completion pre-dated IFPUG version 4.0.
- The size in unadjusted function points is known.
- Development team effort (resource level 1) is known. Our analysis used only the development team's effort.
- Normalized effort and recorded effort are equivalent. This should mean that the reported effort is the actual effort across the whole life cycle.
- The projects are not web projects.

Table 1. Summary statistics for ratio-scaled variables

Variable	Mean	Median	StDev	Min	Max
Size	496	266	699	10	6294
Effort	4553	2408	6212	62	57749
PDR	16.47	8.75	31.42	0.53	387.10

In the remaining set of 909 projects, 231 were all from the same organization and 678 were from other organizations. We only selected the 231 projects from the single organization, as the use of single-company data was more suitable to answer our research questions than using cross-company data. Preliminary analysis showed that three projects were extremely influential and invariably removed from model building, so they were removed from the set. The final set contained 228 projects.

We do not know the identity of the organization that developed these projects.

Release 10 of the ISBSG database provides data on numerous variables; however, this number was reduced to a small set that we have found in past analyses with this dataset to have an impact on effort, and which did not suffer from a large number of missing data values. The remaining variables were size (measured in unadjusted function points), effort (hours), and four categorical variables: development type (new development, re-development, enhancement), primary language type (3GL, 4GL), platform (mainframe, midrange, PC, multi-platform), and industry sector (banking, insurance, manufacturing, other).

Table 1 shows summary statistics for size (measured in unadjusted function points), effort, and project delivery rate(PDR). PDR is calculated as effort divided by size; high project delivery rates indicate low productivity. In [3], the authors examined the project delivery rate and found it changes across time. This finding supports the use of a window.

The projects were developed for a variety of industry sectors, where insurance, banking and manufacturing were the most common. Start dates range from 1994 to 2002, but only 9 started before 1998. 3GLs are used by 86% of projects; mainframes account for 40%, and multi-platform for 55%; these percentages for language and platform vary little from year to year. There is a trend over time towards more enhancement projects and fewer new developments. Enhancement projects tend to be smaller than new development, so there is a corresponding trend towards lower size and effort.

There are two ways in which a window size might be defined: by the number of projects [3], or duration [11]. A window based on duration can be scaled to include only those projects that reflect recent development projects and practices. In contrast, a window based on the number of projects can be scaled to provide enough data for sound analysis. This study defines a window as containing a fixed number of projects.

We adopted the same range of window sizes as [3]. The smallest window size was based on the statistical significance of linear regression with windowed project data: the smallest window size with which all regression models

Table 2. Formulae of weighted functions

Name	Formula
Triangular	$W(x) = 1 - |x|, |x| < 1$
Epanechnikov	$W(x) = 1 - x^2, |x| < 1$
Gaussian	$W(x) = \exp(-(2.5x)^2/2)$
Rectangular (Uniform)	$W(x) = 1, |x| < 1$

were statistically significant was 20 projects. The largest window size was based on the necessary number of testing projects for evaluation. As a result, we used window sizes from 20 to 120.

3.2   Weighted Moving Windows with Linear Regression

Linear regression is one of the popular methods for effort estimation. A typical effort estimation model is as follows:

$$\text{Effort} = b_0 + b_1 \text{Size} + \epsilon. \tag{1}$$

Here, b_0 and b_1 are regression coefficients, and ϵ represents an error term following a normal distribution. The regression coefficients are inferred from a training set so as to minimize the following function:

$$\sum_{i=1}^{n} \left(\text{Effort}_i - b_0 - b_1 \text{Size}_i\right)^2. \tag{2}$$

Here, n denotes the sample size of training set.

Equation 2 assumes that the errors of the training set are to be minimized equivalently. Weighted linear regression controls the importance of training projects via weighting. It minimizes the following function:

$$\sum_{i=1}^{n} w_i \left(\text{Effort}_i - b_0 - b_1 \text{Size}_i\right)^2. \tag{3}$$

Here, w_i represents case weights for the training set.

From this perspective, an unweighted moving window assigns zero-weights to old projects, and equal weights to projects in the window. This formulation also reveals a point that the past study overlooked: it takes into account the chronological order of projects in the window.

This study weights projects in the training set so that a more recent project has a heavier weight. Table 2 shows four weight functions that we examined. We determined x as follows:

$$x = \frac{n_i}{n}. \tag{4}$$

Here, n_i represents a rank of project i in ascending order of date. That is, an older project takes a lower rank and x becomes smaller.

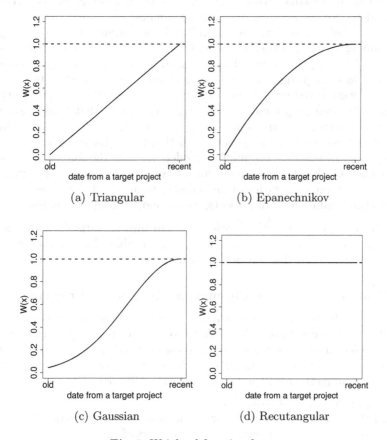

Fig. 1. Weighted function forms

Figure 1 shows the forms of weighted functions. A rectangular function is equivalent to non-weighted moving windows. Different curve functions affect estimation accuracy differently. This study adopted three typical curves: linear, concave, S-shape. These functions are common in local regression [13].

3.3   Modeling Techniques

Weighted linear regression models were built using almost the same procedure as [3]:

1. The first step in building every regression model is to ensure numerical variables are normally distributed. We used the Shapiro-Wilk test on the training set to check if Effort and Size were normally distributed. Statistical significance was set at $\alpha = 0.05$. In every case, Size and Effort were not normally distributed. Therefore, we transformed them to a natural logarithmic scale.

2. Independent variables whose value is missing in a target project were not considered for inclusion in the estimation model.
3. Every model included Size as an independent variable. Beyond that, given a training set of N projects, no model was investigated if it involved more than $N/10$ independent variables (rounded to the nearest integer), assuming that at least 10 projects per independent variable is desirable [14].
4. Models were based on variables selected with Lasso[12] instead of stepwise regression because preliminary investigation showed that Lasso gave more accurate estimates than stepwise; details not presented here (Lasso implementation we used is the "`glmnet`" function from `glmnet` package for R.)
5. To verify the stability of an effort model, we used the following approach: Calculate Cook's distance values for all projects to identify influential data points. Any projects with distances higher than $(3 \times 4/N)$, where N represents the total number of projects, were removed from the analysis.

This procedure performs variable selection, and thus all variables introduced in Section 3.1 are just candidates for independent variables. Models constructed in our experiment can be different for every project.

3.4   Effort Estimation on Chronologically-Ordered Projects

This study evaluated the effects of moving windows of several sizes along with a timeline of projects' history. The effects were measured by performance comparisons beteen moving windows and a growing portfolio. A growing portfolio uses all past projects as the training set. No project ever gets a weight of zero. This evaluation method was performed with the following steps:

1. Sort all projects by starting time
2. Find the earliest project p_0 for which at least $w + 1$ projects, where w is a window size, were completed prior to the start of p_0
3. For every project p_i in chronological sequence, starting from p_0, form four estimates using weighted and non-weighted moving windows, and another using growing portfolio. For moving windows, the training set is the w most recent projects that finished before the start of p_i. For growing portfolio, the training set is all of the projects that finished before the start of p_i.
4. Evaluate estimation results.

3.5   Performance Measures

Performance measures for effort estimation models are based on the difference between estimated effort and actual effort. As in previous studies, this study used MMRE, PRED(25), and MMAE [1] for performance evaluation.

To test for statistically significant differences between accuracy measures, we used the Wilcoxon ranked sign test and set statistical significance level at $\alpha = 0.05$. `wilcoxsign_test` function of `coin` package for R was used with default options. We also controlled false dicovery rate (FDR) of multiple testing [15] with the `qvalue` function of `qvalue` package. FDR is a ratio of the number of falsely rejected null hypotheses to the number of rejected null hypotheses.

Table 3. Mean absolute residuals with different window sizes

Window size (N)	Testing Projects	Growing	(a) MAE	p–val.	(b) MAE	p–val.	(c) MAE	p–val.	(d) MAE	p–val.
20	201	2638	2830	0.107	2829	0.023	2879	0.087	2709	0.140
30	178	2578	2613	0.894	2552	0.917	2648	0.849	2570	0.651
40	165	2541	2599	0.358	2520	0.716	2618	0.342	2523	0.834
50	153	2527	2483	0.973	2423	0.616	2452	0.893	2376	0.460
60	136	2458	2279	0.204	2268	0.302	2262	0.246	2320	0.101
70	126	2300	2147	0.054	2178	0.222	2070	0.087	2060	0.122
80	126	2300	2083	0.011	2033	0.001	2111	0.015	2239	0.084
90	111	2236	2022	0.004	1967	0.001	2074	0.057	2053	0.001
100	88	2314	1930	0.002	2041	0.002	2051	0.041	2192	0.001
110	75	1981	1684	0.004	1771	0.011	1662	0.012	1845	0.000
120	71	1982	1715	0.002	1782	0.006	1696	0.002	1852	0.002

(a) Triangular, (b) Epanechnikov, (c) Gaussian, (d) Rectangular

4 Results

4.1 Accuracy with Different Window Sizes

Tables 3 and 4 show the effects of window sizes on mean absolute residuals and mean MRE. The first column shows window sizes, and the second column shows the total number of projects used as a target project with the corresponding window size. The larger a window size is, the smaller the number of testing projects is. The 3rd column shows accuracy measures with a growing portfolio for the corresponding window sizes. The 4th column shows accuracy measures for the Triangular function. The 5th column shows the p–value from statistical tests on accuracy measures between a growing portfolio and the Triangular function. The remained columns show accuracy measures and p–value for the other weighted functions. The results were computed for all window sizes; the tables only show every tenth window size, due to space limitations. This is still sufficient to show the essential trends.

Figures 2 and 3 show the difference in mean MAE and mean MRE between a growing portfolio and moving windows. The x-axis is the size of the window, and the y-axis is the subtraction of the accuracy measure value with a growing portfolio from that with moving windows at the given x-value. Smaller values of MAE and MRE are better, so the window is advantageous where the line is below 0. Circle points mean a statistically significant difference, in favor of moving windows. Square points mean a statistically significant difference, with moving windows being worse than a growing portfolio. We consider a window is effective if the corresponding q-value is below 0.05 (this means that that the number of falsely rejected hypotheses was at most 5% of rejected hypotheses).

Figures and tables revealed common characteristics among weighted and non-weighted moving windows:

Table 4. Mean MRE with different window sizes

Window size (N)	Testing Projects	Growing	(a) MRE	p–val.	(b) MRE	p–val.	(c) MRE	p–val.	(d) MRE	p–val.
20	201	1.28	1.47	0.171	1.56	0.021	1.53	0.118	1.45	0.100
30	178	1.35	1.45	0.839	1.37	0.664	1.49	0.927	1.26	0.612
40	165	1.35	1.43	0.539	1.37	0.856	1.45	0.426	1.31	0.914
50	153	1.39	1.35	0.917	1.26	0.630	1.39	0.852	1.27	0.316
60	136	1.42	1.23	0.213	1.23	0.364	1.25	0.219	1.23	0.027
70	126	1.48	1.34	0.038	1.37	0.061	1.24	0.037	1.31	0.020
80	126	1.48	1.29	0.000	1.29	0.000	1.29	0.001	1.36	0.001
90	111	1.37	1.20	0.000	1.17	0.000	1.24	0.002	1.17	0.000
100	88	1.36	1.09	0.000	1.13	0.000	1.16	0.007	1.18	0.000
110	75	1.39	1.12	0.000	1.15	0.000	1.14	0.000	1.16	0.000
120	71	1.38	1.12	0.000	1.13	0.000	1.08	0.000	1.18	0.001

(a) Triangular, (b) Epanechnikov, (c) Gaussian, (d) Rectangular

- With smaller windows, all measures are always better using a growing portfolio. Shown in Figs. 2(b) and 3(b), the difference was significant only in one window size. For mean MRE, the difference was found only in the case of using Epanechnikov function.
- In medium windows, moving windows become advantageous. The window size where it becomes advantageous is different among types of weighted functions. Using the Rectangular function becomes advantageous at a smaller window size than using the other functions.
- With larger windows, all measures are always better using moving windows, and the difference was significant in $70 \leq w \leq 120$. Some weighted functions showed significance in smaller windows. Improvements in mean MRE range from 10% to 30%, averaging 20%. Improvements in mean MAE range from 70 to 384, averaging 231. The difference was larger when using gradually weighted functions.

The difference in PRED(25) also showed similar trends, though the results are not shown due to space limitations. With smaller windows, a growing portfolio showed better performance than moving windows. With larger windows, moving windows became advantageous.

4.2   Accuracy Comparisons among Different Weighting Functions

Figures 4 and 5 show the difference in mean MAE and mean MRE between Rectangular and the other functions. Weighted moving windows is advantageous where the line is below 0. Figures 4 and 5 reveal the following:

- With smaller windows, using the Rectangular function is advantageous. The difference was significant around $20 \leq w \leq 50$ for MMRE.
- With medium windows, weighted and non-weighted moving windows are competitive. There was no clear preference between them. There was no significant difference.

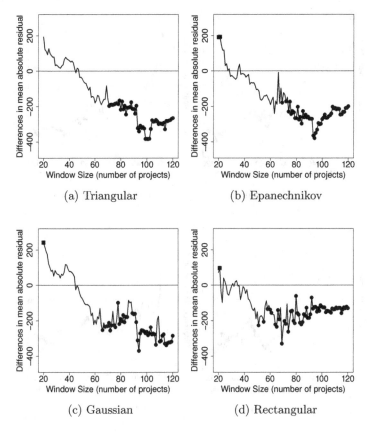

Fig. 2. The difference of accuracy measures between growing and windowing (mean MAE)

- With larger windows, weighted moving windows is advantageous. The range of advantageous window sizes were different among types of weighted functions. The lines in Fig. 4 are always below zero when $w > 90$ for the three functions. The lines in Fig. 5 sometimes rise above zero for Epanechnikov and Gaussian functions. However, statistical tests supported only the weighted functions. For statistically significant windows, improvements in mean MRE range from 1% to 10%, averaging 5%. No significance in case of mean MAE.

The small number of rejected hypotheses might cause the insignificance for mean MAE. With the small number of rejected hypotheses, for instance 10, q-value of 0.05 would limit the number of falsely rejected hypotheses to $0.05 \times 10 < 1$. We expect any of significant windows and can allow looser q-value. With q-value of 0.2, for instance, we could also find significances for mean MAE. Thus, we could say weighted moving windows also had posivitve effects on mean MAE.

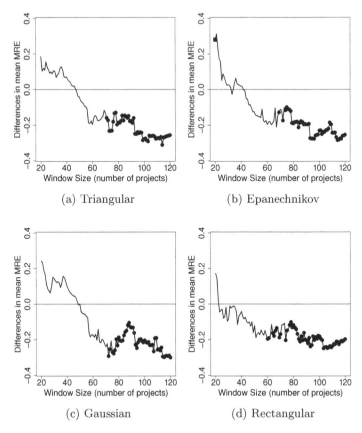

Fig. 3. The difference of accuracy measures between growing and windowing (mean MRE)

5   Discussion

5.1   Answer to RQ1

The null hypothesis was rejected on statistical tests for the difference between all weighted moving windows and a growing portfolio. For Epanechnikov function, for instance, the null hypothesis was rejected in window duration of 20 and 21, and from 69 to 120, based on mean MAE; 21 and from 69 to 120, based on mean MRE. The use of weighted moving windows can affect estimation accuracy against a growing portfolio.

On statistical tests for the difference between weighted and non-weighted moving windows, the null hypothesis was also rejected. For the Triangular function, for instance, the null hypothesis was rejected in window duration from 22 to 51, and from 99 to 120, based on mean MRE. The difference based on mean MAE

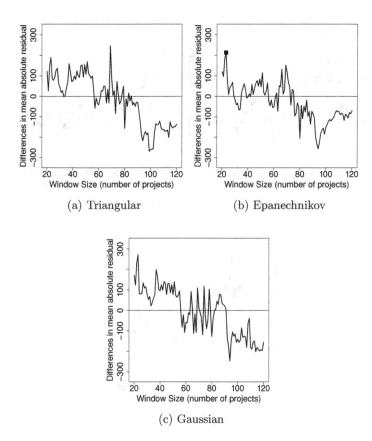

(a) Triangular   (b) Epanechnikov

(c) Gaussian

Fig. 4. The difference of accuracy measures between Rectangular and the other weighted functions (Mean MAE)

was insignificant through all window sizes. However, Fig. 4 depicted positive effects of moving window approach. We thus concluded that the use of weighted moving windows can also affect estimation accuracy against non-weighted moving windows.

5.2 Answer to RQ2

Weighted moving windows showed inferior estimation accuracy when using small windows. The difference was statistically significant, and there is an advantage in using non-weighted moving windows. However, weighted functions perform as well as a growing portfolio: the difference of estimation accuracy between them was insignificant. In contrast, weighted moving windows showed superior estimation accuracy when using larger windows. The difference was also statistically significant, and there is an advantage in using moving windows.

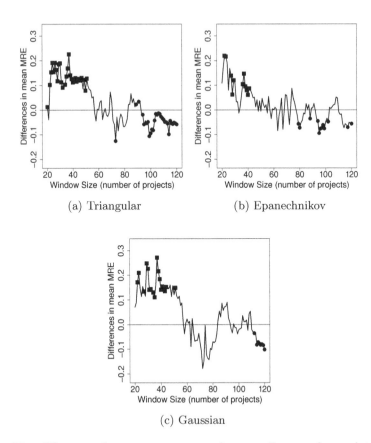

(a) Triangular   (b) Epanechnikov

(c) Gaussian

Fig. 5. The difference of accuracy measures between Rectangular and the other weighted functions (Mean MRE)

The above characteristics can be explained with an interaction between window sizes and the steepness of weighted function curves. The Triangular, Epanechnikov and Gaussian functions assign a small (near to zero) weight to the oldest projects in a window. The other projects receive heavier weights in accordance with distance from the date of a target project within the window. With small size windows, weighted function assigns steeply declining weights. With large window sizes, a weighted function assigns gently declining weights. When the degree of steepness meshes with a window size, a weighted function contributes to improvement of estimation accuracy.

The difference in advantageous window sizes among weighted functions supports the explanation. Figure 1 depicts the difference of steepness among weighted functions. Gaussian is the steepest function, and Epanechnikov is the most gentle function. The steepness of Triangular function is between them. Non-weighted moving windows assigns equal weights and is more gentle than Epanechnikov function. In Figs. 2 and 3, steep functions became advantageous more slowly than gentle functions. Those functions are too steep to reflect the importance of recent projects. With large windows, steep functions meshed with window sizes and improved estimation accuracy significantly. However, the range of significant windows was narrower than that of gentle functions as shown in Figs. 4 and 5.

The results support that weighted moving windows can improve estimation accuracy with appropriate steepness.

6   Threats to Validity

This study shares the same threats to validity as the previous studies.

First, we used only one dataset. The dataset is a convenience sample and may not be representative of software projects in general. Thus, the results may not be generalized beyond the dataset; this is true of all studies based on convenience samples. We trust that numerous potential sources of variation can be removed from the dataset by the selection of a single-company dataset. Since the dataset is large and covers a long time span, we assume it is a fair representation of this organization's projects. The inclusion of the sector as an independent variable helps to allow for variations among sectors in the dataset.

Second, all the models employed in this study were built automatically. Automating the process necessarily involved making some assumptions, and the validity of our results depends on those assumptions being reasonable. For example, logarithmic transformation is assumed to be adequate to transform numeric data to an approximately normal distribution; residuals are assumed to be random and normally distributed without that being actually checked; multi-collinearity between independent variables is assumed to be handled automatically by the nature of Lasso. Based on our past experience building models manually, we believe that these assumptions are acceptable. One would not want to base important decisions on a single model built automatically, without at least doing some serious manual checking, but for calculations such as chronological estimation across a substantial data set we believe that the process here is reasonable.

Third, this study used weighted linear regression. Many effort estimation models have been proposed, and each model can show better accuracy in particular situations. However, linear regression is a popular and accurate effort estimation models. We thus think it is a good choice among major effort estimation models.

7   Conclusion

This paper investigated the use of weighted moving windows as a way to improve non-weighted moving windows. We have shown that it has a statistically significant effect on estimation accuracy in terms of MRE. Although different weighted functions affected estimation accuracy differently, weighted moving windows were significantly advantageous in larger windows. Non-weighted moving windows were significantly advantageous with smaller windows.

What these results suggest is that it can be better to use a weighted window of projects with a weighted function having appropriate steepness. Weighted moving windows gradually decrease the importance of past projects. If a decrease curve is too steep or too gentle, weighted moving windows makes estimation accuracy worse. How to determine appropriate steepness is a crucial question

Our future work involves replication with other datasets such as Maxwell dataset and the CSC dataset used in past studies.

References

1. Port, D., Korte, M.: Comparative studies of the model evaluation criterions mmre and pred in software cost estimation research. In: Proc. of the 2nd ACM-IEEE International Symposium on Empirical Software Engineering and Measurement. ACM (2008)
2. Jørgensen, M., Shepperd, M.: A Systematic Review of Software Development Cost Estimation Studies. IEEE Trans. Softw. Eng. 33(1), 33–53 (2007)
3. Lokan, C., Mendes, E.: Applying moving windows to software effort estimation. In: Proc. of the 2009 3rd International Symposium on Empirical Software Engineering and Measurement, pp. 111–122 (2009)
4. Auer, M., Biffl, S.: Increasing the accuracy and reliability of analogy-based cost estimation with extensive project feature dimension weighting. In: Proc. of International Symposium on Empirical Software Engineering, pp. 147–155. IEEE (2004)
5. Mendes, E., Lokan, C.: Investigating the use of chronological splitting to compare software cross-company and single-company effort predictions: a replicated study. In: Proc. of the 13th Conference on Evaluation & Assessment in Software Engineering (EASE 2009). BCS (2009)
6. Keung, J.W., Kitchenham, B.A., Jeffery, D.R.: Analogy-X: Providing Statistical Inference to Analogy-Based Software Cost Estimation. IEEE Trans. Softw. Eng. 34(4), 471–484 (2008)
7. Li, J., Ruhe, G.: Analysis of attribute weighting heuristics for analogy-based software effort estimation method AQUA+. Empir. Softw. Eng. 13(1), 63–96 (2007)
8. Maxwell, K.D.: Applied Statistics for Software Managers. Prentice Hall (2002)
9. Kitchenham, B., Lawrence Pfleeger, S., McColl, B., Eagan, S.: An empirical study of maintenance and development estimation accuracy. J. Syst. Softw. 64(1), 57–77 (2002)
10. MacDonell, S.G., Shepperd, M.: Data accumulation and software effort prediction. In: Proc. of the 2010 ACM-IEEE International Symposium on Empirical Software Engineering and Measurement. ACM (2010)
11. Lokan, C., Mendes, E.: Investigating the Use of Duration-based Moving Windows to Improve Software Effort Prediction. In: Proc. of the 19th Asia-Pacific Software Engineering Conference, pp. 819–927. IEEE Computer Society (2012)
12. Tibshirani, R.: Regression shrinkage and selection via the lasso. J. Roy. Statist. Soc. Ser. B, 267–288 (1996)
13. Loader, C.: Local Regression and Likelihood. Statistics and Computing. Springer
14. Tabachnick, B.G., Fidell, L.S.: Using Multivariate Statistics. Harper-Collins (1996)
15. Storey, J.D.: A direct approach to false discovery rates. J. Roy. Statist. Soc. Ser. B 64, 479–498 (2002)

Identifying Potential Risks and Benefits of Using Cloud in Distributed Software Development

Nilay Oza[1], Jürgen Münch[1], Juan Garbajosa[2],
Agustin Yague[2], and Eloy Gonzalez Ortega[3]

[1]University of Helsinki, Finland
[2]Universidad Politecnica Madrid, Spain
[3]Indra Software Labs, Spain
{nilay.oza,juergen.muench}@cs.helsinki.fi,
egonzalezort@indra.es, {jgs,agustin.yague}@upm.es

Abstract. Cloud-based infrastructure has been increasingly adopted by the industry in distributed software development (DSD) environments. Its proponents claim that its several benefits include reduced cost, increased speed and greater productivity in software development. Empirical evaluations, however, are in the nascent stage of examining both the benefits and the risks of cloud-based infrastructure. The objective of this paper is to identify potential benefits and risks of using cloud in a DSD project conducted by teams based in Helsinki and Madrid. A cross-case qualitative analysis is performed based on focus groups conducted at the Helsinki and Madrid sites. Participants' observations are used to supplement the analysis. The results of the analysis indicated that the main benefits of using cloud are rapid development, continuous integration, cost savings, code sharing, and faster ramp-up. The key risks determined by the project are dependencies, unavailability of access to the cloud, code commitment and integration, technical debt, and additional support costs. The results revealed that if such environments are not planned and set up carefully, the benefits of using cloud in DSD projects might be overshadowed by the risks associated with it.

Keywords: cloud-based software development, distributed software development, DSD, global software development, case study, empirical software engineering, offshore software development, cloud computing, benefits and risks of using cloud.

1 Introduction

Cloud computing is no longer a new phenomenon. It is now ubiquitous in the industry and is increasingly used to develop software in a distributed environment. In many cases, it seems an obvious choice, especially for new, emerging ecosystems where companies want to involve external developers or external development teams in their own development projects or programs. However, whether cloud-based distributed software development (DSD) really works to address a wide range of technical and non-technical issues in DSD settings has not yet been validated scientifically. In other

J. Heidrich et al. (Eds.): PROFES 2013, LNCS 7983, pp. 229–239, 2013.

words, the expected benefits and risks of developing software in the cloud with distributed teams must be better understood.

Based on the literature [2, 12], we define cloud as the delivery of a stack of hardware or software residing in the data centre as a utility-like service over the network. We particularly focus on DSD in the context of cloud-based computing environments. We refer to DSD in the cloud as "software that is developed on a cloud-based platform across geographically distributed sites in a multi-stakeholder ecosystem."

To examine cloud-based DSD, we conducted an industry-led development project across three multi-site DSD teams. In this paper, we focus solely on what worked (i.e., was beneficial) with respect to cloud and the consequent risks attached to its use in the project. In the DSD project, we present here, our scope is limited to private cloud. Additional analyses of this project are planned or have been performed in parallel, such as the challenges involved in adding a new team to an on-going cloud-based distributed project. The findings of these other analyses are beyond the scope of this paper and will be published separately.

Section 2 describes work related to this paper. Section 3 presents a qualitative case study, including the research questions, the research approach, the context of the study, and the case company. Section 4 presents the results of the analysis of the case data. Section 5 stipulates the limitations and concerns about the validity of the study. Finally, Section 6 summarizes the study and provides an outlook on future research.

2   Related Work

DSD is often carried out in an ecosystem comprised of developers, clients, users, and other key stakeholders. Any new technology adoption will significantly affect such an ecosystem when several stakeholders are involved [17]. The cloud is not different in the sense that it would set DSD at new level of development within a complex multi-stakeholder, people-centric ecosystem [2, 6, 16, and 17].

Technically, cloud enables elasticity, scalability, and flexibility in DSD teams, resulting in overall increased productivity. For example, cloud-based DSD allows teams to perform rapid testing, dynamically scale up or down the required computing infrastructure, and produce working software updates rapidly [13]. Financially, cloud enables cost savings, faster time to market, and benefits of scale [7]. These claims, however, need further empirical validation, particularly because DSD-specific challenges may remain and even intensify in cloud-based development across distributed teams. The results of a few previous studies have already shown the benefits and risks of using cloud in DSD-specific environments [e.g., 2, 4, 8 and 17]. For example, Hashmi et al. [8] used cloud to facilitate DSD challenges, claiming that it would result in benefits for the infrastructure, platform, and provision of software as a service. They [8] also raised several concerns about using cloud in DSD, such as determining different levels of needs in service provision at distributed locations, the availability and subscription of cloud-based services for different types of dependency relationships among cloud users (tenants), and conducting project knowledge transfers across DSD sites. Phaphoom et al. [13] examined a practitioner forum on the benefits of using cloud in software development, finding that practitioners seemed to focus more effort on understanding how to utilize the dynamic scaling of cloud-based resources.

Based on the prototypes showcased for using cloud in DSD, Yara et al. [17], claimed that although the hype about cloud has caused some fear, uncertainty, and doubt (FUD), this infrastructure will bring significant benefits to all key stakeholders in the DSD ecosystem. They also acknowledged other concerns, such as vendor lock-in, SLA control, privacy, reliability, data migration and access, auditing, and norms of regulation compliance.

Further empirical studies conducted in projects using cloud in DSD are required to establish systematically the merits of using cloud in this environment [8, 13 and 17]. In this paper, we contribute to the understanding of using cloud in DSD settings by studying the benefits and risks experienced by two distributed development teams.

3   Case Study

In this section, we present the overall setting of the qualitative study and research methodology adopted.

3.1   Research Question

We present our findings based on our answer to the following research question:

RQ – What are the potential benefits (what works well) and risks (what does not work well) of using a cloud-based infrastructure in a DSD project?

The answer to RQ will focus on the potential benefits and risks of using a cloud-based platform in a DSD project.

3.2   Context

The software factory (i.e., experimental research setting) is a novel software engineering research and education laboratory at the University of Helsinki. It offers a unique setting to conduct applied empirical investigations. All projects in the Software Factory originate from the industry's needs, and their duration is seven weeks. The software factory concept has been adopted by several other universities and companies. The software factories at the University of Helsinki, the Technical University of Madrid (UPM), and Indra are the development sites of the distributed project presented in this paper.

A qualitative study was performed in the context of a distributed development project that included three sites: 1) a software factory at the Indra Software Labs in Madrid, Spain; 2) a software factory at the Technical University of Madrid (UPM), Spain; and 3) a software factory at the University of Helsinki, Finland. The study reports the investigation of the Indra-led DSD project, which used a cloud-based platform. The Helsinki-based team was added for a seven-week development cycle. The qualitative interviews and supplementary data from the Helsinki team (also referred to as the "new team" in the project) are the main focus of the analysis in the proposed study. Working together, the Spanish and Helsinki teams developed solutions for the required massive data analysis by using Hadoop. MapReduce was used for large data calculations. A relevant issue is that the product owner required the quality profile of the resulting product to be commercially usable. Otherwise, the trial would not have been useful. It is also noteworthy that the product owner in the project was from Indra Software Labs. Although this requirement imposed strong pressure on the development teams, it served to reinforce the validity of the results. The project included five project members from the Indra site, seven project members from the UPM site, and eight project members from the Helsinki site. The project also had two dedicated agile coaches, one at Helsinki and one at UPM. The project included one product owner from Indra and three researchers actively involved during the collaborative period. Every engineer that participated in the software factory project had at least two years of software development experience. Based on interviews, they were recruited to align their competencies with the project's needs. An iterative development using the Kanban-based software development process was used [10]. During the seven-week project cycle, seven weekly sprints were conducted, and customer demos and retrospectives were provided after each sprint.

3.3   Research Approach

We use Runeson and Höst's (2009) [15] guidelines for conducting case studies, which comprise five major steps, including study design, preparation for data collection, collecting evidence, analysis of the collected data, and reporting. We also considered validity concerns during the case study.

Regarding the design of the study, the qualitative nature of the examination justified the exploratory nature of the inquiry. The study used the distributed teams across three sites as the units of analysis. The unit of observation was the period of seven weeks, when all teams worked together in the project. Using semi-structured interviews, the direct data were collected from two focus groups, the teams from the Helsinki and Spanish sites. In the semi-structured interviews, topics were provided and approximate times were allocated for each topic. An interview guide was developed to assist the researcher during the interviews. A tape-recorded notice was given. The researcher also ensured the confidentiality and anonymity of the collected information as per the project's research agreement. All the interviews were audio recorded and later transcribed. The researchers also took notes during the interviews when they deemed something particularly relevant. Krueger and Casey's [11] guidelines were followed in the focus group sessions. The indirect data, which consisted of participant observations and notes from retrospective sessions, were stored as a text narrative received from the observer. They were used as complementary sources of information during the data analysis.

We analyzed the transcribed interviews using the "editing approach," recommended by Runeson and Höst [15] for software engineering case studies. In the editing approach, codes are defined based on findings of the researcher during the analysis. A preliminary set of codes was derived and applied to the transcripts. The codebook was then developed. Each statement in the transcribed interviews was given a unique identification and classified by two researchers. The transcribed data was then entered in tables, allowing for the analysis of patterns in the data. The encoding was done using an open coding method [11]. Each statement was analyzed and linked to the codebook. The percentages of statements and linked codes were calculated to generate visualizations of the themes.

4   Results

In this section, we present the key findings of our analysis. We focus mainly on specific findings related to DSD in the cloud infrastructure rather than generic DSD-related issues. In addition, we classify and present the answers to the research question according to the information revealed in the data set.

4.1   RQ: What Are the Key Benefits and Risks of Using a Cloud-Based Infrastructure in a DSD Project?

Our study revealed five major benefits of using a cloud-based platform: rapid development, continuous integration, cost savings, code sharing, and faster ramp-up. In addition, it revealed five major risks of using a cloud-base infrastructure: dependencies, unavailability of access to the cloud, code commitment and integration, technical debt, and additional support costs. Fig. 2 and Fig. 3 provide overviews of the number of times the risks and benefits were mentioned in the qualitative interview.

4.2   Key Benefits of Using the Cloud in DSD

Rapid Development. One of the major benefits experienced by the teams in the project was sharing cloud-based tools across distributed teams. As soon as the team obtained access to the cloud, it was ready to contribute to the development. One of the participants stated "As we did not have to replicate the technical environment, we were able to start development right after the required access was available to the remote infrastructure."

Continuous Integration. The centrality of software development in the cloud brought with it the benefit of continuous integration. Software development in the cloud has a unique benefit in the sense that developers can commit frequent deliveries, even if the other team or unit is not in control of the development environment. One participant commented: "We were directly accessing the remote server where the product code integration happened. We just committed all codes to the main repository."

Cost Savings. Because of near-instant access to development resources and no need to install and configure several tools on local machines, substantial costs of hardware and software were saved at multiple sites.

Code Sharing. The cloud-based platform facilitated the sharing of codes across teams. Although the teams did not use concurrent distributed programming tools, the Spanish team shared the codebase with the Helsinki team, which had the required access controls.

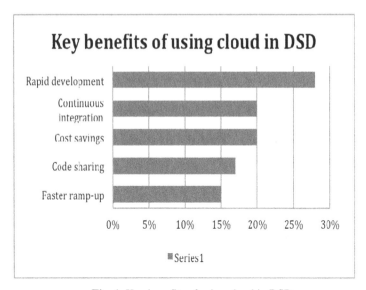

Fig. 1. Key benefits of using cloud in DSD

Faster Ramp-Up. The team felt that although several issues of coordination and organization were encountered in the initial stages of the project, the progress occurred quite rapidly after the initial period. Once the technical environment was understood, the access to cloud-based resources proved very useful in speeding up the software development. One participant said "It took two weeks to really settle on a shared understanding, but then work started, and they (Spanish team) started to see that we could contribute quite a lot…We started to get more work then."

4.3   Key Risks of Using the Cloud in DSD

Dependencies. Dependencies, in terms of both technical and operational issues, created several challenges for the teams to work together. Our analysis indicated dependencies on at least two levels: operational and technical. For example, at times, one team had to wait for the other to catch up, provide feedback, or take specific actions before the development could move to the next stage. One participant said "We had to depend quite a lot on the Spanish team to get lot of things done—sometimes we went into waiting mode or were just not able to implement things, as we had to get something done by the other team." The Spanish team member had a contradicting comment, however, "I saw them more like – 'give me work, I do my work, just my own work'. They were depending on us for one output, one use case." One reason behind this dependency was indicated in the resource imbalance between the Spanish and Helsinki teams, as described above. The Helsinki team worked full time for a seven-week period, whereas the Spanish team worked part time for three or four hours a day.

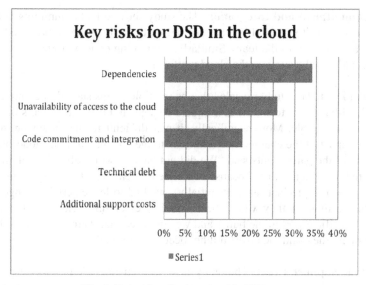

Fig. 2. Key risks of using cloud in DSD

One participant commented "We simply had more people with a full-time work commitment at our end. This meant we could do much more than the other teams thought we could. Probably, some information mismatch happened on how much work capacity was available at our end." Our results also revealed technical dependencies on the codebase as well as the overall complexity of the product's technical environment. This was reflected in the following comment: "There were many applications in the central codebase with linkages to components, etc. It was difficult for us to determine the dependencies of these inter-connected modules, mainly because of the lack of interaction between teams."

Unavailability of Access to the Cloud. The new team, which did not have direct control of the cloud-based platform, were challenged by the lack of accessibility to necessary resources. The results indicated that the new team had to rely completely on the Spanish team to gain access to the cloud-specific resources if they were not previously allocated. The general challenge that we observed was also reflected in some of the team members' comments at the Helsinki site: "The remote server is not controlled by us. If and when we lose access to it (for whatever reason), we have to contact the Spanish team, and only they can re-establish access for us." Another comment revealed a similar challenge: "It is quite difficult to continue working when the team loses access to the cloud. Because of the common codebase and central integration, we have to wait until we are able to get access." The teams also experienced increase in uncertainties when the common cloud-based software was inaccessible. One of the Spanish members commented "infrastructures, when fail, they generate uncertainty. Also, they have created dependency; within these limits, there was a certain dependency. For example, one day, Redmine crashed – and it becomes difficult to keep track on the user histories with the acceptation criteria."

Code Commitment and Integration. The study showed that committing code to the proper code repository could be challenging, particularly if the cloud-based platform was not fully known to the team. Similarly, integrating code with the overall product required additional testing on the cloud platform.

Technical Debt. The study revealed that as multiple teams started to commit changes to the cloud-based platform, the consequent changes in other linked parts of the codebase were not visible. More specifically, it was difficult for the new team to see the evolving impact of the changes and additions to the codebase on the cloud-based platform. One of the participants said "We did not have to worry about the platform, as it was shared by all teams, but because of frequent releases and our lack of understanding of the overall product (at least initially), we had to leave certain changes undone although we thought they would be worth implementing." He further commented "We got specific errors in the build, and we could see that there were errors, but when we told them, they said the errors did not occur at their end".

Additional Support Costs. The study also showed that a cloud-based platform in DSD requires additional managerial and operational support. Although the cloud-based platform has several benefits, additional overhead should be considered.

5   Discussion and Limitations

The results of our study confirmed some earlier findings and provided new insights about using cloud in DSD. The benefits experienced by the distributed teams in our study are similar to those reported in Hasmi et al. [8] and Yara et al. [17]. In particular, cloud-enabling continuous integration in DSD supports Yara et al.'s [17] hypothesis that the cloud could play a "game-changing role" in software testing. The benefits identified in our study also specifically increase the understanding of how cloud could fit into DSD settings, which are highly people-centric, multi-stakeholder ecosystems.

The results specific to the potential risks of using cloud in DSD provided new insights. In particular, potential risks related to dependencies of the DSD teams in addition to the potential increase in technical debt in the software were specifically identified in our study.

Our study extended our initial inquiry into using cloud in a DSD setting as well as if and to what extent it is beneficial. Although the latter questions are beyond the scope of the present study, we could uncover empirically founded insights into the merits of using cloud in DSD.

Our study brings novelty in terms of empirically founded approach to studying benefits and risks of using cloud in DSD and also demonstrating that adoption of cloud still may pose similar threats that were also experienced in DSD projects not based on cloud. One could argue that our findings are potentially the same as they are usually experienced in DSD setting. We, however, note that our study aims to empirically identify benefits and risks of using cloud in DSD rather than claiming any distinct benefits or risks of cloud vs. DSD.

5.1   Limitations

We considered the four validity concerns recommended by [15] in conducting case studies in software engineering. We also followed suggestions for improving the validity of our study [15]: triangulation, developing and maintaining a detailed case study protocol; review of designs, protocols, etc. by peer researchers; review of collected data and obtained results by the case subjects; and spending sufficient time on the case.

One of the limitations of our study is related to subjectivity in the collected qualitative data, which calls into question the validity of our findings. Using the focus group and detailed case study protocol, however, increased confidence in the qualitative data because they were gathered from several persons. In terms of external validity, another limitation concerns the validity of our findings, which resides in the weak generalizability of the results. Although the results could be of high interest to those involved in cloud-based DSD outside the investigated case, the generalizability of the present findings requires further, similar empirical studies. However, the detailed case study protocol and analysis by multiple researchers increased the reliability and replicability of our study in other cloud-based DSD settings, which would help strengthen the generalizable conclusions regarding potential benefits and risks of using cloud in DSD. Furthermore, triangulation was achieved in multiple ways—data were collected from both direct and indirect sources, multiple researchers were used to develop a reliable coding scheme, and case representatives reviewed the results. Although the study was of limited duration, this potential limitation was reduced by the fact that the researchers had a long-term connection with the organization before the present case study was implemented.

6   Conclusions and Future Work

This paper presented a qualitative study that aimed to identify the key benefits and risks of using a cloud-based platform in a DSD project to better understand if and how cloud works in a DSD setting. The study findings indicated that several of the expected merits of cloud computing could be utilized in real DSD projects. In particular, the findings indicated increased development speed, easier integration of development activities, and simplified access to development resources. However, the qualitative analysis also revealed that inherent challenges of DSD, such as lack of informal communication, temporal differences, need for work synchronization, and lack of trust, persist and must be addressed by special measures beyond cloud. A combination of cloud and other measures is needed to address these challenges successfully. In a wider perspective, the use of cloud in DSD would clearly have beneficial effects on development processes and even lead to new types of development processes. These effects are based on advanced cloud's enhanced possibilities for developing software, providing software to customers, and obtaining feedback from customers (e.g., possibilities for continuous integration, continuous global deployment, and live customer feedback). We plan to replicate the study and do further analyses of the data to examine DSD in the cloud to determine what works well and what does not.

Acknowledgments. We sincerely thank our industry partner, Indra Software Lab, for setting up and running the presented DSD project with research-centric interests. We also thank the Finnish technology agency, Tekes, for funding the Cloud Software Factory project, the Cloud Software Program, and the SCABO project, under which the proposed research study was undertaken. Finally, we thank the Spanish Ministry of Science and Innovation for partially sponsoring the project IPT-430000-2010-38 i-Smart Software Factory under the INNPACTO Program.

References

1. Arimura, Y., Ito, M.: Cloud Computing for Software Development Environment. —Inhouse Deployment at Numazu Software Development Cloud Center. Fujitsu Sci. Tech. J. 47(3), 325–334 (2011)
2. Armbrust, M., Fox, A., Griffith, R., Joseph, A.D., Katz, R., Konwinski, A., Lee, G., Patterson, D., Rabkin, A., Stoica, I., Zaharia, M.: A view of cloud computing. Communications of the ACM 53(4), 50–58 (2010)
3. Buyya, R., Yeo, S., Venugopal, S., Broberg, J., Brandic, I.: Cloud computing and emerging IT platforms: Vision, hype, and reality for delivering computing as the 5th utility. Future Generation Computer Systems 25(6), 599–616 (2009) ISSN 0167-739X, 10.1016/j.future.2008.12.001
4. Dillon, T., Wu, C., Chang, E.: Cloud Computing: Issues and Challenges. In: 24th IEEE International Conference on Advanced Information Networking and Applications (2010)
5. Erdogmus, H.: Cloud Computing: Does Nirvana Hide behind the Nebula? IEEE Software 26(2), 4–6 (2009), doi:10.1109/MS.2009.31
6. Garrison, G., Kim, S., Wakefield, R.L.: Success factors for deploying cloud computing. Communications of ACM 55(9), 62–68 (2012)
7. Grossman, R.L.: The Case for Cloud Computing. IT Professional 11(2), 23–27 (2009), doi:10.1109/MITP.2009.40
8. Hashmi, S.I., Clerc, V., Razavian, M., Manteli, C., Tamburri, D.A., Lago, P., Nitto, E.D., Richardson, I.: Using the Cloud to Facilitate Global Software Development Challenges. In: 2011 Sixth IEEE International Conference on Global Software Engineering Workshop (ICGSEW), pp. 70–77 (August 2011), doi:10.1109/ICGSE-W.2011.19
9. Kim, W., Kim, D.S., Lee, E., Lee, S.: Adoption issues for cloud computing. In: Proceedings of iiWAS 2009, pp. 3–6 (December 2009)
10. Kniberg, H.: Kanban and Scrum - Making the Most of Both. Lulu.com (2010)
11. Krueger, R.A., Casey, M.A.: Focus groups: a practical guide for applied research. Pine Forge Press (2009)
12. Mell, P., Grance, T.: Draft - NIST working definition of cloud computing - v15 (August 2009), http://www.nist.gov/itl/cloud/upload/cloud-def-v15.pdf
13. Phaphoom, N., Oza, N., Wang, X., Abrahamsson, P.: Does cloud computing deliver the promised benefits for IT industry? In: Proceedings of the WICSA/ECSA 2012 Companion Volume (WICSA/ECSA 2012), pp. 45–52. ACM, New York (2012), doi:10.1145/2361999.2362007
14. Rimal, B.P., Choi, E., Lumb, I.: A Taxonomy and Survey of Cloud Computing Systems. In: Fifth International Joint Conference on NCM 2009, pp. 44–51 (August 2009), doi:10.1109/NCM.2009.218

15. Runeson, P., Höst, M.: Guidelines for conducting and reporting case study research in software engineering. Empirical Software Engineering 14(2), 131–164 (2009), doi:10.1007/s10664-008-9102-8
16. Voas, J., Zhang, J.: Cloud Computing: New Wine or Just a New Bottle? IT Professional 11(2), 15–17 (2009), doi:10.1109/MITP.2009.23
17. Yara, P., Ramachandran, R., Balasubramanian, G., Muthuswamy, K., Chandrasekar, D.: Global Software Development with Cloud Platforms. In: Gotel, O., Joseph, M., Meyer, B. (eds.) SEAFOOD 2009. LNBIP, vol. 35, pp. 81–95. Springer, Heidelberg (2009)

A Cloud Adoption Decision Support Model
Based on Fuzzy Cognitive Maps

Andreas Christoforou and Andreas S. Andreou

Deprtment of Computer Engineering and Informatics, Cyprus University of Technology
ax.christoforou@edu.cut.ac.cy, andreas.andreou@cut.ac.cy

Abstract. Cloud Computing has become nowadays a significant field of Information and Communication Technology (ICT). Both cloud providers and customers invest time and resources in an endeavor of the former to serve effectively the needs of the latter so as to adopt efficiently such cloud services, based their needs. The decision to adopt cloud services falls within the category of complex and difficult to model real-world problems. Aiming to support the cloud adoption decision process, we propose in this paper an approach based on Fuzzy Cognitive Maps (FCM) which models the parameters that potentially influence such a decision. The construction and analysis of the map is based on factors reported in the relevant literature and the utilization of experts' opinion. The proposed approach is evaluated through four real-world experimental cases and the suggestions of the model are compared with the customers' final decisions. The evaluation indicated that the proposed approach is capable of capturing the dynamics behind the interdependencies of the participating factors.

Keywords: Cloud Adoption, Fuzzy Cognitive Maps, Decision Support.

1 Introduction

The adoption of cloud computing is still a major challenge for organizations daily producing and processing information in the context of their working activities, while a constantly increasingly number of companies includes cloud computing in their short or long term planning. A sufficient number of services that are available on the cloud has surpassed infancy and appears to be quite mature and attractive. Many of the major software developers or service providers have already turned their strategy towards cloud services mostly targeting at increasing their market share. On one hand companies-customers need to consider the benefits, risks and effects of cloud computing on their organization in order to proceed with adopting and using such services, and on the other hand cloud computing providers need to be fully aware of customers concerns and understand their needs so that they can adjust and fit their services accordingly.

Although in recent years the research community has increasingly been interested in this field, a review of the literature on cloud computing, and especially on cloud adoption, revealed that there yet no efficient integrated models or frameworks to support decision making process for adopting cloud services on behalf of customers.

J. Heidrich et al. (Eds.): PROFES 2013, LNCS 7983, pp. 240–252, 2013.

Cloud adoption is a decision involving multiple, conflicting factors with incommensurable units of measurements; therefore, it may be considered as a highly complex process that cannot be satisfied using classical and straightforward methods. Furthermore, the extremely fast-moving nature of the cloud computing environment changes, both to supply and demand, shows how difficult it may be for any procedure to assist the decision making process timely and correctly. This is the reason why a framework or model which supports cloud computing adoption should be quite flexible and dynamically adaptable.

This paper proposes a methodology based on Fuzzy Cognitive Maps (FCM), which attempts to exploit the advantages offered by this model, in such a complex computational environment as that of cloud services. The model is constructed in a systematic manner: Firstly, a study of the most recent and relevant literature on cloud computing and particularly on cloud adoption was performed, through which the identification of all possible factors that influence the final decision was made possible. Next, based on the result of this study a questionnaire was built and distributed to a group of experts so as to capture their knowledge and expertise as regards approving the list of factors already identified and possibly extending the list. In addition, experts were called to define possible relations between factor, the direction of such relations (i.e. form factor A to factor B) and a corresponding weight on a Likert scale. After that, a novel model was developed based on a composite Certainty Neuron Fuzzy Cognitive Map and several hypothetical, as well as real-world scenarios were tested.

The rest of the paper consists of four sections as follows: Section 2 presents related work in the area of cloud computing adoption based on the existing literature and focuses on Computational Intelligent (CI) techniques, such as FCM modeling. In section 3 the methodology of Certainty Neuron Fuzzy Cognitive Maps (CNFCMs) is described, while section 4 introduces the cloud adoption modeling process and discusses and analyses the corresponding experimental results. Finally, section 5 concludes the paper and suggests future research steps.

2   Related Work

Among many definitions of cloud computing, a working definition that has been published by the US National Institute of Standards and Technology (NIST) [5], captured the most common agreed aspects. NIST defines cloud computing as "a model for enabling ubiquitous, convenient, on-demand network access to a shared pool of configurable computing resources (e.g., networks, servers, storage, applications and services) that can be rapidly provisioned and released with minimal management effort or service provider interaction." This cloud model promotes availability and is composed of five essential characteristics, three service models and four deployment models as follows:

- Characteristics: on-demand self-service, broad network access, resource pooling, rapid elasticity and measured service.
- Service models: Software as a Service (SaaS), Platform as a Service (PaaS) and Infrastructure as a Service (IaaS).

- Deployment models: private clouds, community clouds, public clouds and hybrid clouds.

Although it is generally accepted that the adoption of cloud services can offer substantial benefits, many organizations are still reluctant to proceed with it. There is a variety of factors that may influence cloud adoption and it is quite important to properly identify and analyze them aiming to assist customers take the correct decision. Equally important in this study, from the vendors' point of view, is to define which factors should possibly change so as to revert a current negative decision. Our research is mainly focused on the SaaS model investigating both the cloud providers' and the customers' sides.

An investigation of the current literature revealed a relatively small number of papers discussing cloud adoption from the perspective of decision making and also current feasibility approaches fall short in terms of decision making to determine the right decision. We introduce a summary of these studies, examining the contribution of each work to the decision making problem.

In [11] a cloud adoption toolkit is presented which provides a framework to support decision makers in identifying their concerns and match them with the appropriate techniques that can be used to address them. In [12] various issues are examined that impede rapid adoption of cloud computing such as cost, compliance and performance. The authors in [8] attempted to contribute to the development of an explorative model that extends the practical applications of combining Technology Acceptance Model (TAM) related theories, with additional essential constructs such as marketing effort, security and trust, in order to provide a useful framework for decision makers to assess the issue of SaaS adoption and for SaaS providers to become sensitive to the needs of users. Wu [9] explores the significant factors affecting the adoption of SaaS by proposing an analytical framework containing two approaches: the Technology Acceptance Model (TAM) related theories and the Rough Set Theory (RST) data mining. In [13], a solution framework is proposed that employs a modified approach named DEMATEL [14] to cluster a number of criteria (perceived benefits and perceived risks) into a cause group and an effect group, respectively, presenting also a successful case study. Even though all of the above techniques contribute a significant piece to this new open research field, they may be classified as "traditional", single layer approaches which examine only a specific part of the problem.

Techniques that combine fuzzy logic and neural networks seem to improve the way the problem is approached by increasing the flexibility of the related models [15],[16]. FCMs were initially introduced and applied in the field of political science [3] and were also utilized for modeling and simulating dynamic systems in different areas of application, such as analysis of electrical circuits, medicine, organization and strategy planning etc. [4][17][18]. In general, FCMs have shown promising results by modeling real-world problems with success and indicating strong ability to capture the dynamics of complex environments. Therefore, we decided to use FCMs in our decision making modeling environment and through the maps we will search for reasonable answers of practical value to both vendors and customers/users of SaaS.

3   FCM Technical Background

An FCM model provides a graphical representation of the knowledge used to describe a given real-world problem in the form of an acyclic graph comprising cognitive states called concepts [1]. Each concept node is characterized by a numeric state, which denotes the qualitative measure of its presence in the conceptual domain. For example, a high positive numerical value indicates that the concept is strongly present in the analysis, enhances or benefits another node, while a negative value prevents or is harmful to another node. Finally, a zero activation value indicates that the concept is not currently active or relevant to the conceptual domain. The FCM works in discrete steps [5]. When a strong positive correlation exists between the current state of a concept and that of another concept in a preceding period, we say that the former positively influences the latter, indicated by a positively weighted arrow directed from the causing to the influenced concept. By contrast, when a strong negative correlation exists, it reveals the existence of a negative causal relationship indicated by an arrow charged with a negative weight. Two conceptual nodes without a direct link are, obviously, independent.

The activation level of each node of the map and the weighted arrows are set to a specific value based on the beliefs provided by a group of experts. Then, the system calculates the activation levels in a repetitive computational sequence at the end of which the model [5]:

- Reaches equilibrium at a fixed point, with the activation levels, being decimals in the interval [-1 1], stabilizing at fixed numerical values.
- Exhibits limit cycle behavior, with the activation levels falling in a loop of numerical values under a specific time-period.
- Exhibit a chaotic behavior, with the activation level reaching a variety of numerical values in a non-deterministic, random way.

Additional fuzzification to FCMs was introduced via Certainty Neuron Fuzzy Cognitive Maps (CNFCM)[2,[7], which allow for various activation levels of each concept between the two extreme cases, i.e. activation or not. The updating function of a CNFCM is the following:

$$A_i^{t+1} = f(S_i^t A_i^t) - d_i A_i^t \tag{1}$$

$$S_i^t = \sum_{\substack{j=1 \\ j \neq 1}}^{n} A_j^t W_{ij} \tag{2}$$

where A_i is the activation level of concept C_i at some time $(t+1)$ or (t), equation (2) is the sum of the weighted influences that concept C_i receives at time step t from all other concepts, d_i is a decay factor, and (3) is the function used for the aggregation of certainty factors.

$$f_m(A_i^t, S_i^t) = \begin{cases} A_i^t + S_i^t(1 - A_i^t) = A_i^t + S_i^t - A_i^t S_i^t, if\ A_i^t \geq 0, S_i^t \geq 0 \\ A_i^t + S_i^t(1 - A_i^t) = A_i^t + S_i^t - A_i^t S_i^t, if\ A_i^t < 0, S_i^t < 0, |A_i^t| \leq 1, |S_i^t| \leq 1 \\ \frac{(A_i^t + S_i^t)}{(1 - min(A_i^t, S_i^t))}, otherwise \end{cases} \tag{3}$$

4   Modeling the Cloud Adoption Process

4.1   Model Design

The development of an FCM for modeling the cloud adoption decision-making process was implemented based on two methods: (i) Literature study and (ii) Collection of expert opinion through specially prepared questionnaires followed by interviews. More specifically, a small-scale literature review on the subject was conducted in order to identify a number of factors that potentially influence such a decision which would then be used to form the concepts of our model. Each concept in our model is unique in the sense that no overlaps exist between the interpretation of what each concept represents. For example, concept *Compliance* (C5) focuses on functional requirements rather than the issues of security, the latter being addressed by *Privacy and Confidentiality* concept (C8).

Table 1. Conceptual nodes of the proposed model

Id	Name	Definition
C1	Legal	Cloud adoption compliance with all legislative issues. Ability to adjust when legal requirements grow.
C2	Availability	The amount of time that Cloud Services is operating as the percentage of total time it should be operating.
C3	Security	Security of service: data transfer, data stores, web servers, web browsers.
C4	Cost / Pricing	Operational - Running costs, migration costs etc. Cost benefits from Cloud adoption.
C5	Compliance	Business and Regulatory compliance.
C6	Performance/Processing	Does Cloud adoption perform the process to the desire quality?
C7	Scalability	Ability to meet an increasing workload requirement by incrementally adding a proportional amount of resources capacity.
C8	Privacy/ Confidentiality	Privacy and confidentiality coverage.
C9	Elasticity	Ability to commission or decommission resource capacity on the fly.
C10	Data Access / Import-Export	Access to data in various ways.
C11	Technology Suitability	Does cloud technology exhibits the appropriate technological characteristics to support proposed SaaS?
C12	Hardware Access	Degree of cloud Service accessibility, on local hardware.
C13	Audit ability	Ability of cloud service to provide access and ways for audit.
C14	Exit Process	Guarantee and ensure the output process from provider.
C15	Disaster Recovery	Ability of cloud service vendor to provide the required disaster recovery.
C16	Cloud Adoption	Central concept of the model.

The next step involved identifying a group of experts (3) with strongly related background to the subject (i.e. key personnel in cloud providers). An initial list of concepts was then prepared and the experts were asked to evaluate the list and prompted to add or remove concepts based on their expertise and working experience. The last step included one more round with the experts discussing their comments and reaching to consensus as regards the final list of concepts. These concepts were used to form the nodes of the map and are described in Table 1.

Based on the final concept list, the experts were again asked to complete a questionnaire concerning the causal relationships between the nodes of the map and the weights involved, i.e. the degree to which concepts influence each other. The influences were fuzzified using eleven linguistic variables : "negatively very high", "negatively high," "negatively medium," "negatively small," "negatively very small," "neutral," "positively very small," "positively small," "positively medium," "positively high," "positively very high". For simplicity's sake, these variables were encoded in a Likert scale corresponding to integer values within range [-5, 5]. At the same time for each defined relation, the experts would have to declare the value of confidence of their answers by using integer values in range [0, 5] which corresponded to six linguistic variables: "zero", "small", "medium", "high", "very high". The experts' ranking was then combined with their answers in a weighted average scheme and the relationships of the node in the model were represented by the normalized weight matrix shown in Table 2.

Table 2. Causal relationships and weight values between conceptual nodes on a Likert scale from 1 (very low) to 5 (very high) positive and negative - Row influences column.

	C1	C2	C3	C4	C5	C6	C7	C8
C1		0	-2	5	0	3	0	-3
C2	0		0	5	2	0	0	4
C3	-3	0		5	0	-4	0	5
C4	5	5	5		5	5	5	5
C5	5	4	-3	5		0	0	-2
C6	1	0	-2	5	3		0	-4
C7	5	0	0	5	2	3		0
C8	0	2	0	5	4	-3	0	
C9	5	0	-2	5	3	4	0	0
C10	4	3	2	5	2	3	5	3
C11	0	4	-5	4	4	0	0	-4
C12	0	2	-3	5	4	2	0	0
C13	0	5	3	5	4	2	0	2
C14	0	4	0	5	0	0	0	0
C15	0	2	0	5	0	2	0	0
C16	-3	0	-3	5	-3	-3	5	0

Table 2.(*Continued*)

	C9	C10	C11	C12	C13	C14	C15	C16
C1	0	4	3	0	2	0	0	5
C2	0	0	-3	4	4	0	2	4
C3	0	4	-4	-3	-4	0	0	5
C4	3	5	5	5	5	0	5	-5
C5	0	2	4	4	4	2	4	5
C6	3	3	0	0	0	2	0	5
C7	2	5	0	0	0	0	0	5
C8	-2	3	-4	-3	-3	0	0	5
C9		5	0	0	0	0	0	5
C10	4		4	4	4	0	4	5
C11	0	4		0	5	0	0	4
C12	0	4	1		2	0	0	4
C13	0	2	0	2		0	0	3
C14	0	0	0	0	0		0	5
C15	0	5	3	0	0	0		5
C16	0	4	0	0	0	0	0	

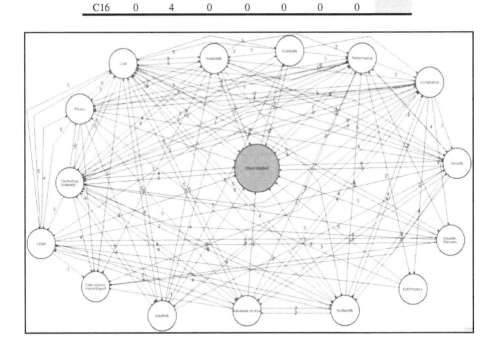

Fig. 1. The cloud adoption CNFCM model

Fig. 1. presents a graphical representation of the map. It is obvious that the structure of the map is quite complex, with 141 total number of connections between nodes. The map is initialized by setting values to the concepts (activation levels) so as to reflect the different scenarios being considered. Each scenario represents a certain situation under modeling as this is described through the activation levels, with the aim being to study the evolution of these levels as follows: After a sufficient number of iterations, if the map succeeds to reach equilibrium at a fixed point, then the final values may be further studied. The most important value is that of the central concept of the map, while at the same time the final values of the rest of the concepts may also provide useful information to decision makers and assist in reaching to important conclusions.

4.2   Experimental Results

Aiming to test and evaluate the performance of the proposed model, two hypothetical scenarios were first conducted representing the so called "extreme cases", that is, a situation where everything would be in favor of cloud adoption (positive scenario) and the opposite case (negative scenario). The target was to reach to equilibrium under known situations and assess the performance of the model proving that the model behaves correctly and as expected to. Next, the map was tested on a number of real-world scenarios, that is, cases collected from real customers of three international cloud services providers with the aid of the same experts that were utilized to construct the map. The two extreme scenarios and the real-world cases experimentation are described below. In all experiments the map was executed for 250 iterations and the results were assessed first to inspect whether they reached equilibrium and then to examine the value of the concept of interest (that is, cloud adoption).

Scenario 1: Positive Case

This case assumes an ideal environment where the cloud services offered perfectly match a customer's needs. Thus, the initial values for each concept were chosen so that they reflect this ideal setting and guide the central concept of interest to a positive value. Following the same logic with linguistic variables as in the case of relationships between the concepts, the initial activation levels for this scenario were defined as listed in Table 3.

The map was executed using the activation level values of Table 3 and the normalized form of the weights listed in Table 2, transformed in the range [-1, 1]. As shown in Figure 2(a), the model reaches an equilibrium state and thus inference is possible. The basic finding here is that the map behaves correctly and leads the central concept of interest to the positive value of 0.795. This means that the model correctly recognized the positive environment and suggested that a decision in favor of cloud adoption should be taken based on the values "read" in the concepts and the current influences between the nodes.

Scenario 2: Negative Case

Working in the same way as with the positive scenario, appropriate initial values for each concept were chosen this time to guide the central node to a negative value. The initial activation levels for the negative scenario are shown in Table 4.

Table 3. FCM initial activation level values of the concepts for the positive scenario

Concept	Linguistic Value	Numerical Value	Normalized Value
C1	positively high	4	0.8
C2	positively high	4	0.8
C3	positively high	4	0.8
C4	negatively high	-4	-0.8
C5	positively high	4	0.8
C6	positively high	4	0.8
C7	positively high	4	0.8
C8	positively high	4	0.8
C9	positively high	4	0.8
C10	positively high	4	0.8
C11	positively high	4	0.8
C12	positively high	4	0.8
C13	positively high	4	0.8
C14	positively high	4	0.8
C15	positively high	4	0.8
C16	zero	0	0

Table 4. FCM initial activation level values of the concepts for the negative scenario

Concept	Linguistic Value	Numerical Value	Normalized Value
C1	negatively high	-4	-0.8
C2	negatively high	-4	-0.8
C3	negatively high	-4	-0.8
C4	positively high	4	0.8
C5	negatively high	-4	-0.8
C6	negatively high	-4	-0.8
C7	negatively high	-4	-0.8
C8	negatively high	-4	-0.8
C9	negatively high	-4	-0.8
C10	negatively high	-4	-0.8
C11	negatively high	-4	-0.8
C12	negatively high	-4	-0.8
C13	negatively high	-4	-0.8
C14	negatively high	-4	-0.8
C15	negatively high	-4	-0.8
C16	zero	0	0

Executing the model using the values for negative the scenario again the map reached equilibrium with its behavior being the one anticipated: the central concept of the map takes the negative value of -0.795 (see Figure 2(b)).

From the above "extreme" scenarios it is evident that the proposed model behaves correctly by recognizing the setting fed and therefore we may now proceed with evaluating its performance on real-world cases.

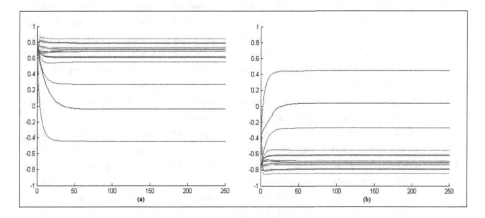

Fig. 2. (a) Positive Case, (b) Negative Case

Real-World Scenarios

As previously mentioned, with the help of cloud providers four different cases were identified: Two customers who decided to proceed with cloud adoption and two cases in which they rejected it. These four cases, along with some related information describing the required cloud services, the size of the organization, the line of business and the final decision regarding cloud adoption, are summarized in Table 5.

Table 5. Brief description of real-world cases

Case	Line of Business	Size (users)	Cloud Services
A	Academic Institution	4500	Mail Server / Mailbox / Mail client
B	Industry	220	Mail Server / Mailbox / Document Management
C	Supplies Industry	85	Mail Server / Mailbox / Mail Client / Document Management
D	Insurance Brokers	125	Mail Server / Mailbox / Mail Client / Custom Business System

A series of interviews was conducted, both with the cloud providers and the customers, so as to identify the initial activation level values for each case separately, which essentially reflected the state of the offered service and the associated factors describing each customer's particular situation at the moment of decision. These initial activation level values for each case are shown in Table 6 in linguistic form, which was found by the people involved in the questionnaires easier to understand and follow.

Table 6. Initial activation level values for real world cases

Concept	Case A	Case B	Case C	Case D
C1	positively very high	positively medium	positively medium	positively medium
C2	positively medium	positively medium	positively medium	positively medium
C3	positively medium	positively medium	positively medium	positively medium
C4	negatively very high	negatively small	positively very small	positively high
C5	positively very high	positively medium	positively medium	negatively very small
C6	positively very high	positively medium	positively medium	negatively very small
C7	negatively high	positively very high	positively very high	negatively medium
C8	positively medium	negatively very high	positively very small	positively very small
C9	positively medium	positively very high	positively very high	negatively medium
C10	positively very high	positively medium	positively medium	negatively small
C11	positively very small	positively medium	positively medium	negatively small
C12	positively very small	positively very small	positively very small	positively very small
C13	positively very small	positively medium	positively very small	negatively medium
C14	negatively very small	negatively very small	negatively very small	negatively high
C15	positively very high	positively very high	positively very high	positively very high
C16	zero	zero	zero	zero

The first case involved an academic institution with a medium to large size which requested a comprehensive solution for email services. In that case easily someone can discern from initial activation level values, that the condition was favorable for a positive decision. The second case described a medium industrial organization which requested for some email cloud services and cloud based document management system. The situation of that organization at that moment can be described as positive too. Third case represents another industrial organization which requested a complete email cloud package and also a cloud based document management system. The decision environment seems to be positive. Finally the fourth case involved a medium insurance broker's organization which requested a complete email cloud package and also a cloud infrastructure to fit a heavy tailored made owned system. In that case, someone can hardly make an assessment of the final decision, based on the initial activation values.

The model was executed again for 250 iterations and reached equilibrium in all cases. The outcome of the model for each of the aforementioned cases is given in Table 7 comparatively with the actual decisions that were taken by the customers.

Table 7. Model's decisions compared with real decisions

Case	Our model's decision	Real decision
A	Yes	Yes
B	Yes	No
C	Yes	Yes
D	No	No

At this point a small discussion on the results should be made. It is evident that the model succeeded in matching its estimation or suggestion with the real decision in three out of four cases. More specifically, in cases A and C our model suggested a positive decision achieving a match with the actual decision. Also, in case D the model estimated a negative decision again in agreement with the real decision. Unlike the previous cases the model failed to coincide with the actual decision taken for real case B. We attempted to investigate the reason for this and after consulting our experts it became evident that this customer should have decided positively given the context of his particular needs; nevertheless, despite the fact that the offered cloud package was fulfilling all requirements the decision was turned negative as a result of the stand towards the cloud environment as a technology taken by the responsible persons, something which on one hand it is definitely beyond the scope of this study and on the other suggests that the result was correct in the first place.

5   Conclusions

This paper proposed a new approach, aiming to improve the cloud adoption decision process. We demonstrated how a new model based on Certainty Neuron Fuzzy Cognitive Maps (CNFCMs) can be constructed and applied to face decision making on the cloud adoption problem, taking the advantages offered by using techniques that combine fuzzy logic and neural networks.

The proposed model was experimentally evaluated on two extreme scenarios, an ideal setting in favor of cloud adoption and a completely negative leading to cloud rejection, showing successful performance. This enabled further experimentation with four real-world scenarios collected form experts/developers in the local mobile software industry. The model succeeded in matching its estimation with the corresponding real decisions in three out of four cases. A more detailed investigation for the case where the model "failed" to suggest the decision that was actually taken revealed that this decision was influenced by human and personal factors that are out of the model's scope and the targets of this research.

Although the results are at a preliminary stage, they may be considered quite encouraging. There are quite a few steps that may be executed in the future so as to enrich and optimize this model. A map analysis, both at a static and a dynamic level, can extract useful information about the behavior of the model. Examples of such an analysis may include the study of the significance of each node in the map by measuring the strength of the connections sourcing by this node, the statistical investigation of a rich number of experimental repetitions using known tests like Pearson correlations, and so on. In addition, more real-world case scenarios could give a helpful feedback for better calibration of the model. Finally, possible expansion of the map will be investigated so as to include more concepts representing better the real cloud environment. Examples of such concepts are the *Return of Investment (ROI)*, *Legislation*, various *Costing Issues* etc. The speed with which current technology evolves underlines the need for periodically studying the model, re-identifying the participating concepts and redefining their causal relationships.

References

1. Kosko, B.: Fuzzy Thinking. The New Science of Fuzzy Logic. Harper Collins, London
2. Tsadiras, A.K., Margaritis, K.G.: Cognitive Mapping and the Certainty Neuron Fuzzy Cognitive Maps. Information Sciences 101, 109–130 (1997)
3. Axelrod, R.: Structure of Decision: The Cognitive Maps of Political Elites. Princeton University Press, Princeton (1976)
4. Alizadeh, S., Ghazanfari, M., Fathian, M.: Using Data Mining for Learning and Clustering FCM. International Journal of Computational Intelligence 4(2), 118–125 (2008)
5. Kosko, B.: Fuzzy Cognitive Maps. International Journal of Man-Machine Studies 24, 65–75 (1986)
6. Taber, W.R., Siegel, M.: Estimation of Expert Weights and Fuzzy Cognitive Maps. In: 1st IEEE International Conference on Neural Networks, vol. 2, pp. 319–325 (1987)
7. Andreou, A.S., Mateou, N.H., Zombanakis, G.A.: Optimization in Genetically Evolved Fuzzy Cognitive Maps Supporting Decision-Making: The Limit Cycle Case. In: Proceedings of International Conference on Information and Communication Technologies: From Theory to Applications, pp. 377–378 (2004)
8. Wu, W.-W.: Developing an explorative model for SaaS adoption. Expert Systems with Applications 38, 15057–15064 (2011)
9. Wu, W.-W.: Mining significant factors affecting the adoption of SaaS using the rough set approach. The Journal of Systems and Software 84, 435–441 (2011)
10. Mell, P., Grance, T.: The NIST Definition of Cloud Computing. National Institute of Standards and Technology (2009)
11. Khajeh-Hosseini, A., Greenwood, D., Smith, J.W., Sommerville, I.: The Cloud Adoption Toolkit: supporting cloud adoption decisions in the enterprise. Software: Practice and Experience 42(4), 447–465 (2012)
12. Kim, W., Kim, S.D., Lee, E., Lee, S.: Adoption issues for cloud computing. In: MoMM 2009, pp. 2–5 (2009)
13. Wu, W.W., Lan, L.W., Lee, Y.T.: Exploring decisive factors affecting an organization's SaaS adoption: A case study. International Journal of Information Management 31(6), 556–563 (2011)
14. Gabus, A., Fontela, E.: World problems, an invitation to further thought within the framework of DEMATEL. BATTELLE Institute, Geneva Research Centre, Geneva, Switzerland (1972)
15. Mateou, N.H., Andreou, A.S.: A framework for developing intelligent decision support systems using evolutionary fuzzy cognitive maps. Journal of Intelligent and Fuzzy Systems 19(2), 151–170 (2008)
16. Papageorgiou, E.I., Papandrianos, N.I., Karagianni, G., Kyriazopoulos, G.C., Sfyras, D.: A fuzzy cognitive map based tool for prediction of infectious diseases. In: IEEE International Conference on Fuzzy Systems, FUZZ-IEEE 2009, pp. 2094–2099. IEEE (August 2009)
17. Andreou, A.S., Mateou, N.H., Zombanakis, G.A.: Evolutionary fuzzy cognitive maps: A hybrid system for crisis management and political decision-making. In: Proc. Computational Intelligent for Modeling, Control & Automation CIMCA, Vienna, pp. 732–743 (2003)
18. Iakovidis, D.K., Papageorgiou, E.: Intuitionistic fuzzy cognitive maps for medical decision making. IEEE Transactions on Information Technology in Biomedicine 15(1), 100–107 (2011)

Modeling and Decision Support of the Mobile Software Development Process Using Influence Diagrams

Pantelis Stylianos Yiasemis and Andreas S. Andreou

Cyprus University of Technology
{pantelis.yiasemis,andreas.andreou}@cut.ac.cy

Abstract. Mobile devices are increasingly becoming one of the most popular and common computing tools with mobile users relying on them for carrying out their everyday working, social and amusement activities. As a result, mobile software has gained the lion's share in the software industry with millions of Dollars/Euros being spent for purchasing mobile applications worldwide. This paper investigates certain aspects of mobile software development through a promising decision making approach, namely Influence Diagrams (ID). Two key models are developed which aim to provide an answer to the questions, "should a developer proceed with producing a new mobile application?" and "what would be the estimated level of user acceptance for a new mobile application?", respectively. The IDs are composed of a number of interrelated factors which were identified through literature review and input received from domain experts. The models are validated against realistic and real-world examples. Their performance is proved quite successful in providing the correct prediction/estimation and therefore may be considered a useful decision making tool.

Keywords: Mobile Software, Development Process, User Acceptance, Influence Diagrams, Decision Support.

1 Introduction

Mobile Software Development has been constantly increasing for the past five years since the introduction of the original iPhone [1] which led to major changes to the whole mobile devices industry. While the number of mobile phones overtook the number of fixed land line phones in 2002, it wasn't until 2007 that a drastic change was observed with mobile software development moving from the closed environment of the device manufacturers to the outer community of software developers. It is estimated that in 2013 the number of people accessing the internet from mobile devices, both mobile phones and tablets, will surpass that of accessing it through PCs [2]. It is clearly visible that there is a shift from traditional PCs to mobile devices for internet access meaning that content needs to be delivered to those users through either cut down versions of websites or dedicated mobile apps. As mobile devices become more popular and provide more capabilities than ever, they seem as a really attractive platform for developers.

J. Heidrich et al. (Eds.): PROFES 2013, LNCS 7983, pp. 253–267, 2013.
© Springer-Verlag Berlin Heidelberg 2013

Mobile devices nowadays have a number of sensors, fast processors and graphic chips, large amount of RAM and storage space, while they are able to connect to the Internet in speeds similar to those in wired broadband connections. While in the PC processor market there are only two major companies competing, in the mobile area more than five companies compete adding and customizing features to their processors in their own specific ways [3]. All these lead to the need for developing more demanding applications and games resembling their desktop counterparts. The Software Development Kits provided for the current mobile devices platforms can be used to develop highly functional and full of features mobile applications with the use of various technologies like JavaScript, Objective C, Java, .Net platform, HTML 5, OpenGL and other [4]. This leads to the creation of a variety of more complex apps, full of features, rich in content that provide innovative ways to display or use it while offering ways to organize and simplify a user's daily routine or just providing entertainment on the go. All the technologies and features provided by the mobile devices, the ease of their development and the simplicity of distributing the apps through the online markets attracted a rich number of development companies and even stand-alone developers. Also, the constant changes in the mobile devices and characteristics, as well as in the development tools and platforms bring more opportunities and constraints to developers of such applications.

Developers are often confronted with a number of difficult decisions they should take before starting the development of a mobile app. They have to assess their options and how they are going to take advantage of all opportunities the mobile environment has to offer in order to develop a successful and profitable app. There are actually a large number of factors that can influence the final decision of proceeding with the development of an app or not and the user acceptance of an app. This paper will attempt to identify them and incorporate them in a decision support model. More specifically we suggest the use of Influence Diagrams (IDs) as a means to assist developers in answering some fundamental questions that put them in distress when choosing between going ahead with the development of a mobile app or not. In this context we created two different models employing IDs to approximate the answer to the following questions:

- Should the development of an app proceed or not? – By examining whether to develop an app or not, which are the factors that influence this decision and how? How would different input values for these factors change this decision?
- Will the level of user acceptance be high for a particular app? Based on different factors like pricing, app functionality and the ability of the app to provide the required functionality, will the level of user acceptance be high?

The benefits of Influence Diagrams supported their choice over other modeling techniques as they can represent mathematical dependencies between complex factors and provide intelligent models to provide answers to the problems in hand.

The aforementioned questions are two of the most significant issues that mobile app developers face when they consider the development of a new mobile app. The significance of this work, therefore, lies with the fact that it offers a model of the mobile software development environment that, to the best of our knowledge, has never been proposed before. The use of real-world scenarios makes this work more important as these real cases reflect the experiences collected by actual developers working in this industry. The questions addressed in this work are considered highly important for anyone tempted to develop a mobile app.

The rest of the paper is structured as follows: Section 2 provides a brief overview of how the factors that influence the development and user acceptance of a mobile app were chosen and present the results of similar studies. Section 3 makes a brief description of the Influence Diagrams and the way they were created in each of the two cases, along with a brief presentation of their modeling philosophy. Section 4 introduces the different scenarios in terms of the experimental values used on the elements of the diagrams described in Section 3. Finally, section 5 provides the conclusions, discusses some of the limitations of the proposed approach and gives some plans for future work in this area.

2   Literature Overview

There are a number of studies which target the factors that influence the mobile user satisfaction, the quality of mobile apps, the quality of experience when using a mobile app, or even the factors influencing the user acceptance of mobile apps. Nevertheless, no previous work exists on defining models to support the decision of developers to go ahead and develop an app or what the user acceptance be, based on a number of factors. This section presents a summary of similar studies focusing on the main factors that may affect the decisions of mobile app developers.

The work of Gerogianni set al. [6] uses Fuzzy Cognitive Maps (FCMs), which essentially constitute a method for knowledge representation and reasoning based on human knowledge and experience, to assess User Satisfaction for smartphones. A FCM model was created to represent users' perceptions of satisfaction from the use of smartphones. The authors derived 24 factors that were found in previous studies to influence user satisfaction and used them to construct their model. These factors include the perceived enjoyment one gets from using a smartphone, the security level the device provides, the complexity of the device, the support for 3G services, a number of features provided by the Operating System, as well as a number of hardware characteristics. With the use of a questionnaire distributed to a number of existing or potential smartphone users the authors assessed each factor as regards the degree of user satisfaction. Based on users' selections they calculated the similarities and dissimilarities between these fuzzy numbers for each factor. The majority of these factors which may influence the decision for developing a mobile application are adopted in this paper too as will be described later on. As tablets are very similar to smart phones in terms of functionality and features, and nowadays both of these categories of devices dominate the mobile computing environment, it is safe for one to suggest that the same factors identified for smartphones apply to tablets as well.

Another work concerned with a similar subject is the one described in [7] which targets the factors influencing the user's Quality of Experience (QoE) for commonly used applications. Both qualitative and quantitative methods were used in a four weeks long user study on 30 users. The focus was on already implemented and operational interactive mobile apps that were available and commonly used on a smartphone. The user study involved a continuous and automatic context data collection on the users' mobile phones through a Context Sensing Software app, gathering user feedback on the perceived QoE with the use of an Experience Sampling Method multiple times a day and a weekly interview with the users. A number of factors that influence the QoE was then distinguished and included the app's interface design, the app's performance, the battery efficiency, the phone features - both in hardware and software - , the app's price and connectivity costs, and finally the user routine and lifestyle. Some of these factors were also included in the model presented in this work as the QoE is a really important factor in the decision of developing or not a mobile app.

The major challenges to mobile web application development were described in the work of Spriestersbach and Springer [8]. They describe the typical challenges in the development of such apps and map them against the ISO 9126 quality standard. Their proposed model was then used to analyze the quality factors of mobile web apps, create an expert evaluation checklist or use it for quality based content adaptation. They concluded the paper by showing that challenges in the mobile web application development can be solved by applying quality assurance methods while the applications are still in the development phase. One of the major challenges of web application development is the large number of different mobile devices and web browsers installed on those devices. The differences in the input form and capabilities strongly influence the use of the apps. Also, the availability of wireless network connections cause even more threats such as limited bandwidth, connection interruptions or increase of latency. The main factors described in the ISO standard are Functionality, Reliability, Usability, Efficiency, Maintainability and Portability. Certain quality factors are also used in the model presented in this paper as they are key issues that influence the decisions to the questions set.

Pocatilu [9] states that software metrics are very important in the software development process as they allow the quantification of the software, the deliverables of all aspects and stages of development and the software processes. He goes on and specifies factors that are associated with metrics for mobile app development. These factors are related with the operating system of the device an app is developed for, the characteristics of the underlying hardware, the network access and finally the application type. Some device-specific factors that may affect the development of an app are memory size, processor speed, screen size and resolution, touch screen availability, accelerometer etc. Compared to traditional (PC-based) software mobile apps have serious limitations regarding the screen size and resolutions, put restrictions to the app size, necessitate the limitation of memory consumption, often present higher complexity compared to the traditional version and require limited data usage. In addition, the testing process of a mobile app requires substantial effort as emulators provided by each SDK cannot test all the features and therefore testing the app on a number of different devices is needed. Another factor that influences mobile software development is the reliability of the final app, that is, the probability that the app is going to work without any failures and according to its specifications. In another work, Pocatilu [10] presents how different app types influence the complexity, size, user interface, processing power needed and knowledge required for developing the app. From this work not only factors that influence the development of an app were extracted and used in the present paper, but also some casual relationships between some of these factors.

The work of Zarmpou et al. [11] focuses on understanding the factors that influence the adoption of specific mobile services by users based on behavioral intention theories like Technology Acceptance Model (TAM), Diffusion of Innovation and Unified Theory of Acceptance, and Use of Technology. Specifically, different variables were identified and a conceptual model was formulated which consisted of the following variables: Behavioral Intention, Perceived Usefulness, Perceived ease of Use, Trust, Innovativeness, Relationship Drivers and Functionality. Data was collected from survey on m-commerce consumers in Greece with the use of questionnaires on a 5-point Likert scale ranging from 1- "Completely Disagree" to 5- "Completely Agree". A number of conclusions from this paper may help developers evaluate their decisions about developing and user acceptance of an app based on the factors that influence its adoption by the users, and thus were incorporated in the proposed models of this work as well. Such factors is the functionality of the app, the ease of use, the personalization of the app to each user's needs and also the personalization of services to create a relationship between the user and the service while being able to use the service from anywhere and at any time. Also, the way the questionnaires were constructed in [11] guided the production of the questionnaires used in this paper.

Gavalas and Economou [12] make an informal survey of 32 mobile-application developers on four different mobile app platforms to highlight the trends and status in current development platforms. Also, they developed a simple game application on all four platforms to show the pros and cons of each of the platforms. Based on their review they assessed the appropriateness of each platform with respect to some critical mobile app development requirements like portability, functionality, development speed and performance. A number of different development issues were described, along with the way each platform addresses a certain issue. Some of the issues addressed in [12] were included in our work, like development platform, community support, development time and development cost.

Summarizing, based on the relevant literature the present paper identified and incorporated 17 factors so as to assess their influence on the final decision for developing or not a mobile app. Some of the factors used were included in more than one study making their choice even more obvious, while a second round of validating the factors was possible with the use of questionnaires handed to mobile app developers. The questionnaires targeted the evaluation of different factors and their weight of contribution to the evaluation of the two models, while also contained comments and suggestions about the inclusion of factors that were not in the initial list, like development time, update/maintenance cost and current market competition. The factors selected to participate in the modeling process, along with the relevant papers from which they were extracted are outlined in Table 1.

Essentially, like with traditional software, mobile app development is affected by numerous factors, some easier to quantify, some harder. The final decision for developing the app is up to the developer but numerous factors like development cost, effort, time, etc. affect directly this decision. Device specific factors, price, complexity of the app, team size and innovation also affect the decision to develop the app or not, but in an indirect way. In addition, a subset of the aforementioned factors may be utilized in modeling the estimation of its market penetration based on the foreseen user acceptance.

Table 1. Factors influencing the development of a mobile app

Factor	Description	Reference
Development Cost	The cost for the development of the mobile app.	[12]
Development Time	The time needed to develop the mobile app.	Experts
Development Effort	The effort needed to develop the mobile app.	[9], [10]
Testing Level	The level of testing that the app to be developed is going to need in order to not contain faults or crash.	[9],[12]
Update/Maintain Cost	The projected cost for updating and maintaining the app after its publication on the market and until its withdrawal.	Experts
Development Platform	The ease of development on the selected platform. When the app type and features are decided then an assessment of the development platform, tools and libraries available can be made to evaluate the ease to develop the app on the selected platform.	[12]
Community Support	The support developers can get from the community of the selected platform. It accounts for the tutorials, online help, forums etc.	[12]
Complexity	The complexity of the app based on the number of classes to be used, the features it uses, the type of the app, the use of Location Based Services, the interaction with other apps etc.	[9]
Quality Factors	These are factors that affect the quality of the app to be developed. They are specified by the developer and are based on the ISO 9126 quality standard. They include Portability, Adaptability, Reliability, Maintainability and Performance.	[8]
Security	The required security to be provided by the app based anticipated levels.	[6], [8],[11]
Device Specific Features	The device specific features the app makes use of, like accelerometer, gyroscope, camera, data connection.	[7], [12]
Competition	The current competition in the market segment the app to be developed aims at.	Experts
Energy Efficiency	The energy efficiency the developer sets for the app. The use of techniques to limit the energy consumption and provide longer battery life to the users.	[6], [7], [9], [10]
Resource Efficiency	The resource efficiency the developer sets for the ap. The good allocation of space and efficient RAM usage does the app provide.	[6], [7], [9], [10]
Team Size	The number of persons in the development team.	[9], [10]
Innovation	The innovative features that are included in the app to be developed and will give an advantage to the app compared to current	[11]

3   The Modeling Process

Influence Diagrams (ID) were first developed in the mid 70s as a decision analysis tool for complicated problems exhibiting high quantitative and qualitative uncertainty. They offer easily understandable and intuitive semantics and they have been designed to bridge the gap between analysis and formulation. Also, they provide both easy communication with experts and decision makers, while they are precise enough for executing formative analysis [13]. IDs represent graphically the uncertain quantities and decisions that reveal probabilistic relationships between them and the flow of information. They are acyclic diagrams represented by a set of nodes and directed arcs. Three different kinds of nodes exist: chance nodes (oval), decision nodes (rectangular) and value nodes (hexagon). An arc that is directed to a chance node indicates a probabilistic dependence, while arcs going to decision nodes represent the information that is available at the time of decision. IDs are compact diagrams which show relationships between the variables while managing to represent a complete probabilistic model of the problem.

Based on the aforementioned advantages we decided to employ IDs for creating our models as their features match our requirements for decision support. In addition, our selection was supported by the fact that influence diagrams provide a number of other computational benefits: (i) An ID model performs all the inference and analysis automatically so that their representation is closer to the decision makers increasing their understandability. (ii) ID can represent a large number of dependencies between a variety of factors that may lead to a decision. (iii) They allow experts to experiment with changing the values of nodes in order to calibrate the model and achieve proper modeling of different scenarios [14]. Using the GeNIe toolbox [15], two different models were created. Their descriptions are as follows:

3.1   Develop Decision Model

The influence diagram in Figure 1 was built to answer the question whether a developer should go ahead and develop a mobile app or not. For clarity purposes we will explain in detail the rationale of this diagram; the philosophy of the other diagram is similar, therefore we will refer only to significant modeling aspects in the second diagram. It should be noted that the values for some of the leaf nodes are not known prior to development (e.g. energy efficiency). Therefore, the desired/anticipated values for these nodes are used.

The *Evaluation* node is used to execute all possible combinations of the value nodes and propose the decision. The latter is primarily dependent on three basic entities, *Update/maintenance cost*, *Development Effort* and *Competition* of the app. Also it is determined by three other nodes, *Development Cost* and *Development Time*, which are influenced directly or indirectly by *Development Effort, and Quality Factors*. A number of other nodes also influence some of the primary factors. Starting from left to right on the diagram, node *App Functionality* is influenced by seven leaf nodes: *Resource Efficiency, Energy Efficiency, Device Specific Features, Quality Factors, Complexity, Security* provided and *Innovation* of the app. All these leaf node values are based on the specifications and requirements of the mobile app as set by the developer. While energy and resource efficiency are included in ISO 9126, we model them independently as they were indicated of great importance by both the experts and the relevant literature. They take the value of low, medium and high and influence the value of *App Functionality* with equal weight; we use a weight scale from 1 to 3 (1 being the lowest). The *App Functionality* node in turn affects *Testing Level*; when *App Functionality* are high then the *Testing Level* increases as well in order to provide adequate testing to all features and characteristics of the App. Both *App Functionality* and *Testing Level* nodes, along with factor *Ease of Development* affect the *Development Effort* for developing the App. While *App Functionality* and *Testing Level* affect positively and increase the value of *Development Effort* with weights of 3 and 1 respectively, *Ease of Development* node decreases *Development Effort*, with a weight of 2, the latter becoming higher as more libraries, tools and online support in general are available to aid in the development of the mobile app. *Community Support*, the amount of help and support a developer can get from the community and forums, and *Development Platform*, the amount of tools, tutorials, libraries provided by the SDK of the platform used, affect *Ease of Development* node; with the same weight of 1. The leaf node *Team Size* influences *Development Time* as well, as larger teams will normally affect (lower, although not always proportionally) the development time of an app when the specifications of the app are stable. While one may argue that *Team Size* affects negatively *Development effort* as more team members introduce communication and coordination overheads, we choose not to model this relationship as both *Team Size* and *Development Effort* affect *Development Time*, so it would be redundant if *Team Size* affected *Development Effort* again. *Development effort* also affects *Development cost*, which in turn affects the final evaluation node.

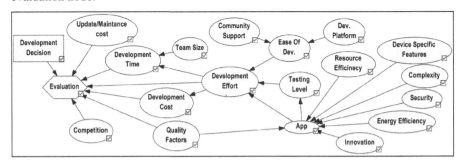

Fig. 1. "Develop or Not" Influence Diagram

Finally, the nodes affecting directly the evaluation node were assigned weights of influence based on experts' judgment as follows: *Competition* and *Development Cost* have the highest influence and thus bear a weight of 3; *Quality Factors*, *Development Time* and *Development Effort* are ranked second in importance and assigned a weight of 2, while *Update/Maintenance cost* is considered the weakest of all and is weighted with 1. It is important to note that all factors directly connected to the *Evaluation* node affect negatively the decision to develop the mobile app: the higher their value the lower the strength of a positive decision. The *Evaluation* node calculates a result in the range of [0, 100] which reflects the answer to our decision problem. A value equal or higher than 70 is interpreted as a clear suggestion that the mobile app should be developed, while a value lower or equal than 30 will mean it should not. Values above 50 and less than 70, or below 50 and above 30 are indications of a "go" and no-go" decision respectively, which become stronger as they move towards the cutoff-values of 70 and 30.

3.2   User Acceptance Decision Model

In order to answer the question whether a mobile app will be highly accepted by potential users the diagram depicted in Figure 2 was created. In this diagram it's visible that four basic entities exist, namely *Pricing*, *App Functionality*, *Innovation* and *Functionality*, which affect the final answer. *Pricing* represents the level of the price decided for the app compared to the current competitors in the market segment; this level may be low(er), average (equal) or high(er) (than the average price of similar apps). *Innovation* is the level of innovative functional features contained in the app and again takes the values low, normal and high by comparing to the current competition. *Functionality* factor represents the level of fulfillment for the desired functionality sought by a user and takes the values low, normal, and high. The decision weights of the four factors were decided once gain based on the opinion of the experts: *Functionality* received a weight of 3, *App Functionality* and *Pricing* of 2 and *Innovation* of 1.

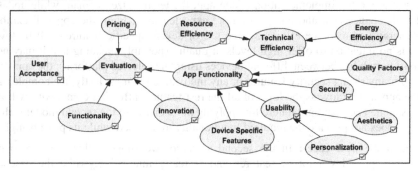

Fig. 2. User Acceptance Influence Diagram

Node *App Functionality* is more complex as it is influenced by a number of other nodes like *Technical Efficiency* (contains both energy and resources efficiency), the quality of the app (node *Quality Factors*), the *Security* level provided by the app, the *Usability* level (taking into consideration *Aesthetics* and *Personalization* issues) and the *Device Specific Features* that the app makes use of. All of these factors take values of low, average and high indicating the level of each feature possessed by the app.

4   Experiments and Results

The models created were based on knowledge elicited through literature review and expert opinion. Certainly, there may be other representations in the same context giving birth to different models than the ones proposed above. Nevertheless, once the validity of the models created is tested and their behavior is proven correct then these models may be put in practice so as to offer significant decision support to the interested parties. To this end, we tested the models created with the two "extremes" of a given situation, that is, with scenarios reflecting an ideal, positive setting with all values in favor of the decision under modeling of test data sets, and right the opposite, a situation with a fully negative picture. If the evaluation node returns a reasonable answer, either positive or negative depending on the case, then we may argue that the modeling process was in general successful and can be further investigated with the use of real-world scenarios.

4.1   Scenarios

Four scenarios were executed on both the IDs for deciding whether to develop or not a mobile app and the user acceptance of the app, based on the developer's desired/anticipated specific features and characteristics of the app and the conditions of the development process (team size, ease of development, etc.) as follows:

Scenario 1 (Worst case): In this scenario, we suppose that the app to be developed will not provide a lot of features or innovation, while the ease of development is low as there is limited community support and the platform does not provide tools and libraries to aid the implementation of the app; the team's size is small, while update and maintenance cost and competition are expected to be high; the app will exhibit low energy and resource efficiency; the use of device specific features will be low; there is no intention to offer high levels of quality (possibly meaning that it may not support portability between different devices using the selected platform); the app will not offer any strong security features or any innovative features; lastly, the complexity of the app will be low as the level of all the rest features affecting complexity will be low as well. The assumption here for applying the scenario to the second model is that the app does not provide the required functionality to the user, while its price is high.

Scenario 2 (Ideal case): In the second scenario, we suppose that the app to be developed provides a lot of features and is really innovative, while the ease of development is high as there is a lot of community support and the platform provides numerous tools and libraries to aid in the implementation of the app; the team's size is large, while maintenance costs are low. There is no competition in the market as there is no app with similar functionality; the app offers high levels of energy and resource efficiency by using intelligent algorithms for their preservation; there is a rich use of device specific features like accelerometer, GPS, data connection, etc.; the app will meet high quality standards meaning that it will support portability, maintainability, efficiency, functionality etc. across different devices; the app will offer high levels of security and will provide highly innovative features compared to similar apps. As the level of app desired features will be high the complexity of the app will be high as well. Lastly the app provides the functionality required by the user, while having a low price.

Scenario 3 (Real case app 1): The third scenario was based on a mobile app that provides interactive drawing and sketching techniques. It also gives information about drawing and sketching lessons in Cyprus. This app has low innovation, while it is energy and resource efficient. It does not require any security as it is an offline app that has no access to user details or to the Internet. It has low use of device specific features, while providing high quality. The complexity of the app is low and the update/maintenance cost is low. In addition, there is almost no competition as no other app provides the same functionality as it is a localized app for a Cyprus sketching lab while it had a low price. Lastly, the team consisted of just one person.

Scenario 4 (Real case app 2): The last scenario was again based on a real-world mobile app that provides information about what to do when in Cyprus, informs users about offers to different kind of stores and restaurants, while also providing locations for them on an interactive map. It offers Augmented Reality to enable the user to find places around him. The app provides high innovation, as uses Augmented Reality to provide information about services in Cyprus. The app did have low energy and resource efficiency due to the use of a high number of Device Specific Features like camera, data connection, accelerometer and compass. It did not provide any security as it has no access to any user details. In addition, the app is of high quality and also complexity. The update/maintenance cost is medium, the competition is low and the team consisted of two persons.

Table 2. Input values for "Develop or Not" diagram

Factors	Term	S1 Worst	S2 Best	S3 Real 1	S4 Real 2
Resource Efficiency	Low	0.8	0	0	0.7
	Medium	0.2	0.2	0.1	0.3
	High	0	0.8	0.9	0
Device Specific Features	Low	0.8	0	0.9	0
	Medium	0.2	0.2	0.1	0.2
	High	0	0.8	0	0.8
Quality Factors	Low	0.8	0	0	0
	Medium	0.2	0.2	0.2	0.3
	High	0	0.8	0.8	0.7
Complexity	Low	0.8	0	0.7	0
	Medium	0.2	0.2	0.3	0.2
	High	0	0.8	0	0.8
Security	Low	0.8	0	0.7	0.8
	Medium	0.2	0.2	0.3	0.2
	High	0	0.8	0	0
Energy Efficiency	Low	0.8	0	0	0.8
	Medium	0.2	0.2	0.2	0.2
	High	0	0.8	0.8	0
Innovation	Low	0.8	0	0.9	0
	Medium	0.2	0.2	0.1	0.3
	High	0	0.8	0	0.7
Dev Platform	Low	0.8	0	0	0
	Medium	0.2	0.2	0.3	0.3
	High	0	0.8	0.7	0.7
Community Support	Low	0.8	0	0	0
	Medium	0.2	0.1	0.2	0.2
	High	0	0.9	0.8	0.8
Competition	Low	0	0.8	0.9	0.9
	Medium	0.2	0.2	0.1	0.1
	High	0.8	0	0	0
Update/Maintenance Cost	Low	0	0.8	0.8	0
	Medium	0.2	0.2	0.2	0.3
	High	0.8	0	0	0.7
Team Size	Small	0.8	0	1	0.8
	Medium	0.2	0.2	0	0.2
	Large	0	0.8	0	0

The quantitative values of the factors in Tables 2 and 3 were converted from their qualitative counterparts obtained from the experts using seven linguistic variables: "very low", "low", "low-medium", "medium", "medium-high" "high" "very high,". For simplicity's sake, these variables were encoded in a Likert scale to values within range [0, 1].

4.2   Develop a Mobile App or Not?

Table 2 presents the input values used in the experiments for development or not of an app. The values reflect the values described in the previous four scenarios; columns S1, S2, S3 and S4 represent the four scenarios executed.

4.2.1 Results

In the Worst-case scenario (S1), the Influence diagram computed the value of 40.1. This means that the developer should not go ahead with the development of the app. As the input values for this scenario correspond to a not so promising app with not many features and with high update/maintenance costs and competition, the developer should not proceed with developing the app. The Best-case scenario (S2) returns the value of 66.34. The developer should go ahead and develop the app according to the diagram: the specified app contains a lot of features, it is of high quality, the support of the community is high, it provides high levels of security, the competition is low as well as the cost for updating and maintaining the app, while it provides efficient memory and power features. Based on these input values we can conclude that the developer should develop the app, something which is verified by the proposed ID for this question. Since the two "extreme" cases worked well the next step is to test the proposed model on the real-world scenarios.

The first real case scenario (S3) returns the value of 68.47 for developing the app which means that the developer correctly developed the app according to the diagram. The app is really simple and with low update\maintaince cost, low competition, small team and exhibiting high platfrom and community support as it is an iOS app. The second real case scenario (S4) returns the value of 61.97 for developing the app. This score is translated to a decision possibly favoring development; the app's characteristics though do not give a clear picture thus the developer needs to be cautious and give it a second though. Looking into the causes of this cautiousness we can see that this app requires a lot of development effort based on the its characteristics, the team is relatively small, it has high update\maintainance costs, but on the other hand it faces a low competition, something which surely accounts in favor. Again the development platform is iOS providing high values for platform and community support. These factors influence the evaluation of the ID in a way that the proposed answer is on the positive side; therefore in this case too the original developer decision was correct. A short validation round with the developers revealed that in the first case the app is already considered successful as it has a high number of downloads, while in the second case, which is also considered successful in terms of user response, it was a quite tough application to develop, and moreover, it slipped a bit outside the planned release thus confirming the somewhat skeptisism of the ID, but the lack of competition was worth the shot; thus the model was right after all.

The findings on the above scenarios suggest that the proposed model is quite successful and can be trusted for taking safer decisions as regards proceeding with the development of a mobile app.

4.3 User Acceptance of Mobile App

User acceptance of an app was modeled using the diagram of Figure 2, again utilizing the four scenarios described in section 4.1 to demonstrate its applicability and performance based on the app's characteristics, price and functionality.

Table 3 presents the input values of the factors for evaluating User Acceptance of an app reflecting the previous four scenarios. Columns S1, S2, S3 and S4 represent the four scenarios executed.

Table 3. Input Values for User Acceptance Diagram

Factors	Term	S1 Worst	S2 Best	S3 Real 1	S4 Real 2
Resource Efficiency	Low	0.8	0	0	0.7
	Medium	0.2	0.2	0.1	0.3
	High	0	0.8	0.9	0
Energy Efficiency	Low	0.8	0	0	0.8
	Medium	0.2	0.2	0.2	0.2
	High	0	0.8	0.8	0
Quality Factors	Low	0.8	0	0	0
	Medium	0.2	0.2	0.2	0.3
	High	0	0.8	0.8	0.7
Security	Low	0.8	0	0.7	0.8
	Medium	0.2	0.2	0.3	0.2
	High	0	0.8	0	0
Aesthetics	Low	0.8	0	0.2	0
	Medium	0.2	0.2	0.6	0.3
	High	0	0.8	0.2	0.7
Personalization	Low	0.8	0	0.9	0.8
	Medium	0.2	0.2	0.1	0.2
	High	0	0.8	0	0
Device Specific features	Low	0.8	0	0.9	0
	Medium	0.2	0.2	0.1	0.2
	High	0	0.8	0	0.8
Innovation	Low	0.8	0	0.9	0
	Medium	0.2	0.2	0.1	0.3
	High	0	0.8	0	0.7
Functionality	Low	0.8	0	0	0
	Medium	0.2	0.2	0.2	0.2
	High	0	0.8	0.8	0.8
Pricing	Low	0	0.8	0.9	0.8
	Medium	0.2	0.2	0.1	0.2
	High	0.8	0	0	0

4.3.1 Results

The Influence diagram computed the value of 19.7 for the Worst-case scenario (S1). This translates to a minimum user acceptance. The Best-case scenario (S2) on the other hand returned the value of 80.7 when indicating a very high user acceptance. Both results are perfectly logical and expected. Therefore, it would be interesting to examine the results of the model on the real cases. The diagram showed that both real-world scenarios would be quite successful among the users; the first yielding the value of 65.63 for user acceptance while the second the value of 73.34. As previously mentioned, this is indeed confirmed by the high number of downloads of both apps performed so far and a positive feedback and rating received.

By examining the findings on these scenarios and the results provided by the IDs, we may conclude that the proposed model is also successful and can be used for assessing user acceptance of a mobile app.

5   Conclusions

Mobile Software Development has been on the rise for the last five years, since the introduction of the original iPhone. Since then there has been a spectacular increase in features, innovation and processing power of mobile devices that transformed them to a very important tool for entertainment, business and daily tasks. In 2012 over 9 billion U.S. Dollars were spent by software companies on mobile app development. Before initiating, though, the development of any mobile app there are a number of serious questions to answer and difficult decisions to take, like for example "which platform should the app target?", "what would be a proper price that will not drive away users and make profit?", "how well will the users accept the app?"

This paper focused on investigating the factors that influence mobile software development. We isolated two decisions-questions that we found to have high importance to the area of mobile development: (i) Proceed with developing a certain mobile app or not?, (ii) What will the user acceptance of the app be? A number of factors were collected through review of the relevant literature enhanced by expert knowledge. These factors constituted the basis for constructing two different models based on Influence Diagrams, one for each question posed. Four scenarios were then constructed, one representing the worst case scenario, one the best and two scenarios based on real-world apps developed and released in the market by the experts. Our purpose was to assess the results of the diagrams so as to check if they provided reasonable and verified guidance to the questions in hand. The findings of both models on the worst and best case scenarios were as expected, providing indications that the proposed approach is quite successful. Next we ran the models using the real-world cases and analyzed the results. Our findings confirmed that we can trust such models and we may use them to guide us in deciding if we should develop a mobile app and predict what the user acceptance of the app would eventually be.

Future work will concentrate on automating the value input method for the leaf nodes as in the current stage it is a very time and effort consuming task. In addition, evolutionary computing, like genetic algorithms, will be combined with ID so as to provide simulation analysis of hypothetical scenarios: The ID model will be executed with a set of values describing a situation and then we will have the evolutionary algorithm search and find the proper connections and influences that can drive the evaluation node produce the desired answer to the questions; then this genetically evolved diagrammatic alteration will be studied so as to guide decision makers how to move towards the right direction for achieving this desired value, for example changing the weights representing the significance of each of the nodes directly influencing the evaluation node. Finally, we will gather more real-world examples from the mobile software industry and continue validating and calibrating the proposed models, possibly using information available at the App Store and Google Play related to rankings and downloads of various applications hosted.

References

1. Kerris, N., Dowling, S.: Apple Reinvents the Phone with iPhone. Apple (January 9, 2007), http://www.apple.com/pr/library/2007/01/09Apple-Reinvents-the-Phone-with-iPhone.html (accessed January 26, 2013)
2. Standage, T.: In 2013 the internet will become a mostly mobile medium. Who will be the winners and losers?: The Economist (November 21, 2012), The Economist: http://www.economist.com/news/21566417-2013-internet-will-become-mostly-mobile-medium-who-will-be-winners-and-losers-live-and (retrieved February 5, 2013)
3. Miller, M.J.: Forward Thinking - Mobile Core Wars: How the Chip Makers Stack Up (March 13, 2012), PcMag.com: http://forwardthinking.pcmag.com/cell-phones/295297-mobile-core-wars-how-the-chip-makers-stack-up (retrieved February 8, 2013)
4. Amalfitano, D., Fasolino, A., Tramontana, P.: A GUI Crawling-Based Technique for Android Mobile Application Testing. In: Software Testing, Verification and Validation Workshops (ICSTW), pp. 252–261. IEEE, Berlin (2011)
5. Holzer, A., Ondrus, J.: Trends in Mobile Application Development. In: Hesselman, C., Giannelli, C. (eds.) Mobilware 2009 Workshops. LNICST, vol. 12, pp. 55–64. Springer, Heidelberg (2009)
6. Gerogiannis, V.C., Papadopoulou, S., Papageorgiou, E.I.: A Fuzzy Cognitive Map for identifying User Satisfaction from Smartphones. In: 16th Panhellenic Conference on Informatics (2012)
7. Ickin, S., Wac, K., Fiedler, M., Janowski, L., Hong, J.H., Dey, A.K.: Factors influencing quality of experience of commonly used mobile applications. IEEE Communications Magazine 50(4), 48–56 (2012)
8. Spriestersbach, A., Springer, T.: Quality Attributes in mobile Web Application Development. In: Bomarius, F., Iida, H. (eds.) PROFES 2004. LNCS, vol. 3009, pp. 120–130. Springer, Heidelberg (2004)
9. Pocatilu, P.: Influencing Factors of Mobile Applications' Quality Metrics. Economy Informatics, 1–4 (2006)
10. Pocatilu, P.: Mobile Applications Design. In: ACTTM International Symposium, Bucuresti (2005)
11. Zarmpou, T., Saprikis, V., Markos, A., Vlachopoulou, M.: Modeling users' acceptance of mobile services. Electronic Commerce Research, 225–248 (2012)
12. Gavalas, D., Economou, D.: Development Platforms for Mobile Applications: Status and Trends. IEEE Software 28(1), 77–86 (2011)
13. Shachter, R.D.: Evaluating Influence Diagrams. Operations Research, 871–882 (1986)
14. Papatheocharous, E., Trikomitou, D., Yiasemis, P., Andreou, S.A.: Cost Modelling and estimation in agile software development environments using influence diagrams. In: 13th International Conference on Enterprise Information Systems (ICEIS(3)), Beijing, pp. 117–127 (2011)
15. Laboratory, D.S.: Graphical Network Interface (GeNie). University of Pittsburgh (2013), GeNIe&SMILE: http://genie.sis.pitt.edu (retrieved January 15, 2013)
16. Maximilien, E.M., Pedro, C.: Facts, trends and challenges in modern software development. International Journal of Agile and Extreme Software Development, 1–5 (2012)

Authoring IEC 61508 Based Software Development Process Models

Ivan Porres, Jeanette Heidenberg, Max Weijola,
Kristian Nordman, and Dragos Truscan

Åbo Akademi University,
Department of Information Technologies,
Joukahaisenkatu 3-5 A, 20520 Turku, Finland
`givenname.surname@abo.fi`

Abstract. During software procurement, a development process is usually present whether it is well defined or not. If the goal of the software is to be used in safety-critical systems, compliance to a standard (such as the IEC 61508) might be required. In order to map the current state of safety compliant development, a survey within the RECOMP project was conducted, showing a need for promoting the use of formal process descriptions. To meet this need, the software related parts of the IEC 61508 standard, have been regarded as a process and modeled using the SPEM meta-model. Having the standard available in this format, facilitates reading, communicating and customizing the standard. Moreover, it eases the adaption of any process that is modeled in SPEM to the IEC 61508 standard.

Keywords: software process authoring, process modelling, safety critical development, IEC 61508, SPEM.

1 Introduction

The IEC 61508 standard is commonly used in the development of safety-critical systems, especially when safety functions are realized by software. General requirements of IEC 61508, which is a process based standard, demand that the development process is documented rigorously. Therefore, there is a clear benefit for companies wishing to certify their products against IEC 61508 to use formal process descriptions. Contrary to this, a conducted survey (see Sect. 3) showed that informal and semi-formal descriptions are often used in favor of formal ones.

Regarding approaches for complying with the standard the survey showed that it was most common to either adapt the own development process or use the standard as the process. In view of this mindset, it was recognized that modeling the IEC 61508 standard itself, as a process by a formal description, would ease both the usage of the standard as well as promote formal process descriptions. Firstly, having the standard available in such format, provides those who follow the standard as a process with a good starting point. Moreover, as the conventional format of the standard is a set of documents, a more flexible

J. Heidrich et al. (Eds.): PROFES 2013, LNCS 7983, pp. 268–282, 2013.

format can aid readability. Finally, using a general format by which it is simple to model various development processes, facilitates the possible adaption of these processes to the standard, since process and standard then share a common representation.

2   Background

2.1   Process Modelling and the SPEM Meta-model

In order to make different software processes comparable, the term *software process model* is often used to represent software processes on an abstract level [1]. A concrete software process model representation is often called a *process description* [1]. The four most important objectives [1,2] for a process description are: effective communication, facilitated reuse, support for process evolution and facilitated process management.

For software process modelling, the most popular meta-model is SPEM [3], which is based on UML [4]. SPEM divides its modelling elements into *method content* and *process patterns*. Method content consists of reusable elements which can be combined into different processes. SPEM also uses the notion of *method configurations* for configuring and targeting the same model at different audiences.

2.2   The Eclipse Process Framework (EPF) Composer

In order to utilize SPEM, a specific implementation has to be selected. In this work, the EPF Composer [5] is the chosen implementation due to its many benefits: the EPF Composer is free, open-source and available on multiple platforms. There exists readily modelled processes available for free download and use, such as SCRUM and OpenUP (an open-source Rational Unified Process alternative). The EPF Composer has been used in previous research [1,6] and supports extensive HTML export functionality for easy sharing and use of created processes.

2.3   Safety Critical System Development

Fundamental activities of safety critical development include identifying and reducing the likelihood of possible *harm*, caused by the system being developed. Harm is often defined as damage to health of people, property or environment. A central goal is that the combination of severity and occurrence of harm, called *risk*, is reduced to a tolerable level. In order to achieve this, safety standards are applied [7,8].

The general approach of safety standards is to introduce *functional safety*. This approach entails the specification of safety requirements, and how to implement these by safety functions, in order to ensure that the system operates within acceptable risk.

In order to prove the functional safety of a product, the developer collaborates with a certifying body. The task of the certifying body is to aid the developer in correct interpretation of a standard, since safety standards usually need adoption and interpretation into specific contexts [9]. Standards can be either product or process centered. Arguments have been presented why software safety standards often are process centered [9].

2.4   IEC 61508

IEC 61508 is a generic, process oriented, safety standard that deals with functional safety when implemented by Electrical / Electronic and Programmable Electronic systems [10]. It is mainly used in the development of system components as opposed to system integration [11]. Furthermore, it is considered one of the best generic standards for functional safety in software [12].

The IEC 61508 standard is divided into seven parts, out of which parts one to four are normative. Parts five to seven are informative and consist of guidelines on how to use the standard. Out of the four normative parts, part one contains general requirements, while part two and three deal with realization of hardware and software, respectively. Part four contains definitions and abbreviations, and not direct requirements. In the different parts, information is organized into a hierarchy of clauses and associated support material, such as figures and tables.

Safety Integrity Levels. General requirements prescribed by the IEC 61508, include a hazard and risk analysis. One result of the analysis, is the necessary amount of risk reduction for the system. Depending on the needed amount of reduction, safety requirements prescribe a level of *safety integrity* for the safety functions. There are four levels, SIL 1–SIL 4, where conforming to the standard in a SIL 4 aspect achieves the greatest risk reduction and safety functions that are least probable to fail.

For each SIL, normative recommendations are given for some of the clauses in the realization parts of the standard. Concerning software safety requirements, the recommendations constitute requirements on measures and techniques that should be used. In the standard, SIL recommendations are provided in tables of multiple cross-referencing annexes. Part IEC 61508-3, annex A presents ten tables of methods, refering to clauses concerned with the activities of the software safety lifecycle. Annex B of the same part has nine additional non-normative tables that give more detailed recommendations on some of the techniques described in the A annex. Additionally a third informative annex, classifies techniques according to their effectiveness, with the aim of giving guidance and rationale for technique selection. Finally, textual descriptions of techniques are given in the seventh part of IEC 61508.

Safety Lifecycle. In order to have a clear structure, IEC 61508 motivates the presentation of its requirements in the perspective of a V-model/plan-driven development process, called *the safety lifecycle*. At the same time, it is stressed that any process can be used for development of safety functions as long as they "fulfill the requirements of the standard" and "provided that a statement of equivalence is given in the safety plan". There is however no guidance given for how to assure that a custom development process fulfills the requirements.

2.5 Previous Work

Work related to our work of interpreting the IEC 61508 standard as a process is found in, e.g., [13]. The model presented is, however, tightly dependent on that the standard's reference process is followed, something that limits the model's usability. Another approach is presented in [14], where the main focus is to improve the readability of the standard. This is done by interpreting selected parts of the standard as "safety patterns", i.e. groups of process patterns that are to make grasping the standard easier. The work in [12] takes yet another approach in that it prioritizes the collection evidence for the certification process.

Similar to these works, our presented model aims to ease readability and the communication between certifier and developer. In contrast to the related work, we present a model where the aim is to not introduce any interpretation or simplification of the standard, with focus on process authoring

3 Currently Used Processes and Standard Compliance Strategies in Safety-Critical Software Industry

We performed a survey among the software producing companies in the RECOMP project [15] during the spring and summer of 2011. The purpose of the survey was to gather information about how the partner companies are currently describing their processes.

The participants in the study were invited to join the survey by means of an email sent out to the consortium contact person of the companies in question. The email explained the purpose of the survey, explained what kind of experience we wished for the respondent to have as well as the expected effort needed by the respondent.

As we were aware of the differences in practices and terminology between the companies, we considered that a web survey would not be sufficient. We thought it would be difficult to formulate questions that would be understood in the same way by all participants. For this reason, we decided to use one hour semi-structured interviews over the phone for data collection. The results from the subsequent analysis is illustrated in Fig. 1 and discussed in the following subsections.

3.1 Population

A total of 17 organizations completed the survey. The respondents varied in size and market.

The percentage of software developers in the organizations varied from close to zero up to over 90%. There were quite a few organizations that had a very small ratio of software developers, while only one company could be seen as a pure software house with the ratio of software developers nearing 90%. The numbers close to zero come from companies that have a handful of software developers in an organization of several thousands.

The type of software developed by the organizations includes embedded controllers (6), embedded or real-time operating systems (3), aerospace or avionics software (2), development tools (2), signal processing (1), industrial software (1), platform for automotive solutions (1), and simulation (1). It is interesting to note that products that can be seen as enablers for other products, i.e., operating systems, tools and platforms make up an equally large part of the answers (3+2+1) as the most common answer (embedded controllers).

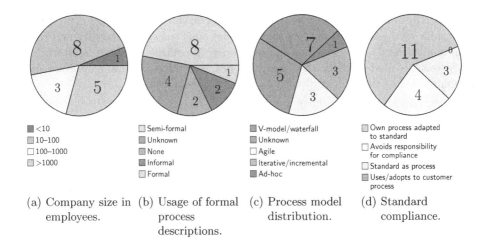

(a) Company size in employees.   (b) Usage of formal process descriptions.   (c) Process model distribution.   (d) Standard compliance.

Fig. 1. The results of the survey

3.2   Formal Process Descriptions

Based on the interview material, we classify the process description into five classes: *None*: No process description exists; *Informal*: The process is described in text documents or similar media; *Semi-formal*: Some formal elements exist, such as UML diagrams; *Formal*: The process is described using a formal process description language, such as SPEM; *Unknown*: We were not able to discern the type of process description based on the interview or the respondent did not know how the process is described.

Only one (1) respondent stated that they use a formal description language. The largest category is the semi-formal description format, containing eight (8) of the replies. The categories for none and informal hold equal shares of two (2) replies. In four (4) cases, we were not able to discern the format based on the interview.

3.3 Process Model

We also classify the type of process(es) used. In case several different processes were used in the organization, we select multiple categories for the organization in question. The five categories for process type are: *Unknown*: We were not able to discern the type of process used based on the interview or the respondent did not know what process is used; *Ad-hoc:* The process varies from project to project and is not standardized within the organization; *V-model / waterfall*: A waterfall type of process is used; *Iterative, incremental*: An iterative, incremental (but not agile) type of process is used; *Agile*: An agile type of process is used.

A wide variety of processes are in use. When the individual categories are added up, it is also clear that some companies use more than one process type, depending on the project. In five (5) cases, we were not able to identify the process based on the interview. The V-model / waterfall approach is the most common (7). As agile methods are also iterative and incremental, it is interesting to note that the total of iterative, incremental methods (3+3) constitute almost as large a share as the waterfall category. Only one (1) organization can be said to have ad-hoc processes.

3.4 Standard Compliance

Lastly, we categorized the strategy used for standards compliance into four different groups: *Standard as process*: By using the standard as the development process, the organization expects to be compliant with the standard; *Own process adapted to standard*: By modifying or extending the organization's existing process with necessary practices, artifacts and roles from the standard, the organization expects to be compliant; *Uses/adapts to customer process*: By incorporating the customer's process into their own process, the organization expects to be compliant with the standard; *Avoids responsibility for compliance*: The organization can avoid responsibility for compliance by, e.g., expecting the customer to have the responsibility to demonstrate compliance.

Most respondents choose to adapt their existing process to the standard (11), while almost equal shares use the standard as their process (3) and avoids responsibility altogether (4). The zero in (d) of Fig. 1 reflects that none of the organizations use the customer's process in order to conform to standards.

4   Extracting Method Content and Process Patterns from IEC 61508 Clauses

Section 2 presented how SPEM divides modelling elements into method content and process patterns. This is done among other things for the sake of reusability. In this section, we propose a three-stage process (Stage A, B, C) that extracts method content elements and combines them into process patterns so that a SPEM/EPF Composer model is obtained out of parts one and three of the IEC 61508 standard. The separation between content and processes, does not only ease reusability but also creates a natural divider between normative requirements and the substitutable reference process in which these are presented. Fig. 2 illustrates the separation and gives an overview of the mapping.

4.1 Stage A: Mapping Clauses to Method Content

Step 1 – Classification and Filtering of Clauses. The clauses of the standard can be classified into different groups. One group, those that contain "shall", "must" or equivalent wording are classified as *requirements*. Besides requirements, the standard also contains clauses of type *introduction* and *objective*. These describe the structure or clarify the representation of surrounding clauses. Having this classification in mind, each clause is further marked as applicable or not applicable for inclusion in the mapping process.

Clauses of the requirements type, found in a normative part of the standard, are classified as applicable. Introductions and objectives are on the other hand classified as non-applicable.

Example 1. An applicable clause:

3:7.4.7.1 – Each software module shall be verified as required by the software module test specification that was developed during software system design ...

Example 2. A non-applicable clause:

1:1.5 – Figure 1 shows the overall framework of the IEC 61508 series and indicates ...

References to clauses used in the examples follow the notation [**part of standard**]:[**clause**].

Step 2 – Mapping Applicable Clauses to Method Content. The applicable clauses from the filtering are now to be mapped into method content element types. Available types of elements are: *task, work product, role* and *guidance element*. Clauses associated with an activity, naturally map to task elements. On the other hand, clauses associated with results, documents and outcomes map to work product elements. Requirements describing or relating to persons or roles map to role elements.

In the simplest cases, clauses provide a one-to-one mapping, such that one clause may immediately be turned into a method content element. In many cases however, clauses are ordered in a hierarchy of clauses and subclauses. As such, they are not independent statements and must thus be analyzed together when mapped to method content, in a many-to-one mapping. Moreover, when a set of connected clauses is found, any near-by objective clause is reinterpreted as applicable if it contains information concerning the particular set.

Subclauses that become part of the same method content element may map to different sub-items of the parent element. In a task, a subclause may e.g. become

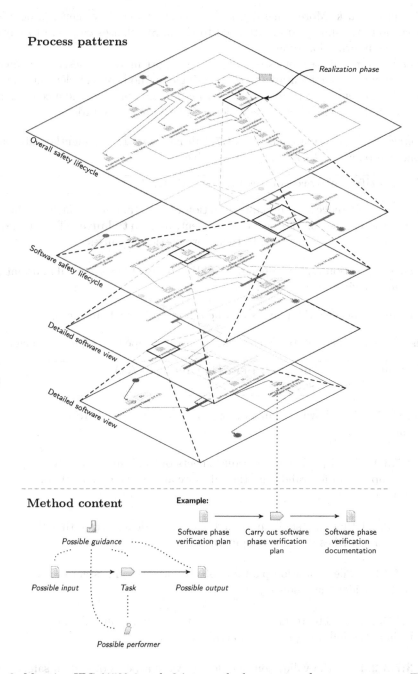

Fig. 2. Mapping IEC 61508-1 and -3 into method content and process patterns. The method content centers around tasks that map normative requirements of the standard. The process patterns are based on the IEC 61508 reference process.

a *step* in the task. More generally, method content may have general, detailed and version meta-information attached to them. Subclauses can map to any of these meta-information types.

Finally, some clauses, or especially their support material, describe common information that is not suitable to tie to a single method content element. In this case it is more suitable to map that information as a unique guidance element, that can be linked to all concerned elements later on in the process.

Example 3. Considering clause **3:7.4.7.1** in Example 1, a straightforward one-to-one mapping to a task element is possible:

Task	**Verify software requirements (3:7.4.7.1)**

Note that a reference to the mapped section of the standard, is included in the name of the created method content element, as (**part:clause**). This makes it possible to trace elements back to their corresponding clauses.

Example 4. Section **A.1** in appendix A of IEC 61508-1 gives general information on document kinds, e.g. "plan":

Plan — specifies the plan as to when, how and by whom specific ...

This is an example of data that is conveniently wrapped in a guidance element:

Guidance	**Document kind: plan (1:Annex A, A1)**
	Plan — specifies ...

Example 5. The following clauses represent a set that needs to be analyzed as one entity:

3:7.3.1 The objective of the requirements of this subclause is to develop a plan for validating the safety-related software aspects of system safety.

3:7.3.2.1 Planning shall be carried out ... to demonstrate that the software satisfies its safety requirements.

3:7.3.2.2 The validation plan for software aspects of system safety shall consider the following a) ... i) ...

3:7.3.2.3 ... The technical strategy for the validation ... shall include the following information: a) ... d) ...

3:7.3.2.4 ... the validation plan for software aspects of system safety shall be agreed with the assessor ...

3:7.3.2.5 The pass/fail criteria for accomplishing software validation shall include: a) ... c) ...

From these clauses information may be grouped into requirements that describe how to conduct the validation planning, **3:7.3.2.1**, **3:7.3.2.3** and **3:7.3.2.5** and on the other hand, into requirements regarding the validation plan: **3:7.3.2.2** and **3:7.3.2.4**. Hence a task and a work product are generated:

Task	**Develop validation plan for software (3:7.3.1)**
	Step 1 Specify steps for demonstrating that software satisfies safety requirements (3:7.3.2.1)
	Step 2 Choose strategy and specify rationale for chosen strategy (3:7.3.2.3)
	Step 3 Determine pass/fail criteria (3:7.3.2.5)

Work product	**Software validation plan (3:7.3.1)**
	General information (3:7.3.2.2)
	Detailed information (3:7.3.2.4)

Carrying out the above mapping process, for IEC 61508-1 and -3, the most common content type was recognized as task, resulting in 65 task elements. The number of work product elements, guidance elements and role elements were 51, 18 and 2, respectively.

Step 3 – Creating Dependencies between Method Content Elements. As seen in the previous step, it is sometimes possible to map subclauses into a single method content element, maintaining their inherent dependency. Creating tasks consisting of steps was one such possibility. On the other hand, some associations are lost as clauses map to different elements. In order to preserve these connections, elements need to be linked together.

Fig. 2 shows how task elements have a central role when specifying associations for method content. Roles perform tasks, work products are input to, or output from tasks. Guidance elements can be related to any method element, as additional information.

Example 6. In Example 5, the task "Develop validation plan for software" and the work product "Software validation plan" were generated from a set of related clauses. In order to model their missing connection, the work product is defined as an output of the task. Moreover, since the work product is a document of type "plan", the guidance element for "Document kind: plan" created in Example 4 is linked to the work product.

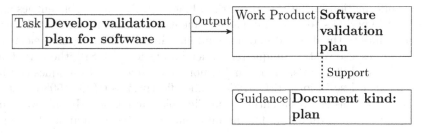

4.2   Stage B: Combining Method Content into Process Patterns

Section 2.4 introduced the reference process used in the standard for providing a context to the requirements. On the one hand, modelling the reference process is essential, since it gives a clear context to the method content, in the same way as it is motivated in the standard. On the other hand, it is not compulsory to follow the reference process in order to comply with the standard. In fact, it might not be desirable since the standard itself refers to its process as a "waterfall" procedure. Hence, there should at least be a distinct separation between the method content that arose from normative requirements and the elements we choose for modelling the process. Conveniently, SPEM and the EPF Composer provide a suitable division as reference processes may be modelled via *process patterns* in a *delivery process*.

The standard presents its reference process as a hierarchy of safety lifecycles. As depicted in Fig. 2, at the top layer one finds the overall safety lifecycle which is described in part one of the standard. The realization phase of this pattern, contains both the software and hardware realization. The software safety lifecycle relates to part three of the standard, while the hardware realization relates to part two. As such, it is only the software realization phase that has been modelled in this work. The software realization itself contains sub-phases and more detailed process views. Finally at the "bottom layer", links to specific tasks appear. The most frequently used component in the process patterns is the *phase*, which contains other phases or tasks. The relationships between the contents of a phase may be visualized through activity diagrams, as seen in the layers of Fig. 2.

4.3   Stage C: Mapping SIL Recommendations

SIL recommendations are given in the scope of activities in the realization phases of the safety lifecycle. As such, they naturally map to the process patterns produced in the previous stage. For this work, software realization and thus the annexes of the third part are of primary interest. Considering the guiding nature of the SIL recommendations, they are favorably modelled as guidance elements.

Fig. 3 shows an illustration of how the SIL recommendations, in the annexes of the third part, have been modelled. Starting from tables in the A annex, a table is split into four guidance elements, each containing the recommendations for a single SIL level.

One of the benefits when using the EPF Composer is that guidance elements contain information in the HTML markup language. As such, table entries can consist of hyperlinks to other guidance elements. In this way, an A table may efficiently link to the detailed information found in a B table guidance element. Since B tables also contain unique recommendations for each SIL, there are four versions created of them as well. Furthermore, recommended techniques can be linked to their descriptions (IEC 61508-7) and effectiveness (IEC 61508-3 Annex C) guidelines. This creates a natural and clickable reading flow. In this way, the EPF Composer plug-in allows for the information in the three appendices and

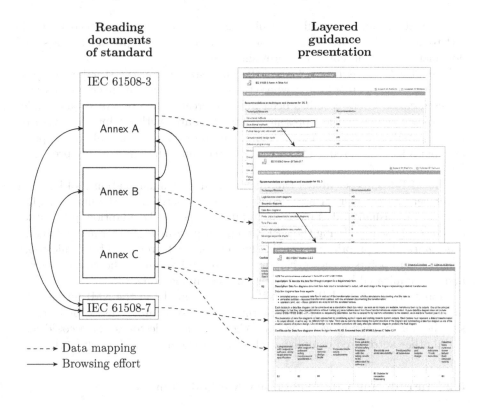

Fig. 3. Mapping of SIL recommendations

the descriptions in the seventh part, to be merged. Comparing this to manually looking up the cross-references in the document version of the standard, a more reader-friendly presentation is hence obtained.

Carrying out the above mentioned SIL mapping process resulted in a total of 237 additional guidance elements. The large number of created elements comes as a direct consequence of creating unique guidance elements for each SIL. This namely forces some of the information to be duplicated. Duplicated information is however a neglectable drawback considering the configuration options that are available when having the information separated. In order to make use of this capability, method configurations were created, so that the standard may be exported with a specific SIL in mind. Then, the exported data will only contain the recommendations for the chosen level.

5   Applications

5.1   Understanding, Applying and Communicating IEC 61508

Standards are usually regarded as difficult to understand [12,14]. To start with, they need interpretation to be applied in a specific setting. Moreover, this interpretation has to coincide with the interpretation of the certifier. Additionally, they might use an inaccessible terminology which can require considerable effort to get familiar with. Furthermore standards are often provided as a set of documents requiring noticeable browsing effort.

The EPF Composer model eases the understanding of the standard by providing the contents in a format where the information can be linked, and as such browsed easily. Great care has been put into creating the proposed base model with only the information present in the standard, with no interpretation or non-essential information. Furthermore, method configurations allows the plug-in exports to be tailored, so that, e.g., SIL recommendations are only presented for a chosen level.

The EPF Composer model can also be used as communication tool between developer and certifier, or as a "contract" as is described for the model in [12]. Certification usually takes places in iterative steps, as the adaption of the standard is discussed [9]. Using the EPF Composer plug-in, a certifier may introduce *milestones* at appropriate stages in the development process. These milestones can represent points in the development where work products should be reviewed and communicated between developer and certifying body.

Moreover, since the EPF Composer saves the model in the XMI format, the model presents an easily parsable format of the standard. This is for instance suitable for extracting work product checklists at milestones. This could also entail other automated compliance checks as done in previous work [13,12].

5.2   Introducing Complementary Method Content

Having the standard available in the flexible format of an EPF Composer plug-in, it can be extended to include other interesting factors, such as environmental awareness or multi-core technology considerations. In this work we have modelled results from the RECOMP project as complementary method content. The complementary method content consists of guidance elements that are linked to other related method content. The guidance elements are grouped into their own *content packages* allowing for extensions to be turned on or off through method configurations.

5.3   Combining the Plug-in with Other EPF Plug-ins

An additional strength of particularly using the EPF Composer is the good availability of ready to use plug-ins for different processes. Among the plug-ins found on the official EPF Composer homepage [5], XP (Extreme Programming), SCRUM and OpenUP are freely available for download.

There is no need to rigorously plan plug-in usage beforehand, as any plug-in can be used as a base and several plug-ins can be imported into the EPF Composer dynamically during process authoring. As the IEC 61508 standard does not describe any product development process, authoring a complete IEC 61508 compliant development process can be achieved by combining our proposed IEC 61508 EPF Composer plug-in with other plug-ins.

5.4   Authoring New IEC 61508 Based Process Models

While section 5.3 introduced the possibilities for plug-ins as base material for process authoring, we now explore how new process models can be authored.

The EPF Composer tool allows for great flexibility in the process authoring work and it is possible to start with creating either method content or process patterns [16,17]. In this section we present an example of how a smaller development organization can use the IEC 61508 plug-in to author a development process for component development, that needs to comply with only select parts of the IEC 61508 standard

Example 7. Authoring a custom development process by combining the IEC 61508 and OpenUP plug-ins:
In this example, a smaller company is developing software for a bigger, safety critical system, developed by another organization. To create a complete development process compliant with the needed parts of the standard, the company can create an own plug-in and import both the IEC 61508 and OpenUP plug-ins alongside. Existing process descriptions can be used as base and, depending on the format, either be modelled as either process patterns or method content. From the OpenUP plug-in, method content such as roles can be included to perform development tasks. At appropriate stages in the development process, select lifecycle phases from the IEC 61508 plug-in can be introduced. During communication with the certifying body, milestones for continuous follow-up is introduced.

6   Conclusion

In this paper we have presented a method for extracting and modelling parts of the IEC 61508 standard as a SPEM representation in the EPF Composer tool. The EPF Composer model of the standard can be used by development organizations to author complete processes for development of safety critical products. One possibility is to combine the EPF Composer plug-in for IEC 61508 with other readily available process plug-ins.

With the EPF Composer model of the IEC 61508 standard we want to support the process authoring of companies aiming to develop IEC 61508 compliant products. A survey of currently used processes and standard compliance strategies showed that only one company used formal process descriptions and eight used semi formal process description out of 17 organizations in the survey.

The decomposition and modelling of the standard was done in three stages. In stage A, clauses from the standard was mapped as reusable method content. Stage B combined the method content from stage A into process patterns corresponding to the reference process described in the IEC 61508 standard. Finally, in stage C, SIL recommendations were added to concerned process elements.

Additionally, complementary method content was created for considerations regarding development of systems with multi-core technology in safety critical applications as a part of the RECOMP[15] project.

Acknowledgement. The authors would like to thank RECOMP for making this work possible. The authors would like to extend gratitude to Espen Suenson for helping to conduct the survey, as well as Vicky Wong, Risto Nevalainen and Oscar Slotosch for valuable ideas and feedback.

References

1. Holmström, P.: Ideas for the next generation process authoring tool (2009)
2. Kellner, M.I.: Representation formalisms for software process modelling. SIGSOFT Softw. Eng. Notes 14(4), 93–96 (1988)
3. Ruiz-Rube, I., Dodero, J.M., Palomo-Duarte, M., Ruiz, M., Gawn, D.: Uses and applications of spem process models. A systematic mapping study. Journal of Software Maintenance and Evolution: Research and Practice (2012)
4. Object Management Group, Software & systems process engineering meta-model specification, v.2, http://www.omg.org/spec/SPEM/2.0/
5. The Eclipse Foundation, Eclipse process framework project, http://eclipse.org/epf/
6. Borg, A., Patel, M., Sandahl, K.: Extending the openup/basic requirements discipline to specify capacity requirements. In: 15th IEEE International Requirements Engineering Conference, RE 2007, pp. 328–333. IEEE (2007)
7. Knight, J.: Safety critical systems: challenges and directions. In: Proceedings of the 24th International Conference on Software Engineering, ICSE 2002, pp. 547–550 (May 2002)
8. Medoff, M.D., Faller, R.I.: Functional Safety – An IEC 61508 SIL 3 Compliant Development Process (2010)
9. Squair, M.J.: Issues in the application of software safety standards. In: Proceedings of the 10th Australian Workshop on Safety Critical Systems and Software, SCS 2005, vol. 55, pp. 13–26. Australian Computer Society, Inc. (2006)
10. IEC, Functional safety of electrical/electronic/programmable electronic safety-related systems (IEC 61508), 2nd edn. (2010)
11. Gall, H.: Functional safety iec 61508/iec 61511 – the impact to certification and the user. In: IEEE/ACS International Conference on Computer Systems and Applications, AICCSA 2008, March 31-April 4, pp. 1027–1031 (2008)
12. Panesar-Walawege, R., Sabetzadeh, M., Briand, L., Coq, T.: Characterizing the chain of evidence for software safety cases: A conceptual model based on the iec 61508 standard. In: 2010 Third International Conference on Software Testing, Verification and Validation (ICST), pp. 335–344. IEEE (2010)
13. Chung, P., Cheung, L., Machin, C.: Compliance flow–managing the compliance of dynamic and complex processes. Knowledge-Based Systems 21(4), 332–354 (2008)
14. Vuori, M., Virtanen, H., Koskinen, J.: Safety process patterns in the context of iec 61508-3
15. ARTEMIS JU RECOMP – Reduced Certification Costs Using Trusted Multi-core Platforms, http://atc.ugr.es/recomp/
16. Haumer, P.: Eclipse epf overview – part 1, http://eclipse.org/epf/general/EPFComposerOverviewPart1.pdf
17. Haumer, P.: Eclipse epf overview – part 2, http://eclipse.org/epf/general/EPFComposerOverviewPart2.pdf

Challenges in Flexible Safety-Critical Software Development – An Industrial Qualitative Survey

Jesper Pedersen Notander, Martin Höst, and Per Runeson

Software Engineering Research Group, Dept. of Computer Science,
Lund University, Sweden
{jesper.pedersen_notander,martin.host,per.runeson}@cs.lth.se

Abstract. Context. Development of safety-critical systems is mostly governed by process-heavy paradigms, while increasing demands on flexibility and agility also reach this domain. **Objectives.** We wanted to explore in more detail the industrial needs and challenges when facing this trend. **Method.** We launched a qualitative survey, interviewing engineers from four companies in four different industry domains. **Results.** The survey identifies human factors (skills, experience, and attitudes) being key in safety-critical systems development, as well as good documentation. Certification cost is related to change frequency, which is limiting flexibility. Component reuse and iterative processes were found to increase adaptability to changing customer needs. **Conclusions.** We conclude that agile development and flexibility may co-exist with safety-critical software development, although there are specific challenges to address.

Keywords: Software Engineering, Qualitative Survey, Safety-Critical Software.

1 Introduction

The development of safety-critical systems is traditionally governed by document-driven, process-heavy paradigms. Safety standards, such as IEC61508 for automation and EN50126 for railways, assume extensive documentation and strictly defined processes for the product safety certification, including risk analysis, change control and traceability. Consequently, the pace of change is lower in this type of systems, making them less flexible with respect to changing requirements from customers and markets.

In her book "Engineering a Safer World" [8], Leveson identifies several types of changes to the safety-critical systems we build, for example, fast pace of technological change, increasing complexity and coupling, and complex relationships between humans and automation. She concludes that there is a need for a paradigm change in the development to achieve safer systems, which she then proposes in the book. While we share the general description of the changes, we see a need for a more systematic exploration of the industrial context and needs in the development of safety-critical systems in different industry domains.

J. Heidrich et al. (Eds.): PROFES 2013, LNCS 7983, pp. 283–297, 2013.

Therefore, we launched a qualitative survey on industry practices and problems. We particularly focus on how the system development and safety certification processes relate to each other, when developing safety-critical systems. A viewpoint of particular interest is the ability to support flexibility in the development to meet changing customer needs and technological changes. We interviewed five safety and software engineers from four companies in different industries: Aerospace, Automation, Robotics and Transportation. The interviews were transcribed, coded, and qualitatively analyzed. We conclude from the study that human factors and the quality of requirements are as essential for development of safety critical systems, as they are for non-critical systems. In addition, we observe that the cost of certification is proportional to the number of releases, thus creating an incentive for few releases with many changes, which adversely affects flexibility. Furthermore, component reuse and iterative processes were found to increase adaptability to changing customer needs.

The paper is outlined as follows. We define the problem background and related work in Section 2. In Section 3 we present the methodology used for the study, including a characterization of the studied companies. In Section 4 we present and discuss the resulting findings. Section 5 concludes the paper.

2 Background and Related Work

Developers of safety-critical systems are increasingly using software to implement system functions, both safety-critical and non-critical. The inherent flexibility of software, enables system developers to rapidly adapt to changes in customer and market needs, without paying the high costs associated with hardware. It also supports reuse of existing functionality in new products as well as evolution of existing solutions.

Although increasingly used in safety-critical systems, the extent to which software is adopted by industry differs between different domains. In some domains, software has been used extensively for many years in safety-critical parts, e.g. Aerospace, whereas in other domains it has primarily been used for non-safety critical parts, e.g. Robotics. The trend, however, clearly points towards using more software, with increasing complexity, in safety-critical functions.

Safety-critical systems have the potential of causing harm to people and the environment [8]. *Safety-critical software* is used in a safety-critical system to realize a safety-critical function, e.g. the flight control algorithm in an airplane. Software in itself cannot harm people or the environment but unanticipated behavior of the software, either resulting from faults in the requirements specification, failure to implement requirements according to specification or not following operation requirements, can propagate into the physical world and there cause harm.

Safety-critical systems are regulated systems in the sense that system developers are mandated by law or strongly recommended to show compliance with an applicable standard. For example, in the European Union industrial robots need to show compliance with the Machinery Directive by following the ISO10218 standard. Several industries have their own standards that are applicable for specific systems, e.g. medical devices, aircraft systems, railway systems etc. Some standards are general in scope and apply to a broader range of systems, e.g. ISO61508 that covers electric, electronic and programmable electronic safety-related systems, whereas other standards are industry or even system specific, e.g. ISO10218 that only applies to robots and robotic devices.

Standards can be classified, for instance by their scope, generic vs. domain-specific as mentioned earlier, but also whether they are *means-prescriptive* or *objective-prescriptive*. A means-prescriptive standard, e.g. ISO61508, focuses on the *means* to achieve certain high-level safety goals and typically provides lists of methods and suggestions that a developer would be recommended or forced to include in their development process. An objective-prescriptive standard on the other hand, e.g. RTCA/DO-178, defines (low-level) objectives that should be reached, but does not necessarily define how to reach them. High-level safety goals are achieved when the objectives are fulfilled.

Common for all standards regarding safety-critical software, which are applicable in the context of this study, are that they consider software as a deterministic artifact, whose failures can only be caused by residual specification, design or implementation faults. Thus, safety is assured through the application of a standard-dependent design assurance process consisting of process-based and product-based development activities [1].

Although we do not claim to have done an extensive literature study, it would seem that there is a lack of empirical research in safety-critical software development, which investigates the flexibility aspect of safety-critical software from a holistic point of view. Land *et al.* [7], investigated component reuse in safety-critical systems through an industrial case study as well as action research. They identified challenges of component reuse with the aim of getting an overall picture of safety-critical development. They addressed flexibility by means of component reuse and provide a broad picture of challenges, including component interfaces and abstraction, traceability and certification, but they do not address the development process as such.

McHugh *et al.* [9] address flexibility from a process perspective, basing their work on an industrial survey, in which they investigated barriers preventing the adoption of agile practices in safety-critical medical device development. They found that the barriers they identified were tightly coupled with current regulatory constraints on medical software, but they emphasized that the barriers were not insurmountable even with todays best practices and standards. Kornecki and Zalewski [6] approach flexibility through an industrial survey of software tool support in the development and verification of safety-critical systems. Due to the increasing use of software tools in modern, highly complex, safety-critical systems development, the authors wanted to identify issues and concerns in software tool qualification and certification.

There exist several papers that present insights, into safety-critical development and related areas, which were gained from analytical and design research performed as academic case studies, sometimes basing the case on real world

Table 1. Research steps

Research step	Result
Definition of research questions	3 questions
Planning of interviews	9 main questions
Conducting interviews	$\sim 5 \times 1$ h interview recordings
	Interview transcripts
Definition of codes	19 initial codes
Coding	Coded transcripts,
	13 additional codes
Analysis of coded transcripts	Reduced code set to 27 codes,
	7 clusters of related codes,
	additional areas of interest
Summary of areas of interest	Identified themes among clusters,
	Thematic conclusions

situations with industrial data but in equal amounts on fabricated, but plausible, data. For instance, Hawkings *et al.* [4] present a safety argument pattern catalog, which was evaluated in two case studies. The two cases were based on industrial data from two real products. The presented pattern catalog is an appealing way of aiding the construction of safety cases in a repeatable and consistent way, which might be of benefit in a situation were safety-critical systems are composed of flexible components.

3   Research Method

In this section we present the research method used in the study, the case companies and the interviewees. We also discuss the validity of the study in relation to the used method and selected companies.

The research is based on a qualitative survey using interviews for data collection [3]. The methodology in a qualitative survey resembles that of a multiple case study [11,5], but the cases are not studied in depth in the survey. The objective of the research was to identify potential conflicts between safety certification procedures and more flexible methods for composition and development of software intensive systems. A significant part was to understand todays practices. By *composition* we mean integration and configuration of reusable components with the specific aim of creating variants of a system, whereas by *development* we mean the activities that is undertaken to create the components and the system design.

Because qualitative methods were used, our conclusions are based on an *understanding* of the collected data, created through a structured and systematic reading-process. The different steps in the research study, which are based on the guidelines of Runeson *et al.* [11], are summarized in Table 1, and described in more detail below.

3.1 Definition of Research Questions

Based on the objective, the following research questions were defined, which were recorded in a case study protocol:

RQ1 What are the challenges related to flexibility and safety in *software development* for software-intensive safety-critical systems, with respect to *agile practices*?

RQ2 What are the challenges related to flexibility and safety in *system composition* for software-intensive safety-critical systems, with respect to *safety certification*?

RQ3 What is the role of *system and software architectures* with respect to *flexibility and safety* in software-intensive safety-critical systems development?

3.2 Planning of Interviews

Based on the research questions, a set of interview questions were derived. The following top-level questions were defined:

IQ1 What is your role at the company, particular in relation to the certification process?

IQ2 How much experience do you have with the current certification process?

IQ3 Could you describe the product and outline the main challenges regarding the safety certification of it?

IQ4 Could you give a brief description of the certification process in general and for software in particular?

IQ5 How does the certification process impact the development process?

IQ6 What is the role of the system and software architecture in the certification process?

IQ7 What are the main concerns with the current certification process?

IQ8 What are the main driving forces behind the introduction of more flexibility?

IQ9 What is the next step towards more flexibility in the certification process?

We also derived, for most of the main questions, 3–4 additional sub-questions, which have more explicit connection to the three research questions (RQ1–3). These are not presented in detail in this paper due to space constraints.

3.3 Conducting Interviews

Interview candidates were selected with the aim of acquiring a diversified view from different industries and companies, see Section 3.6, as well as different roles, see Table 2. The identification and selection of interviewees was an ongoing process throughout the study.

The interviews were semi-structured, which means that open ended questions were asked about specific areas [11, Chapter 4]. Questions were not necessarily asked in the same order as presented in Section 3.2 and tended to be more

Table 2. Summary of interviewee characteristics

ID Role	Experience	Responsibilities
I1 System Architect	18 years, 5 with safety	Safety related issues at a system level.
I2 Safety Manager	30 years, 4-5 in current role	Coordinates the company safety and certification activities.
I3 Software Architect	14 years	Manages the development of a software based safety framework as well as working as the project liaison to I2.
I5 Safety Manager	10 years, 5 in current role	Responsible for the implementing, evolving and enforcing the software development process at of the company.
I4 Safety Manager	10 years, 5 in current role	Manages certification activities and contact with the certification authorities.

open at the end of the interviews. Interviewees were not interrupted when their answers diverged from the asked question, as long as the answer was within the scope of the study. The researchers kept track of the interviewees answers and tried to take that into account when additional questions were asked, so as not to ask a question that had already been covered.

In total, five interviews were held with interviewees from four different companies. The five interviewees could roughly be classified into three roles: safety managers, system architects and software architects. All interviews were conducted with two researchers each except for interview I5, and were recorded and later transcribed for further analysis.

3.4   Analysis

Definition of codes. Initially, a set of codes was defined based on the interview questions, the study objective and the knowledge that was gained during the interviews and from the transcription process. A set of 19 codes were found, see Column S_{ci} in Table 3.

Coding. The coding was done in two steps. In the first, the interview transcripts were compiled into a list of codeable text segments corresponding roughly to a paragraph in the source transcript. In the second step, each text segment was assigned a set of codes, i.e. a segment could be given any number of codes ($\leq 19 + 13 = 32$). The maximum number of codes assigned to a segment was 7, the minimum 1 and the median 2. The coding was conducted by two of the researchers. One researcher coded three transcripts and the other two.

While coding the two first interview transcripts, 13 additional codes were defined, as reported in Column S_{ce} in Table 3. After coding, non-used codes were removed, as well as specialized codes that were subsets of other codes. The final set contains 27 codes, see Column S_{cf} in Table 3.

Table 3. Code sets during the stages of the analysis, including the code clusters. An x means the code is member of the set, r and c indicate whether a code was in the row or column cluster set in the "heat map", b if in both.

Id	Name	S_{ci}	S_{ce}	S_{cf}	Substitute	C_1	C_2	C_3	C_4	C_5	C_6	C_7
C1	Certification Process	x	x	x						c	b	c
C2	Development Process	x	x	x				r		c	c	b
C3	Safety-Critical	x	x	x		c		r				
C4	Standard	x	x	x						c	b	c
C5	Stakeholders	x	x	x						c	b	
C6	Safety Analysis	x	x	x					r	b	r	
C7	Variants	x	x	x					b			
C8	System	x	x	x					b		r	
C9	Component	x	x		C14				b			
C10	Software	x	x	x					r	b	r	
C11	Challenges	x	x	x		c	r					r
C12	Activity	x	x	x			b					r
C13	Artifact	x	x	x			b				r	
C14	Architecture & Design	x	x	x			b		r			
C15	Safety	x	x	x		c	r					
C16	Tools & Methods	x	x	x			b					
C17	Composition	x	x		C7							
C18	Flexibility	x	x	x					r	b	r	
C19	Future	x	x		C18							
C20	Economy	x	x				b	r				r
C21	Quality	x			None							
C22	Verification & Validation	x	x					b				r
C23	Skills & Experience	x	x				b					r
C24	Safety Case	x	x						r	b	r	
C25	Requirements	x	x					b	c			r
C26	Safety Awareness	x	x			r						r
C27	Company Culture	x	x			b						r
C28	Hardware	x	x						r	b		
C29	COTS & OSS	x	x						r	b	c	
C30	Late Fault Identification	x			C11, C22							
C31	Legal Responsibility	x	x								b	
C32	Roles	x	x					r			b	

Count: 19 32 27 Unique pairs: 18 15 63 15 24 27 26

Analysis of Coded Transcripts. When all transcripts were coded, we began searching for code patterns, i.e. themes, in the coded transcripts. Although, we already had an impressions of which code patterns were more frequent than others, we sought a more systematic approach.

To guide our reading, we created an overview of how different codes were related and to what degree, by calculating a relative *overlap* score for each possible pairs of codes, defined for any two codes A and B as:

$$\text{overlap}(A, B) = \frac{\#\text{ text segments with both code } A \text{ and code } B}{\#\text{ text segments with code } A}$$

The score is a measure of the overlap that describes the number of occurrences of the pair (A, B) relative the total number of occurrences of code A. An overlap score of one means that code A is a true subset of B, i.e. A occurs only together with B.

We visualized the overlap scores for all possible code pairs in a "heat map", and identified clusters of pairs, i.e. groups with high pair-wise scores, using hierarchical clustering and manual inspection. In total, 7 clusters were identified, see Table 3. The clusters were used to select text segments for further analysis. A segment was selected if it was coded with a pair belonging to the cluster or if it had only one code and that code was in a pair belonging to the cluster.

By reading the segments thus selected, in-depth and in their context, the aim was to identify themes for each cluster. In total only four themes were found, partially due to content overlap between clusters and that some clusters were lacking in cohesiveness.

Summary of Areas of Interest. In this last step of the analysis the result of the previous step was summarized for each area of interest by contrasting different interviewees' statements. The result of this step is presented in Section 4.

3.5   Analysis of Threats to Validity

The validity of the research is discussed based on the design presented above, based on Runeson *et al* [11].

Construct validity. The construct validity concerns how well the researchers and the interviewees are able to communicate the real underlying phenomena under study. There is a risk of being misunderstood, e.g. if the interviewees did not have the same construct in mind as we researchers when talking about terms like 'safety', 'security', 'flexibility', etc. However, during the interviews we were aware of this risk, and much of the purpose of the interviews was to understand what the interviewed people and organizations mean with these constructs, and thus the threat is reduced.

Internal Validity. The internal validity threat is mainly concerned with causal relationships. Since this study is primarily descriptive, these threats are not applicable.

External Validity. The external validity threat concerns to what extent the results are valid in other contexts than the cases that were studied in the presented research. Since the study is carried out in a limited set of organizations it is not possible to widely generalize to other organizations without considering the differences. However, the selected organizations represent different domains that use different safety standards. In addition to this, the interviewees represent different roles in their organizations. Thus, the findings must be confirmed in larger studies, before generalizing them.

Table 4. Summary of company characteristics

ID Domain	Standard(s)	Product
C1 Robotics	ISO10218	Industrial robots and service robots. Off-the-shelf components for system integrators.
C2 Transportation	EN50128	Railway signal systems. System and component provider. Mainly government customers.
C3 Automation	IEC61508	Process controllers. Off-the-shelf components for system integrators.
C4 Aerospace	RTCA/DO-178B	Aircraft systems. End-user products. Government customers.

Reliability. This concerns how the analysis and the results depend on the researchers. We have followed strict protocols for the conduct and analysis, which are openly reported. Additionally, all findings that were derived by one of the researchers were reviewed by the other researchers, which we argue limits the reliability threat.

3.6 Case Description

In this section, the companies in the survey are described in more detail. Our classification of the companies and the presented characteristics are based on data collected during the interviews.

The four companies come from different industries: Robotics (C1), Transportation (C2), Automation (C3) and Aerospace (C4), and are subject to different certification standards. They employ different business models, some are market driven whereas others work in tight collaboration with governments and large organizations. See Table 4 for a summary of the characteristics of the four participating companies. In total, five interviews were held, one at each of the companies C1, C3 and C4, and two at C2.

C1 belongs to a division of a global company which has long experience developing industrial robotics and recent experience with service robotics. Applicable standards for industrial robots are ISO10218. One interview (I1) was held at this company with a system architect. Software is used extensively by the company for non safety-critical functionality, although not for safety-critical functions. The development can be seen as system integration of software and hardware components, either in-house or acquired from third-party sources. The company does not provide end user certificates for their products.

C2 belongs to a national branch of a global company. They develop train-signaling systems for several countries. Applicable and mandatory standards for railway signaling systems in the European Union is EN50128. At this company two interviews were held, (I2) and (I3). One with a safety manager and one with a software architect. The company has several years of experience in developing safety-critical software, and they recently changed development process from a version diversity based process to a single version unit test based process. The company has customers in several countries all over the world, as a result their products must be able to comply with different legislation as well as specific customer needs.

C3 belongs to another division of the same corporation as C1 but develops automation solutions. The company is subject to the ISO61508 standard. We conducted one interview (I4) at this company with a safety manager who was responsible for contact with certification authorities and quality assurance of the development process. They have a strong focus on software, both non-critical and safety-critical. Their customers are end-users, which integrate the company's products into larger systems, e.g. processing plants.

C4 belongs to a multinational company in the defense & aerospace industry. The company base their development process around the RTCA/DO-178B standard. One interview (I5) was held at this company, with a safety manager responsible for the software development process. The company has a long history of developing avionics, i.e. aircraft software, and works in close collaboration with the national authorities responsible for certifying aircraft systems. They consider themselves system integrators and deliver a product that is intended to be used directly by end-users. All customers are governments.

4   Results and Discussion

This section presents the results from our study, as well as our interpretations of the result. The four themes presented in this section were identified during the transcript analysis.

For each theme, we first present our conclusions, then our analysis and finally the supporting evidence for our claims. References to RQs are given in the analysis, while the direct responses to RQs are summarized in Section 5.

4.1   Human Factors – Skills, Experiences and Attitudes

This theme covers skills and knowledge among developers and managers, as well as their attitudes towards safety critical development, and how this impacts the development and certification process. From a flexibility point of view, human factors affect team composition and the performance of employees.

Development of safety-critical systems is not about writing code. It is about understanding the problem that should be solved by the system and be aware of the special nature of safety-critical systems, i.e. that they can cause harm to people. For instance, several interviewees mentioned that the quality of testing was depending on good knowledge about the system, its intended functionality and about safety-critical development in general. This was exemplified by I2 stating: *if you do not ask the right questions you will not get the right answers.* Having employees with the right knowledge profile was explicitly considered by two of the interviewees as the main asset of their company. I5 emphasized, that there is a big knowledge difference between developers doing normal application code and those that make safety-critical code. I3 considered that developers should work across the system-software boundary to get a better understanding of the product domain and intended system functionality. Agile team practices help achieving these goals (RQ1).

It is essential to document the knowledge in a way that can be accessed by the ones using it. Especially in an organization that change process model or reassigns experienced personnel to other projects and products. For instance, I1 pointed out that undocumented knowledge might be a challenge when going from one process model to another. This was further supported by I3 who thought that getting information out about novel development concepts and how to apply them posed a challenge. I5 strongly emphasized that information should be documented and be freely accessible by all concerned parties. This is both an advantage and a challenge of agile practices, which focus on communication, but not on documentation (RQ1). One key challenge that was identified by several of the interviewees was to keep the organizations' safety awareness high and how to improve it, i.e. that the people in the company should always be aware of that the product is safety-critical and have the potential of causing harm, and base their actions on this awareness (RQ2). It was considered to be both difficult and time consuming. For instance, interviewee I1 said that it cannot be forced upon the organization; it has to grow with time.

From a managerial perspective, safety awareness, or lack of it, will greatly impact the development. For instance in one of the case companies, management pushed for shortcuts and reduced staffing of key personnel, which in the short term might have led to some reductions in cost but in the long run adversely affected the company's ability to certify larger changes in their products. The reverse case, when management is too aware, is perhaps not ideal either. Although, a low level of safety awareness might lead to costly decisions, a too high level might result in fear of change, as was implied by I1. Though, the latter case would probably be better from a safety perspective, however, less so from a flexibility point of view (RQ2).

Although not directly connected with flexibility, human factors play an important role in safety-critical development. To be successful, a flexible process should consider these factors and provide adequate support for knowledge sharing. As identified in [2], agile practices (XP), seems to support developers motivational needs (RQ1). Their motivational needs included, among others: knowledge sharing, support for the less experienced and knowledge acquisition.

4.2   Requirements and Verification

This theme is related with testing, requirements engineering and how the requirements are elicited during the development process.

Good requirements and a complete requirement specification is the key to safety critical software development, or any kind of development for that matter. Without the right requirements, on the right level, verification and validation becomes hard to do in any meaningful way. A complete set of requirement is perhaps not practical or even possible which means that the gaps must be filled by other means. In this regard, testing plays an important role by finding implementation and design errors. To get good quality test cases the testers need to be knowledgeable about the system, the problem domain and the development process. This view is strongly supported by both I2 and I3. For instance, I3 described how requirements specifications on the functional level were used to develop unit test cases, and, as a consequence because the testers needed more information to adequately test the units, additional data (requirements) were attached to the function specifications. The result was that testing became more occupied with finding discrepancies between the code and the specification rather than finding actual errors in the source code. Agile practices, with their focus on working code over rigorous documentation may counteract this (RQ1).

From our study we must conclude that formal methods are not used widely by industry. Only in C2 were formal methods used and only in a specific case. I2 expressed a wish to increase the use of formal methods because they had problems finding certain kinds of errors related to logic and combinatorics. When speaking about the software architecture and system properties, I4 explained that they did not use formal methods although they followed modeling guidelines when building their architecture model.

Safety related requirements are described, in all four cases, to be elicited through an iterative process, starting with a new design or change request. Then some form of risk analysis technique is applied, e.g. FMEA in the C1 case and HAZOP in the C2 and C3 cases.

Interviewee I4 explains that they find requirements engineering challenging because they are required by their standard to finalize the design before starting to write code. One explanation for this could be that the same engineers do both design and coding, as explained by I4, which is in sharp contrast to agile practices (RQ1). No other interviewee reported on having this difficulty.

A closely related topic is requirements traceability. Traceability is mandated by the safety standards and must be maintained for safety-critical systems (RQ2). I4 described traceability as a time consuming and labor intensive task that would probably not have been performed if the standard did not require it. In contrast, I5 gave the impression that traceability was a well integrated activity, but also agreed that it was time consuming. In both cases tool support existed as well as a functional specification that traced product requirements through system functions down to components, but in the C3 case the specification was seen as making tracing harder as opposed to the view of it as a helpful tool in the C4 case. One explanation of the different views might be that the level of detail in the functional specification is too high in the C3 case.

From a flexibility point of view requirements engineering and verification & validation are essential. If these activities are not aligned with the process or the architecture, flexible development or composition of system variants might not be feasible. For instance, one limiting factor today, that was reported by I4, is that the cost, in terms of certification overhead, of changing a safety-critical system, i.e. make a new release, is proportional to the number of releases rather than the implementation effort of the releases (RQ2). This means that there is an incentive to have few releases with many changes, which is in conflict with the idea behind agile processes (RQ1).

4.3 Agile Development

This theme covers the trend towards more iterative and agile development processes and standard related challenges.

Agile processes, at least agile inspired processes, are being introduced or have been used for some time in safety-critical development. Although, only the C4 case explicitly followed an agile process model both the C2 and C3 cases made use of iterative development processes that seemed to share some characteristics of an agile process (RQ1). Interviewee I2 described their process as working back and forth in 14 days test release cycles. This agile interpretation is further supported by interviewee I3, who had previous experiences of working with Scrum, at another company, and did not think that the development process of C2 was any different from previous experiences. The C4 case used Scrum in their project teams.

Some challenges were identified by the interviewees. For instance interviewee I4 stated that there is a conflict between their need to adopt a more agile process and their certifier's insistence on conformance with the standard, which is means-prescriptive and prescribes a waterfall-based process (RQ2). Another challenge that was identified by interviewee I5 is maintaining independence in the development teams, i.e. a person is not allowed to produce and review the same artifact. This was resolved by keeping track of who did what.

A common belief is that agile processes are in conflict with the requirements of safety standards [12]. Our conclusion is that this might be the case when it comes to means-prescriptive standards, e.g. C3, but not for objective-prescriptive standards, e.g. C4. In fact, interviewee I5 saw Scrum primarily as a project management tool for work planning and did not seem to think that it was, in any way, in conflict with RTCA/DO-178 (RQ2).

4.4 Variants and Components

The last theme we identified covers system variants and how reusable components are handled by the case companies.

Reusable software components have the potential of reducing development time and the cost of certification, at least in the presence of system variants. In both case companies that had variants, C2 and C4, efforts were made to isolated software functions into reusable components or frameworks (RQ3). In the two other cases, C1 and C3, variants did not exist and little or no effort was put into creating reusable components.

There are different approaches towards creating reusable software components. For instance, interviewee I2 described their layered software architecture that has a generic bottom layer and more specific adaptation layers at the top

(RQ3). Each layer can be considered as a reusable component that can be certified and reused in other situations, although it would still be necessary to certify the integrated system finally delivered to the customer. A change to a higher layer does not force a re-certification of a lower level, however, the reverse is not true (RQ2). Interviewee I5 explained another approach, where they considered a solution with a main system containing all functions for all variants. A variant would then be an instance of the main system with some functions deactivated. They also considered a solution where common functions were put into components that were declared to a suitable criticality level. Sufficient evidence could then be collected for each component and be used repeatedly whenever the component was integrated into a system variant.

Reusable components seem to be one of the keys to enable flexibility in safety-critical development (RQ3). At least interviewee I5 states this directly but it is evident that in the C2 case the fact that they can reuse their layers in different variants enables them to be very flexible when it comes to system composition and to meet the needs of their customers. It is also interesting to note that component reuse is encourage by, at least, the RTCA/DO-178B standard (RQ2).

5   Conclusions and Future Work

We launched a qualitative survey of companies developing safety-critical systems with software, in four different industry domains. Although governed by different standards, the characteristics are very similar across the domains. Based on interviews with five practitioners (safety managers, system and software architects) we conclude that human factors and quality of requirements are central for safety-critical systems, as they are for non-critical systems.

We conclude that issues related to *agile methods* (RQ1) include aspects, which are in line with safety goals, for example, their focus on communication, teamwork across boundaries, developer motivation and good code. Challenging issues of combining agility and safety include less focus on documentation, tight collaboration between development and test, in contrast to independent test teams, and many releases, which conflicts with certification procedures required for each release. Practice demonstrated the feasibility of combining agile and safety. One of the surveyed companies, C4, used agile processes, while C2 and C3 cases used iterative development processes.

Regarding system composition and *safety certification* (RQ2) we observe that safety awareness is a key human aspect. However, a challenge is that it may lead to fear of change, hindering flexibility. Traceability, as mandated by the safety standards, may support flexibility since it helps identifying dependencies to handle during evolution. The cost of maintaining traceability is high, as is the costs for safety certification, although both being a necessary condition for making safety-critical systems. The use of agile processes is possible to combine with safety standards, although some implicitly assume waterfall processes.

The role of the *software and system architectures* (RQ3) is primarily to harness reusable components, which is a key strategy to make safety-critical systems development and composition more efficient. A layered architecture may also help isolate changes, and thus the need for re-certification.

We conclude that agile development and flexibility may co-exist with safety-critical software development, although there are specific challenges to address by research and industry practice. Future work includes e.g. designing modeling concepts that may reduce the certification overhead for software changes, under kept standard compliance [10].

Acknowledgements. The work in this paper was funded by the Swedish Foundation for Strategic Research under a grant to Lund University for ENGROSS-ENabling GROwing Software Systems.

References

1. Baufreton, P., Blanquart, J.P., Boulanger, J.L., Delseny, H., Derrien, J.C., Gassino, J., Ladier, G., Ledinot, E., Leeman, M., Quéré, P., Ricque, B.: Multi-domain comparison of safety standards. In: Proceedings of the 5th International Conference on Embedded Real Time Software and Systems (ERTS2), Toulouse, France (2010)
2. Beecham, S., Sharp, H., Baddoo, N., Hall, T., Robinson, H.: Does the XP environment meet the motivational needs of the software developer? An empirical study. In: AGILE 2007, pp. 37–48. IEEE CS (2007)
3. Flink, A.: The survey handbook, 2nd edn. SAGE Publications (2003)
4. Hawkins, R., Clegg, K., Alexander, R., Kelly, T.: Using a software safety argument pattern catalogue: Two case studies. In: Flammini, F., Bologna, S., Vittorini, V. (eds.) SAFECOMP 2011. LNCS, vol. 6894, pp. 185–198. Springer, Heidelberg (2011)
5. Jansen, H.: The logic of qualitative survey research and its position in the field of social research methods. Forum Qualitative Sozialforschung/Forum: Qualitative Social Research 11(2) (2010)
6. Kornecki, A., Zalewski, J.: Software certification for safety-critical systems: A status report. In: International Multiconference on Computer Science and Information Technology, vol. 3, pp. 665–672. IEEE Computer Society (2008)
7. Land, R., Åkerholm, M., Carlson, J.: Efficient software component reuse in safety-critical systems – an empirical study. In: Ortmeier, F., Lipaczewski, M. (eds.) SAFECOMP 2012. LNCS, vol. 7612, pp. 388–399. Springer, Heidelberg (2012)
8. Leveson, N.: Engineering a safer world: systems thinking applied to safety. MIT Press, Cambridge (2011)
9. McHugh, M., McCaffery, F., Casey, V.: Barriers to adopting agile practices when developing medical device software. In: Mas, A., Mesquida, A., Rout, T., O'Connor, R.V., Dorling, A. (eds.) SPICE 2012. CCIS, vol. 290, pp. 141–147. Springer, Heidelberg (2012)
10. Pederson Notander, J., Runeson, P., Höst, M.: A model-based framework for flexible safety-critical software development – a design study. In: Proceedings of the 28th Symposium on Applied Computing, Coimbra, Portugal (2013)
11. Runeson, P., Höst, M., Rainer, A., Regnell, B.: Case Study Research in Software Engineering – Guidelines and Examples. Wiley (2012)
12. Turk, D., France, R., Rumpe, B.: Assumptions underlying agile software development processes. Journal of Database Management 16(4), 62–87 (2005)

Improving Process of Source Code Modification Focusing on Repeated Code

Ayaka Imazato, Yui Sasaki, Yoshiki Higo, and Shinji Kusumoto

Graduate School of Information Science and Technology, Osaka University,
1-5, Yamadaoka, Suita, Osaka, Japan
{i-ayaka,s-yui,higo,kusumoto}@ist.osaka-u.ac.jp

Abstract. There are various kinds of repeated code such as consecutive if-else statements or case entries in program source code. Such repeated code sometimes require simultaneous modifications on all of its elements. Applying the same modifications to many places on source code is a burdensome work and introduces new bugs if some places to be modified are overlooked. For these reasons, it is necessary to support modifications on repeated code. Appropriate supports for repeated code can improve process of source code modification. In this paper, as a first step for supporting modifications on repeated code, we investigate how repeated code are modified during software evolution. As a result, we revealed that, 73-89% of repeated code were modified at least once in their life and 31-58% of modifications on repeated code were simultaneous ones for all of their elements.

1 Introduction

Recent studies have revealed that a significant fraction (between 7% and 23%) of program source code has become code clones [2,14]. A code clone is a code fragment in source code that is similar to or identical to other code fragments [15]. Code clones are introduced into source code because of various reasons such as copy-and-paste programming [10]. An advantage of copy-and-paste programming is that: we can implement necessary functions quite rapidly. However, if the copied code includes a latent bug, copy-and-paste programming unintentionally scatters the bug into its pasted places [1,9,11]. Moreover, code clones often require simultaneous modifications. If we overlook some code clones to be modified simultaneously, new bugs are introduced to the overlooked code fragments [7,12].

Authors are thinking that the same problems have been occurring in repeated code. Repeated code means a list of the same instructions such as consecutive case entries or if-else statements. If an element of repeated code requires a modification, we may need to modify the other elements of the repeated code in the same way simultaneously; besides, if the number of repetition is large, manual modifications on every element of the repeated code is a burdensome and error-prone operation. Some research efforts investigated program source code and found that there are many repetitions in it [6,13,16]. Figure 1 shows actual repeated code in Java source code found in the investigation of literature [6]. As shown in this figure, various instructions in source code can become repeated code.

J. Heidrich et al. (Eds.): PROFES 2013, LNCS 7983, pp. 298–312, 2013.

```
case Project.MSG_ERR:
    msg.insert(0, errColor);
    msg.append(END_COLOR);
    break;
case Project.MSG_WARN:
    msg.insert(0, warnColor);
    msg.append(END_COLOR);
    break;
case Project.MSG_INFO:
    msg.insert(0, infoColor);
    msg.append(END_COLOR);
    break;
case Project.MSG_VERBOSE:
    msg.insert(0, verboseColor);
    msg.append(END_COLOR);
    break;
```

(a) case entries

```
public static boolean isAbstract(int access_flags) {
    return (access_flags & ACC_ABSTRACT) != 0;
}

public static boolean isPublic(int access_flags) {
    return (access_flags & ACC_PUBLIC) != 0;
}

public static boolean isStatic(int access_flags) {
    return (access_flags & ACC_STATIC) != 0;
}

public static boolean isNative(int access_flags) {
    return (access_flags & ACC_NATIVE) != 0;
}
```

(b) method declarations

```
if (null != storepass) {
    cmd.createArg().setValue("-storepass");
    cmd.createArg().setValue(storepass);
}

if (null != storetype) {
    cmd.createArg().setValue("-storetype");
    cmd.createArg().setValue(storetype);
}

if (null != keypass) {
    cmd.createArg().setValue("-keypass");
    cmd.createArg().setValue(keypass);
}
```

(c) if blocks

```
out.println();
out.println("-------------------------------------");
out.println(" ANT_HOME/lib jar listing");
out.println("-------------------------------------");
doReportLibraries(out);

out.println();
out.println("-------------------------------------");
out.println(" Tasks availability");
out.println("-------------------------------------");
doReportTasksAvailability(out);
```

(d) method invocations

```
e = ccList.elements();
while (e.hasMoreElements()) {
    mailMessage.cc(e.nextElement().toString());
}

e = bccList.elements();
while (e.hasMoreElements()) {
    mailMessage.bcc(e.nextElement().toString());
}
```

(e) while blocks

```
src = attributes.getSrcdir();
destDir = attributes.getDestdir();
encoding = attributes.getEncoding();
debug = attributes.getDebug();
optimize = attributes.getOptimize();
deprecation = attributes.getDeprecation();
depend = attributes.getDepend();
verbose = attributes.getVerbose();
```

(f) assign statements

```
private MenuBar iAntMakeMenuBar = null;
private Menu iFileMenu = null;
private MenuItem iSaveMenuItem = null;
private MenuItem iMenuSeparator = null;
private MenuItem iShowLogMenuItem = null;
private Menu iHelpMenu = null;
private MenuItem iAboutMenuItem = null;
```

(g) variable declarations

```
} catch (final ClassNotFoundException cnfe) {
    throw new BuildException(cnfe);
} catch (final InstantiationException ie) {
    throw new BuildException(ie);
} catch (final IllegalAccessException iae) {
    throw new BuildException(iae);
}
```

(h) catch blocks

Fig. 1. Repeated code in Java source code (, which were identified in the investigation of literature [6])

It is generally said that switch statements, where repeated code often occur, are not recommended instruction in object-oriented design [5]. There are some research efforts that have proposed ways to transforms switch statements and consecutive if-else statement into multiple classes using polymorphism [4].

Consequently, paying special attention to repeated code can improve source code modification process. For example, firstly identifying repeated code in source code in an automatic way; then, if an element of repeated code is modified, the same modifications are (semi-)automatically applied to the other elements of the repeated

```
947    excludes = new String[ 0 ];        947    excludes = new String[ 0 ];
948  }                                     948  }
949                                        949
950  filesIncluded = new Vector();        950  filesIncluded = new ArrayList();
951  filesNotIncluded = new Vector();     951  filesNotIncluded = new ArrayList();
952  filesExcluded = new Vector();        952  filesExcluded = new ArrayList();
953  dirsIncluded = new Vector();         953  dirsIncluded = new ArrayList();
954  dirsNotIncluded = new Vector();      954  dirsNotIncluded = new ArrayList();
955  dirsExcluded = new Vector();         955  dirsExcluded = new ArrayList();
956                                        956
957  if( isIncluded( "" ) )               957  if( isIncluded( "" ) )
958  {                                     958  {
```

(a) Before   modification   (revision   (b) After   modification   (revision
270,290)   270,291)

Fig. 2. Actual modification on repeated code in file DirectoryScanner.java of Software Ant. Consecutive object generations were changed to ArrayList fromVector.

code. those kinds of supports would be helpful for programmer. In this research, as a first step of modification support for repeated code, we investigate how repeated code are modified and evolved. Finding and analyzing their modification/evolution patterns will make it possible to propose useful ways of modification supports for repeated code.

As a result of the investigations we conducted on open source software, we obtained the following knowledge, which are main contributions of this paper:

- elements forming repeated code were too small to be detected by existing code clone detection tools;
- 73-89% of repeated code were modified at least once;
- 31-58% modifications on repeated code were applied to all the elements of repeated code simultaneously;
- any instruction type of repeated code was modified. Especially, try block, while block and variable declarations were more likely to be modified than the others; and,
- the lesser repetitions repeated code had, the higher the ratio of simultaneous modifications on all the elements of them was.

The remainder of this paper is organized as follows: Section 2 shows actual modifications on repeated code, which motivated us to conduct this research; Section 3 explains how we investigated modifications applied to repeated code; Section 4 shows the investigation result on three open source software systems; then, Section 6 describes some threats to validities on the investigation; finally, Section 7 concludes this paper.

2   Motivation

Figures 2 and 3 show actual modifications on repeated code in Ant. In Figure 2, six assignment statements creating Vector objects were changed to ones creating ArrayList objects simultaneously. In Figure 3, a parameter was added to every method invocation in repeated code.

```
135   private File[] getAnt1Files() {
136     List files = new ArrayList();
137     addJavaFiles(files, TASKDEFS_ROOT);
138     addJavaFiles(files, new File(TASKDEFS_ROOT, "compilers"));
139     addJavaFiles(files, new File(TASKDEFS_ROOT, "condition"));
140     addJavaFiles(files, DEPEND_ROOT);
141     addJavaFiles(files, new File(DEPEND_ROOT, "constantpool"));
142     addJavaFiles(files, TYPES_ROOT);
143     addJavaFiles(files, FILTERS_ROOT);
144     addJavaFiles(files, UTIL_ROOT);
145     addJavaFiles(files, new File(UTIL_ROOT, "depend"));
146     addJavaFiles(files, ZIP_ROOT);
147     addJavaFiles(files, new File(UTIL_ROOT, "facade"));
148     addJavaFiles(files, INPUT_ROOT);
149
150     files.add(new File(PACKAGE_ROOT, "BuildException.java"));
```

(a) Before modification (revision 272,635)

```
135   private File[] getAnt1Files() {
136     List files = new ArrayList();
137     addJavaFiles(files, TASKDEFS_ROOT, false);
138     addJavaFiles(files, new File(TASKDEFS_ROOT, "compilers"), true);
139     addJavaFiles(files, new File(TASKDEFS_ROOT, "condition"), true);
140     addJavaFiles(files, DEPEND_ROOT, true);
141     addJavaFiles(files, TYPES_ROOT, true);
142     addJavaFiles(files, FILTERS_ROOT, false);
143     addJavaFiles(files, UTIL_ROOT, false);
144     addJavaFiles(files, new File(UTIL_ROOT, "depend"), false);
145     addJavaFiles(files, new File(UTIL_ROOT, "facade"), true);
146     addJavaFiles(files, ZIP_ROOT, true);
147     addJavaFiles(files, INPUT_ROOT, true);
148
149     files.add(new File(PACKAGE_ROOT, "BuildException.java"));
```

(b) After modification (revision 272,636)

Fig. 3. Actual modification on repeated code in file Builder.java of Software Ant. The number of parameters of consecutively invoked methods were increased.

As shown in these examples, all the elements forming a repeated code are modified on the same way simultaneously. The authors are thinking that there are two problems in such modifications:

- applying modifications to multiple (even many) places is a time-consuming and burdensome task;
- they introduce new bugs if some places to be modified are overlooked.

Consequently, modification supports on repeated code are necessary. For example, the following support may be useful: if we modify an element in a repeated code, (semi-) automatic modifications are performed on the other elements in the repeated code. In this paper, as a first step of modification support on repeated code, we investigate how repeated code are modified during software evolution.

3   Investigating Modifications on Repeated Code

Herein, we introduce a method for investigating how modifications were applied to repeated code during software evolution. The input and the output of the method are as follows.

INPUT repository of the target software.
OUTPUT data related to repeated code, for example the followings are distilled:
- instruction types included in repeated code;
- number of repetitions in repeated code;
- number of modifications applied to repeated code.

The investigation method consists of the following steps:

STEP1 identifying revisions where source files were modified;
STEP2 distilling data related to repeated code modified between every consecutive two revisions, each of which was identified in STEP1;
STEP3 making evolutional data from the results of STEP2.

In the reminder of this section, Subsections 3.1, 3.2, and 3.3 explain each step of the investigation method, respectively. Then, Subsection 3.4 describes software tool that we have developed based on the investigation method.

3.1   STEP1: Identifying Revisions Where Source Files Are Modified

In STEP1, the method identifies revisions where one or more source files were modified. Source code repositories contain not only source files but also other files such as manual or copyright files, so that there are revisions that no source files were modified in software repositories. The purpose of STEP1 is eliminating revisions where no source files were modified because we focus on only modifications on source files.

Herein, we assume that:

- R is a target repository;
- there are n revisions where at least one source file was modified in R;
- index i represents the order of revisions included in R, that is, r_i means that its revision is the i-th oldest in R.

By using the above assumptions, repository R can be defined as:

$$R = \{r_1, r_2, \cdots, r_{n-1}, r_n\} \tag{1}$$

3.2   STEP2: Distilling Data Related to Repeated Code Modified between Every Consecutive Two Revisions

Differences between two consecutive revisions r_i and r_{i+1} ($1 \leq i \wedge i < n$) are analyzed for finding whether repeated code were modified or not.

If repeated code were modified, the following information is distilled:

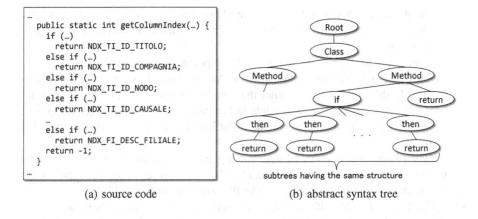

(a) source code　　　　　　　　(b) abstract syntax tree

Fig. 4. An Example of constructing AST and finding repeated structures in it

```
1: A
2: B
3: line will be changed 1
4: line will be changed 2
5: C
6: D
7: line will be deleted 1
8: line will be deleted 2
9: E
10: F
11: G
12: H
```

```
1: A
2: B
3: line changed 1
4: line changed 2
5: C
6: D
7: E
8: F
9: G
10: line added 1
11: line added 2
12: H
```

```
3,4c3,4
<   line will be changed 1
<   line will be changed 2
---
>   line changed 1
>   line changed 2
7,8d6
<   line will be deleted 1
<   line will be deleted 2
11a10,11
>   line added 1
>   line added 2
```

(a) before modification　　　(b) after modification　　　(c) diff output

Fig. 5. A simple example of comparing two revisions of a source file with `diff` (changed region is represented with identifier 'c' like 3,4c3,4, deleted region is represented with identifier 'd' like 7,8d6, and added region is represented with identifier 'a' like 11a10,11. The numbers before and after the identifiers show the corresponding lines)

- instruction types forming the modified repeated code;
- numbers of repetitions of the modified repeated code;
- token numbers of elements of the modified repeated code;
- whether the modified repeated code sustained repeated structure or not.

We find whether repeated code were modified or not with the following steps.

STEP2A: Identifying repeated code in revisions r_i and r_{i+1} by using AST generated from the revisions. AST sibling nodes are sorted in the order of the appearance on the source code. If there are consecutive similar structures in the sibling nodes, their code are regarded as repeated structure.

　　– In the case that the sibling nodes are leaves, conditions for satisfying the similarity are (1) they are the same type nodes in AST and (2) they are textually similar to each other. For the 2nd condition, we use *Levenshtein* distance.

- In the case that the sibling nodes are branches, the whole subtrees under the branches have the similar structures. That is, structure similarity is checked recursively.

Repeated structures in AST are regarded as repeated code in source code.

Figure 4 shows an example of constructing AST and identifying repeated structures from it. In this case, subtrees under the if node in Figure 4(b) are the same structure, so consecutive if-else statements in the source code are regarded as repeated code. After identifying repeated code, their location information (line number) is distilled.

AST used herein is not a usual one. We applied some heuristics to AST for easily identifying repeated structures. If readers have an interested in the detail of the specialized AST and repeated code identification, see literature [16].

STEP2B: In order to identify where were modified in the source files between revisions r_i and r_{i+1}, we use UNIX diff command. Figure 5 shows an example of diff output. As shown in Figure 5, it is easy to identify line number modified between two revisions. All we have to do is just parsing the output of diff so that the start line and end line of all the modifications are identified.

STEP2C: By comparing the result of STEP2A and STEP2B, we find whether repeated code in revision r_i were modified or not. If modified, the above information is distilled.

3.3   STEP3: Making Evolutional Data by Using the Results of STEP2

In this step, we track repeated code through all the target revisions by using diff information between every consecutive two revisions (the result of STEP2). Tracking repeated code allows us to obtain the following data:

- when a given repeated code appeared and disappeared;
- the number of modifications applied to a given repeated code.

We used the method proposed in literature [3] for tracking repeated code.

Finally, evolutional data related to repeated code is output textually. In this step, any visualization of the data is not performed. If necessary, user can create some graphs or perform statistical tests for understanding data by themselves.

3.4   Implementation

We have developed a software tool based on the investigation method. In the tool, we are using

- JDT (Java Development Tool) for Java source code analysis, and
- SVNKit for handling Subversion repositories.

That is, currently the tool is just a prototype, and it can be applied to only Java software managed with Subversion. Output of STEP3 is in CSV format, which is intended for analyzing data with Excel or R.

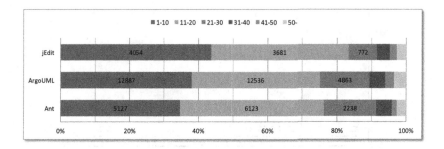

Fig. 6. Distribution of Element Size (number of tokens) on the End Revision

4   Investivation on Open Source Software

In order to reveal how repeated code is modified during software evolution, we investigated three open source software systems. We chose Ant, ArgoUML, and jEdit as our targets because they are well-known and widely-used systems. Table 1 shows the detail information of the systems.

In this investigation, we reveal the followings:

RQ1 how large are elements of repeated code?
RQ2 how often are repeated code modified during software evolution?
RQ3 what is the rate of simultaneous modifications on repeated code?

In the reminder of this section, we describe the experimental results and answer the RQs.

4.1   Answer to RQ1 (How Large Are Elements of Repeated Code?)

Figure 6 shows distributions of element sizes (the number tokens) on the end revision. We can see that small size dominates a large part: 1-10 are between 35-44%; 11-20 are between 37-41%; 21-30 are between 8-15%. Totally, 1-30 elements dominate 89-92% for all the elements. Code clone detection tools take a threshold of minimal size of code clones to be detected. In many cases, "30 tokens" is used for the threshold [8]. Of course, we can use smaller thresholds in code clone detection. However, if we use smaller thresholds, tools would detect a large amount of code clones, which include many false positives. Extracting necessary code clones from a large result is not an easy task. That is, code clone detection techniques are not suited for identifying repeated code.

Table 1. Overview of Target Software

Software	Start revision (date)	End revision (date)	# of target revisions	LOC of end revision
Ant	267,549 (2000-1-13)	1,233,420 (2012-1-20)	12,621	255,061
ArgoUML	2 (1998-1-27)	19,893 (2012-7-10)	17,731	369,583
jEdit	3,791 (2001-9-2)	21,981 (2012-8-7)	5,292	183,006

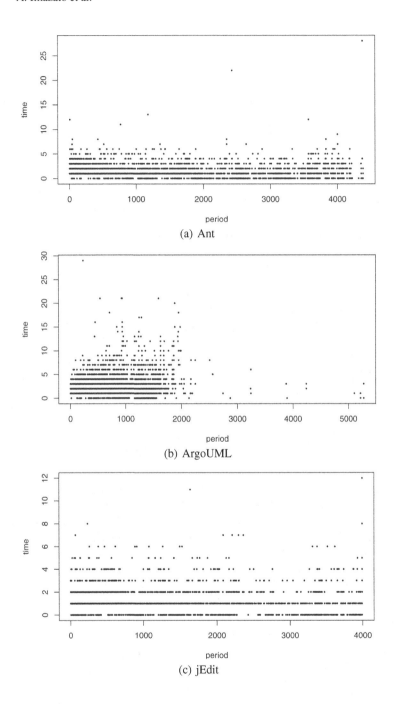

Fig. 7. Relationships between survival period and the number of modifications. Y-axis is the number of modifications, and X-axis is survival period.

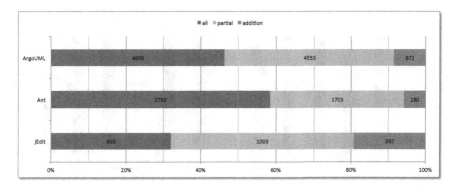

Fig. 8. Ratio of the three types of modifications on each target system

Consequently, in order to identify repeated code, it is necessary to use a technique that are tailored to detect repeated code. In this paper, we proposed a method using similarities of AST subtrees for identifying repeated code. The method is scalable, so that we could finish repository analysis of the target software within 30 hours, 65 hours, and 18 hours from 12,621, 17,731, and 5,292 revisions of source code, respectively.

4.2 Answer to RQ2 (How Often Are Repeated Code Modified during Software Evolution?)

Figure 7 shows relationships between survival period and the number of modifications: Y-axis is the number of modifications and X-axis is survival period. A dot locating on 1 or above of Y-axis means its repeated code was modified at least once. We can see the following from this figure:

- 84%, 89%, and 73% repeated code were modified at least once,
- there was no correlation between survival period and the number of modifications.

The numbers of modifications on repeated code were 4,776, 10,123, and 2,063, respectively. By dividing them with the number of target revisions, we obtained 0.438, 0.395, and 0.356. That is, repeated code were modified every two or three revisions.

4.3 Answer to RQ3 (What Is the Rate of Simultaneous Modifications on Repeated Code?)

We analyzed modifications on repeated code and classified them as follows:

all all the elements in a repeated code were modified simultenously;
partial only a part of elements was modified;
addition existing elements of a repeated code were not modified but new elements were added to the repeated code.

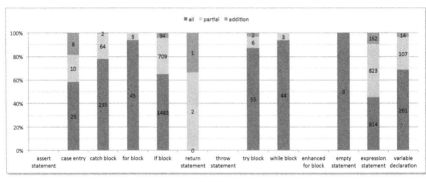

(a) Ant

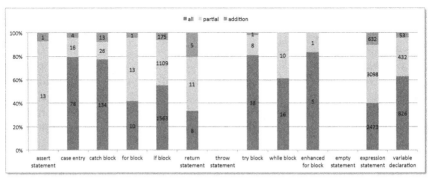

(b) ArgoUML

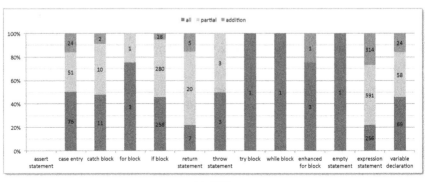

(c) jEdit

Fig. 9. Ratio of the three types of modifications by focusing on instruction types in repeated code

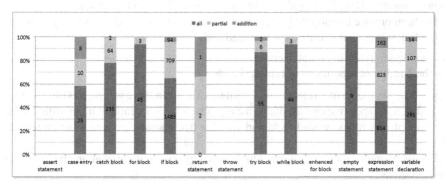

(a) Ant

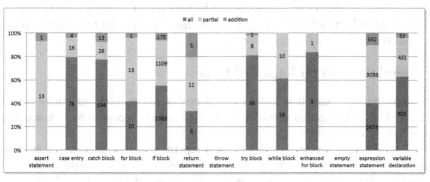

(b) ArgoUML

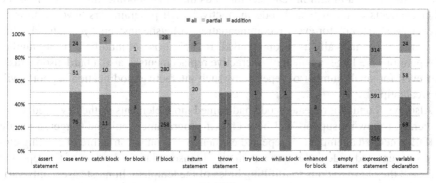

(c) jEdit

Fig. 10. Ratio of the three types of modifications by focusing on the number of repetitions of repeated code

Figure 8 shows ratio of the three types of modifications. There were many *all* modifications on all the target systems. The numbers were 663, 2,793, and 4,698, respectively. They dominated 31%, 58%, and 46% for the modifications on repeated code.

Furthermore, we investigated the ratio of the three types of modifications by focusing on the followings characteristics of repeated code:

- instruction types in repeated code;
- the number of repetitions of repeated code.

Figure 9 shows the former result. Areas with no bars mean there was no modification on the instruction types. We can see that some types have a higher ratio of *all* modifications. For example, try block, while block, and variable declarations are near to or more than 50%.

Figure 10 shows the latter result. The followings are common phenomena in all the target systems.

- The lesser number of repetitions is, the higher ratio of *all* modifications is.
- The higher number of repetitions is, the higher ratio of *addition* modifications is. Repeated code including many repetition are more likely to get new repetitions than repeated code with a few repetitions.

5   Useful Support on Repeated Code

In this research, we found that 73-89% of repeated code was modified at least once in their life. Thus, modification supports on repeated code is necessary to reduce cost of source code modification.

We found that if a repeated code has lesser repetitions, all of its elements are more likely to be modified simultaneously. Thus, we are thinking that interactive modification completions are useful for repeated code. For example, if an element of a repeated code is modified, a plugin in IDE recommends the same modification for each of the other elements of the repeated code interactively. All programmers have to do is to answer "yes" or "no" for every recommendation. If he/she answers "yes", the element is modified automatically as recommended. If "no", it is not modified. If the number of repetitions are large, a bunch of interactive replacements is also a burdensome task. However, for small number of repetitions, such interactive modification supports will be great helpful.

Also, we found that repeated code had gained more elements as they evolved. Consequently, following support will be useful: if programmers pull the trigger, a plugin of IDE generated a template of repeated element based on the structure of existing elements of repeated code and it was automatically inserted to the bottom of the repeated code. All they have to do is to fulfilling holes of the template. In most cases, only variable names or method invocations are inserted to holes.

6   Threats to Validity

6.1   Number of Target Systems

In this investigation, the number of target systems was only three. In order to generalize the investigation result, we have to conduct experiments on more software systems.

Currently, we can investigate only Java software managed with Subversion due to the implementation limitations. In the future, we are going to extend the tool for other programming languages such as C/C++ and other version control systems such as git for investigating various software systems.

6.2 Not Regarding Modification Types

In this investigation, we did not take care of modification types. For example, in the case of variable declaration statement, there may be a modification that inserts a single white space between its operand and its operator. Such modification does not have a direct impact on program behavior. Consequently, if we extracted and used only the modifications that are bug fixes or function additions, the investigation result would be different from the investigation result of this paper.

6.3 Disappearing Repeated Code

In this investigation, we regarded that a repeated code had disappeared if it satisfied either of the conditions:

- the repeated code is completely removed from the source code;
- the number of its repetition became one.

In the latter case, an element of repeated code remains in the source code after modifications. Hence, the latter case should not be regarded as disappearance of repeated code. If we conducted the investigation with the setting, the investigation result would be changed.

7 Conclusion

In this paper, we investigated how repeated code had been modified during software evolution as a first step for improving modification process on repeated code.

We selected three famous open source software systems, Ant, ArgoUML, and jEdit as experimental targets. As a result, we obtained the following knowledge.

- Element size of repeated code was too small to be detected with code clone detection tools.
- 73-89% of repeated code were modified at least once.
- 31-58% of modifications were simultaneous modifications for all the elements of them.
- Any instruction type of repeated code was modified. Especially, try block, while block and variable declarations were more likely to be modified than the others.
- The lesser repetitions repeated code had, the higher the ratio of simultaneous modifications on all the elements of them was.

Acknowledgment. This work was supported by MEXT/JSPS KAKENHI 24680002 and 24650011.

References

1. Aversano, L., Cerulo, L., Di Penta, M.: How clones are maintained: An empirical study. In: Proceedings of the 11th European Conference on Software Maintenance and Reengineering, CSMR 2007, pp. 81–90. IEEE Computer Society, Washington, DC (2007)
2. Baker, B.S.: On finding duplication and near-duplication in large software systems. In: Proceedings of the Second Working Conference on Reverse Engineering, WCRE 1995, pp. 86–95. IEEE Computer Society, Washington, DC (1995)
3. Canfora, G., Cerulo, L., Penta, M.D.: Identifying changed source code lines from version repositories. In: Proceedings of the Fourth International Workshop on Mining Software Repositories, MSR 2007, p. 14. IEEE Computer Society, Washington, DC (2007)
4. Ducasse, S., Demeyer, S., Nierstrasz, O.: Transform conditionals to polymorphism. In: Proceedings EUROPLOP 2000 (5th European Conference on Pattern Languages of Programming and Computing, 1999), pp. 219–252. UVK Universitätsverlag Konstanz GmbH, Konstanz (2000)
5. Fowler, M.: Refactoring: improving the design of existing code. Addison-Wesley Longman Publishing Co., Inc., Boston (1999)
6. Higo, Y., Kamiya, T., Kusumoto, S., Inoue, K.: Method and implementation for investigating code clones in a software system. Inf. Softw. Technol. 49(9-10), 985–998 (2007)
7. Higo, Y., Kusumoto, S.: How often do unintended incosistencies happend? –deriving modification patterns and detecting overlooked code fragments–. In: Proceedings of the 2012 28th IEEE International Conference on Software Maintenance, ICSM 2012, pp. 222–231. IEEE Computer Society, Washington, DC (2012)
8. Kamiya, T., Kusumoto, S., Inoue, K.: Ccfinder: A multilinguistic token-based code clone detection system fo r large scale source code. IEEE Transactions on Software Engineering 28, 654–670 (2002)
9. Kapser, C.J., Godfrey, M.W.: "Cloning considered harmful" considered harmful: patterns of cloning in software. Empirical Softw. Engg. 13(6), 645–692 (2008)
10. Kim, M., Bergman, L., Lau, T., Notkin, D.: An ethnographic study of copy and paste programming practices in oopl. In: Proceedings of the 2004 International Symposium on Empirical Software Engineering, ISESE 2004, pp. 83–92. IEEE Computer Society, Washington, DC (2004)
11. Kim, M., Sazawal, V., Notkin, D., Murphy, G.: An empirical study of code clone genealogies. In: Proceedings of the 10th European Software Engineering Conference Held Jointly with 13th ACM SIGSOFT International Symposium on Foundations of Software Engineering, ESEC/FSE-13, pp. 187–196. ACM, New York (2005)
12. Li, Z., Lu, S., Myagmar, S., Zhou, Y.: Cp-miner: Finding copy-paste and related bugs in large-scale software code. IEEE Trans. Softw. Eng. 32(3), 176–192 (2006)
13. Murakami, H., Hotta, K., Higo, Y., Igaki, H., Kusumoto, S.: Folding repeated instructions for improving token-based code clone detection. In: Proceedings of the 2012 IEEE 12th International Working Conference on Source Code Analysis and Manipulation, SCAM 2012, pp. 64–73. IEEE Computer Society, Washington, DC (2012)
14. Roy, C.K., Cordy, J.R.: An empirical study of function clones in open source software. In: Proceedings of the 2008 15th Working Conference on Reverse Engineering, WCRE 2008, pp. 81–90. IEEE Computer Society, Washington, DC (2008)
15. Roy, C.K., Cordy, J.R., Koschke, R.: Comparison and evaluation of code clone detection techniques and tools: A qualitative approach. Sci. Comput. Program. 74(7), 470–495 (2009)
16. Sasaki, Y., Ishihara, T., Hotta, K., Hata, H., Higo, Y., Igaki, H., Kusumoto, S.: Preprocessing of metrics measurement based on simplifying program structures. In: International Workshop on Software Analysis, Testing and Applications, pp. 120–127 (December 2012)

Assessing Refactoring Instances and the Maintainability Benefits of Them from Version Archives

Kenji Fujiwara[1], Kyohei Fushida[2], Norihiro Yoshida[1], and Hajimu Iida[1]

[1] Nara Institute of Science and Technology,
8916-5 Takayama, Ikoma, Nara Japan
{kenji-f,yoshida}@is.naist.jp, iida@itc.naist.jp
[2] NTT DATA Corporation
Toyosu Center Bldg. Annex, 3-8, Toyosu 3-chome, Koto-ku, Tokyo, Japan
fushidak@nttdata.co.jp

Abstract. For the development of high quality software, process quality assessment should be applied into development organization. So far, several process quality assessment methodologies are proposed and applied into a lot of organizations. In this paper, we propose an approach to assess instances of refactoring that is one of the key processes for quality improvement. The proposed approach can be done semi-automatically by investigating version archives in a configuration management system. We applied our proposed method to the Columba project which is an open source software project. The result of our preliminary case study shows that the frequency of defect introduction tends to decrease in the term after frequent refactoring.

Keywords: Refactoring, Mining software repositories, Process assessment.

1 Introduction

So far, our research group has proposed several reasonable approaches for fine-grained assessment of the development process from version archives [6,8]. These approaches can assess ongoing or past development processes and compare their expectations by analyzing version archives of configuration management systems (e.g., CVS, Subversion). Refactoring is a sort of processes, which is defined as the process of changing a software system in such a way that it does not alter the external behavior of the code, yet improves its internal structure[4]. Because the appropriateness of refactoring affects product quality, as well as other sort of processes, project managers must consider the following:

- Did the previous refactoring instances improve the quality of the product?
- Were the previous refactoring instances performed based on the original intention of the developers?
- Was any additional unintentional refactoring performed?

J. Heidrich et al. (Eds.): PROFES 2013, LNCS 7983, pp. 313–323, 2013.

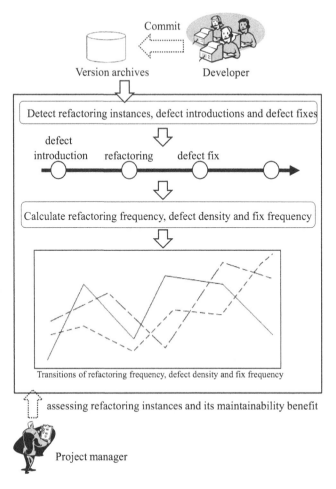

Fig. 1. An overview of our research

However, manual finding of version archives (e.g., commit logs, source code changes) is time consuming for developers, especially project managers who have a little knowledge of the source code of the project.

In this paper, we propose an approach to help a project manager who assess refactoring instances from version archives in a configuration management system (see Figure 1). In our approach, first refactoring instances are detected by the UMLDiff algorithm, then, frequencies of refactorings, defect introductions, and defect fixes are computed for a certain period. Finally, a comparison is performed among the evolutions of those computed frequencies. In addition, we show a preliminary case study of an open source software project Columba to confirm the appropriateness of our approach.

The results of our preliminary case study show that once refactoring instances appear frequently, the frequency of defect introduction tends to decrease.

2   Background

2.1   Refactoring

Refactoring is a technique for improving software design. It is defined as the process of changing the structure of a program without changing its behavior[4]. Various typical refactoring patterns have been cataloged by Fowler[3], who describes that one of refactoring effects is the decrease of software defects.

2.2   Refactoring Detection

We need to investigate when and how refactoring was performed in software development. Approaches to detect refactoring activities are categorized into four types[7]:

Type (a) Using log messages recorded in version control systems.
Type (b) Analyzing source code changes.
Type (c) Observing developers' activity.
Type (d) Tracking usage of refactoring tools.

A type (a) approach detects evidences of refactorings by searching for the word "refactor" and possibly for related words such as "rename" or "extract" from log messages recorded in version control systems. The method assumes developers write performed refactorings into log messages in the version control system. Type (b) analyzes difference of source code between two versions. As a result, evidences of refactorings such as "Rename Field" or "Extract Method" are detected. The method allows us to detect more refactorings than type (a) because it can recover undocumented refactorings. On type (c), researchers observe how developers perform refactoring. Its range of application is narrow because it needs human resources or observation tools. In contrast, it allows us to collect detailed information of refactorings. Type (d) tracks when developers use a refactoring support feature and what part of the source code is changed.

Types (a) and (b), are possible to be applied to existing software projects that adopt a version control systems. However, their results are not complete because they are estimation from development histories. On the other hand, type (c) and (d) cannot be applied to existing projects because they require preparation. For which, we consider the adoption of these types of refactoring detection techniques is highly costly for software development organizations.

3   Investigation Method

3.1   Metrics

In our investigation method, we introduce three metrics:

- *refactoring frequency*: the number of performing of the refactoring within a certain period

- **defect density**: the number of introductions of the defect within a certain period
- **fix frequency**: the number of fixes of the defect within a certain period

In order to define these metrics, we denote the set of revisions recorded in the version control system by V and each revision by v_i. Therefore, V is denoted by $V = [v_1, v_2, \cdots, v_n]$. Then, we let op_i be a source code change from revision v_i to v_{i+1}. In addition, we define the function $r(op_i)$ which returns whether op_i contains a refactoring. $r(op_i)$ returns the value one if op_i contains a refactoring, zero otherwise. Furthermore, we define *refactoring frequency* to be $f_r(j, k)$ as follow:

$$r(op_i) = \begin{cases} 1 & (\text{if } op_i \text{ contains a refactoring}) \\ 0 & (\text{otherwise}) \end{cases}$$

$$f_r(j, k) = \frac{\sum_{i=j}^{k-1} r(op_i)}{k - j} \qquad (j < k, \quad v_j, v_k \in V)$$

Similarly, we define the function $d(op_i)$ which returns whether op_i contains a defect introduction and defect density to be $f_d(j, k)$, we also define the function $f(op_i)$ which returns whether op_i contains a fix of the defect and fix frequency to be $f_f(j, k)$ as follow:

$$d(op_i) = \begin{cases} 1 & (\text{if defects are introduced at } v_{i+1}) \\ 0 & (\text{otherwise}) \end{cases}$$

$$f_d(j, k) = \frac{\sum_{i=j}^{k-1} d(op_i)}{k - j} \qquad (j < k, \quad v_j, v_k \in V)$$

$$f(op_i) = \begin{cases} 1 & (\text{if defects are fixed at } v_{i+1}) \\ 0 & (\text{otherwise}) \end{cases}$$

$$f_d(j, k) = \frac{\sum_{i=j}^{k-1} f(op_i)}{k - j} \qquad (j < k, \quad v_j, v_k \in V)$$

3.2   Locating Refactoring Changes

In order to measure **refactoring frequency**, we need to know when refactorings were performed to the software. Our method uses the refactoring detection method based on the UMLDiff algorithm[12] designed by Xing et al[13]. The UMLDiff algorithm takes two revisions of the source code and derives the difference among two revisions. It recovers design information from each revision of the source code to derive the difference. In detail, it firstly extracts source code entities such as classes and methods from each revision. Then, it derives the relationships among entities. Finally, it detects the differences such as method/class additions and method/class renames.

Xing et al. also designed the refactoring detection method based on the UMLDiff algorithm[13]. It detects refactorings which performed on the changes from one revision to another one by analyzing the output of the UMLDiff algorithm. The method takes two revisions as input of the UMLDiff algorithm and applies the algorithm. Then, it analyzes the output to search the set of differences which is a candidate for an evidence of refactoring. It is promising to derive only refactoring instances and ignore non-refactoring changes because the detection mechanism in the UMLDiff algorithm follows refactoring patterns written by Fowler[4].

In this paper, we locate changes which contain refactoring instances by the following steps:

Step 1. Divide all revisions by every n revisions into k groups.

Step 2. For each k group, use the first revision and the final revision as inputs for the UMLDiff algorithm and apply the algorithm.

Step 3. Locate the refactoring change which contains refactoring instances detected in the previous step.

3.3 Locating Fix and Fix-Inducing Changes

Our method measures **defect density** (which is the number of introductions of defect within a certain period). In order to measure **defect density** and **fix frequency**, we need to know when defects were introduced to the software and when defects were fixed. Śliwerski et al. designed the SZZ algorithm which is an algorithm to extract fix-inducing changes from version control systems[10]. Their algorithm links information recorded in the issue tracking system and the version control system. We consider fix-inducing changes as introductions of defects.

The SZZ algorithm links the issue and commit by following steps:

Step 1. Firstly, the SZZ algorithm searches candidates of the fix commits by using commit messages. For instance, it search the keyword which related to the fixes such as "fixes", "closed" and so on. If the commit message contains the keywords, SZZ searches defect ID from the commit message.

Step 2. Then, it filter out suspected candidates. SZZ use the criterion of filtering as follow.

  − Does the defect ID exist in the issue tracking system?
  − Has the fix completely done?

As a result of this step, we got the link of defects and commits.

Step 2. Finally, SZZ trace the changes to detect when the fix-inducing change was introduced by using the version control system.

3.4 Requirements of Target Projects

The target project of our method requires to be adopted the version control system and the issue tracking system. In addition, to apply the SZZ algorithm, the project needs to collaborate with the version control system and the issue tracking system.

4   Case Study

We applied our proposed method to the Columba[1] project which is an open source software project. Table 1 shows an overview of the Columba project. The Columba project uses Subversion[2] which is a version control system and an issue tracking system provided by SourceForge.net.

Table 1. An over view of the Columba project

category	development period	#revisions	LOC of the final revision
Mail Client	2006/7/9 – 2011/7/11	458	192,941

4.1   Study Procedure

We measured three the metrics described in Section 3 from the development history of the Columba project by the following steps:

Step 1. Located refactoring changes by the UMLDiff based refactoring detection method.

Step 2. Located fix and fix-inducing changes by the SZZ algorithm.

Step 3. Calculated three metrics from the results of the Step 1 and Step 2. Each metric was calculated every 25 revisions. For instance, we calculated a refactoring frequency from revision 25 to 50.

Step 1. Locating Refactoring Changes. Using the procedures described in Section 3.2, we detected refactoring changes from the archive of the Columba. When using the UMLDiff algorithm, we used the following approaches to realize precise detection of refactoring instances.

(a) Give the first and the last revisions to the UMLDiff algorithm for input.
(b) Pick-up every five revisions from the archive, and then give each pair of the picked-up revisions next to each other.

In order to locate refactoring changes from the result of the UMLDIff algorithm, we manually analyzed source code archives by using the browsing differences feature of Subversion. At that time, we removed false positives. For instance, an Extract Method refactoring was detected by the UMLDiff algorithm, but it was not an actual refactoring because the name of the extracted method was similar to an the existing method, but its body was quite different.

Step 2. Locating Fix and Fix-Inducing Changes. In order to locate fix and fix-inducing changes, we used a tool implemented the SZZ algorithm. The columba project has a rule of commit log strictly. For a bug fix commit, the tag word [**bug**] or [**fix**] is added to the log. Therefore, we recognized a commit whose log contains those tag words as a fix change. Then, we located the fix-inducing change from those fix changes.

---

[1] http://sourceforge.net/projects/columba/
[2] http://subversion.apache.org/

Table 2. List of detected refactorings

Kind of refactoring	#Refactorings		
	Approach A	Approach B	total
Convert top level to inner	1	0	1
Die-hard/legacy classes	1	1	1
Downcast type parameter	3	0	3
Encapsulate field (get)	1	0	1
Extract class	2	1	2
Extract method	7	2	7
Extract subsystem/package	3	2	3
Extract super interface	0	6	6
Generalize type (method)	10	9	10
Generalize type (field)	2	2	2
Generalize type (parameter)	42	40	42
Information hiding	6	0	6
Inline subsystem/package	1	2	2
Move method/field/behavior	0	12	12
Move subsystem/package/class	0	12	12
Pull-up method/field/behaivior	5	4	5
Push-down method/field/behaivior	1	0	1
total	85	93	116

4.2 Result

Table 2 shows the result of the UMLDiff based refactoring detection method. The result does not include false positives. The columns of *Approach A* and *B* correspond to the approaches described in the previous section. *Total* column represents the union of the result of approaches A and B. 14 kinds of refactorings were extracted, and the total number of extracted refactoring was 116. As a result of the SZZ algorithm, 322 fix changes and 243 fix-inducing changes were extracted.

Figure 2 shows the transition of the *refactoring frequency*, *defect density* and *fix frequency* of the Columba project. X-axis indicates the revision number, and y-axis indicates the value of three metrics. As described in the previous section, each value of three metrics was calculated and plotted every 25 revisions. For instance, the value of the *fix frequency* from revision 250 to revision 275 is 0.2.

5 Discussion

We confirmed following two characteristics from Figure 2.

(a) **Defect density** tends to decrease from the most refactored period (from 150 revision to 175 revision).

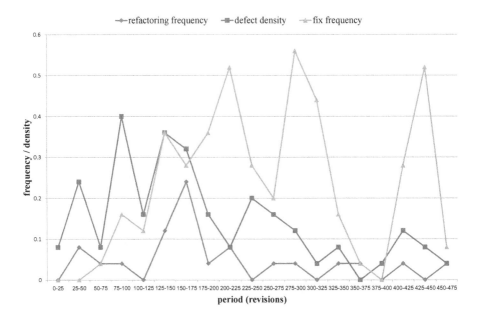

Fig. 2. Transition of the refactoring frequency, defect density and fix frequency in the Columba

(b) ***Fix frequency*** tends to decrease after the refactoring frequency is high through out the project.

The average of the ***defect density*** from revision zero to revision 175 is 0.23. In contrast, the average from revision 175 to revision 458 is 0.09. Furthermore, commit logs in the most refactored period (from revision 150 to revision 175) include evidence of big refactoring[3]. We consider that the decrease of the defect density after a big refactoring is due to improvement of the source code by performing refactoring. On the other hand, we also consider that defect density decreased because the Columba project has entered to the maintenance phase. However, the version 1.4 of the Columba was released in the revision after about 100 revisions from the point a big refactoring occurred.

We consider that the performing of refactoring improved source code readability and then the developers could find and fix defects easily, however, we also consider developers performed refactoring in order to be source code more flexible and then performed fixes. In contrast, there is a possibility these fixes are due to failure of refactorings.

---

[3] The commit logs from revision 151 to revision 155 were exactly same. These were *[intern] big refactoring of the filter stuff. There was a interface created and all the required interfaces moved to core-api. After that all classes which using the filter stuff now refactored to use the interfaces instead the implementation. Now the mail-api compiles without problems with maven2.*

6   Threats to Validity

Preciseness of the Refactoring Detection Method. Our proposed method relies on preciseness of the refactoring detection method. The preciseness depends on the granularity of the divisions of the revisions. In fact, the result of *Approach A* and *B* were different. Thus, we probably left out some refactoring changes (e.g., file addition after revision r_n, delection before revision r_m where (r_n, r_m) denotes the input of the UMLDiff Algorithm). However, we believe that our result will not change dramatically if we can add detect ignored refactorings.

Preciseness of the SZZ Algorithm. Our proposed method also relies on preciseness of the fix and fix-inducing detection method. In our case study, that preciseness depends on the accuracy of the developers record activities because we located fix changes based on the commit logs of the Columba project. Some studies report the accuracy of existing detection methods for locating fix and fix-inducing changes based on commit logs depend on the quality of commit log and data in bug tracking systems[1,2]. Hence, they also report that these methods cannot recover all fix and fix-inducing changes completely. For locating fix-inducing changes, the SZZ algorithm traces back changes of the source code by using version control systems. Thus, the algorithm does not support certain type of changes which consist in only deletions. However, our result does not suffer from those changes because such cases are rare.

Granularity of Refactorings, Defects and Fixes. Our proposed method focuses on whether a refactoring, a defect introduction and a fix are performed in each change. Therefore, our method treats a single refactoring change and a multiple refactoring change in the same manner. We consider that treating the number of refactoring in our proposed method is not appropriate because the kinds of refactoring detected by the UMLDiff based method has much granularity. Similarly, for fix and fix-introducing changes, we focused on whether those changes were performed or not.

7   Related Work

Ratzinger et al. analyzed the relationship between refactorings and defects[9]. They used log messages in a version control system to detect refactoring. They reported that when the number of refactorings is high over a certain period of the software project, defect introducing changes would decrease over successive period. Therefore, they concluded that refactoring reduces defect introduction. However, they did not refer to the effect of development that continues to use low-quality source codes which requires refactoring. We evaluate the effect of lack of refactorings by using bad smells. In addition, we investigate details of time relation between refactorings and defects.

Kim et al. investigated the role of refactorings among three open source software[5]. They extracted refactoring histories from the software development history, and then evaluated the role from the following viewpoints:

- Are there more bug fixes after refactorings?
- Do refactorings improve developer productivity?
- Do refactorings facilitate bug fixes?
- How many refactorings are performed before major releases?

As a result, they reported that the bug fix rate of 5 revisions before refactoring is around 26.1% for Eclipse JDT, and refactorings decrease time of bug fixes. In addition, they reported refactorings tend to be performed together with bug fixes and there are many refactoring before major releases. Their research focused on the effect of the refactorings on the bug fixes. On the other hand, our approach focused on the effect on the defect introducing changes.

In order to detect refactorings, Weißgerber and Diehl presented a method by using syntactical and signature information of the source code[11]. Their method extracts refactoring candidates by that information, and then ranks them based on code clone detection technique. Compared with the method based on the UMLDiff algorithm, their method can detect less kinds of refactoring(10 kinds). In our study, we use the method based on the UMLDiff algorithm because the method can detect 33 kinds of refactoring.

8   Conclusion and Future Work

We proposed an approach to assess refactoring instances from version archives. Our proposed method detects refactoring instances using a refactoring detection method based on the UMLDiff algorithm. It also detects defect introductions and defect fixes using the SZZ algorithm.

As a result of our preliminary case study using the Columba project, our method is promising to support the assessment of the assessing refactoring instances and its maintainability benefit.

As a future work, we plan to apply our method to another open source software project. However, in the case study, the run-time for the UMLDiff algorithm based refactoring detection was approximately 19 hours. The computation time of the detection method is roughly proportional to the scale of the target project. Therefore, in order to apply our method to the project which is larger than the Columba project, we need to develop a refactoring detection tool which detect refactoring instances among two versions more quickly.

Acknowledgments. This research was supported by Japan Society for the Promotion of Science, Grant-in-Aid for Scientific Research (No.22500027).

References

1. Bachmann, A., Bird, C., Rahman, F., Devanbu, P., Bernstein, A.: The missing links: bugs and bug-fix commits. In: Proc. the Eighteenth ACM SIGSOFT International Symposium on Foundations of Software Engineering (FSE 2010), p. 97 (2010)

2. Bird, C., Bachmann, A., Aune, E., Duffy, J., Bernstein, A., Filkov, V., Devanbu, P.: Fair and balanced?: bias in bug-fix datasets. In: Proc. the 7th Joint Meeting of the European Software Engineering Conference and the ACM SIGSOFT Symposium on the Foundations of Software Engineering (ESEC/FSE 2009), pp. 121–130 (2009)
3. Fowler, M.: Refactoring home page, http://refactoring.com/
4. Fowler, M.: Refactoring: improving the design of exsiting code. Addison Wesley (1999)
5. Kim, M., Cai, D., Kim, S.: An empirical investigation into the role of api-level refactorings during software evolution. In: Proc. the 33rd International Conference on Software Engineering (ICSE 2011), pp. 151–160 (2011)
6. Kula, R.G., Fushida, K., Kawaguchi, S., Iida, H.: Analysis of bug fixing processes using program slicing metrics. In: Ali Babar, M., Vierimaa, M., Oivo, M. (eds.) PROFES 2010. LNCS, vol. 6156, pp. 32–46. Springer, Heidelberg (2010)
7. Murphy-Hill, E., Black, A.P., Dig, D., Parnin, C.: Gathering refactoring data: a comparison of four methods. In: Proc. the 2nd ACM Workshop on Refactoring Tools (WRT 2008), pp. 1–5 (2008)
8. Ohkura, K., Goto, K., Hanakawa, N., Kawaguchi, S., Iida, H.: Project replayer with email analysis – revealing contexts in software development. In: Proc. the 13th Asia Pacific Software Engineering Conference (APSEC 2006), pp. 453–460 (2006)
9. Ratzinger, J., Sigmund, T., Gall, H.C.: On the relation of refactorings and software defect prediction. In: Proc. the 5th Working Conference on Mining Software Repositories (MSR 2008), pp. 35–38 (2008)
10. Śliwerski, J., Zimmermann, T., Zeller, A.: When do changes induce fixes? In: Proc. the 2nd International Workshop on Mining Software Repositories (MSR 2005), pp. 1–5 (2005)
11. Weißgerber, P., Diehl, S.: Identifying refactorings from source-code changes. In: Proc. the 21st IEEE/ACM International Conference on Automated Software Engineering (ASE 2006), pp. 231–240 (2006)
12. Xing, Z., Stroulia, E.: UMLDiff: an algorithm for object-oriented design differencing. In: Proc. the 20th IEEE/ACM International Conference on Automated Software Engineering (ASE 2005), pp. 54–65 (2005)
13. Xing, Z., Stroulia, E.: Refactoring Detection based on UMLDiff Change-Facts Queries. In: Proc. the 13th Working Conference on Reverse Engineering (WCRE 2006), pp. 263–274 (2006)

Evaluation of Standard Reliability Growth Models in the Context of Automotive Software Systems

Rakesh Rana[1], Miroslaw Staron[1], Niklas Mellegård[1], Christian Berger[1],
Jörgen Hansson[1], Martin Nilsson[2], and Fredrik Törner[2]

[1] Chalmers/ University of Gothenburg
rakesh.rana@gu.se
[2] Volvo Car Corporation

Abstract. Reliability and dependability of software in modern cars is of utmost importance. Predicting these properties for software under development is therefore important for modern car OEMs, and using reliability growth models (e.g. Rayleigh, Goel-Okumoto) is one approach. In this paper we evaluate a number of standard reliability growth models on a real software system from automotive industry. The results of the evaluation show that models can be fitted well with defect inflow data, but certain parameters need to be adjusted manually in order to predict reliability more precisely in the late test phases. In this paper we provide recommendations for how to adjust the models and how the adjustments should be used in the development process of software in the automotive domain by investigating data from an industrial project.

1 Introduction

Software plays a significant role in modern cars. In past few decades the amount and importance of software in cars has increased exponentially [1], to the extent that today's premium cars carry more than 70 ECUs and software of the order of over ten million lines of code [2]. Software is not only replacing traditional models of control systems but today it is at the heart of providing new functionality and driving innovation. With the rapid growth in significance of software in automotive industry there are a number of challenges the industry faces in developing and maintaining good software for modern cars [2, 3].

Automotive software differs from software in other sectors due to stringent demands for rapid development, need for cost effectiveness, high demand for innovation and need of high reliability. To ensure that cars are safe for drivers, occupants and other road users as well as to maintain the consumer confidence, the quality and reliability demand for safety critical software is very high. The functional safety standard (such as ISO 26262, [4]) provide strict guidelines for the development of software for safety critical applications within automotive domain with significant emphasis on ensuring reliability.

Software reliability growth models (SRGMs) have been used to assess the maturity of software for a number of years. Efficient estimation of latent defects in software is

J. Heidrich et al. (Eds.): PROFES 2013, LNCS 7983, pp. 324–329, 2013.

valuable information, test managers can use this information to make important decisions not only to ensure optimal resource allocation but also to decide when the given software is ready for release [5]. Applying SRGMs for estimating reliability in industrial applications needs careful consideration to the applied model assumptions, data availability and predictive power, but proper use of SRGMs provides several benefits for developing high quality and reliable software.

2   Related Work

Over the years, a number of SRGMs has been presented [6], although there is still need for wider evaluation of these models in industrial, domain-specific applications. This is especially true for the automotive sector. Different industrial domains have very different demands for its software and the development process also varies to a large extent, hence not all SRGMs would be suited for every sector. Ullah et al. [7] applied and compared different SRGMs on 50 failure data sets and evaluated goodness of fit, prediction accuracy and correction. They found that the Musa-Okumoto model performs better than the rest on the industrial datasets, while Gompertz works better for Open Source datasets. Woods [8] applied eight SRGMs on software products from industry and showed that defects predicted based on cumulative defects inflow profiles matches well with after release defects. Staron and Meding [9] evaluated SRGMs on large software projects in the telecom sector and proposed a new model based on historic trends data. In this paper we apply common SRGMs on a project from automotive sector and evaluate it on the simplest fit measure. The applications of SRGMs in automotive software projects are very scarce and with increasing dominance of software in the automotive industry, the importance of such studies is apparent.

In [10], authors present a review of common Non-Homogeneous Poisson Process (NHPP) based software reliability models and compare their performance on a real time control system. We evaluate SRGMs with maximum three parameters, which are easy to implement and intuitive to understand. This also means that these models can be easily adopted in industry.

The automotive domain in itself is quite unique, firstly the industry due to various reasons including the historic factors is driven by the "V" development model with high dependence on suppliers, this has also became true to a large extent for the development of software within this domain. Secondly automotive unlike some other industries and like many other similar sectors have widely adopted the model based development approach. Additionally within the Original Equipment Manufacturers, there exist numbers of different departments/teams (for example Powertrain, Central Electric Module, Infotainment etc.) which develops quite different type of software products and works in quite different working environments. Currently there is also a significant trend within automotive domain towards being more agile in their software development. In this paper we give a way forward for effective implementation of SRGMs in the automotive sector, what challenges need to be addressed and what would lead to optimal software reliability modeling in this domain.

3   Research Context and Method

We use data from a large project within the development of an active safety function from our industrial partner, Volvo Car Corporation (VCC) from the automotive sector. Department of Active Safety within VCC develops functions/features such as driver alert control, collision warning, lane departure warning etc. The defect data has been used earlier in [11] for a study that introduced a new lightweight defect classification scheme. In this paper we use dynamic software reliability growth models reported in earlier studies, summarized in Table 1.

Table 1. Software reliability growth models used in this study

Model Name	Model Type	Mean Value Function	Ref.
Models with 2 parameters			
Goel-Okumoto (GO)	Concave	$m(t) = a(1 - e^{-bt})$	[12]
Delayed S-shaped model	S-shaped	$m(t) = a(1 - (1 + bt)e^{-bt})$	[13]
Rayleigh model	S-shaped	$m(t) = a(1 - e^{-(t/b)^{\wedge}2})$	[14]
Models with 3 parameters			
Inflection S-shaped model	S-shaped	$m(t) = \dfrac{a(1 - e^{-bt})}{(1 + \beta e^{-bt})}$	[10]
Yamada exponential imperfect debugging model (Y-ExpI)	Concave	$m(t) = \left(\dfrac{ab}{\propto + b}\right)(e^{\propto t} - e^{-bt})$	[15]
Yamada linear imperfect debugging model (Y-LinI)	Concave	$m(t) = a(1 - e^{-bt})\left(1 - \dfrac{\propto}{b}\right) + \propto at$	[15]
Logistic population model	S-shaped	$m(t) = \dfrac{a}{1 + e^{-b(t-c)}}$	[16]
Gompertz model	S-shaped	$m(t) = ae^{-be^{-ct}}$	[17]

To fit the models to our data we use non-linear regression routine of the commercially available statistical software package, IBM SPSS. The starting values provided were same for all models and iterations are done until the reduction between successive residuals errors is less than 1.0*E-08. Models with two and three parameters are used in fitting of the curves as these parameters could be interpreted empirically (for instance with respect to the testing effort or maximum number of defects). The models are built based on the data set from all the development phases of the system starting at requirement analysis and ending with vehicle production testing (i.e. excluding the post-release defects).

4   Results and Interpretation

The fitting of different SRGMs (two and three parameter models) on actual data is presented in Fig. 1. Due to confidentiality reasons the scale of the Y-axis is not presented and the time scale is trimmed at beginning and end representing only partial data for illustrating the fit of the used models.

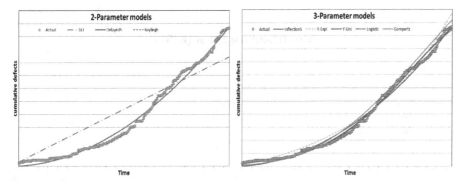

Fig. 1. Two and three parameter software reliability growth models applied to data set from automotive software project[1]

Although (as shown in Fig. 1) concave type models fit the data, they have a tendency of growing exponentially. The exponential growth gives unrealistically high values of asymptotes (maximum predicted defects); such growth is not possible in practice – the defect discovery rate is slow at the start and the number of defects discovered late in the projects decreases over time, thus giving the well-known S-shape of the cumulative defect inflow profile. This shortcoming can be overcome by using three parameter models which include the $\alpha(t)$ parameter. The additional parameter is meant to describe the function of test progress over time, and therefore provide more accurate results with logical empirical explanations.

The analysis of the models and their fit, as shown in Fig. 1, suggests that the $\alpha(t)$ parameter is promising and will be used in our further analyses. Using the Mean Square Error (MSE) measure to analyze the goodness-of-fit of the models (shown in Figure 2) we observed that models that fitted the data best were the logistic model (used to model population growths in general) and the InflectionS model.

MSE presented in Fig. 2 for the simplest and one of the earliest Goel-Okumoto (GO) model was approximately 10 times larger than the rest of the models thus we excluded it from the chart to rescale it and focus on the remaining models. It is interesting to note that two parameter models (DelayedS and Rayleigh model with exception of GO) fits better than the three parameters Yamada exponential imperfect debugging model and Yamada linear imperfect debugging model. Both Yamada models attempt to account for the testing effort using the third parameter. This means that our initial results should be complemented with a more accurate model of the testing effort

Another significant observation is with respect to the three parameter general logistic model, which performs best among models used in this study with respect to minimum MSE criteria, despite this model not being widely used for software reliability modeling. Our observation suggests that traditional three parameter models such as logistic and Gompertz provide superior fit to our data from automotive domain software project. InflectionS model also does very well in MSE fit criteria with MSE only higher than logistic and lower than that using Gompertz model.

---

[1] Scales on X and Y axis have been removed due to confidentiality reasons. The time domain is also trimmed at the beginning and end to show only the partial data, however full data was used to fit the models.

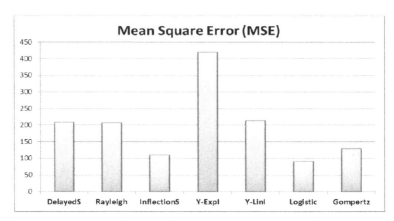

Fig. 2. The mean-square error for each of the models, note that the GO model is excluded in this figure

5   Conclusions and Further Work

A number of SRGMs have been proposed and evaluated over time. It is noted here that despite software being dominant in modern automotive industry there is a gap in studies evaluating the application of SRGMs in this domain. In this paper we take a step in direction of addressing this gap by applying eight common SRGMs on defect data from an automotive software project and evaluating their fit using MSE criteria. Further we provide a way forward for effective application of SRGMs in automotive software reliability modeling as follows:

- It was observed that simple two parameters models can provide good fit (with exception of the GO model), but the asymptotes obtained might be unrealistic;
- Logistic and InflectionS models had the best fit to our data among the different models tried;
- Since one of the important factors for successful use of SRGMs is to use appropriate time scale, we identify that modeling the change of testing effort over time (generally done using parameter $\alpha(t)$) will be critical in applying SRGMs within automotive sector;
- Using parameter estimates from two parameter models and based on historic values one could also model/predict the testing effort i.e. $\alpha(t)$ for the current project which would give useful insight to managers for optimizing the resource allocation going forward.

Realistic accounting of testing effort will help us to fit the SRGMs to actual defect inflow data. Finding the models which provide the best fit, have superior predictive power, and use the data in its available form will significantly enhance the adoption of software reliability modeling in industries where software is starting to play a critical role. And customizing the SRGMs to conform to given industrial domains such as automotive sector will provide a powerful tool to test and quality managers within these industries to use them for optimal resource management, increasing the quality, reliability, and ensuring timely delivery of high quality software.

Acknowledgement. The research presented here is done under the VISEE project which is funded by Vinnova and Volvo Cars jointly under the FFI programme (VISEE, Project No: DIARIENR: 2011-04438).

References

1. Liggesmeyer, P., Trapp, M.: Trends in embedded software engineering. IEEE Software 26, 19–25 (2009)
2. Broy, M.: Challenges in automotive software engineering. In: Proceedings of the 28th International Conference on Software Engineering, pp. 33–42 (2006)
3. Grimm, K.: Software technology in an automotive company: major challenges. In: Proceedings of the 25th International Conference on Software Engineering, pp. 498–503 (2003)
4. ISO 26262:2011 Road vehicles - Functional safety (2011)
5. Stringfellow, C., Andrews, A.A.: An empirical method for selecting software reliability growth models. Empirical Software Engineering 7, 319–343 (2002)
6. Lyu, M.R.: Software reliability engineering: A roadmap. In: Future of Software Engineering, FOSE 2007, pp. 153–170 (2007)
7. Ullah, N., Morisio, M., Vetro, A.: A Comparative Analysis of Software Reliability Growth Models using Defects Data of Closed and Open Source Software. In: 2012 35th Annual IEEE Software Engineering Workshop (SEW), pp. 187–192 (2012)
8. Wood, A.: Predicting software reliability. Computer 29, 69–77 (1996)
9. Staron, M., Meding, W.: Predicting weekly defect inflow in large software projects based on project planning and test status. Information and Software Technology 50, 782–796 (2008)
10. Pham, H.: Software reliability and cost models: Perspectives, comparison, and practice. European Journal of Operational Research 149, 475–489 (2003)
11. Mellegård, N., Staron, M., Törner, F.: A light-weight defect classification scheme for embedded automotive software and its initial evaluation (2012)
12. Goel, A.L., Okumoto, K.: Time-dependent error-detection rate model for software reliability and other performance measures. IEEE Transactions on Reliability 28, 206–211 (1979)
13. Yamada, S., Ohba, M., Osaki, S.: S-shaped reliability growth modeling for software error detection. IEEE Transactions on Reliability 32, 475–484 (1983)
14. Kan, S.H., et al.: Metrics and Models in Software Quality Engineering, 2nd edn. Pearson Education India (2003)
15. Yamada, S., Tokuno, K., Osaki, S.: Imperfect debugging models with fault introduction rate for software reliability assessment. International Journal of Systems Science 23, 2241–2252 (1992)
16. Taghi, M.K., Edward, B.A.: Logistic regression modeling of software quality. International Journal of Reliability, Quality and Safety Engineering 6, 303–317 (1999)
17. Ohishi, K., Okamura, H., Dohi, T.: Gompertz software reliability model: Estimation algorithm and empirical validation. Journal of Systems and Software 82, 535–543 (2009)

A Tool for IT Service Management Process Assessment for Process Improvement

Anup Shrestha, Aileen Cater-Steel, Wui-Gee Tan, Mark Toleman, and Terry Rout

University of Southern Queensland, Toowoomba, Australia
{anup.shrestha,aileen.cater-steel,wui-gee.tan,
mark.toleman}@usq.edu.au, terry.rout@griffith.edu.au

Abstract. Process assessments can improve IT service management (ITSM) processes but the assessment method is not always transparent. This paper outlines a project to develop a software-mediated process assessment tool to enable transparent and objective ITSM process assessment. Using the international standards for ITSM and process assessment, the tool is being developed following the goal-question-metric (GQM) approach in collaboration with academics, standards committee members and ITSM practitioners.

Keywords: ITSM process assessment tool, ISO/IEC 20000, ISO/IEC 15504, ITIL, Goal-Question-Metric approach.

1   Introduction

The IT Service Management (ITSM) discipline promotes a process approach in managing IT services. IT Infrastructure Library (ITIL) is a widely accepted approach to ITSM using best practice guidelines. The international standard for ITSM: ISO/IEC 20000 [1] can be used to certify ITSM capabilities in organisations. One of the central themes of ITSM is continual service improvement (CSI). Improvement in ITSM processes as part of CSI can be measured using ITSM process assessments.

Organisations would normally engage consulting firms to perform process assessments [2]. However, process assessments are costly and their outcomes are often dictated by proprietary assessment models [3]. An alternative is to develop a software tool that organisations can use to self-assess their ITSM processes. The clear advantage of the tool is its utility in understanding process gaps to resolve before a formal assessment. We propose this approach as Software-mediated Process Assessment (SMPA): a semi-automatic approach where a software tool can facilitate data collection to determine process capabilities and provide improvement recommendations. Using software can result in more efficient process assessments and the SMPA tool can be aligned with the international standard for process assessment ISO/IEC 15504 [4] to address objectivity and transparency issues in assessments. The use of the standards provides justification for a non-proprietary and transparent assessment.

Several ITSM Process Assessment frameworks have been proposed: Tudor's ITSM Process Assessment (TIPA) provides an overall approach to conducting

J. Heidrich et al. (Eds.): PROFES 2013, LNCS 7983, pp. 330–333, 2013.
© Springer-Verlag Berlin Heidelberg 2013

process assessment based on ITIL and ISO/IEC 15504 [2]; Standard CMMI Appraisal Method for Process Improvement (SCAMPI) is based on the appraisal requirements for Capability Maturity Model Integration (CMMI) using CMMI-SVC [5]; and the ITIL Process Maturity Framework (PMF) works with ITIL processes to define maturity levels [6]. While most of the approaches rely on process-specific indicators that demonstrate objective evidence of process capabilities, the point of differentiation with our research is to develop a SMPA tool that provides a top-down approach where each IT service process is defined with a goal and then assessment is guided by explicit questions and metrics that are set to goal attainment. A top-down approach in ITSM process assessment ensures that the measurement is specific to the business context and objectives for process and service improvements in ITSM. This approach is guided by the Goal-Question-Metric (GQM) approach [7].

The research team comprises academics with expertise in ITIL, ISO/IEC 20000 and ISO/IEC 15504. The team also includes three partner organisations: **Assessment Portal** in using its software platform to develop the tool; and the Queensland Government ICT division (**CITEC**) and the Toowoomba Regional Council (**TRC**) in Queensland, Australia in providing sites to implement and evaluate the tool. After the research questions are stated, the methodology and the tool development are reported.

2   Research Questions

There are software tools available to support the activities of several ITSM processes. However, little is available to assist in a transparent process assessment. To address this problem, we propose the development of a SMPA tool using the international standards. The first research question (**RQ1**) explores: *to what extent does the use of international standards facilitate the development of a SMPA tool?* Past research has shown that new IT projects that alter existing practices can be problematic in implementation. The second research question (**RQ2**) asks: *what factors impact on the SMPA tool implementation?* Following from RQ2, the final research question (**RQ3**) is: *to what extent does the use of the SMPA tool facilitate CSI in ITSM?* If the tool is a proprietary design, it behaves as a black box as the rationale of analysis may be unknown. Hence, the advantage of ISO/IEC 15504 is the uniformity in the assessment.

3   Research Methodology

We use Design Science Research Methodology (DSRM) [8] to develop the tool. The project comprises four phases: **phase 1** (6 months) a structured literature review to research primary studies on ITSM process assessment; **phase 2** (9 months) researching the international standards and relevant frameworks to develop the SMPA tool; **phase 3** (4 months) tool demonstrated in the two case study organisations with a baseline ITSM process assessment; **phase 4** (14 months) tool evaluation with three checkpoint assessments to ascertain the utility of the SMPA tool and its impact on improvement. Fig. 1 shows the research approach with the DSRM phases mapped to the research questions in this project. The requirements for a transparent ITSM process

assessment and the technology features to address such requirements will be considered to develop the tool which will then be demonstrated in a case study research to
evaluate the utility of the tool and its effectiveness in process improvement.

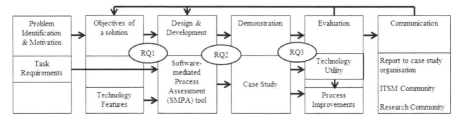

Fig. 1. Research Project Approach (adapted from [9])

4   Development of the Tool

We are currently in phase 2 with the focus on the SMPA tool development. The GQM
approach to software metrics defines a measurement model on three levels: conceptual (goal), operational (question) and quantitative (metric) [7]. While the GQM approach has been applied in the software industry for over two decades, use of this
approach to develop a SMPA tool in ITSM is novel. The process reference model
from ISO/IEC 20000 defines each process in terms of purpose and outcomes following the guidelines for process definition in ISO/IEC TR 24774. Attainment of the
process purpose by meeting the outcomes and thereby continually improving the
process capabilities defines the "goal" component of the SMPA tool.

The process assessment model for ITSM in ISO/IEC 15504-8 [10] provides a set of
base practices to fulfill the process outcomes and a set of generic practices for process
management, standardisation, quantitative measurement and innovation. In the context of a formal ISO/IEC 15504 assessment, these would be used as indicators to enable a formal evaluation of the process capabilities. In the context of this project, the
emphasis is on less formal assessment to provide information that can drive improvement of ITSM processes. These indicators are translated into a set of assessment
questions. The SMPA tool loads these questions and facilitates allocating them to the
respondents of three process roles in ITSM: process performers, process managers
and process interfaces. This defines the "question" component of the SMPA tool.

Finally the assessment questions are grouped to determine process capability levels
1-5 and every question is rated using the scale: 'Not', 'Partially', 'Largely', 'Fully'
and 'Not Applicable' as defined in ISO/IEC 15504. This rating is an opinion metric of
the ITSM process stakeholders. Rather than the assessment team making a subjective
choice of the indicator rating based on objective evidence, the SMPA tool has a "metric" component to collect and objectively measure experience feedback of the stakeholders directly. These metrics can be collectively used with the process metrics
defined by ITIL for process improvements leading to CSI in ITSM.

The industry partner provided the software platform for ITSM process assessment.
The online tool is developed using the Microsoft Azure® cloud platform with features

to automate online survey tracking and a facilitator console to manage the surveys for assessment. The tool also collects the response metrics to generate contextual recommendations for ITSM process improvement.

5   Conclusion

The existing guidelines for ITSM process assessment lack transparency and objectivity. We are developing a SMPA tool aligned with the international standards of ITSM and process assessment to overcome this problem. A collaborative effort between academic researchers and industry practitioners has facilitated the tool development. The design of the tool is currently being validated before its implementation. This will be followed by the evaluation of the tool at two organisations to demonstrate its utility and impact on process improvement. The SMPA tool is expected to provide a transparent ITSM process assessment so that process capabilities are aligned with improvement metrics consistently enabling benchmarking and service improvements.

References

1. ISO/IEC, ISO/IEC 20000-1:2011 – Information technology – Service management – Part 1: Service management system requirements 2011, International Organization for Standardization, Geneva, Switzerland (2011)
2. Barafort, B., Betry, V., Cortina, S., Picard, M., St-Jean, M., Renault, A., Valdès, O.: ITSM Process Assessment Supporting ITIL. Van Haren Publishing, Zaltbommel (2009); P.R.C.H. Tudor (ed.)
3. Fayad, M.E., Laitnen, M.: Process Assessment Considered Wasteful. Communications of the ACM 40(11), 125–128 (1997)
4. ISO/IEC, ISO/IEC 15504-2:2004 – Information Technology – Process Assessment– Part 2: Performing an Assessment 2004, International Organization for Standardization, Geneva, Switzerland (2004)
5. CMMI, CMMI® for Services, Version 1.3 2010. Software Engineering Institute, Carnegie Mellon University, MA, USA (2010)
6. MacDonald, I.: ITIL Process Assessment Framework 2010. The Co-operative Financial Services, Manchester (2010)
7. Basili, V.R., Caldiera, G., Rombach, H.D., van Solingen, R.: Goal Question Metric (GQM) Approach. In: Marciniak, J. (ed.) Encyclopedia of Software Engineering, vol. 1, pp. 578–583 (2002)
8. Hevner, A.R., March, S.T., Park, J., Ram, S.: Design Science in Information Systems Research. MIS Quarterly 28(1), 75–105 (2004)
9. Peffers, K., Tuunanen, T., Rothenberger, M.A., Chatterjee, S.: A Design Science Research Methodology for Information Systems Research. Journal of Management Information Systems 24(3), 45–77 (2007)
10. ISO/IEC, ISO/IEC TS 15504-8 Information technology - Process assessment - Part 8: An exemplar process assessment model for IT service management 2012, International Organization for Standardization, Geneva, Switzerland (2012)

Making Sense Out of a Jungle of JavaScript Frameworks

Towards a Practitioner-Friendly Comparative Analysis

Daniel Graziotin and Pekka Abrahamsson

Free University of Bozen-Bolzano, Italy
{daniel.graziotin,pekka.abrahamsson}@unibz.it

Abstract. The field of Web development is entering the HTML5 and CSS3 era and JavaScript is becoming increasingly influential. A large number of JavaScript frameworks have been recently promoted. Practitioners applying the latest technologies need to choose a suitable JavaScript framework (JSF) in order to abstract the frustrating and complicated coding steps and to provide a cross-browser compatibility. Apart from benchmark suites and recommendation from experts, there is little research helping practitioners to select the most suitable JSF to a given situation. The few proposals employ software metrics on the JSF, but practitioners are driven by different concerns when choosing a JSF. As an answer to the critical needs, this paper is a call for action. It proposes a research design towards a comparative analysis framework of JSF, which merges researcher needs and practitioner needs.

Keywords: Web Development, JavaScript Framework, Comparative Analysis.

1 Introduction

Technologies like HTML5, CSS3, and JavaScript (JS) are maturing in a way that it is possible to substitute entire Desktop applications with counterparts running in a Web browser. Innovation is certainly not stopping here. Many argue that it is necessary for the industry to follow the momentum. JS is the most popular programming language for the browser [5]. Although it is possible to write pure JS code while constructing websites and Web applications, this is typically avoided with a JavaScript Framework (JSF). A JSF should abstract the longest and complex operations, ensure cross-browser compatibility, and speed up program comprehension and software development.

As of today, according to Jster.net, thousands of JS libraries are available for different purposes. Examples include *jQuery*, *Backbone.js*, *YUI*. When developing a Web application it is necessary to choose which framework to apply [2] as soon as possible as it introduces bindings and constraints. Software developers face difficulties when evaluating a JSF. Specialized websites like StackOverflow.com are full of beginner's questions on the topic[1].

---

[1] For example, http://fur.ly/9fp8

J. Heidrich et al. (Eds.): PROFES 2013, LNCS 7983, pp. 334–337, 2013.

The focus of existing research is on the complexity and the quality of JS source-code (e.g. [2]). Software benchmarks lead on-line comparisons, to the point that Web browser vendors claim superior performance over the competitors by benchmarking performance on running JS code [4]. While benchmarks are able to measure different aspects of performance, their results may not be representative of real Web sites at all [4].

We note that practitioners seems interested in different aspects than those of academic research. For example, the Wikipedia page <http://en.wikipedia.org/wiki/Comparison_of_JavaScript_frameworks> compares 22 JSF without considering software metrics at all. Some of the criteria are the age of the latest release, the size of the JSF, the license, presence of features (e.g., Ajax, JSON Data Retrieval) and the browser support. Additionally, we note that the ability to obtain a JSF by expressing the concerns to be solved also seems useful for practitioners. Jster.net is an online catalog of JSF and libraries, where each project can be reached through semantic tags related to concerns (e.g., DOM traversing, Math Libraries, Routing, and UI Components).

It appears that the research interests in the academia are diverging from practitioners' interests. While this is not entirely uncommon, for this end, we call for action and propose a research design towards a comparative analysis framework of JSF. The resulting comparison framework will combine researcher's interests with the practitioner's interests in order to meet the best of the two worlds. We aim to expand an already proposed academic solution consisting of software metrics of JSF [2] with practitioner-related concerns.

2   Related Work

As far as we know, the literature consists in a single proposal. Gizas et al. [2] have attempted to compare six JavaScript Frameworks (JSF) using software metrics on the frameworks. They compare ExtJS, Dojo, jQuery, MooTools, Prototype, and YUI. They evaluate what they describe as the core version of each framework, namely DOM manipulation, selectors, Ajax functionalities, form elements, functions for event handling, and compatibility support. They test different aspects of quality, validation, and performance. The *quality* is expressed in terms of size metrics – i.e., statements, lines, comments, and related ratios, complexity metrics – i.e., branches, depth, McCabe's Cyclomatic Complexity, and maintainability metrics – i.e., Halstead metrics and Maintainability Index. The *validation* tests were performed by using the tools JavaScript Lint and Yasca. The *performance* tests were measurements of the execution time of the JSF with SlickSpeed Selectors test framework. The proposal is recent, in the form of a short paper.

3   Research Design

The proposal by Gizas, et al. [2] will be extended in two different measurement directions: one related to research and the other one to practitioners. (1) Their proposed metrics on code validation, quality, and performance will be employed on the JSF as they suggest, but also on the same Web application implemented with the different JSF. (2) Measurements related to practitioner concerns will emerge from in-field studies and interviews of developers. The GQM method [1] will be employed to find the most appropriate metrics to represent the practitioner concerns.

3.1   Pilot Study

We contacted four front-end Web developers to obtain their views on how to choose a JSF. The discussions were related to the criteria employed when choosing a new JSF or how a currently employed JSF was chosen. The preliminary results support the expected divergence between the proposed software metrics and the practitioner's criteria when selecting a JSF.

Three criteria were mentioned by all the participants: adequacy of the documentation, community participation, and "code less, do more" factor – i.e., the pragmatics of a JSF. Other emerged concerns are the maturity of the JSF and the frequency of the updates - i.e., its "freshness". How a JSF fulfills these concerns is subjectively perceived by inspecting the source code, code examples, and the documentation.

When asked about the metrics proposed by Gizas et al. [2], the respondents showed mild interest about measurements of performance and admitted having a poor understanding of the other metrics. We were recommended to perform measurements on the same software project implemented using different JSF instead of measuring the JSF alone. A suitable project for this end is TodoMVC [3]. It enables practitioners to study and compare MV* (Model-View-Anything) JSF through source-code inspection of the same TODO-list Web application, developed by experienced Web developers employing their favorite JSF. TodoMVC provides a rigorous set of requirements, HTML/CSS templates, coding style and other specifications[2]. In order to be accepted in the TodoMVC catalog, the applications are first reviewed by the project leaders and then by the open-source community.

The participants suggested some measurements that would be beneficial for them. For example, the ratio of answers over questions related to a JSF on StackOverflow is perceived as being representative of the community involvement while traditional measurements like the frequency of commits in the version control system of the JSF represents both the community participation and the freshness of the JSF.

3.2   Proposed Framework

A high level view of the comparison framework is represented in Figure 1. The current proposal was born after the analysis of the pilot study data. The framework is organized in two layers, one related to research and the other related to practitioners. The blue boxes are the categories of metrics proposed by Gizas et al. [2] while the orange boxes are the extensions suggested by this study.

Each JSF will be measured using measurements relevant for academia and practitioners. Empirical data coming from the corresponding TodoMVC project will enforce the theoretical claims (thus, the blue boxes are surrounded by orange borders).

---

[2]   Complete TodoMVC instructions and specifications: http://fur.ly/9fp7

In-field studies will improve the practitioner area of the framework. The GQM model will be employed to find the most appropriate metrics to represent the practitioner needs.

Fig. 1. Comparison Framework

4   Conclusion

We are entering a new era of Web Development, in which JavaScript (JS) is becoming more and more crucial for the Information Technology industry. So far, research interests have not been aimed at supporting the task of finding a suitable JavaScript framework (JSF) to improve the current state of Web development.

We set a call for action in this paper. We presented a research design towards a comparative analysis framework of JSF suitable for researchers and practitioners. The framework will extend a recent proposal to analyze JSF technically, using software metrics. These metrics will also be collected on the same software product produced using the different JSF. Empirical data from practitioners will be collected to understand and validate what are their needs when choosing a JSF. Therefore, research-related metrics will be complemented by practitioners-friendly metrics in a modern, updated database of JSF.

The resulting comparison framework will be a step forward in conciliating software engineering research and practitioners of software development. It will allow a quick selection of a JSF, thus saving time and resources of Web development firms.

References

1. Basili, V., Weiss, D.: A methodology for collecting valid software engineering data. IEEE Transactions on Software Engineering 10(6), 728–738 (1984)
2. Gizas, A.B., et al.: Comparative evaluation of javascript frameworks. In: Proceedings of the 21st International Conference Companion on World Wide Web, pp. 513–514 (2012)
3. Osmani, A.: Learning JavaScript Design Patterns. O'Reilly Media (2012)
4. Ratanaworabhan, P., et al.: JSMeter: Comparing the behavior of JavaScript benchmarks with real web applications. In: Proceedings of the 2010 USENIX Conference on Web Application Development, p. 3 (2010)
5. Yue, C., Wang, H.: Characterizing insecure javascript practices on the web. In: Proceedings of the 18th International Conference on World Wide Web - WWW 2009, p. 961. ACM Press, New York (2009)

Software Processes with BPMN: An Empirical Analysis

Andre L.N. Campos and Toacy Oliveira

Federal University of Rio de Janeiro, COPPE, Brasil
andrecampos@ufrj.br, toacy.oliveira@cos.ufrj.br

Abstract . BPMN 2.0 is a widely used notation to model a business process that has associated tools and techniques to facilitate process management, execution and monitoring. As a result using BPMN in the context of Software Development Process (SDP) can improve by leverage on the BPMN's infrastructure to improve SDP quality. This work presents an analysis of BPMN notation in modeling software processes.

Keywords: Process modeling, BPMN, Modeling notations, Software process, CMMI.

1   Introduction

Software development organizations need to continuously improve the quality of their products, while facing challenges such as the rapidly change in the technologies involved in building the software. To address these challenges organizations are effortlessly looking for ways to improve the software development process [1]. A common manner to foster comprehension is through modeling the process software. There are several process modeling languages that could be used to do software processes models. However, SPEM 2.0 (Software & Systems Process Engineering Meta-Model) [2] expected to become the dominant technology in this area, because it has broad tool support, like EPF Composer [3]. Despite expectations, the SPEM does not provide concepts or tools for modeling process behavior precisely. Consequently, SPEM fails to address process execution, optimization and simulation [4], which are important activities used in process analysis and improvement. This work presents a qualitative study about the use of the Business Process Modeling and Notation (BPMN) to represent a Software Development Process, because modeling is the first step in this path that starts at the understanding of the process and goes up to the implementation of this process. We utilize an empirical inquiry because the persons involved in process of modeling could play a role in the result [5].

2   Software Process

Much effort has been made in recent decades to make the process of software easy to understand and improve. All this effort has produced several standards, models and methods related to software process. For example, there are the ISO 9.000, MIL-STD-

J. Heidrich et al. (Eds.): PROFES 2013, LNCS 7983, pp. 338–341, 2013.

498, IEEE 1074, CMMI, Extreme Programming, Scrum, Adaptive Software Development, Crystal, OPEN, RUP, OOSP, and others standards or guides to good practices, which sometimes are called "software process". The software process of an organization is the standard model of the development process and software maintenance, including activities to be performed, the artifacts produced and consumed, and the actors involved. This model serves as a basic infrastructure that can be used in its original state or adapted to meet a given project [6]. So, first of all, we need to model the organization's software process properly, to understand it and improve it. Is BPMN notation suitable to do that?

3   BPMN

The Business Process Modeling and Notation (BPMN) is devoted to represent business processes in a graphical way so that end-users can understand processes' concepts such as flow of activities, used information and role allocation. Despite the primary objective of BPMN is to be understandable by humans, BPMN stands on a formal meta-model, allowing the development of an ecosystem of tools that support its adoption, and has a formal structure that supports processing by machine [7]. The objectivity, clarity and ease of understanding of BPMN notation, is probably the reason why BPMN has become one of the most widely used notations for modeling work processes [8] [9]. Moreover, BPMN notation is open, standardized and maintained by the OMG [10], which is the same organization that maintains SPEM. As result, likewise SPEM, BPMN has a graphical notation and an associated textual representation based on XML that is utilized to save the model. It is also important to mention that BPMN has built in extension mechanisms [11], wich allows to define additional modeling elements to improve BPMN's expressiveness.

4   Evaluation of BPMN in Software Process

We wanted to use a process simple to modeling, but minimally complete. Then we chose the OpenUP (Open Unified Process), because it is an Open Source initiative derived from the Unified Process (UP), minimalist, extensible, and can become a common denominator for software projects [12].

To form analysis from opinion we prepared a questionnaire with criteria defined by previous works in this area such as shown in [7]: 1) The notation had all necessary elements to represent software processes; 2) There was possible drill down processes by sub layers of representation; 3) The BPMN was enough to represent processes software. It is not necessary to improve that notation for this purpose; 4) It is possible to get good results in BPMN modelling without any training; 5) It is possible to get good results in BPMN modeling with just a little training; 6) Complex processes could be easily modeled with BPMN; 7) It is possible to represent software requirements linked to activities; 8) It is possible to represent adaptable processes; 9) It is possible to represent reusable processes. The answer for each question should be in a gradual manner: 1 - Strongly Disagree, 2 - Having to disagree, 3 - I tend to agree,

4 - I totally agree. Furthermore, we decided to analyze each model built, to verify a minimal quality in its construction. To help us in this hard work, we created a set of issues, as follows: Were at least all macro processes from OpenUP represented? Were at least 7 artifacts from OpenUP represented? Did the workflow in the models built makes sense? Was there a lack of representation of OpenUP objects? If yes, which object?

We conducted three case studies, two in the academic environment and one in the business environment. We call each one of these case studies a phase. The first phase involved five subjects from the academic setting, on Federal University of Rio de Janeiro. The second phase was conducted with ten subjects in a real environment at the Oswaldo Cruz Foundation, an important public health and research institution in Brazil. The third phase included nine subjects from the same institution in the first phase, but the subjects were different from the first phase.

5   Results

We evaluated each of the built models, to verify if the models were correct, or if they made sense as software processes. The result was YES for all issues, except for "There was lack of representation of OpenUP objects?" which we found two NO. We conclude that it was possible to model the process of software from OpenUP model using BPMN notation. Despite that conclusion, the process modeling expert assessed the models produced and compared these models to OpenUP, and he concluded that the models described properly the process OpenUP.

The questionnaire was responded based on a scale, as previously explained. The answers were grouped by issues. All subjects completed the questionnaire. We made a synthesis of the results by calculating the median of responses for each question. The median result per question help us to define the grades between 1.0 and 2.49 as NO, and results between 2.50 and 4 as YES. Whereas the scale goes from 1 to 4 instead of 0 to 4, the cutoff value was regarded as the average of the scale, namely 2.5. In questionnaire responded by subjects, we have three additional questions related to the capacity of representation of BPMN, which are questions 1, 2 and 3. For these questions we have a YES from all questions for first and third phases (case studies), and a NO for all questions in the second phase. Just to remember, the first and third phases were run with students, and the second phase was run in the business environment. From answers to questions 4, 5 6 we realize that to use the BPMN notation we must provide adequate training beforehand. The subjects answered the questions 7, 8 and 9 positively in most phases, which tells us that the BPMN notation has mechanisms to connect diagrams to each other, besides enabling the adaptation and reuse of processes.

6   Conclusion

This paper presented the fundamental concepts related to software process and evaluated qualitatively the possibility of modeling these processes with BPMN notation. If BPMN is suitable to modeling software processes, then it would allow bringing the benefits achieved by business areas of Business Process Management (BPM). For this, we conducted three case studies both with students and with practitioners. This paper presents indications that the BPMN notation is suitable for modeling software processes. As mentioned, the representation was well assessed. Responses indicated a trend of the groups agreeing that BMPN is suitable for modeling this type of process. Future studies may evaluate the impact of training in BPMN notation on the results of process modeling software. We could analyze the degree of progress reported by participants, compared to this work. Still dealing with the possibility of future work, this study realized the probable need to extend the BPMN notation for use in the full process modeling software. Studies have been conducted in this direction [11], but further studies will explore the issue further.

References

[1] Magdaleno, A.M., Werner, C.M.L., Araujo, R.M.: Reconciling software developmento models: a quasi-systematic review. The Journal of Systems and Software (2011)
[2] OMG: Software Process Engineering Metamodel (SPEM) 2.0 Specification (2008)
[3] E. Foundation: Eclipse Process Framework Project (EPF) (2013),
    http://www.eclipse.org/epf (acesso em February 2013)
[4] Bendraou, R., Combemale, B., Crégut, X., Gervais, M.P.: Definition of an eXecutable SPEM 2.0. IEEE Computrer Society, Nagoya (2007)
[5] Easterbrook, S., Singer, J., Storey, M.-A., Damian, D.: Selecting Empirical Methods for Software Engineering Research. In: Guide to Advanced Emprirical Software Engineering, pp. 285–311. Springer, London (2008)
[6] Araujo, R., Cappelli, C., Gomes Jr., A., Pereira, M., Iendrike, H.S., Ielpo, D., Tovar, J.A.: A definição de processos de software sob ponto de vista da gestão de processos de negócio (2004)
[7] Campos, A.L.N., Oliveria, T.C.: Modeling work processes and software development: Notation and tool. In: ICEIS 2011 - Proceedings of the 13th International Conference on Enterprise Information Systems 3 ISAS, China, pp. 337–343 (2011)
[8] van der Aalst, W.M.P.: Process mining - discovery, conformance and enhancement of business processes. Springer (2011)
[9] Chinosi, M., Trombetta, A.: BPMN: An introduction to the standard. Computer Standards & Interfaces, 124–134 (2011)
[10] Object Management Group, Business Process Model and Notation (BPMN) (2010)
[11] Pillat, R.M., Oliveira, T.C., Lattario, F.: Introducing Software Process Tailoring to BPMN: BPMNt. In: Proceedings of 7th International Conference on Software and System Process (2012)
[12] Bertrand, C., Fuhrman, C.P.: Towards defining software development processes in DO-178B with OpenUP. In: Electrical and Computer Engineering, pp. 851–854 (2008)

A Generalized Software Reliability Model Considering Uncertainty and Dynamics in Development

Kiyoshi Honda, Hironori Washizaki, and Yoshiaki Fukazawa

Waseda University, 3-4-1, Okubo, Shinjuku-ku, Tokyo, 169-8555 Japan
khonda@ruri.waseda.jp, {washizaki,fukazawa}@waseda.jp

Abstract. Development environments have changed drastically in recent years. The development periods are shorter than ever and the number of team has increased. These changes have led to difficulties in controlling the development activities and predicting the end of developments. In order to assess recent software developments, we propose a generalized software reliability model based on a stochastic process, and simulate developments that include uncertainties and dynamics, such as unpredictable requirements changes, shortening of the development period, and decrease in the number of members. We also compare our simulation results to those of other software reliability models. Using the values of uncertainties and dynamics obtained from our model, we can evaluate the developments in a quantitative manner.

Keywords: Software Reliability Model, Prediction of bugs, Stochastic Process.

1 Introduction

The logistic curve and Gompertz curve[1] are well-known software reliability growth curves. However, these curves cannot account for the dynamics of software development. Developments are affected by various elements of the development environment, such as the skills of the development team and changing requirements. Examples of the types of software reliability models include Times Between Failures Models and Failure Count Models.[2] We use the Failure Count Model, which is based on counting failures and using probability methods. This type of models is represented by the Goel-Okumoto NHPP Model and the Musa Execution Time Model. Most models of this type cannot account for the dynamics of development, such as drastic changes in the members of a development team or significant reductions of the development time. However, our approach can handle these dynamic elements and simulate developments more accurately.

Recent studies by Tamura[3], Yamada[4] and Zhang[5] have attempted to describe the dynamics of developments using stochastic differential equations. These studies only use linear stochastic differential equations, but our approach uses non-linear stochastic differential equations, leading to more elaborate equations that can model situations more realistically. Our model can quantify uncertainties that are influenced by random factors such as the skills of teams

J. Heidrich et al. (Eds.): PROFES 2013, LNCS 7983, pp. 342–346, 2013.

and development environments. The quantification of uncertainties is important for predicting the end of developments more accurately and for optimizing the development teams or environments.

2   Generalized Software Reliability Model

For our software reliability model, we extend a non-linear differential equation that describes fault content as a logistic curve to an Ito type stochastic differential equation. We start with the following equation, which is called the logistic differential equation.

$$\frac{dN(t)}{dt} = N(t)(a + bN(t)) \tag{1}$$

The $N(t)$ is the number of detected faults at t, a defines the growth rate and the b is the carrying capacity[2].

We extend equation (1) to a stochastic differential equation because actual developments do not correctly obey equation (1) due to numerous uncertainties and dynamic changes. We consider such dynamic elements to be time-dependent and to contain uncertainty, and express them using a. The time-dependence of a can be used to describe situations such as skill improvements of development members and increases of growth rate. The uncertainty of a can describe parameters such as the variability of development members. We analyze the growth of software with a focus on the test phase by simulating the number of tested cases. We assume software development to have the following properties.

1. The total number of bugs is constant.
2. The number of bugs that can be found is variable depending on time.
3. The number of bugs that can be found contains uncertainty, which can be simulated with Gaussian white noise.

Considering these properties, we extend equation (1) to an Ito type stochastic differential equation with $a(t) = \alpha(t) + \sigma dw(t)$ as shown below.

$$dN(t) = (\alpha(t) + \sigma^2/2 + \beta N(t))N(t)dt + \gamma(t) \tag{2}$$

$N(t)$ is the number of tested cases at t, $\alpha(t) + \sigma^2/2 + \sigma dw(t)$ is the differential of the number of tested cases per unit time, $\gamma(t) = N(t)\sigma dw(t)$ is the uncertainty term, σ is the dispersion, β is the carrying capacity term which is non-linear. This equation has two significant terms, α and dw; α affects the end point of development, and dw affects the growth curve through uncertainties, especially $dw(t)$ relates $N(t)$, this means uncertainties depend on the number of tested cases. We compare the $\gamma(t) = N(t)\sigma dw(t)$ with other two types, $\gamma(t) = \sigma dw(t)$, not related with $N(t)$, and $\gamma(t) = 1/N(t)\sigma dw(t)$, related with inverse of $N(t)$. We vary these two terms, $\alpha(t)$ and the coefficient of $dw(t)$, and simulate models using equation (2). We summarize the types of $\alpha(t)$ and of the coefficient of $dw(t)$ and the corresponding situations in Table 1. Using our model, it is necessary to choose the types in Table 1 and calculate the parameters by using past data.

Table 1. $\alpha(t)$ is the number of tested cases per unit time. $dw(t)$ is the uncertainty term.

	$\gamma(t) = N(t)\sigma dw(t)$	$\gamma(t) = \sigma dw(t)$	$\gamma(t) = 1/N(t)\sigma dw(t)$
$\alpha_1(t) = a_1(\text{const.})$	The number of tested cases per unit time is constant, and the uncertainty increase near to the end. This model is similar to a logistic curve. (**Model 1**)	The number of tested cases per unit time is constant, and the uncertainty is constant at any given time.	The number of tested cases per unit time is constant, and the uncertainty is greater at the start of the project than at the end (e.g. the team matures over time).
$\alpha_2(t) = a_2(t < t_1)$ $\alpha_2(t) = a_3(t \geq t_1)$	The number of tested cases per unit time changes at t_1, and the uncertainty increases near to the end (e.g. new members join the project at time t_1). (**Model 2**)	The number of tested cases per unit time changes at t_1, and the uncertainty is constant at any given time.	The number of tested cases per unit time changes at t_1, and the uncertainty is greater at the start of the project than at the end.
$\alpha_3(t) \propto t$	Both the number of tested cases per unit time and the uncertainty increase near to the end (e.g. increasing manpower with time). (**Model 3**)	The number of tested cases per unit time increases, and the uncertainty is constant at any given time.	The number of tested cases per unit time increases, and the uncertainty is greater at the start of project than at the end.

3   Simulation and Discussion

Three of the cases in Table 1 are modeled and plotted in Fig. 1. The difference between these three models is the parameter $\alpha(t)$. Based on **Model 1**, we defined that $a_2 = a_1$, $a_3 = 2a_1$ and $t_1 = t_{max}/2$ in **Model 2**, and $\alpha_3(t) = a_1 t$ in **Model 3**. The situation corresponding to **Model 2** is that at time t_1 the number of members of the development team doubles. The situation corresponding to **Model 3** is that the members' skills improve over time, effectively doubling the manpower by the time t_{max}. The purpose of the simulations is to confirm that our approach can assess software reliability under dynamic changes and uncertainties in development, and that it can adapt to the three models above and produce appropriate results. We use a Monte Carlo method to examine these models.

In **Model 1**, the number of tested cases per unit time is constant, and the uncertainty increases near to the end. As we predicted, the simulation result for **Model 1** fits the logistic curve. This result cannot be obtained simply by using other stochastic models that do not include a non-linear term.

In **Model 2**, the number of tested cases per unit time changes at t_1, and the uncertainty increases near to the end. In agreement with our predictions, the resulting curve sharply rises at t_1 and then converges quickly. Other models cannot describe such a time-dependent curve involving a non-linear term.

In **Model 3**, both the number of tested cases per unit time and the uncertainty increase near to the end. We expected the resulting curve to show a steeper increase than **Model 1**, but that was not the case. The reason for this is that the non-linear term pulls the curve down because of the increasing growth rate.

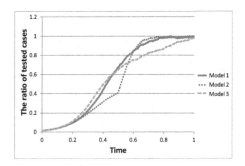

Fig. 1. The ratio of the total number of tested cases at time t to the total number of tested cases for the entire project is plotted. The x-axis represents time in arbitrary units, where 1 corresponds to t_{max} and 0.5 to t_1. In **Model 1**, the number of tested cases per unit time is constant. In **Model 2**, the number of tested cases per unit time changes at t_1. In **Model 3**, the number of tested cases per unit time increases.

4   Conclusion and Feature Work

Using our model, we were able to simulate developments containing uncertainties and dynamic elements. We obtained the time-dependent logistic curve and growth curve, which was not possible using other models. Our model can be used to predict the end of projects where team members drastically change during development.

For future work, we will propose ways to quantitatively evaluate teams or team members taking uncertainties into account, and to optimize the teams to suit particular projects using our model. By using the past data, we can calculate the uncertainties of our model and predict the end of the project.

References

1. Yamada, S., et al.: S-Shaped Reliability Growth Modeling for Software Error Detection. IEEE Transactions on Reliability R-32(5), 475–484 (1983)
2. Goel, A.: Software Reliability Models: Assumptions, Limitations, and Applicability. IEEE TOSE SE-11(12) (1985)

3. Tamura, Y., et al.: A exible stochastic differential equation model in distributed development environment. EJOR 168, 143–152 (2006)
4. Yamada, S., et al.: Software Reliability Measurement and Assessment with Stochastic Differential Equations. IEICE TFECCS E77-A(1), 109–116 (1994)
5. Zhang, N., et al.: A Stochastic Software Reliability Growth Model with Learning and Change-point. In: CDC (2010)

Orienting High Software Team Performance: Dimensions for Aligned Excellence

Petri Kettunen

University of Helsinki
Department of Computer Science
P.O. Box 68, 00014 University of Helsinki, Finland
petri.kettunen@cs.helsinki.fi

Abstract. Modern software development teams are by nature striving for high performance. However, it is not often straightforward to understand, what excellent performance means for the specific team, and how to achieve that in the particular context. This work addresses those objectives by proposing a holistic performance analysis frame supported by a provisional team self-monitoring instrument. The frame guides software development organizations to position and consequently improve their teams in multiple key dimensions (business, operational, growth). The cases demonstrate how the proposed frame and instrument could facilitate such performance analysis of different teams in practice.

Keywords: software teams, new product development, process improvement, organizational design, performance management.

1 Introduction

High-performing teamwork has been investigated in many fields over the years. In particular, the success factors of new product development (NPD) teams are in general relatively well known. However, the specific performance aims and concerns of modern software development teams are essentially less understood in particular in larger scales. Such an understanding would help organizations to steer their teams more systematically in total. This paper approaches those issues by proposing a holistic performance steering frame supported by provisional instrumentation for software teams. The impacts are twofold: Software development organizations can gauge the teams with it towards their strategic performance excellence, and software teams themselves may utilize it for their own performance management accordingly.

2 High-Performing Software Teams

Industrial-strength software product development is almost always done in teams, even in globally virtual set-ups. In general, it is not reasonable to attempt to define (high) performance of software teams without taking into account the context. In all, the domain of the software (products) sets the main performance criteria.

J. Heidrich et al. (Eds.): PROFES 2013, LNCS 7983, pp. 347–350, 2013.

In general, there is no one universal measure of software team performance. Typically software team performance is associated with productivity [1]. However, software development teams have usually multiple stakeholders – including the team members themselves – and consequently multiple different dimensions of performance. Different teams may have different targets even in same organizations. Multivariate measures are thus usually more applicable. Prior literature has described many such possible software team performance measures [2]. The measurement systems can be developed based on existing general-purpose frameworks to begin with [3].

There is no universal recipe for creating and improving high-performing software teams. In addition to the context, no two teams are in practice equal inside since teams consist of individual persons with different skills, competencies, and personalities [4]. In practice there are usually many ways to achieve and affect the (high) performance in software teams [5]. At the software team level, the Team Software Process (TSP) is one of the most well-established development approaches.

3   Framework for Orienting

Following the related work in Sect. 2, software team performance should be seen in a multidimensional space. Table 1 charts such a conceptual dimensioning grid. The reasoning for choosing those dimensions is to cover a wider range than basic software engineering by incorporating business and organizational traits in particular from NPD and Lean. The Growth dimension captures longer-term capability development.

Table 1. Dimensioning software team performance

DIMENSION	Key Field / Discipline	Focus Areas
Business Excellence	Business Competence	customer value; outputs meeting / exceeding standards and expectations; delivering (ever-improving) value
Operational Excellence	Software Engineering	value stream, flow, pull; developmental and production efficiencies; robustness
Growth	Organizational Concepts	organizational and personal learning, experiences; assets, capital (intellectual); foresight

In order to operationalize the approach proposed above, we can utilize our earlier investigations of analyzing high-performing software teams with a self-assessment Monitor instrument [6]. By selecting and combining a distinct subset of the Monitor elements, we can produce indicative performance orientation views of software development teams following the frame in Table 1. Table 2 presents such a view of the Monitor question items. The rationale column explains how the items address the focus areas in each dimension plotted in Table 1.

The basic configuration devised here can be specialized further based on the organizational context and business model aims. The framework can then be linked to continuous organizational development by selecting current improvement traits in Table 1. Furthermore, the software development process can be tailored accordingly.

Table 2. Software team performance Monitor configuration (partial)

ITEM	Rationale
Business Excellence	
How do you appraise the following team outcomes and impacts? • *Getting the business benefits (value)*	The value creation and capture drives the software development. The business mindset is incorporated to the software teams.
Operational Excellence	
How important are the following for your team? • *Getting the products done well (effective and disciplined delivery)*	The software production is results-driven. The activities are aligned towards the delivery targets.
Growth	
How do you rate the following aspects from your point of view? • *We have a clear, compelling direction that energizes, orients the attention, and engages our full talents.*	Finding (the) most significant and meaningful problems and opportunities to be solved with software is emphasized.

4   Case Exhibits

The Monitor tool has been utilized earlier in various other case studies to survey software teams for high performance [6]. We can now revisit that raw data to appraise the new conceptual frame proposed here by reviewing the data with the configuration defined in Table 2. Table 3 presents such an excerpt of the Monitor data of three case teams. They applied agile-oriented development models, but the organizational contexts were dissimilar. Note that some respondents skipped some questions.

Table 3. Business Excellence dimension performance perceptions (partial)

How do you appraise the following team outcomes and impacts?	Key	Important	Relative	Some little	Little	n/a
Getting the business benefits (value)						
Student team (customer-driven)	0	0	3	1	0	0
Industrial R&D team (B2B)	0	2	1	1	0	0
Industrial (IT) PM team (internal)	5	4	1	0	0	0

In essence, the Monitor views tabulated in Table 3 exhibits, how the case software teams perceived their current performance space with respect to Table 1. We can now reflect their views with respect to Table 2 like follows: The business perspective is by nature less significant for the student team. The industrial R&D team working on system components may not see their role clearly in the total value constellation. The industrial IT team serves the business more directly. As an example of a consequent improvement action, the industrial R&D team could be engaged more closely to their system product business management. In a similar way, more constructive analysis can be done by discussing together with the teams based on their detailed contextual and situational information.

5   Discussion

The aim of this investigation is to build systemic understanding of the key dimensions of high-performing teams with the aid of probing and catalytic questions. The rationale is not to replace existing models but to probe a wide range of key performance areas in a lightweight way to trigger potential team performance improvement actions like illustrated in the case exhibits. The key advantage and implication here is to guide organizations to see their software team performance in their overall product development performance constellation. Each company should continuously manage and develop the performance portfolio of their teams accordingly as a socio-technical system, including relevant team distribution and cultural factors while (re)organizing. Furthermore, team members should steer their personal performance in alignment.

A limitation is that we profile how the team perceives its performance orientation, but we do not measure how the team is in its performance. It must be measured otherwise. Consequent improvement actions must also be devised. That would also provide more validating evidence of actual longer-term benefits of the proposed model.

6   Conclusion

In this paper, we have proposed a performance orientation framework with provisional instrumentation support for high-performing software teams. The performance frame aims to guide software development organizations to position and consequently improve their teams in those key dimensions towards comprehensive excellence. We encourage software organizations to engage their teams to such orienting discussions.

Acknowledgements. This work was supported by the Finnish National Technology Agency TEKES (SCABO project no. 40498/10).

References

1. Petersen, K.: Measuring and predicting software productivity: A systematic map and review. Information and Software Technology 53, 317–343 (2011)
2. Kasunic, M.: A Data Specification for Software Project Performance Measures: Results of a Collaboration on Performance Measurement. Technical report TR-012, CMU/SEI (2008)
3. Staron, M., Meding, W., Karlsson, G.: Developing measurement systems: an industrial case study. J. Softw. Maint. Evol.: Res. Pract. 23, 89–107 (2010)
4. Lu, Y., Xiang, C., Wang, B., Wang, X.: What affects information systems development team performance? An exploratory study from the perspective of combined socio-technical theory and coordination theory. Computers in Human Behavior 27, 811–822 (2011)
5. Sawyer, S.: Software Development Teams. Communications of the ACM 47(12), 95–99 (2004)
6. Kettunen, P., Moilanen, S.: Sensing High-Performing Software Teams: Proposal of an Instrument for Self-monitoring. In: Wohlin, C. (ed.) XP 2012. LNBIP, vol. 111, pp. 77–92. Springer, Heidelberg (2012)

An Experience Report: Trial Measurement of Process Independency between Infrastructure Construction and Software Development

Noriko Hanakawa[1] and Masaki Obana[2]

[1] Hannan University
[2] Nara Institute of Science and Technology
5-4-33, Amami-Higasi, Matsubara, Osaka, 580-8502
Japan
hanakawa@hannan-u.ac.jp

Abstract. Recently, large-scale computer system including software and hardware becomes complicated more and more. Software is not only application software but also middleware like database, web server, and file server. Software and hardware are deeply influences each other. Relationship between software and infrastructure influences the whole system quality. Therefore, we propose Process independency. Process independency presents strength of relationship between software development process and infrastructure construction process. Process independency was applied to two practical projects. As a result, we confirmed that process independency may be related with software faults caused by infrastructure problems.

Keywords: process independency, software quality, infrastructure quality, software faults caused by infrastructure, communication.

1 Introduction

Recently, large-scale computer system including software and hardware becomes complicated more and more. Software is not only application software but also middleware like database, web server, and file server. In addition hardware is not only server computers but also various type client computers such as smartphone, mobile terminal, and various network equipment such as router, and access point, and switching hub. Computer system troubles are also complicated more and more. Engineers have to find causes of troubles of the computer system with high knowledge and effort. Therefore, we propose process independency between infrastructure construction process and software development process. A basic idea is based on separation of two processes; software development process and infrastructure construction process. If the two processes independently execute without communication such as discussions and meetings, the processes independency is high. If process independency is high, software development is not influenced by infrastructure construction process. Independency of processes between software development process and infrastructure construction process is measured by communication such as discussion in meeting.

On the other hand, various techniques for design infrastructure or system architecture have been proposed. Clements et al. proposed an advanced design method for

J. Heidrich et al. (Eds.): PROFES 2013, LNCS 7983, pp. 351–354, 2013.
© Springer-Verlag Berlin Heidelberg 2013

infrastructure named ATAM (Architecture Tradeoff Analysis Method) [2]. Hasegawa et al. proposed an infrastructure design method for quickly changing technology [3]. A feature of the design method is iterative design process. These design methods are discussed only infrastructure design and technologies. We focus on relationship between software process and infrastructure process. Research viewpoints are different. Some researches deal with infrastructure as service. An infrastructure design method of cloud computing service has been proposed [4]. The design method is devised, whereby numbers of servers, routers and communication bandwidth can be calculated through considering both infrastructure costs and business losses incurred by service level agreement violations. Touzi et al. proposed an architecture design for collaborative services in different organizations [5]. The method is based on a collaborative architecture according to Model-Driven Architecture (MDA) principles. These infrastructure design methods include considerations or trade-offing of various services. Services generally include not only software but also hardware (infrastructure). Therefore, a service regards as a package of software and hardware in these researches. In our research, we regard software development and infrastructure construction as different works. Software engineers and infrastructure engineers independently work in separated schedule and processes. Strength of relations of software development and the infrastructure development is our originality.

In this paper, at first, we propose Process independency, after that, we measure values of Process independency in practical projects. Then, we discuss usefulness of Process independency.

2   Process Independency

Projects of large-scale computer system including software and hardware have two main processes; software development process and infrastructure construction process. The two processes are different because of different targets, and different engineers. Software development process normally includes analysis work, outline design work, detail design

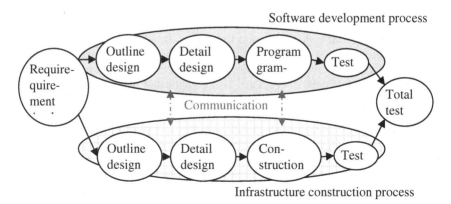

Fig. 1. A basic idea of process independency

work, programming work, test work, total test work. Infrastructure construction process also includes analysis work, outline design work, detail design work, construction work, test work, total test work (See Figure 1)[1]. Our basic idea is that communication is measured as process independency. Communication means interaction between software development process and infrastructure construction process. When the communication is less, process independency is high. When the communication is much, the process independency is low. If the communication is less (process independency is high), the two processes are not influenced each other. Therefore, the two processes smoothly execute without disturbance from other process. In constant, if communication is much (process independency is low), the process does not smoothly execute with disturbance from other process. The disturbance means discussions for influences, revision of design, and re-programming and re-setting.

The proposed process independency is as follow;

$$\text{Process independency} = \text{COM/PARALLEL} + \text{FA} \tag{1}$$

COM: the number of communication topic between software development process and infrastructure construction process during independent execution. If a value of COM is small, process independency is high.

FA: the number of software faults caused by infrastructure and the number of infrastructure faults caused by software in total test phase. If a value of FA is small, process independency is high.

PARALLEL: a ratio of independent execution period between software development and infrastructure construction to a whole project period. If a value of PARALLEL is 1, software development is completely independent from infrastructure construction, that is, process independency is high.

3   Application of Process Independency

Values of Process independency are measured in two finished projects; Project A and Project B. The three elements; COM, FA, and PARALLEL are shown Figure 2. The values of Process independency are shown Figure 3. The values of PARALLEL of the projects are extracted from master workflow management tables. The values of PARALLEL of project A and project B are almost same. Parallel development periods (See Fig.2) are 57% - 59%. Next, values of FA were extracted from trouble management tables of project A and project B. The trouble tables include all kinds of troubles such as software bugs, infrastructure troubles, specification errors, and pending problems in all phases. For FA, we counted troubles that occurred in total test phase (See Fig.1). The value of FA of project A is one, the value of FA of project B is two. Both values of FA are very low. In addition, the values of COM were extracted from meeting records from the outline design phase to the test phase (See Fig.1). The meetings were independently held in software development process or infrastructure construction process. Basically, engineers are different between software development and infrastructure construction. Therefore, meetings were separately held in each process. In meetings for software, we counted topics that are discussed infrastructure. COM of Project A is 9, COM of Project B is 11. As a result, a value of

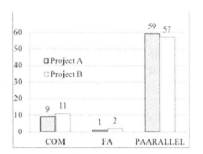

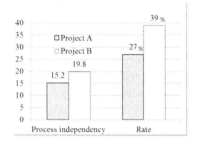

Fig. 2. Values of the three metrics of the two projects

Fig. 3. Comparison between Rate and Process independency

Process independency of Project A is 15.2, a value of Process independency of Project B is 19.8. Project B is better than Project A in viewpoint of Process independency.

In addition, Figure 3 also shows Rate. The values of Rate are calculated as follow;

Rate = Num. software faults caused by infrastructure problems/ Num. of all faults   (2)

A value of Rate of Project A is smaller than a value of Rate of Project B. Because data is only two projects, we are not able to be clear the relationship between Rate and Process independency. However, at least, in the two projects, Process independency between the two projects is similar to Rate between the two projects.

4   Summary

We proposed Process independency for software development process and infrastructure construction process. Process independency was applied to two projects. As a result, the values of Process independency are similar to rate value of software fault caused by infra problem. In future, process independency will be applied to many projects. Relationships between values of process independency and software faults caused by infrastructure problems will be correctly clarified. The metric of process independency will be refined.

References

1. ISO 9000 Quality Systems Handbook - updated for the ISO 9001:2008 standard
2. Clements, P., Kazman, R., Klein, M.: Evaluating a Software Architecture. Addison Wesley (2002) ISBN 0321154959
3. Hasegawa, M., Ishida, E., Ogawa, H.: The establishment of the method for designing infrastructure to cope with changes quickly. IBM Provision (50), 68–75 (2006)
4. Shi, H., Zhan, Z.: An optimal infrastructure design method of cloud computing services from the BDIM perspective. In: Asia-Pacific Conference on Computational Intelligence and Industrial Applications, PACIIA 2009, November 28-29, vol. 1, pp. 393–396 (2009)
5. Touzi, J., Benaben, F., Pingaud, H., Lorré, J.P.: A model-driven approach for collaborative service-oriented architecture design. International Journal of Production Economics 121(1), 5–20 (2009)

How to Configure SE Development Processes Context-Specifically?

Philipp Diebold

Fraunhofer Institute for Experimental Software Engineering,
Fraunhofer-Platz 1, 67663 Kaiserslautern, Germany
philipp.diebold@iese.fraunhofer.de

Abstract. In software engineering there is no silver bullet available for software processes. Instead many technologies can be used in the development and it is difficult to find the best for specific needs. It is necessary to distinguish among software projects and specific aspects such as project-specific development processes need to be addressed individually. To address this, a framework for project-specific process configuration is presented. It provides technology ranking, selection, and combination as well as process configuration. A preliminary evaluation of the framework was conducted.

Keywords: process config., technology selection, technology combination.

1 Introduction

The domain of software engineering (SE) has advanced rapidly over the last decades. Today, software is a part of every domain, such as automotive or health care [1]. To address their requirements, a large number of different technologies have evolved. Some address the whole development process whereas others address a small aspect. Each technology is assumed to have a specific impact on product quality, costs, or schedule. In many domains, aspects of quality are becoming important key performance indicators along with costs and schedule [2].

Complicating the situation, "there is no one-size-fits all [...] silver bullet" [3] available in SE. This implies that it is almost impossible to find a technology that supports all required elements of individual software projects. Thus, the combination of appropriate technologies to be used for a project is a challenging task.

Some technologies fit better for specific projects than others. This leads to the problem of finding most appropriate project-specific technologies. This choice is difficult because of different selection criteria, e.g. quality aspects. All aspects have to be considered when configuring a best-fit development process. This complex task of selecting the technologies is often applied manually by experts.

To solve this and the technology transfer problem [4], we propose a means for supporting the selection of well-suited technologies for configuring a context-specific process: the Process Configuration Framework. It focuses on combining the most appropriate project-specific technologies in order to configure well-suited processes.

J. Heidrich et al. (Eds.): PROFES 2013, LNCS 7983, pp. 355–358, 2013.

2   Background and Related Work

For the framework described in this paper, a generic technology categorization schema is needed because it covers technologies from all life-cycle phases.

In the literature, we found a huge number of existing schemas, which overlap or have merged over time. The technology schema development started in the late 1980s with [5] and the framework for software reuse. This was refined twice and enlarged to encompass the experience factory approach in [6]. Simultaneously with this approach, the SEI published [7], which provides a catalogue of around 60 technologies. The experience factory approach resulted in several publications. The SEI evolved contrary and was used first in [8]. This publication merged both lines into one schema the first time. The schema predating of our research is [2] which merge most other schemas, therefore we adapted it for our needs.

3   Process Configuration Framework

The Process Configuration Framework (PCF) presented in this paper is a static approach based on the five SE phases. It is divided into these stages:

Prerequisite	-	Technology Categorization
Stage I	-	Technology Ranking
Stage II	-	Technology Combination
Stage III	-	Process Configuration

The *Technology Categorization* is the prerequisite of the framework because it provides a repository and a schema including technology, context and impact model, which are adapted from [2]. The technology model contains the information about technologies. The context model includes details about where the technology has been applied and the impact model includes the context-dependent impact. Each technology can be connected with an arbitrary number of context-impact tuples. More detailed information regarding the three models can be found in [10].

This *Technology Ranking* stage deals with the ranking of all technologies. Therefore, it requires the repository with the schema, because the ranking is based on the attributes. The process of ranking all the technologies could be done in parallel because of their independence. Nonetheless, the individual ranking has a specific order. This results in the following steps:

1. Technology ranking based on *Application Domain*, *Project*, *Impact on Quality of Product*, *Impact on Development Costs*, and *Impact on Development Schedule*
2. Technology ranking based on *Environment*
3. Technology ranking based on parts of *Static Context*

Before explaining the three steps, we need to introduce the ranking of the three steps. Our approach works with a ranking value for each technology-context-impact triple because one technology might have several contexts and impacts. Each value is based on a percentage interval scale, initialized with zero and incrementally increased.

The first step uses the information, which can be selected or entered by the users directly. Selection inputs are related to attributes within a specific range, entered inputs to attributes with a numeric value. Then the ranking is performed based on different attributes of the environment element, the selection of single-value attributes and multi-value attributes. The last step is very similar to the previous one because there is again a selection of static context attributes, the training, qualification, and experience attributes.

The *Technology Combination* stage of the framework deals with the combination of the technologies over the different SE phases and consists of these steps:

---

4. Creation of all Technology Chains
5. Technology Chain restriction based on *Preset Technologies, Interdependencies,* and *existing SE Objects*
6. Technology Chain ranking based on *Static Context*
7. Technology Chain ranking based on *Dynamic Context*
8. Extending the Technology Chain with Quality Assurance (QA) Technologies

---

In the first step, all Technology Chains are created based on the SE phases assigned to the technologies. Even if this results in a huge number, this is no issue because the chains do not differ among projects and can be calculated statically. Additionally, many combinations will be eliminated in the next step. The restriction step uses three attributes for decreasing the number of chains. The Preset Technologies keeps Technology Chains which use the specified technologies. The next restriction checks all technologies in a chain in terms of negative interdependencies. Last, we reduce the chains by using the existing SE object. The Technology Chain ranking also uses a percentage value composed of the technology ranking values and a combination value, which is calculated in the next two steps. First, the ranking is performed based on the Static Context element, mainly the interface matching. Then, dynamic aspect increases the combination value. In the last step, it is possible for the user to extend the standard Technology Chain with QA technologies for each phase.

This *Process Configuration* stage of the framework deals with the configuration of the process and is based on the following steps:

---

9.   Using the generic Process Component Diagram (PCD)
10. Extending the PCD by new components
11. Instantiating the PCD with the Technology Chain
12. Defining the corresponding process patterns

The first two steps are generic as they form the PCD, which models the SE lifecycle by using ports that provide the input and output documents. The process components of the PCD are instantiated by the technologies of the chain. The last step of the process configuration provides the SPEM process patterns. These can then be plugged together to build an individual process for each software project.

4   Summary and Conclusions

Since most software projects differ from each other and require project-specific aspects, the presented PCF addresses this problem by building a project-specific process based upon appropriate technologies. It is thus important to not only well-known technologies. The framework presented uses a generic technology schema, which allows better understanding and facilitates combination. Moreover, the PCF automatically performs technology ranking, selection, and combination, allowing project managers to see which technologies best fit their needs. It transfers the technology combination to a specific process covering the project-specific needs. In the initially case study [10] the results of four domain experts were compared with the PCF results. They indicate that experts select similar technologies as the PCF provides.

In addition, there are other usage scenarios for the framework, such as identifying problems in the current processes, because of worse technology interfaces. Future work aspects will focus on improving the PCF, finding scenarios for its use and performing a more sound evaluation.

Acknowledgments. This paper is based on research being carried out in the ARAMiS project (BMBF O1IS11035Ü), funded by the German Ministry of Education and Research.

References

1. Birk, A.: Modelling the application domains of software engineering technologies. In: 12th IEEE International Conference on Automotive Software Engineering, pp. 291–292. IEEE, Incline Village (1997)
2. Jedlitschka, A.: An Empirical Model of Software Managers' Information Needs for Software Engineering Technology Selection. Fraunhofer IRB Verlag, Stuttgart (2009)
3. Fraser, S., Mancl, D.: No Silver Bullet: Software Engineering Reloaded. IEEE Software 1, 91–94 (2008)
4. Redwine, S.T., Riddle, W.E.: Software Technology Maturation. In: 8th International Conference on Software Engineering, pp. 189–200. IEEE Computer Soc. Press, Los Alamitos (1985)
5. Basili, V., Rombach, H.-D.: Towards A Comprehensive Framework for Reuse: A Reuse-Enabling Software Evolution Environment. In: 19th Annual Software Engineering Workshop, Maryland, USA (1988)
6. Basili, V.R., Caldiera, G., Rombach, H.: Experience Factory. In: Encyclopedia of Software Engineering 2001, pp. 511–519. John Wiley & Sons, New York (2001)
7. Software Engineering Institute (SEI): SEI C4 Software Technology Reference guide - A Prototype, Pittsburgh, PA, USA (1997)
8. Birk, A.: A Knowledge Management Infrastructure for Systematic Improvement in Software Engineering. Fraunhofer IRB Verlag, Stuttgart (2000)
9. International Organization for Standardization (ISO): ISO 12207 - Systems and Software engineering - software life cycle processes, Geneva, Switzerland (2008)
10. Diebold, P.: A framework for goal-oriented Process Configuration, Masterthesis, TU Kaiserslautern (2012), https://kluedo.ub.uni-kl.de/frontdoor/index/index/docId/3366

Improving IT Service Operation Processes

Marko Jäntti[1] and Terry Rout[2]

[1] University of Eastern Finland, School of Computing
ITSM Research Group, P.O. Box 1627, 70211, Kuopio, Finland
`marko.jantti@uef.fi`
[2] Institute for Integrated and Intelligent Systems, Nathan Campus
Griffith University, 170 Kessels Road, QLD 4111, Australia
`t.rout@griffith.edu.au`

Abstract. IT organizations often start improving IT service management from the processes that are closely related to customer interface,
such as incident management, service request management and problem
management. These processes belong to the service operation phase in
IT service management. However, many IT organizations encounter difficulties while adopting service operation practices. The research problem
in this study is: How service operation processes are performed in IT
service provider companies and what types of challenges exist in these
companies regarding service operation?

Keywords: Service operation, incident, problem management.

1   Introduction

Many IT organizations start the IT service operation improvement by using
IT Infrastructure Library (ITIL). IT service management is a growing research
field that has strong relationship with IT industry. Previous studies on IT service
management field have dealt with problem management [1], success factors in
ITIL implementations [2], reasons why ITIL projects fail [3], combining ITIL
and CMMI frameworks [4], and IT service management process maturity [5].
Similarly, Tan, Cater-Steel and Toleman [2] have explored success factors of
ITIL projects. There are also studies that have focused on improving service
support processes [6] and improving service quality measurement framework [7].

The **main contribution of this study** is to describe how service operation processes are performed in IT service provider organizations, identify what
types of challenges exist in service operation processes from different perspectives: service desk; incident management, service request management, problem
management and continual improvement, and explore how continual improvement activities (measurement, reporting, managing improvement suggestions)
are visible in service operation.

The remainder of the paper is organized as follows. In Section 2, the research
methods of this study are described. In Section 3, we present service operation
methods, continual improvement methods and IT service operation challenges
in three cases. The discussion and the conclusions are given in Section 4.

J. Heidrich et al. (Eds.): PROFES 2013, LNCS 7983, pp. 359–362, 2013.

2 Research Methods

The research problem in this study is: How service operation processes are performed in IT service provider companies and what types of challenges exist in these companies regarding service operation? The research problem was further divided into following research questions: How service operation processes are performed in IT service provider organizations? What types of challenges exist in service operation? How continual improvement is visible in service operation processes?

A case study research method with three cases was used to answer the research problem. The case Alfa is the IS Management unit of a government agency. The case Beta provides IT services for a large bank in Finland and the case Gamma is one of the largest IT service provider organizations in Finland. A case comparison analysis technique defined by Eisenhardt [8] was used to analyze the collected case study data. Data from cases was collected by using documents, archival records, interviews and discussions, participative observation and physical artifacts.

3 Improving IT Service Operation Processes

In this section, the results of the case study are presented. The results have been organized according to research questions.

3.1 How IT Service Operation Processes Are Performed?

Alfa: The user support services unit performs the service operation processes by providing support services for the use of the IT and management of production environment. There were several groups in several locations responsible for handling incidents and service requests. The 1st-line support is provided by the service desk. Remote support operates on 1st and 2nd level and handles incidents on 1st level during busy days. The Operations Bridge (Valvomo) manages and coordinates the investigation of infrastructure related incidents. Application support provides user support on application-related questions and user rights management manages access rights.

Beta: Beta's internal customers are employees of banks and insurance companies. The first-level support is carried out mainly by five units: process services (bank service processes, customer service support), user support team,the service desk of the IT provider, the telephone service of insurance business and business service numbers. Incidents may be reported by internal and external customers, employees (on bank and insurance domain), management and third party providers.

Gamma: Customers may contact the Gamma service desk by phone, by email or by creating an incident from the web portal. The incident management has been divided into three lines: first-line that is responsible for communicating with customers and recording the service desk contacts, second-line that has specialized technical knowhow but does not answer the phone calls from customers and third-line specialist that have a deeper technical knowhow and participate in planning and implementing changes to for customers.

3.2   How Continual Improvement Is Visible in Service Operation?

Alfa: In Alfa, continual improvement regarding service operation is based on effective measurement of customer support and feedback collection. Feedback is collected frequently both from staff and customers. Customers are able to give feedback on service desk case resolutions. Feedback can be quantitative (4-10 scale) and open feedback. Service desk and support engineers can also record feedback to the service desk tool. The service manager of user support services analyzes the feedback and initiates improvement actions.

Beta: In Beta, we identified a role 'improvement owner' that is responsible for continual improvement, such as identifying improvement areas. Employees may report the improvement ideas regarding processes to those improvement managers that shall present them further to the CSI steering group. The Steering group directs the continual service improvement activities, decides annually on where improvements should be focused and improvement goals. Managers of Beta had also used Lean Six Sigma.

Gamma: Customer feedback and formal complaints on IT services come from customers through customer service managers that contact the production managers or management. A documented investigation is done for complaints and feedback is discussed in groups in order to identify the root cause and corrective actions. There is a documented process for managing feedback. Gamma frequently uses external auditors to benchmark their service operation processes.

In Alfa, Beta and Gamma, the measurement of service operation processes was performed by using the following metrics: Number of opened and closed service desk cases by type, number of major incidents, number of phone calls to service desk, ervice desk case resolution raten, number of SLA breaches in user support services, number of service desk cases by submission channel, and call response time.

3.3   What Types of Challenges Exist in Service Operation?

The following challenges were identified in case organizations' service operation: Lack of time to record support cases; lack of good metrics for problem management; interfaces between different ITSM processes are challenging; SLAs when a case is assigned to the 2nd level; lack of major incident definition; no responsible person for the service feedback; feedback reports are difficult to read; lack of rules for reopened cases; classification of incidents and service requests, terminology challenges; problems related to 3rd party service provider's quality, a large number of contact points, lack of problem management procedures, and lack of automated reporting.

4 Discussion and Conclusions

The main objective of this study was to answer the research problem: How Service Operation processes are performed in IT service provider companies and what types of challenges exist in these companies regarding Service Operation?

First, we showed the similarities and differences regarding two organizations' service operation methods. Differences were found especially in use of Service Level Agreements and problem management. Second, we explored continual improvement in service operation. Examples of continual improvement methods included collecting feedback on service desk case resolutions, using Lean Six Sigma to remove bottlenecks from ITSM processes, using PDCA philosophy, and benchmarking service operation processes. Third, the key service operation challenges were related to measurement and reporting of service operation processes, classifying incidents, challenges caused by third party service providers, challenges related to managing feedback and interfaces between IT service operation processes.

Acknowledgment. This paper is based on research in KISMET project funded by the National Technology Agency TEKES, European Regional Development Fund (ERDF), and industrial partners.

References

1. Kajko-Mattsson, M.: Corrective maintenance maturity model: Problem management. In: Proceedings of the International Conference on Software Maintenance (ICSM 2002), p. 486. IEEE Computer Society, Washington, DC (2002)
2. Tan, W.G., Cater-Steel, A., Toleman, M.: Implementing it service management: A case study focussing on critical success factors. Journal of Computer Information Systems 50(2) (2009)
3. Sharifi, M., Ayat, M., Rahman, A.A., Sahibudin, S.: Lessons learned in itil implementation failure. In: International Symposium on Information Technology, ITSim 2008, vol. 1, pp. 1–4 (2008)
4. Latif, A.A., Din, M.M., Ismail, R.: Challenges in adopting and integrating itil and cmmi in ict division of a public utility company. Computer Engineering and Applications 1, 81–86 (2010)
5. Niessink, F., van Vliet, H.: Towards mature it services. Software Process - Improvement and Practice 4(2), 55–71 (1998)
6. Jäntti, M.: Defining requirements for an incident management system: A case study. In: Proceedings of the Fourth International Conference on Systems (ICONS 2009). IEEE Computer Society (2009)
7. Lepmets, M., Cater-Steel, A., Gacenga, F., Ras, E.: Extending the it service quality measurement framework through a systematic literature review. Journal of Service Science Research 4, 7–47 (2012)
8. Eisenhardt, K.: Building theories from case study research. Academy of Management Review 14, 532–550 (1989)

A Security Assurance Framework
for Networked Medical Devices

Anita Finnegan, Fergal McCaffery, and Gerry Coleman

Regulated Software Research Centre, Dundalk Institute of Technology & Lero,
Dundalk, Co Louth, Ireland
{anita.finnegan,fergal.mccaffery,gerry.coleman}@dkit.ie

Abstract. This paper presents work for the development of a framework to assure the security of networked medical devices being incorporated. The paper focuses on one component of the framework, which addresses system development processes, and the assurance of these through the use of a Process Assessment Model with a major focus on the security risk management process. With the inclusion of a set of specific security controls and assurance processes, the purpose is to increase awareness of security vulnerabilities, risks and controls among Medical Device Manufacturers with the aim of increasing the overall security capability of medical devices.

1 Introduction

The increase in networked Medical Devices (MDs) proves to be beneficial from both a business and medical point of view. However, there is a growing awareness of new security risks, threats and vulnerabilities associated with their use. The concern among the MD community is that technology has advanced but the security processes have not yet [1]. This became evident following a number of controlled hacking demonstrations where security researchers proved the vulnerability of MDs [2], [3], [4]. Also the Government Accountability Office (GAO) inquiry into the FDA's assessment of MDs in 2012 [5] highlighted the lack of consideration for security vulnerabilities during the FDA's MD approval processes. This paper discusses one of the two components of the security assurance framework: the process assurance. The other element of this framework deals with final product assurance [6] but is outside the scope of this paper. Section 2 describes the process assurance and discusses key standards. Section 3 concludes the paper and details the expected impact this research will have both on MDMs and regulatory compliance.

1.1 Overview

The key objective is the development and implementation of a Process Reference Model (PRM), a Process Assessment Model (PAM) (including a Process Measurement Framework in compliance with IEC/ISO 15504-2 [7]) for the assurance of MDMs development processes and the establishment of a process capability level.

J. Heidrich et al. (Eds.): PROFES 2013, LNCS 7983, pp. 363–366, 2013.

The aim is to positively impact MDMs in their design decisions during the development of MDs. Figure 1, shows a high level architecture for the security assurance framework.

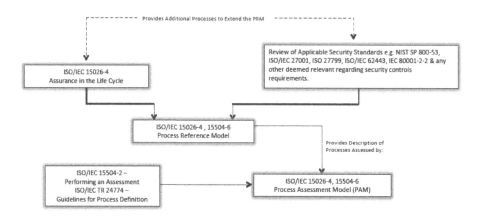

Fig. 1. Security Assurance Framework

2   Security Process Assurance

2.1   The Process Assessment Model in Compliance with ISO/IEC 15504

The International standard for Software Process Improvement and Capability determination (ISO/IEC 15504) is used to establish the development process capability level. Compliance with ISO/IEC 15504 results in the following outputs: a PRM, and a PAM (including an aligned Measurement Framework). ISO/IEC 15504-6 [8] details an exemplar PAM that contains two dimensions: the Process Dimension and the Capability Dimension. The Process Dimension utilizes the processes as defined in ISO/IEC 15288 [9] (which is a system development life cycle standard) and describes these in terms of their 'Purpose' and 'Outcome'. The PAM expands the PRM with the use of Performance Indicators called Base Practices (BP) and Work Products (WP). Base Practices are the basic activities addressing the process purpose and describe 'what' should be done. Work Product performance indicators are process outputs and are used to review the effectiveness of each process. Combined evidence of Work Practice characteristics and the performance of Base Practices provide the objective evidence of achievement of the 'Process Purpose'. The Capability Dimension, as set out in ISO/IEC 15504-2, utilizes six Capability Levels from Level 0, 'Non Performing' to Level 5, 'Optimizing'. These are the measurable characteristics required to manage and improve each process. ISO/IEC 15504-6 will form the foundation of the model as it contains the most suitable processes (ISO/IEC 15288) necessary for the development of networked MD system.

2.2   Building Additional Assurance into the PAM

Due to the criticality of medical device security, additional assurance during the development life cycle is achieved with the inclusion of processes in the PRM from ISO/IEC 15026-4 [10]. ISO/IEC 15026-4 provides a process framework for systems that need assurance for particular critical properties. Critical properties are usually associated with substantial risk concerning safety, dependability, reliability or security. The standard presents a set of processes, activities and tasks intended to build upon the Agreement, Project and Technical processes as set out in ISO/IEC 15288. Therefore conformance to this standard is achieved through the demonstration of these additional processes as well as conformance with ISO/IEC 15288. For this reason, demonstration of additional assurance specifically addressing security is suitable to enhance the PAM as set out in ISO/IEC 15504-6.

2.3   Security Controls for the Risk Management Process

To specifically address security as the system critical property focus is placed on the Risk Management Processes where we introduce new considerations and tools to be utilized during risk management activities. IEC/TR 80001-2-2 [11] is a technical report which sets out to promote the communication of security controls, needs and risks of medical devices to be incorporated into IT networks between MDMs, IT vendors and HDOs. This technical report presents 20 security capabilities for networked MDs. It forms the foundation for the security risk management process. The capabilities defined in IEC/TR 80001-2-2 have become part of the risk management process that the MDM must address and document.

A security control mapping across an array of industry security standards has been conducted to strengthen the security risk management process. An exhaustive list of security controls from all security standards (as shown in Figure 1) has been compiled and these controls are mapped to their attributing IEC/TR 80001-2-2 capability. Subsequently, a gap analysis is being carried out to identify further capabilities that should be included in IEC/TR 80001-2-2. This will be achieved through the use of expert opinion (i.e. expert users from industry and the FDA). The validated security controls, plus the existing IEC/TR 80001-2-2 security capabilities, will form the foundation for the security risk management process and this will be detailed in a upcoming Technical Report (a work in progress).

3   Conclusion

This paper presents a framework for the assurance of networked MDs in terms of security. The solution combines an array of international standards and guidance documents to create a step-by-step process for MDMs. The result is a tailored PAM for system life cycle processes (ISO/IEC 15504-6 using ISO/IEC 15288 as the PRM) with a focused risk management process (IEC/TR 80001-2-2) and additional processes for security assurance (ISO/IEC 15026-4). Currently there is no method to address the security development processes of networked MDs. This is the primary focus of this work. It is envisaged that the output of this research will positively impact the MD domain in both the EU and the US by building awareness of security vulnerabilities, threats and related risks for MDMs [6].

Acknowledgements. This research is supported by the Science Foundation Ireland (SFI) Stokes Lectureship Programme, grant number 07/SK/I1299, the SFI Principal Investigator Programme, grant number 08/IN.1/I2030 (the funding of this project was awarded by Science Foundation Ireland under a co-funding initiative by the Irish Government and European Regional Development Fund), and supported in part by Lero - the Irish Software Engineering Research Centre (http://www.lero.ie) grant 10/CE/I1855.

References

1. DHS, Attack Surface: Healthcare and Public Heath Sector (2012)
2. Radcliffe, J.: Hacking Medical Devices for Fun and Insulin: Breaking the Human SCADA System (2011)
3. Infosecurity Magazine, Pacemaker virus could lead to mass murder (2012)
4. Goldman, J.: Security Flaws Found in Philips Xper Hospital Management System (2013), http://www.esecurityplanet.com
5. GAO, Medical Devices, FDA Should Expland Its Consideration of Information Security for Certain Types of Devices (2012)
6. Finnegan, A., McCaffery, F., Coleman, G.: Development of a process assessment model for assessing security of IT networks incorporating medical devices against ISO/IEC 15026-4. In: Healthinf 2013, Barcelona, Spain (2013)
7. ISO/IEC, 15504-2: 2003 Software Engineering - Process Assessment - Performing an Assessment (2003)
8. ISO/IEC, 15504-6: 2008 Information technology — Process assessment — An exemplar system life cycle process assessment model (2008)
9. ISO/IEC, 15288 - Systems engineering — System life cycle processes (2008)
10. ISO/IEC, 15026-4: Systems and Software Engineering - Systems and Software Assurance - Assurance in the Life Cycle (2012)
11. IEC, TR 80001-2-2 - Guidance for the disclosure and communication of medical device security needs, risks and controls. International Electrotechnical Committee (2011)

Model-Based Transition from Requirements to High-Level Software Design

Hermann Kaindl

Vienna University of Technology
Gußhausstr. 27–29, 1040 Vienna, Austria
kaindl@ict.tuwien.ac.at

Abstract. How can the application domain and the requirements be better understood using object-oriented (OO) modeling? How do scenarios / use cases fit together with functional requirements? How can a domain model be used for a model-based transition to a design model?

This tutorial addresses these questions in the following manner. It shows how each requirement given in natural language can be viewed itself as an object and modeled as such. This approach facilitates both a hierarchical organization (by grouping requirements instances into classes and subclasses) and explicit association (by relating requirements through OO associations). While scenarios / use cases can somehow illustrate the overall functionality, additionally functional requirements for the system to be built should be formulated and related to them appropriately. All kinds of requirements make statements about the application domain, which should be first represented in a domain model of conceptual classes, in order to make the requirements better understandable. This tutorial explains a seamless transition to a high-level design model, where design classes are abstractions of implementation classes. This transition from requirements to software design is also investigated in model-driven terms, whether it is a transformation or just a mapping. In addition, the influence of non-functional requirements for selecting an architecture is explained.

Keywords: Requirements, software design, model-based transition.

1 Tutorial Objective and Target Audience

The primary objective of this tutorial is to improve software development in practice regarding the difficult and important transition from requirements to high-level software design.

The target groups are software development practitioners, such as requirements engineers, software designers and project leaders. Also educators will benefit from this tutorial. The assumed attendee background is some familiarity with object-oriented concepts as well as interest in requirements, analysis or software design.

2 Key Learning Outcomes

The participants will understand several key problems with current object-oriented (OO) methods and how they can be resolved. In particular, they will see how scena-

J. Heidrich et al. (Eds.): PROFES 2013, LNCS 7983, pp. 367–369, 2013.
© Springer-Verlag Berlin Heidelberg 2013

rios and use cases can be utilized for requirements engineering and software design. But they will also see the additional need to specify the functional requirements for the system to be built. In addition, they will be able to distinguish between domain objects and software objects. They will experience UML as a language for representing OO models, but also the need to be clear about what kind of objects are represented. This is important for the model-based transition from requirements to design.

3   Outline

- Introduction and Background
  - Requirements
  - Object-oriented core concepts
  - Use cases
- Business and domain modeling using objects and UML
  - Business process — Business Use Case
  - Domain model
- Functional requirements, goals and scenarios / use cases
  - Functional requirements
  - Goals
- Requirements and UML models
  - Types of requirements
  - Non-functional / quality requirements
  - Conflicts between quality requirements
  - OOA (object-oriented analysis) model
  - Requirements vs. requirements representation
  - Software Requirements Specification
- Transition to software design
  - Animated transition example
  - OOD (object-oriented design) model and architecture
  - Sequence diagrams for OOA vs. OOD models
  - Transition recommendations
  - Model-based transition
- High-level software design
  - Software architecture
  - Selection depending on non-functional requirements
- Summary and conclusion

4   CV of the Presenter

Hermann Kaindl joined the Institute of Computer Technology at the Vienna Univ. of Technology in early 2003 as a full professor, where he also serves in the Senate. Prior to moving to academia, he was a senior consultant with the division of program and systems engineering at Siemens AG Austria. There he has gained more than 24 years of industrial experience in software development and human-computer interaction. He has published five books and more than 150 papers in refereed journals, books and conference proceedings. He is a *Senior Member* of the IEEE, a *Distinguished Scientist* member of the ACM, a member of the AAAI, and is on the executive board of the Austrian Society for Artificial Intelligence.

References

1. Kaindl, H.: How to Identify Binary Relations for Domain Models. In: Proceedings of the Eighteenth International Conference on Software Engineering (ICSE-18), pp. 28–36. IEEE Computer Society Press, Los Alamitos (1996)
2. Kaindl, H.: A Practical Approach to Combining Requirements Definition and Object-Oriented Analysis. Annals of Software Engineering 3, 319–343 (1997)
3. Kaindl, H.: Difficulties in the transition from OO analysis to design. IEEE Software, 94–102 (September/October 1999)
4. Kaindl, H.: A Design Process Based on a Model Combining Scenarios with Goals and Functions. IEEE Transactions on Systems, Man, and Cybernetics (SMC) Part A 30(5), 537–551 (2000)
5. Kaindl, H.: Adoption of Requirements Engineering: Conditions for Success. In: Fifth IEEE International Symposium on Requirements Engineering (RE 2001), Toronto, Canada (August 2001)
6. Kaindl, H.: Is object-oriented requirements engineering of interest? Requirements Engineering 10, 81–84 (2005)
7. Kaindl, H.: A Scenario-Based Approach for Requirements Engineering: Experience in a Telecommunication Software Development Project. Systems Engineering 8, 197–210 (2005)
8. Kaindl, H., Falb, J.: Can We Transform Requirements into Architecture? In: Proceedings of the Third International Conference on Software Engineering Advances (ICSEA 2008), pp. 91–96. IEEE (2008)
9. Kaindl, H., Kramer, S., Kacsich, R.: A Case Study of Decomposing Functional Requirements. In: Proc. Third International Conference on Requirements Engineering (ICRE 1998), pp. 156–163. IEEE (April 1998)
10. Kaindl, H., Svetinovic, D.: On confusion between requirements and their representations. Requirements Engineering 15, 307–311 (2010)

Software Effort Estimation and Risk Management

Jens Heidrich

Fraunhofer Institute for Experimental Software Engineering (IESE)
Kaiserslautern, Germany
`jens.heidrich@iese.fraunhofer.de`

Abstract. Every software business has to be able to budget and plan its software development projects realistically. Since software projects are usually fraught with uncertainty, they inherently involve planning risks right from the start. Consequently, it is important to manage cost-related risks in order to monitor them and implement adequate contingency plans when a crisis occurs. Since not all projects are equal, it is important to identify the specific factors (cost drivers) that have a positive or negative influence on productivity. Thus, the use of appropriate cost estimation approaches does not only contribute to accurate project planning and successful risk management, but also to improved software processes and overall organization maturity.

1 Introduction

The tutorial teaches the basics of systematic effort estimation and risk management for software development projects. Participants will learn about different estimation approaches (such as Delphi Approach, CoCoMo II, and CART) and their practical usage. Moreover, approaches for determining the size of a development project (such as functional size measurement with IFPUG function points) at early stages will be discussed as one major input of estimation models. Finally the CoBRA® approach for creating risk-based effort estimation models will be presented. The participants will obtain an overview on how to create their own estimation models and conduct systematic effort estimation and risk management.

Target groups are managers of software development organizations, members of Software Engineering Process Groups (SEPG), project managers and planners as well as quality managers.

2 Outline

- Effort Estimation Basics
    - Why effort and cost estimation?
    - Common mistakes in practice
    - Overview of estimation approaches
    - When to use which approach?

J. Heidrich et al. (Eds.): PROFES 2013, LNCS 7983, pp. 370–371, 2013.

- Functional Sizing
  - Basics of functional size measurement
  - IFPUG Function Points and COSMIC FFP
  - FP versus LOC
  - Productivity Measurement
- The CoBRA® Approach
  - Develop custom-tailored estimation models
  - Effort estimation
  - Risk management
  - Benchmarking
- Industrial Case Study and Summary

3   CV of the Presenter

Dr. Jens Heidrich is head of the processes management division at the Fraunhofer Institute for Experimental Software Engineering (IESE) in Kaiserslautern, Germany. His research interests include project management, quality assurance, and measurement. He received his doctoral degree (Dr. rer. nat.) in Computer Science from the University of Kaiserslautern, Germany. He is lecturer at the University of Kaiserslautern and gives seminars on software measurement and effort estimation.

References

1. Trendowicz, A., Heidrich, J., Münch, J., Ishigai, Y., Yokoyama, K., Kikuchi, N.: Development of a Hybrid Cost Estimation Model in an Iterative Manner. In: Proceedings of the 28th International Conference on Software Engineering, Shanghai, China, pp. 331–340 (2006)
2. Trendowicz, A.: Software Cost Estimation, Benchmarking, and Risk Assessment: The Software Decision-Makers' Guide to Predictable Software Development. The Fraunhofer IESE Series on Software and Systems Engineering. Springer, Heidelberg (2013)

Author Index

Aaramaa, Sanja   20, 123
Abrahamsson, Pekka   50, 334
Accioly, Paola   65
Aleixo, Fellipe A.   153, 169
Amasaki, Sousuke   214
Andreou, Andreas S.   240, 253
Aranha, Eduardo   65

Basili, Victor   184
Bauer, Thomas   80
Berger, Christian   324
Borba, Paulo   65

Campos, Andre L.N.   338
Campos Neto, Edmilson   65
Cater-Steel, Aileen   330
Christoforou, Andreas   240
Coleman, Gerry   363

da Silva, Bruno C.   199
Diebold, Philipp   355

Eldh, Sigrid   35

Feldt, Robert   93
Finnegan, Anita   363
Florén, Dan   93
Freire, Marília   65
Fujiwara, Kenji   313
Fukazawa, Yoshiaki   342
Fushida, Kyohei   313

Garbajosa, Juan   229
Gimenes, Itana M.S.   169
Gonzalez Ortega, Eloy   229
Gorschek, Tony   93
Graziotin, Daniel   50, 334

Hanakawa, Noriko   351
Hansson, Jörgen   324
Heidenberg, Jeanette   268
Heidrich, Jens   370

Higo, Yoshiki   298
Honda, Kiyoshi   342
Höst, Martin   283
Hyysalo, Jarkko   20

Iida, Hajimu   313
Imazato, Ayaka   298

Jäntti, Marko   359

Kaindl, Hermann   367
Kasurinen, Jussi   5
Kelanti, Markus   20
Kettunen, Petri   347
Kinnunen, Tuomo   123
Kläs, Michael   80
Knapp, Alexander   138
Kuhrmann, Marco   138
Kulesza, Uirá   65, 153, 169
Kusumoto, Shinji   298

Laine, Risto   5
Lampasona, Constanza   184
Lehto, Jari   20, 123
Lokan, Chris   214
Lundqvist, Kristina   35

Maciel, Rita Suzana Pitangueira   199
McCaffery, Fergal   363
Mellegård, Niklas   324
Méndez Fernández, Daniel   108, 138
Münch, Jürgen   229

Nilsson, Martin   324
Nordman, Kristian   268

Obana, Masaki   351
Ocampo Ramírez, Alexis Eduardo   3, 184
Oliveira, Toacy   338
Oliveira Junior, Edson A.   153, 169
Oza, Nilay   229

Pazin, Maicon G.   169
Pedersen Notander, Jesper   283
Pernståhl, Joakim   93
Porres, Ivan   268

Ramalho, Franklin   199
Rana, Rakesh   324
Rout, Terry   330, 359
Runeson, Per   283

Sasaki, Yui   298
Shrestha, Anup   330
Sizílio, Gustavo   65
Smolander, Kari   5
Staron, Miroslaw   324
Sundmark, Daniel   35

Tan, Wui-Gee   330
Taušan, Nebojša   123
Tiberi, Ubaldo   80
Toleman, Mark   330

Törner, Fredrik   324
Truscan, Dragos   268

Wagner, Stefan   1
Wang, Xiaofeng   50
Washizaki, Hironori   342
Weijola, Max   268
Wieringa, Roel   108
Wiklund, Kristian   35

Xenis, Christos   4

Yague, Agustin   229
Yiasemis, Pantelis Stylianos   253
Yoshida, Norihiro   313